INFORMATIO[N]

Management
in Action

Wiley Series in Computing and Information Processing

Hugh J. Watson, University of Georgia-Athens, Series Editor

INFORMATION SYSTEMS

Management Principles in Action

ROBERT K. WYSOCKI
Bentley College

JAMES YOUNG
Wheeler Group

WILEY

JOHN WILEY & SONS

New York ☐ Chichester ☐ Brisbane ☐ Toronto ☐ Singapore

Library of Congress Cataloging in Publication Data:
Wysocki, Robert K.
   Information systems : management principles in action / Robert K. Wysocki,
      James Young.
      p. cm.
   Bibliography: p.
   Includes indexes.
   ISBN 0-471-60302-3
   1. Management information systems. I. Young, James, 1947-
II. Title.
T58.6.W972   1989
658.4'038--dc20

Printed in the Republic of Singapore

10 9 8 7 6 5 4 3

about the authors

□

ROBERT K. WYSOCKI, PH.D

Dr. Wysocki is the Director of the MBA Program and Adjunct Associate Professor of Computer Information Systems at Bentley College. He has more than 20 years of professional experience as an educator and administrator in graduate business programs, as an independent consultant, and as an internal systems consultant for Texas Instruments, Inc. He has several years of experience as an information systems manager and had developed and implemented two degree programs in computer and information systems. An active member of the Data Processing Management Association, he has several journal publications and professional presentations in the areas of information systems and management sciences. He holds degrees in mathematics and mathematical statistics from the University of Dallas and Southern Methodist University, respectively.

JAMES YOUNG

Mr. Young is the Vice President of Information and Telecommunications Systems for the Wheeler Group, a unit of Pitney Bowes in Hartford, Connecticut, His 17 years of experience includes data processing management positions in government (U.S. Marine Corps), management consulting (Arthur Young), and private industry (Barry Wright) as well as other management assignments. He has worked in a diversity of environments; large mainframe, minicomputer, and microcomputer, both centralized and decentralized.

Mr. Young holds degrees in engineering (B.S. from the U.S. Naval Academy), computer science (M.S. from the U.S. Naval Postgraduate School), business administration (M.B.A. from the Havard Business School) and the CDP. He frequently speaks on professional issues to groups such as ASM, EDPAA, IBM, Netron, and others. Mr. Young has written extensively on data processing issues and has been a contributing columnist for Computerworld since 1983. He is also currently visiting lecturer on MIS concepts in the graduate program of Clark University in Worcester, Massachusetts.

about the authors

ROBERT K. WYSOCKI, PH.D.

JAMES YOUNG

preface

This book and the messages that it hopes to convey are products of the authors' feelings of affection and concern for the growing discipline of information systems (IS), which has commanded the better part of our working lives. We have seen that those who have been faithful in their service to IS have been rewarded with improvements in their organization's products and technology, increased influence within those organizations, and a larger, more visible professional role within society. In this affection we are definitely not alone; many other people feel similarly. Although the vision of early IS pioneers—of a world in which information and related technologies occupy a dominant positionis still evolving, the enthusiasm of IS practitioners is enduring. It reflects a positive response, not only to the emergence of a very successful field of work and study, but also to the important personal contributions that many professionals have made to IS. Their labor, we have seen repeatedly, bears significant fruit.

Paradoxically, the evolution of IS gives rise to a significant concern. The process of expansion has required a gradual modification of our work habits, our perspective, and more inclusively, our management techniques. This has entailed a more ambitious or global conception of IS as well as the development of different sorts of relationships with non-IS individuals. Unfortunately, in many cases IS professionals have failed to keep up with their own creation; they have not gone through necessary shifts in attitude and have too often responded reluctantly to change. Moreover, although realigning IS production and management processes depends heavily on the "tribal knowledge" of experienced and battle-scarred IS managers, no broad scientific tradition of IS management reflecting such cumulative knowledge has evolved or at least has not been well-published. There is as yet no reliable road map for up-and-coming IS managers to follow.

We believe instinctively in the future success and expanding effectiveness of the IS discipline. But also we know that this success will occur only if our profession solves the problems of IS management. Until IS management addresses more effectively the needs and imperatives of organizations, technologies, and society, IS will not realize its full potential.

PURPOSE

The purpose of this text is to close the gap between future IS management needs and current IS management skills. A basic principle of this book is that IS management may be the single most important determinant of future successful IS use. Therefore, the watchword will be management—not technology, not procedural practice, not application. These issues are valuable to IS only in so far as they relate (as they frequently do) to various management tasks. Although as many specific IS practices as possible will be included, a fundamental doctrine of this text is that IS management is not a grab bag of tricks learned through experience, nor is it a function of arcane knowledge. It reduces to the ability to make decisions in the light of a complex array of influences, pressures, and considerations. This book attempts to acquaint the reader with this array and to illustrate how various factors contribute to successful IS management.

DIRECTION

While this text will be highly practical in its focus, we have not ignored established research tradition. IS theory and scholarship have directed our presentation, often bringing clarity to complicated issues. Research findings help us build a framework with which the student can better grasp the more esoteric IS functions and interrelate the diverse components of IS.

In some areas, differing views will be offered and the strengths and weaknesses of each contrasted. Presenting alternative ways to think about IS issues is a useful means of reinforcing another fundamental tenet: There is no "right answer." Several contrasting approaches may be equally effective. Depending on variations and nuances, two similar problems may require very different solutions. Varying methods of implementation too, can make diverse approaches successful. In this spirit, this text tries to take a comprehensive look at <u>all</u> aspects of each IS issue raised in its pages. Students' personal input and evaluation of strengths and weaknesses of diverse viewpoints should generate lively discussions—or at least constructive reflection.

ORGANIZATION

We have organized the book to correspond to the structure of organizations. Specifically, we discuss the relationship of the IS department at the corporate level, at the functional business unit level, and at the end-user level. At each level of the organization we examine the role, responsibility, issues and opportunities for IS management. Other texts have chosen less cohesive structures for their presentation. It is our belief that the rapid evolution taking place in the application of information technology (IT) at all levels in the organization strongly suggests the approach we have taken. Furthermore, it gives the student a more organized perspective with which to understand the principles of management as applied to the IS department.

Discussion questions have been used sparingly. None are of the "list the 10 causes of the Civil War" type questions. Rather, they are comparatively more difficult than the norm; they are designed to be thought-provoking and intended more for class discussion than as homework assignments to be collected and graded. In that vein they are a rich source of additional lecture and discussion material for the instructor.

Accompanying each of the five parts of the text are Suggested Student Projects and a Supplementary Reading List. The projects require that the student relate classroom study to the real world. In that sense they are not unlike semester projects that instructors will often assign as part of the course requirements. The Supplementary Reading List provides the student with a source of materials from the academic and trade journals. No claim is made for completeness. These readings give further avenues of exploration for both instructor and student.

To reinforce the belief that the "right answer" emanates from a thoroughgoing assessment of all sides of a question, a companion casebook, *Information Systems: Management Practice in Action*, has been prepared. The book consists of short vignettes, or "Situations" as we call them, that are derived from realistic experiences of the authors and other IS professionals. We have preserved the anonymity of the individuals and organizations described in these Situations for several reasons. First, we believe that many environments are too motivated to publicize their technical successes to share basic management problems. Moreover, when such problems are in fact exposed, distilling them into their essential features—those components useful for classroom discussion—is difficult if the real-world participants must be identified and discussed in detail. Finally, the "right answer" is too often suggested to students by actions eventually taken or results eventually ensuing in real life, which, if known, can prejudice the objectivity of that assessment process we value so highly. In short, we feel that anonymity allows the introduction of a realistic level of ambiguity found in most problems and in most problem-solving activities. The Situations are intended to permit a wide range of opinions to emerge; they offer enough information to provide a supporting foundation but not so much misleading or superfluous detail to distract from the fundamental aspects of a problem that each Situation seeks to highlight.

We also recognize the importance of more comprehensive case analyses to many instructors. The Instructor's Manual contains several references to cases from the Harvard Business School. We have classified approximately 100 information systems related cases according to the chapter of the text for which they are most appropriate.

ASSUMPTIONS AND AUDIENCE

Because this book is dedicated to the exploration of the sophisticated and yet inadequately developed area of IS management, it proceeds on the assumption that the reader is well versed in the basics of IS. Specifically, students' familiarity with fundamental IS terminology is assumed, as is a basic understanding of essential management practices. This knowledge should be obtainable through industry experience or introductory courses in management principles, organizational behavior, and IS required in graduate and undergraduate business programs.

The text has been prepared for upper-division and graduate students of IS programs who are interested in the evolving issues and challenges of IS management. It is equally applicable to the technical professional aspiring to more managerial duties, or to the general management student who is preparing to practice management in the burgeoning IS field. We hope that the text will also be valuable to the student whose management ambitions lie in some other discipline but who is wise enough to foresee that familiarity with major IS issues will be of value in almost any management career. If our aims are realized, this text will help its users deal with important IS issues effectively, whether those users are functional managers or chief executive officers of an organization. Although we address many topics dealing with specialized issues, nowhere do we dignify proprietary or parochial topics by inclusion; each area treated here has been included because it is important enough to affect the contributions of IS to an organization. Therefore, we expect that this text should be of value to any member of an organization's management team concerned about the role of IS.

It is our hope that each reader will find here something of value to assist him or her in the quest for enhanced IS management skills and improved IS efficiency, effectiveness, and strategic impact.

ROBERT K. WYSOCKI
JAMES YOUNG

January 1989

contents

□

PART IV
INFORMATION SYSTEMS AS A USER-SUPPORT ENTITY   349

fifteen
THE ROLE OF INFORMATION SYSTEMS AS A
USER-SUPPORT ENTITY   351

sixteen
END-USER APPLICATIONS DEVELOPMENT   371

seventeen

ORGANIZING INFORMATION SYSTEMS TO SUPPORT END-USER
COMPUTING   393

eighteen

INFORMATION SYSTEMS AS A USER-SUPPORT ENTITY: ISSUES
AND OPPORTUNITIES   415

PART V

THE FUTURE AND INFORMATION
SYSTEMS MANAGEMENT   431

nineteen

QUALITY OF WORK   433

PART I

OVERVIEW OF INFORMATION SYSTEMS MANAGEMENT

In this, the first of five parts of the text, we lay the groundwork for our study of the management of the information systems (IS) function in the information-age organization. The story that we unfold is of a profession that has grown too rapidly and has consequently made some significant errors along the way. The story began with the realization by corporate America that the computer was a marvelous tool for handling labor-intensive organizational functions and for improving productivity. This recognition brought on a flood of requests for computerization, many of which could not be met effectively; indeed, in the early days of computerization, systems development methods and programming tools were crude and not well understood. And, complicating matters, many computer programmers were enamored of the attention they received. They made large promises that could not be kept, thereby disappointing functional managers (those in marketing, production, personnel, etc.) and encouraging skepticism in other branches of the organization.

Fortunately, the story has not remained gloomy. The computer profession has matured and has emerged as an essential player in the organization of the future. As organizations vie for improved competitive positions, they have turned again to the computer professional for creative insights into strategic uses of computer technology. New challenges and opportunities have arisen for the information-age IS manager. Many of the challenges have no clear resolution, as you will observe. What is clear, however, are the needs of the organization—and the fact that the IS manager is expected to make a bottom-line contribution.

CHAPTER 1
The Scope and Role of Information Systems Management

CHAPTER 2
Foundation of Information Systems Management

SUGGESTED STUDENT PROJECTS

SUPPLEMENTARY READING LIST

one

☐

The Scope and Role of Information Systems Management

As a name, information systems (IS) has gone through a series of permutations that reflect the discipline's evolution. Originally, the term data was used as the descriptor of computerization in an organization—as in automated data processing (ADP), electronic data processing (EDP), or just plain data processing (DP). However, such phrasing suggested a very limited role for computerization, confining it to purely technical realms. With the recognition that computerization requires incursions into areas of operational application and, ultimately, of organizational strategy, the term *information* began to be used as a more accurate descriptor of what was happening in practice. Similarly, the term *systems* started to replace *processing* as a way of signifying that more than just computer programs were involved; it related procedures, people, practices, and processes (manual and other). Indeed, as Robert Waterman and his colleagues (1980) have observed, *organizational systems* is a pervasive and potentially dominant factor in the evolution of the name.

Hence, the phrase *information systems* was coined to describe that part of any organization that is responsible for the management of the organization's informational resources—*all* its collective knowledge—and of the systems that make use of these resources. Some organizations attached the modifier *management* to the term,— that is, *management information systems* (MIS). However, the current trend is to remove this modifier, as it denotes only one dimension (and a poorly exploited one at that) of the role that IS practitioners play in the handling of an organization's informational resources. And, although certain organizations use the term *information services,* we will see that it too tends to be limiting; it overemphasizes the passive role of the "technology department" and ignores the crucial aspects of leadership and guidance. *Information systems* will therefore be used in this text to describe all of an organization's computer-related informational resources. Although the responsibility for these resources may not be undertaken by a department of this name in a given organization, from a top-management perspective this responsibility certainly is the essential challenge facing the IS manager.

This chapter begins by taking a broad view of the importance of IS in organizations and the leverage these systems provide for organizations that exploit them effectively. Next, we look at the direction of IS growth and the crucial need for IS management, particularly in light of the fact that users are now customers. After sketching the nature of particular IS managerial skills, we end by discussing the changing boundaries of IS within the modern organization.

THE GROWING IMPORTANCE OF INFORMATION SYSTEMS

With the decline of the manufacturing and agricultural sectors as sources of employment in our economy, employment growth has been supported almost entirely by needs in the service sector, and the information sector as shown in Exhibit 1-1. According to Porat (1977), the information sector in particular grew from 22 percent in 1950 to 57 percent in 1977. The growth in information technology (IT) in one sense can be seen as being caused by the needs of this particular area.

We might then expect that IS professionals believe their discipline is becoming more significant every day. However, it is more meaningful and less biased to report on how senior executives respond to the increasing presence of IS in their organization. Exhibit 1-2 indicates that executives find IS to be the most difficult and costly function to manage. Moreover, the fact that senior managers tend to rank IS low on a scale of corporate priorities would seem to indicate a potentially serious problem in attitude. Perhaps because of the steadily increasing cost of IS, upper management has tended to treat it as a necessary evil—a generator of expenses, not benefits. Many experienced IS professionals believe that IS ranks low in importance in the eyes of some senior managers because of how they use it; these managers are not yet aware of its huge potential to confer benefits. A

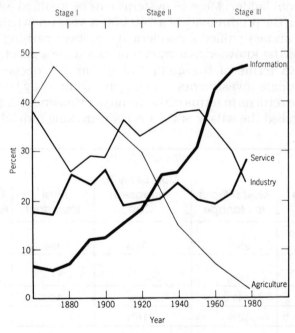

EXHIBIT 1-1 Percentage aggregation of the U.S. workforce.

major challenge for IS managers, therefore, is to change that perception.

What do IS benefits amount to? We will discuss them in later chapters, but for now we can say that they boil down to one important feature: organizational leverage. As an increasing percentage of the national workforce uses automation, the investment made by organizations in computer technology provides proportionately larger returns. In a very general sense, if 60 percent of a company's budget is devoted to personnel but only 10 percent of its staff uses computers, expenditures on IS can improve the effectiveness of only 6 percent of that organization's budget. This means that, unless investments in IS can deliver substantial productivity gains, they will remain modest. However, when half the organization's staff uses automation, investments in IS technology can positively affect 30 percent of that organization's budget. In such cases, projects that have less return on investment will make sense because benefits can be increased by a factor of five (30 percent instead of 6 percent).

This leveraging of investments increases as one goes up the organizational ladder. More IS systems can be justified as a means of improving the productivity of a $50,000-a-year knowledge worker than they can be justified for a clerical employee earning $25,000. Moreover, if the knowledge worker's or executive's effectiveness is measured in terms of the quality of his or her decisions, even disproportionate investments in computer technology become reasonable; the returns in terms of the quality or timeliness of a decision typically exceed the salary of the decision-making individual.

Corporate Staffs				
Function	**Most Difficult to Manage**	**Most Likely To Increase in Cost**	**Most Important**	**Largest Function**
Information Systems	23%	34%	9%	23%
Human Resources	16%	—	11%	—
Finance	14%	—	44%	20%
Legal	13%	16%	—	—
Planning	—	—	9%	—

EXHIBIT 1-2 The importance of information systems to senior management.

Source: American Productivity Center and the consulting firm of Cresap, McCormick, and Paget, "Positioning Corporate Staffs for the 1990s," Computerworld, September 22, 1986. Copyright 1986 by CW Publishing Inc., Framingham, MA 01704. Reprinted from Computerworld.

The Direction of Information Systems Growth

Information Systems are becoming increasingly essential to more and more parts of many organizations. Automation is finding applications not only in "number-crunching" areas such as accounting but also in major operational areas such as marketing and manufacturing, which increasingly depend on IS-related services. Although IS critics (who are still numerous) might see this development as the unruly spread of technology, astute observers recognize that often this spread is resisted: It occurs with the reluctant approval of senior managers—and then only after clear benefits have been amply demonstrated. We will touch on this reluctance later in this chapter.

Exhibit 1-3 illustrates some of the directions of IS applications. In what is by now a familiar part of our story, computer technology's applications were initially in operational areas, where manual processes were replaced with automated ones. As the technology became more familiar and as superficial opportunities for operational applications were exhausted, managerial applications in such areas as spending control and market analysis began to crop up. These applications were made possible by the existence of the underlying automated operational systems that were their forerunners, but their real impetus was the recognition that integrating and transferring information opened up entirely new possibilities. The importance of shared and repeatedly used data led to the notion of

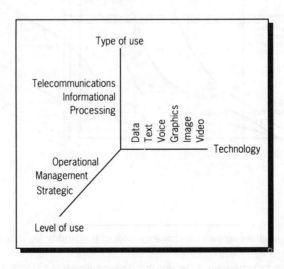

EXHIBIT 1-3 Directions of information systems growth.

information as a part of a system—a concept that was critical to the emergence of IS management as an important corporate function.

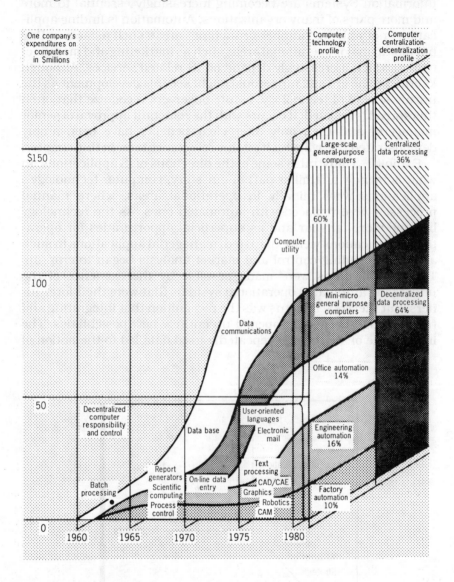

EXHIBIT 1-4 Changing computer technology and responsibility for automation in the organization.

Source: Reprinted by permission of the *Harvard Business Review*. An exhibit from "Managing Information Systems by Committee" by Richard L. Nolan (July-August 1982). Copyright © 1982 by the President and Fellows of Harvard College; all rights reserved.

The IS function has become a complex of interacting technologies, application trends, and management concerns. It is important that you understand this complexity, for much of our discussion of management issues will draw on it. One method is to categorize the type of technology being managed: data, text, voice, graphics, image, or video, such as is shown in Exhibit 1-3. Another is to concentrate on where various technologies are applied. For example, Exhibit 1-4 shows the sizable presence of automated systems in areas at one time uncomputerized and illustrates how these areas together dwarf the primarily technical areas of data processing. Many of these new applications have grown with distributed control and responsibilities, thereby focusing the role of the IS manager on diplomacy, informal leadership, influence, and negotiation—all of which require particular and distinctly nontechnical skills.

THE NEED FOR INFORMATION SYSTEMS MANAGEMENT

If the IS function is ever larger and more costly, and if the perceptions of senior management regarding IS need monitoring, then the duties of the IS manager are of necessity increasingly managerial. Whether this person's actual title is vice president, director, manager, or even supervisor, if his or her job entails responsibility for the organization's IS functions (either explicit or implied), then this person's historic dedication to technology will no longer be appropriate. We will attempt to characterize the needed repositioning of IS managers as an opportunity, which indeed it is——but the unfortunate consequences of a failure to reposition should not be ignored. To quote the futurist, Alvin Toffler (1981): "The next ten years contain the opportunity for the corporate computer executive to become obsolete. He is controlling dinosaurs while the ants are swarming over his world." Toffler's words are still valid even as we approach the twenty-first century.

In 1986, IS managers were asked to rate their top concerns (Datamation, 1986). The following is a list of the top seven concerns:

Aligning MIS with business goals
Data utilization
Educating senior personnel
Software development
Productivity

Planning

Integration of technologies

Only toward the end of this list do technical issues appear; most of the concerns require managerial skills and managerial attention. Mastery of technology, as we will see, plays only a small part in contributing to the accomplishment of IS goals and tasks. Unfortunately, most IS managers have evolved within technical disciplines. Even though some have learned managerial skills as they advance, the fact remains that the senior management components of the most important IS jobs are not stressed, nor is a managerial focus common in IS training programs.

The foregoing list of concerns helps us to delineate the various management challenges facing today's IS manager. There are three basic roles that IS adopts in an organization: that of a corporate entity, that of a user support entity, and that of a functional entity. Most contemporary IS management problems relate to one of these three roles, and most of the concerns that IS managers rank as important are related to these roles. For instance, insofar as IS is a corporate entity, IS managers need to address the concerns of aligning IS with business goals, educating senior personnel, and planning (among others). Insofar as IS is a functional entity, managers must focus on software development and productivity. And in today's competitive environment, it is paramount that IS managers recognize new management opportunities by focusing on IS as a user support entity. Let us take a brief look at this last issue.

Users As Customers

Information systems professionals have not always been considerate of the needs of the system user. The view of some IS professionals that "we know better than they do" has various rationales, some more persuasive than others, but the end result has been uniformly negative: Too many non-IS professionals have become disenchanted with IS. However, wise IS professionals recognize that without end-users, IS would not exist. They also see that without properly used systems, company processes will not function and the benefits of automation will not be achieved. They treat end-users appropriately by doing the following

- Listening to their needs when building or selecting systems.
- Paying careful attention to training in initiating systems.

- Believing that users must be satisfied with the technology or they will not embrace it enthusiastically.
- Ensuring that IS understands how the system must perform for users and then committing to deliver that performance.
- Providing consistently understandable communication to users.
- Providing education on technical subjects.
- Building sound user/IS team relations.

Progressive IS departments have recognized that the term "user" has taken on negative connotations. They have begun to use the term "customer" or "client" to describe someone to whom the IS department provides services. In a certain sense it is also the recognition that IS is a profit center and is operating in an openly competitive environment. Although agreeing wholeheartedly with this sentiment, we will refer to this group as "users" in this text to avoid confusion with a company's outside customers and in appreciation of the fact that this term is widely used and need not have disagreeable implications.

A new term for user becomes quite reasonable in light of the dramatic transformation of users of IS services in recent years. The earliest users of computer systems were clerical-level employees performing repetitive tasks for high-volume data transactions. Both the information and the task of using the system were usually well defined. However, as systems evolved, a different type of user began to emerge. At present, users are likely to be managers dealing with ill-defined information and systems that are quite flexible. The volumes of data transactions are likely to be small, but the effect of their use—in a financial simulation, for instance—could be high. These users must have a broader, better-defined understanding of information systems. Their needs are not as easy to encompass as were those of earlier clerical staffs.

In the future, the executive user is likely to become prominent. She or he will have only a passing understanding of the technology and will use it minimally. However, the importance of such users' basic queries, the variety of their interests, and the need for a simplicity that can encourage their dialogue with computers, will necessitate clever design and software selection by the IS department.

All these diverse users as well as assorted hybrids will exist within any organization. In such user diversity lies numerous challenges and opportunities for the IS manager: This user community constitutes a demanding audience.

By being both knowledgeable and assertive, some members of this community have ushered in stand-alone systems. In environments that have allowed such autonomy (and many have), users unhappy with the speed or quality of IS response to their needs have seized the initiative and acquired turnkey systems that require little or no programming to use. In hindsight, many of these decisions to "go stand-alone" will prove to be flawed. Because the alternative might have been no system at all, it is hard to criticize these decisions as a complete mistake; however, the fact that they have been made at all should demonstrate to the IS professional that today's user is impatient for results and knowledgeable enough to proceed independently. Such a user may well consider many technical solutions other than the central IS department's pet answers.

Regardless of the autonomy of a given user, the IS manager is ultimately responsible for the long-range appropriateness of an organization's uses of technology—or condemned to pick up the pieces. To live up to this responsibility, the IS manager needs to recognize and respect the current variety of end users.

Information Systems Management Skills

How do we define the skills needed by these new IS managers? Some observers have called for a recasting of the traditional picture of this individual's role and skills. Richard Nolan (1983) has described what he calls the computer function executive (CFE) and suggests that this role has developed as the needs of the organization have changed. It is a position, he carefully points out, that must be earned by the incumbent through proper exercise of executive skills. One view of these skills is given by John Rymer (1983), who lists the skill requirements of the chief information officer (CIO), a title frequently used to describe this new and more executive IS manager. That list includes the following:

- The CIO's most important attribute must be an *understanding of the corporation* and its business.
- Top executives have *political, organizational, and communication skills*, and a CIO must match them.
- A CIO must have experience in managing various aspects of organizations, particularly *sales and production functions*.
- Although a CIO need *not be technically oriented*, he or she must be able to manage specialists in hardware, software, networking, and other technical functions.
- A CIO must be a *member of the corporate inner circle* to be effective. This status will require that they be able to manage not only line employees, but other managers as well.

- A CIO must be a *strategic planner* concerned with the long-range implications of new technology.
- A CIO must ensure that the effects *of new technologies on people* are positive and productive.

The term CIO has been used so expansively that some feel it connotes an executive position in addition to that of IS manager, as there could conceivably be too many skills and duties to include in one position. Others strongly maintain that to be properly deployed, these skills have to reside within one position and perhaps even within one individual. All would agree, however, that the addition of such skills to an organization adds a heretofore nonexistent set of strengths to a chief executive's arsenal. Enlightened CEOs recognize this and are moving to acquire these skills.

THE CHANGING BOUNDARIES OF INFORMATION SYSTEMS WITHIN THE ORGANIZATION

As computers and software become less expensive, more varied, sophisticated, and functional, user skills and computer literacy have improved. In many cases this has allowed users to acquire systems without having to follow traditional IS procedures or gain the approval of an IS department. The result, in some organizations, is a central IS department surrounded by many unrelated pockets or islands of technology.

But even where the central IS department has no immediate technical responsibilities, the organization does still need the following:

- Identification of total IS spending.
- Independent identification of benefits of the proposed system at the senior management level.
- Promotion of isolated system successes.
- Education about unsuccessful solutions so as to avoid them in the future
- Consistent approaches, coordinated where necessary and shared where possible.
- Long-range evolution of diverse applications.
- Passive support for uses outside mainstream business activities.
- Assignment of priorities for alternative investments in technology.
- Joint planning process with user departments.

The real challenge for IS management is to progress beyond managing a central information-resource function and to provide, at the corporate level, the services just listed.

Many organizations seek to bring together diverse systems so that they may share data, functionality, and common facilities. This makes sense when the team nature of any organization is considered. However, although it is wise to keep this in mind when devising automation solutions for distributed areas, the need for expediency or functionality, or even the absence of technical opportunity may make integration impossible. In these circumstances IS management is required in order to "retrofit" integration. The approach taken might be to position an organization to benefit from anticipated technical advances. Regardless of the specific approach, oversight and guidance are necessary—which is where IS steps in.

CONCLUSION

It has been relatively few years since the explosive growth of IS systems within organizations began. Therefore, it is understandable that the IS managerial skill base needed to support a demanding managerial challenge is not yet fully in place. The IS profession may be criticized, however, for failing to adjust its conception of an organization's IS needs to the reality and urgency of those needs. In particular, the lack of efficient IS-user relationships remains a significant impasse. Perhaps a new generation of managers is required to meet this challenge. The following chapters attempt to orient and prepare the new IS manager for the assumption of what are in many cases overdue responsibilities.

DISCUSSION QUESTIONS

1. Under what conditions would it be wise for an organization to have a CIO responsible for all corporate IS systems—a person to whom the manager of the central computing department reports? What would be the disadvantages of such an arrangement?

2. Compare and contrast the IS function with the other functions in Exhibit 1-2.

3. How important is the actual name of the corporate function responsible for exploiting computer technology? Explain.

4. What might business organizations do if IS professionals fail to develop the proper management skills?

5. How has the new breed of IS end user made the IS management job harder? How might it have made this job easier?

6. How does one account for the poor image of IS in the eyes of some senior managers? Is their view fair?

REFERENCES

"MIS Rates the Issues," *Datamation* (November 1986).

Nolan, Richard L. (1983). *Stage by Stage*, vol. 3, nos. 2 and 3 (Summer/Fall) Lexington, Mass.: Nolan, Norton, and Co.

Porat, M. U. (1977). *The Information Economy*, Washington, D.C.: U.S. Department of Commerce, Office of Telecommunications Policy.

Rymer, John (1983). "Executives to Unlock Technology's Promise," *Computer Decisions* (September 15), pp. 135–147.

Toffler, Alvin (1981). Interview in *Software* (January), p. 24.

Waterman, Jr., Robert H., et al. (1980). "Structure Is Not Organization," *Business Horizons* (June), pp. 14–29.

two

□

Foundation of Information Systems Management

Models of Information Systems Management

A Taxonomy of Application Systems

The Modern Information Systems Manager

Conclusion

Discussion Questions

References

Information systems have evolved through several stages since the mid- to late 1950s, when computers were first used commercially in organizations. This evolution dramatically affected organizations at all levels. In the functional departments, computers began to be used to automate manual systems and processes and thus to change departmental structures and operations in radical ways. At first, senior management played little part in computerization other than to go along with it and approve hardware and software acquisitions. Eventually, however, senior managers had to step in, imposing controls and resolving disputes that arose between the user and the IS department.

With the rapid and unceasing spread of computer use, IS managers themselves have evolved, and their roles and interactions at all levels of the organization are still in a certain degree of fluctuation. In this chapter we develop a conceptual foundation that will enhance our understanding of the practical limits of IS management. We begin by looking at several models of the evolution of IS and its management, the first of which fills in some important history. Next, we summarize several taxonomies for application systems, briefly trace the evolution of software and hardware technology, and discuss how systems development methods have become increasingly effective. After looking at some changes in both the user community and organizational needs for information management, we wind up with a sketch of the modern IS manager—a picture to be elaborated in future chapters.

MODELS OF INFORMATION MANAGEMENT SYSTEMS

The Stages Hypothesis

Perhaps the most widely known explanation of the evolution of IS is the so-called stages hypothesis (Nolan and Gibson, 1974; Nolan, 1979). Nolan (1979) argued that IS develops in six stages, as shown in Exhibit 2-1. We will describe these stages historically, that is, from the vantage point of a modern IS organization that has gone through all but the last stage.

Stage 1: Initiation   In this stage the computer was introduced into the organization. In the late 1950s the data processing (DP) unit typically consisted of a supervisor (sometimes called the lead programmer), a data entry clerk, and perhaps an operator. The department was usually attached to the accounting or finance area. Not too surprisingly, then, the first applications were accounting-related (for instance, general ledger, accounts payable, accounts receivable, and payroll). Such accounting activities were well defined, operated with a fixed set of rules, and consisted of a repetitive set of operations. Being labor intensive, they were excellent candidates for the first automated systems.

The initiative for developing such systems came almost exclusively from the DP unit. The analysis, design, and programming tools available to automate manual accounting processes were crude, labor intensive, and cryptic to all but a few. Systems development methodologies were not yet sophisticated enough to allow for reasonable definitions of systems requirements and development. Actual

GROWTH PROCESSES	Stage 1 Initiation	Stage 2 Contagion	Stage 3 Control	Stage 4 Integration	Stage 5 Data administration	Stage 6 Maturity
Applications portfolio	Functional cost-reduction applications	Proliferation	Upgrade documentation and restructuring of existing applications	Retrofitting existing applications using data base technology	Integration of applications	Application Integration "mirroring" information flows
DP organization	Specialization for technological learning	User-oriented programmers	Middle management	Establish computer utility and user account teams	Data administration	Data resource Management
DP planning and control	Lax	More lax	Formalized planning and control	Tailored planning and control systems	Shared data and common systems	Data resource strategic planning
User awareness	"Hands off"	Superficially enthusiastic	Arbitrarily held accountable	Accountability learning	Effectively accountable	Acceptance of joint user and data-processing accountability
Level of DP expenditures				Transition point		

EXHIBIT 2-1 Six stages of data processing growth.

Source: Reprinted by permission of the *Harvard Business Review*. An exhibit from "Managing the Crises in Data Processing" by Richard L. Nolan (March-April 1979). Copyright © 1979 by the President and Fellows of Harvard College; all rights reserved.

project completion times were far from the estimated times.

During this stage both the DP staff and system users were learning about the new technology. Because users had no concept of what to expect, they had no reason to be dissatisfied with what they got or with the time required to get it. During this stage—a classic case of the blind leading the blind—both user and programmer were initially quite tolerant of the process, however.

The IS manager (usually called the ADP or DP supervisor at this point) was following what might be called a hero strategy: Simply rush ahead and secure the needed resources. Taking this approach typically did not represent either a sound management decision or a good business decision, but at the time, the new user community was determined to computerize any corporate activity with high labor costs. Most requests for automation were approved by senior management with little in-depth evaluation. Indeed, senior managers had no alternative but to approve the many requests they received; they did not know what kind of questions to ask and would not have known how to evaluate the answers. Eventually, of course, this pattern had to come to an end.

Stage 2: Contagion As information systems were put into production, users became increasingly enthusiastic about new possibilities. As a result, the demand for more computer applications increased. In some cases the EDP group (by now raised to the status of a department) aggravated the situation by overselling computerization. It was not uncommon to hear EDP personnel promise sophisticated systems that would literally replace the manager with a button. Computers were going to make all the decisions.

We now know how unrealistic those promises were, but they did create great excitement among a somewhat naive user community. The contagion stage in the evolution of IS is often characterized as a period of unbridled growth, first in the volume of requests for new systems and then in the volume of requests from EDP departments for more and better hardware. Because computing was typically treated as an overhead expense, users felt no need to restrict their requests. There was little in the way of managerial control. During this stage the general perception was that one had to be a mathematician to learn the special languages of the computer and that few people could refute the arguments of technical wizards for more equipment. The EDP department usually had its way.

Stage 3: Control The inevitable began to happen: missed deadlines, cost overruns, and the like caught the attention of senior management, which had no choice but to ask for some rationale for the money being spent and some reckoning of the benefits being realized. EDP managers began to find their budget requests being closely scrutinized. Senior management was finally paying attention and quickly learned that it was possible to manage an EDP department in much the same way as an engineering department. During this stage the EDP manager was asked to assign priorities with respect to existing and proposed applications; doing so required the implementation of some system of measurement and control. A new way of doing business was emerging for the EDP manager. At the same time, users were being asked to justify their systems development requests. Charge backs to users for computing resource use became popular. The free ride was over.

Senior managers seeking to make informed decisions in the computer and systems area just as in other areas of the organization were now gaining control of the EDP function. They dictated to the EDP manager what was to be done and by when. The EDP manager's role had evolved; at first strongly proactive (the EDP manager took the initiative in computerization), it gradually became reactive (the EDP manager had to answer requests from senior management and to defend most activities).

As the organization entered the 1970s, computing became increasingly more sophisticated. New tools were available. The user community was growing comfortable with the technology and consequently was requesting more sophisticated applications. The term "management information systems" (MIS) replaced EDP. The new MIS field and the MIS manager were maturing. This stage was marked by repeated promises that everything could be computerized.

Many MIS managers tried hard to regain the proactive position that had been lost a decade earlier. However, in too many cases they were trying to become empire builders. The seeds of a problem that would flourish in the early 1980s—autonomous actions on the part of the user community—were being planted.

Stage 4: Integration   During the 1970s the computer industry expanded rapidly as technology raced ahead. Data and systems integration came about as a direct result of centralization of the MIS function under a single management structure. New software technologies in the form of data bases, data-base management systems, and fourth-generation languages made this integration possible. The microcomputer and the first commercially successful spreadsheet package ushered in a new era in computing for the user as the organization entered the 1980s. The broken promises and crippling applications-development backlog of MIS departments could now be circumvented. Users now had tools that would allow them to do much of their own development work. They no longer had to line up at the door of systems and programming offices to request high-priority action on their proposals; they could do their own thing, often without having to request additional monies. The costs of microcomputing hardware and software was falling within reach of many user budgets.

Thus, along with revolutionary changes in technology came equally significant changes in the role of both the user and the IS department (the M was dropped from MIS about this time). During the integration stage there was clear movement toward an IS department that was in effect a utility and service organization for the user, who in turn had access to various tools for systems development. The IS department was evolving from a tightly controlled, centralized structure into a decentralized one. With this evolution, the strong corporate power base that the IS manager had developed over the years became further weakened. End-user and departmental computing were replacing the more traditional systems and programming groups. Both users and the IS department were initiating new systems for the benefit of the organization.

Many diehard IS managers had a difficult time dealing with this evolution. This stage was one of unrest for both the user and the IS department as each tried to determine its respective role in the organization.

Stage 5: Data Administration   In this, the current stage of evolution for most IS organizations, the IS department has recognized that information is a corporate resource that must be made available to all users. For this to happen, information must be managed appropriately. Data must be stored and maintained so that all users have access to them as a shared resource. This stage is characterized by the ascendancy of the user, who now has chief responsibility for the integrity and proper use of organizational information resources. Few organizations have moved beyond the data administration stage.

Stage 6: Maturity   This stage might be called the frontier. If the organization has reached this stage, it has completely woven its information resources into the overall strategic fabric of the organization. The IS manager—or chief information officer (CIO), as he or she is known in some organizations—is a member of the senior management team and a significant contributor to decisions regarding how the computer is to be used for competitive advantage. This person is a strong influence over how the organization does its business and even, in fact, what business it does. Not many organizations have reached this stage; most are at some point between stages 4 and 5.

The stages hypothesis has often been applied to a single organization to determine the development of IS within the existing corporate structure and to indicate appropriate IS strategy. However, because the model is historical, some of the early stages are no longer relevant to organizations just getting involved with computerization. For example, the ready availability of user-friendly software allows the first-time user to begin working productively with sophisticated data-base applications. It would be incorrect to assume that every organization must now pass (or even could pass) through every stage of the model. It is common for companies to skip stages or for different parts of a company to be in different stages simultaneously.

The Nolan and Gibson model is dated, but it is nonetheless of important strategic value to the IS manager. Knowing the stage that an organization, division, department, or user group is in can help the IS manager formulate policy and strategy. Some questions that the model can help the IS manager answer include:

- Are management practices consistent with the stage the company is in?
- Is the organization ready to take advantage of a particular technology?
- Is the systems and programming group technically prepared to support the new strategic directions?

Throughout the book we will discuss material relevant to the answers for these questions.

Critical Success Factors

The Nolan and Gibson hypothesis gives us a good evolutionary view of IS management, especially as it relates to the functional units of the organization. As we have seen, the emergence of the microcomputer in the late 1970s, coupled with the introduction of spreadsheet software, ushered in the era of the end user. It was now possible for the individual manager to access information and begin using it productively and efficiently.

The work of John Rockart and his colleagues (1979) at the Center for Information Systems Research at the Sloan School of Management at the Massachusetts Institute of Technology gave managers a major tool, called critical success factors (CSFs), to help them define their information needs and to link these with general business needs. CSFs, also called strategic success factors by Paul Tom

(1987), are defined as those few areas of business activity that are measurable, have business value, are easily understood, and must go well in order for the organization to succeed. CSFs differ from industry to industry, from organization to organization (even in the same industry), and from one time period to another (even in the same organization). Five prime sources of CSFs have been identified (Bullen and Rockart, 1981):

1. *The industry.* There are usually a few CSFs common to every organization in a particular industry.

2. *Competitive strategy and industry position.* Numerous factors distinguish one organization from another in a given industry. Size, location, and market niche are some of the possible differentiating factors. It is through such differences that CSFs unique to a particular business arise.

3. *Environmental factors.* A number of exogenous factors can often give rise to CSFs. Recent changes in the balance of trade or exchange rates are two examples. These factors are outside the control of the organization.

4. *Temporal factors.* As a result of some extraordinary event a particular CSF may be important, or even primary, but usually only for a short period of time.

5. *Managerial position.* CSFs can also be defined for the functional units of an organization. These may be generic to that organizational level, as well as specific to that functional area.

Some examples of CSFs given in the work of Rockart and his colleagues follow.

Automobile industry

Image
High-quality dealer system
Cost control
Compliance with energy standards

Computer industry

Choice of market niche
Technological leadership
Orderly product development
Service and stability
Attraction and retention of high-quality personnel

Organizations in the same industry may have differing sets of CSFs. Exhibit 2-2 lists, in decreasing order of importance, the CSFs from three different medical group practices. Bullen and Rockart (1981) provide details on the interview process used to define the CSF set for a particular organization or department.

Even if the organization does not use CSFs in its planning process, individual departments can still use them for their own planning activities. And individual managers can use CSFs to develop departmental strategic plans and identify their own information needs.

The Strategic Grid

The strategic grid (Exhibit 2-3), developed by F. W. McFarlan and coworkers (1983), is a tool for connecting the strategic position of the entire organization, its planning environment, and the appropriate management of information technology. (As used here, the term *information technology* (IT) refers only to hardware and software systems.) The grid contains four main categories into which organizations can be placed.

The Support Category   The support role played by IS has its roots in the beginnings of commercial data processing; when transaction-based processes were automated. For organizations in this category,

Clinic 1	Clinic 2	Clinic 3
Government regulations	Quality and comprehensive care	Efficiency of operation
Efficiency of operations	Federal funding	Staffing mix
Patient's view of practice	Government regulations	Government regulations
Relation to hospital	Efficiency of operations	Patient's view of practice
Malpractice insurance effects	Patient's view of practice	Relation to community
Relation to comunity	Satellite versus patient service	Relation to hospital
	Other providers in community	
	Relation to hospital	

EXHIBIT 2-2 Example of critical success factors for three different medical group practices.

Source: Reprinted by permission of the *Harvard Business Review.* An exhibit from "Chief Executives Define Their Own Data Needs" by John Rockart (March-April 1979). Copyright © 1983 by Richard D. Irwin, Inc.

the objective of the IS department is cost reduction and the IS manager's success hinges on the achievement of this objective. Organizations in this category are usually well-established manufacturing or manufacturing-related firms.

The Turnaround Category Organizations tend to move from the support category to the turnaround category as a result of both external and internal factors and pressures. Newer and more cost-effective computer products and services as well as industry dynamics are the two major external factors. Through enlightened management as well as growing pressures from its end-user groups, the organization may move into the turnaround category. This category represents, however, only a temporary strategic position. If the organization does not follow-up with additional development of strategic systems, it will move into the factory category. However, should such follow-up activity occur, the organization may eventually move into the strategic category. The turnaround category is thus seen as a transitional category. The appropriate action for the IS manager in a turnaround-category organization will be to continue encouraging changes that have strategic value.

The Factory Category Organizations in the factory category have implemented systems with a definite strategic impact, although no new systems in the development portfolio are so labeled. The

		Strategic impact of existing application systems	
		Low	High
Strategic impact of applications systems under development	High	Turnaround	Strategic
	Low	Support	Factory

EXHIBIT 2-3 Strategic impact of application systems.

Source: Reprinted by permission of Richard D. Irwin, Inc. an exhibit from *Corporate Information Systems Management* by F. W. McFarlan and J. L. Kenny. Copyright © 1983 by Richard D. Irwin, Inc.

activities of the IS department in organizations in the factory category are more sophisticated than in the support category, but the IS department's role is still limited to current operational activities. The challenges are to improve existing strategic systems and sustain the strategic thrust of the organization through education programs and additional efficiency/effectiveness initiatives. Some of these efforts may require a technology push rather than a business pull.

The Strategic Category　In organizations in the strategic category, the IS department acts in true partnership with senior management in strategy set formation. The IS manager is the information expert on the management team and, in that capacity, is expected to identify, recommend, and implement information and technology changes that will affect the strategic direction of the organization. Continual effort will also be required to protect the organization's current strategic position. The framework for accomplishing this must be collaborative. The IS manager also works with functional area managers to maintain and improve products and services in the strategic portfolio.

The strategic grid is a much more powerful tool for the IS manager than might be obvious at first. To exploit it fully, the IS manager must first determine in which category the organization finds itself and then take appropriate action. For example, if the organization is in the factory category and the IS manager is trying to allocate the departmental budget across various competing projects, he or she should favor allocations to activities that maintain and improve existing systems rather than investing in new technologies and new applications. It is possible, however, that new technologies should be acquired if they contribute directly to the efficiency and effectiveness of existing systems. On the same theme, an appropriate planning system would be one that reacts to the existing business plan rather than one that blazes new trails. (We return to this topic in Chapter 5.)

The strategic grid has other applications for the IS manager. The support and factory categories are static, whereas the turnaround and strategic categories are dynamic. Similarly, the support and factory categories are concerned with present operations, whereas the turnaround and strategic categories are concerned with future operations. Budget decisions should roughly favor operations in the case of support- and factory-category organizations and development in the case of turnaround- and strategic-category organizations. The choice of an appropriate planning system will follow a similar pattern. In general, IS planning will be reactive for organizations in the support and factory categories and proactive for those in the turnaround or strategic categories.

The Benefit/Beneficiary Matrix

It was through the efforts of Cyrus Gibson and Michael Hammer (1985) that the stages hypothesis, the CSF method, and the strategic grid were synthesized into the benefit/beneficiary matrix (Exhibit 2-4). Their creation is in essence an operational tool. It makes use of a "domain" scheme to categorize an organization's use or need for information technology.

Domain 1 For organizations in the initiation and contagion stages of the Nolan and Gibson model, the primary purpose of computing is to improve the efficiency of functional departments. Most systems are initially developed to reduce the labor cost associated with highly repetitive activities (primarily in the accounting functions). As organizations advance in subsequent stages, they use automation to increase effectiveness in other functional areas. Domain 1 in the benefit/beneficiary matrix contains functional units as the beneficiaries and efficiency and effectiveness as the benefits.

Domain 2 As the Nolan and Gibson model shows, the introduction of the microcomputer and other end-user tools gave rise to a new beneficiary, the individual user. Spreadsheets offer managers a

Information Technology as a Strategic Weapon			
Benefits \ Beneficiary	Individuals	Functional units	Whole organization
Efficiency / Effectiveness	Domain 2	Domain 1	Domain 3
Transformation			

EXHIBIT 2-4 Benefit/beneficiary matrix.

Source: Cyrus F. Gibson and Michael Hammer, "Now That the Dust Has Settled, A Clear View of the Terrain," *Indications*, vol. 2, no. 5, July, 1985, Index Group, Inc., Cambridge, Mass.

means of improving the quality and timeliness of their decisions. And, by using the CSF method, managers can define their own information needs and thereby improve their effectiveness. Clerical workers, too, can use word processing to improve both the speed and accuracy of their work. Domain 2 therefore contains individuals as beneficiary and efficiency and effectiveness as benefits.

Domain 3   Michael Porter (1980) developed a value system model as an extension of value chain analysis. The model examines the relationships between an organization and its suppliers and customers. One of the outcomes from this examination is the identification of information technology applications that have the potential of strengthening these relationships. Information could be used to develop systems that expanded and redefined the responsibilities of individuals and functional units. Information could also create linkages to external forces in the value system. In summary, the strategic use of information can transform the organization both internally and externally. Organizations will realize some competitive advantages as a result. As an example consider making a customer's order status available to them electronically. This creates linkages for the customer with sales, production, and shipping and strengthens ties to that customer. Each of these functions is changed in order to accommodate the new system and realize the competitive advantages that result.

Uses of the Benefit/Beneficiary Matrix   As we have seen, the matrix synthesizes the evolutionary development of IS in the organization. It is an excellent conceptual foundation for strategy set (mission, goals, objectives, strategy) development based on existing and new information technologies. It can also be used as an operational tool for exploiting IT by redefining it in terms of the nine cells shown in Exhibit 2-5. To use the matrix, a manager will first determine what problem he or she wishes to solve and whether the beneficiary of the solution, whatever it will be, is an individual, a functional unit, or the organization. By determining the benefits, the manager can position the problem in one of the nine cells in the matrix and then focus on the appropriate technology to solve the problem.

A TAXONOMY OF APPLICATION SYSTEMS

In addition to the IS management environment, it is instructive to consider the applications environment. Two popular classification schemata for applications systems are Dickson's systems hierarchy

(Dickson, 1968) and the Gorry and Scott-Morton decision taxonomy (Gorry and Scott-Morton, 1971).

The Systems Hierarchy

In 1968 Gary Dickson proposed a model of IS development (Exhibit 2-6) that centered on the structure of the organization and its information needs at various levels. In Dickson's model, applications systems are categorized as clerical, information, decision support, and programmed. These constitute the entity now known as MIS. Each is briefly discussed next.

Level 1: Clerical Systems Computerized systems at this level simply replace certain manual operations. The earliest commercial systems were of this type and were almost exclusively accounting related. Accounting applications, which are oriented largely toward transactions, have well-defined inputs, outputs, and processing rules and are thus prime candidates for computerization. Historically, the IS department took the initiative in suggesting computerization of accounting; the user's role was passive and seldom involved

Benefit/Beneficiary Matrix			
Benefits \ Beneficiary	Individual	Functional unit	Organization
Efficiency	Task mechanization	Process automation	Boundary extension
Effectiveness	Work improvement	Functional enhancement	Service enhancement
Transformation	Role expansion	Functional redefinition	Product innovation

EXHIBIT 2-5 Type of application by matrix cell.

Source: Cyrus F. Gibson and Michael Hammer, "Now That the Dust Has Settled, A Clear View of the Terrain," *Indications*, vol. 2, no. 5, July, 1985, Index Group, Inc., Cambridge, Mass.

more than input/output specification and ceremonial sign-offs at development milestones.

Clerical systems are characteristic of the initiation and contagion stages of the Nolan and Gibson model and of the support category in McFarlan's strategic grid.

Level 2: Information Systems   For managers, the ability to store and retrieve data is a tool for control and effective decision making. Information systems (as the term is used by Dickson) exist primarily to assist the manager with control and/or decision-making activities. The system provides summarized data that the manager synthesizes into information for control and/or decision making. The information, per se, is therefore external to the system.

Initially, the user played only a token role in the development of information systems, even though the motivating force behind such systems was often not the IS manager but rather user managers or senior managers. A major problem in developing these information systems, therefore, was determining how to give users a larger role in all phases of the systems development cycle. These information systems are characteristic of the control stage of the Nolan and Gibson model.

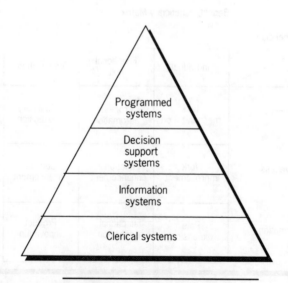

EXHIBIT 2-6 The systems hierarchy.

Source: Reprinted from W. Gary Dickson, "Management Information-Decision Systems," *Business Horizons,* vol. 11, no. 12, December 1968. Copyright 1968 by the Foundation for the School of Business at Indiana University. Used with permission.

Level 3: Decision Support Systems Application systems at this level are almost exclusively interactive manager-machine systems. The decision-making situations that these systems address are relatively complex; that is, reaching a decision involves both processing data according to fixed rules and algorithms (which computers accomplish very well) and synthesizing information according to heuristics or just plain "gut feeling" (which a manager can do). The actual decision is usually the result of repeated loops between the computer and the decision-maker.

Decision support systems (DSS) are characteristic of systems developed in the integration and data administration stages of the Nolan and Gibson model. DSS have definite strategic value and are therefore also characteristic of organizations in the turnaround and strategic categories. It is worth noting that the computer professional and the user form a team that initiates and develops the DSS. In a certain sense they are both proactive, as neither one acting alone could accomplish the result.

Level 4: Programmed Systems Decisions that can be made on the basis of a condition defined according to a set of rules are addressed by so-called programmed systems. The most sophisticated of these systems are based on concepts from the field of artificial intelligence. The development of application systems at this level requires that the IS manager be a member of the senior management team. The IS manager must have a keen sense of the business and of creative ways to apply computer technology to gain competitive advantage and augment market share. Programmed systems thus involve the IS manager in a very proactive role and are characteristic of organizations in the strategic category.

Taxonomy of Decision-making Situations

On the assumption that information systems exist only to assist managers in decision-making exercises, we can look at the characteristics of the decision-making situation itself as a framework for considering the development of information systems. H. A. Simon (1960) provides a useful taxonomy of decision-making situations by placing them on a continuum ranging from programmed to unprogrammed. However, the more common terms are structured (algorithmic or determined) and unstructured (heuristic or random), so these are the terms we will use.

Initially, applications systems were developed for those decision-making situations classified as structured. As hardware and software became more sophisticated and as systems development methods became better understood, more challenging decision-making situations could be computerized. As a result, more and more applications were developed for situations that tended toward the unstructured.

Nearly 25 years ago, R. N. Anthony (1965) introduced a three-part taxonomy of managerial activities that remains useful today

1. *Operational control:* The process of ensuring that specific tasks are carried out effectively and efficiently.

2. *Management control:* The process by which managers ensure that resources are obtained and used effectively and efficiently in the accomplishment of the organization's objectives.

3. *Strategic planning:* The process of deciding on the organization's objectives, changes in these objectives, the resources used to attain them, and the policies governing the acquisition, use, and disposition of these resources.

Gordon Davis (1974) extended Anthony's taxonomy by adding a more basic activity called operations. However, Anthony's taxonomy has become a standard, so we will use it here. By combining Simon's taxonomy of decision-making situations with Anthony's taxonomy of managerial activities, we arrive at the IS framework shown in Exhibit 2-7. This framework is useful because it clearly indicates that in the past most IS activity centered on structured decision-making situations. The traditional systems development cycle suited structured applications in which users typically had played a reactive role; developers and users interacted only when the developer needed the user to sign-off on an analysis or design phase. Often the user did not really understand what was being done but was under pressure to cooperate so as not to cause further project delays. As development tools became more sophisticated, senior management directed IS managers to develop systems for operational and managerial control. Initially, these systems involved structured decision-making situations (e.g., budget analysis), but they soon began to involve semistructured situations (e.g., inventory control, production scheduling).

The roles of the user, the systems developer, and the IS manager thus started to change on the basis of whether the decision-making situations were structured, semistructured, or unstructured. The traditional systems development cycle quickly became ineffective (Keen, 1980), and the user began to play a more active role, in many cases assuming responsibility for the design of the system (Lucas, 1986). The nature of certain decision-making situations forced an alliance that at first was uneasy; neither user nor system developer could get along without the other. The user needed the developer to translate certain problems into computer code, and the developer needed the user to describe the problem or situation to be addressed (Keen, 1980).

As the taxonomies just discussed reveal, important factors contribute to the role changes experienced by users, developers, and managers (both IS and corporate). These factors are the evolution of new hardware and software technology, more effective systems development methods, a more sophisticated user community, and changing organizational needs. Each is discussed in the sections that follow.

	Operational Control	Management Control	Strategic Planning
Structured	Accounts receivable	Budget analysis— engineered costs	Tanker fleet mix
	Order entry	Short-term forecasting	Warehouse and factory location
	Inventory control		
Semistructured	Production scheduling	Variance analysis— overall budget	Mergers and acquisitions
	Cash management	Budget preparation	New product planning
Unstructured	PERT/COST planning systems	Sales and production	R&D

EXHIBIT 2-7 A framework for information systems.

Source: Reprinted from "A Framework for Management Information Systems," by Anthony Gorry and Michael S. Scott-Morton, *Sloan Management Review*, Fall 1971, p. 62, by permission of the publisher. Copyright © 1971 by Sloan Management Review Association. All rights reserved.

Evolution of Hardware and Software Technology

To think that we have moved from paper tape and punch cards to both touch- and voice-activated systems in a little over three decades is staggering. Keeping up with new technologies while interacting with user and senior management has posed a significant challenge for the IS manager.

Of all the new technologies, the most significant are the personal computer (PC), a collection of user-friendly software packages, and micro-to-mainframe communications. The emergence of the microcomputer in the mid-1970s was at first ignored by the business community. Many viewed the PC as a toy, not a device that could have any measurable value for the organization. The picture quickly changed, however, with the introduction of Visicalc in 1976. Monthly ledgers, budgets, balance sheets, and various standard forms could be quickly constructed and modified for a variety of planning and analysis needs. The PC did find a place in the business world and gave users a sound tool for developing their own applications. PC hardware and software was relatively inexpensive, and their acquisition could go relatively unnoticed. Every department could buy its own microsystems and begin development right under the nose, so to speak, of the IS manager.

Most IS managers initially tried to ignore the proliferation of PCs, thinking that they represented a fad that would soon disappear. However, as a wide range of easy-to-use software packages became available, the PC became more functional. Users were at last able to break the shackles of the applications backlog and take charge of their own applications development. Gradually, the more visionary IS managers began devising strategies to capitalize on user initiatives. (A detailed discussion of these strategies is found in Part IV.)

Further advances in office automation, CAD/CAM, factory automation, and desktop publishing have added yet another layer of complexity to IS management. These so called "islands of technology" were (and still are) developed totally outside the traditional boundaries of IS. In many cases they have their own hardware, software, staff, and budgets. (In Chapter 10 we examine these "islands" and consider organizational and chain-of-command questions.)

As applications of artificial intelligence begin to find their way into organizations, the IS manager will have opportunities to increase their value to the organization. By the mid-1980s artificial intelligence had developed to the point where commercially available "expert system" shells were available for constructing sophisticated systems to deal with unstructured decision-making situations.

These systems had applications at the operational, managerial, and strategic levels of the organization and offered the promise of significant effects on profitability and market share. Here was a chance to use computer technology to create new products, new services, and new ways of doing business. Using artificial intelligence tools to develop expert systems, IS managers have an opportunity to contribute to the automation of heuristic decision processes at lower levels in the organization and eventually to decision-making at the executive level.

Artificial intelligence certainly seems to make Nolan's and Gibson's maturity stage attainable. To reach that stage, however, the IS manager will need to act creatively and aggressively and to forge a new partnership with senior management. This is not to say that IS will always jump on the new technology. Such action will frequently result in senior management becoming more skeptical. In Part II we discuss this new partnership.

More Effective Systems Development Methods

Initially, systems development methods involved little user-developer interaction. As users became more comfortable with the computer and as IS professionals became more familiar with business functions, however, shared efforts were undertaken during the specification and design phases, and users began to play a more active role in the entire process. As organizations moved into the control stage, the systems being developed were essentially the information systems of Dickson's model. They often addressed decision-making situations and applications that bordered on the semistructured, such as production planning. During the control stage, senior management became very directive toward IS management, forcing the IS manager to give the user a more meaningful role in specification and design.

Prototyping (see Chapters 15 and 16), an adaptive design technique that involves repetitive feedback loops from user to designer as the system takes shape, soon emerged as a development methodology to be used in semistructured decision-making situations. The user assumed equal responsibility with the systems developer—and sometimes even more, as Lucas (1986) points out. Moreover, with micro-based nonprocedural languages, the aggressive user had tools that made it very tempting to assume fully the role of the systems developer. A dramatic turning point had been reached.

An entirely new strategy for managing the IS function is now emerging, one that takes into account changing end-user capabilities. The results are very encouraging. Organizations are at last on the threshold of exploiting the computer in creative, effective, and productive ways.

A More Sophisticated User Community

In the early 1980s experienced users began helping new users "get up to speed." User groups were formed, and departmental computing units were established with their own hardware and function-specific applications development teams. By the mid-1980s the user community had generally matured. It was now placing more demands on the IS department for accountability and for opportunities to participate in long-range systems planning.

Some IS managers, realizing that these end users were an untapped resource that could be used to reduce the applications backlog, took the initiative and established information centers. Initially, these were places for the new user to go for introductory training in PC and applications package use, as well as help in deciding what hardware and software were best suited for various applications. IS managers had a hidden agenda, too: by establishing information centers, they opened the door for the implementation of standards in hardware/software acquisition and data definition for end users.

It was not long, however, before users discovered that by linking into the corporate data base they could develop even better systems for managerial decision making (Rockart and Treacy, 1982). They began to insist that their PCs be connected to corporate mainframes so that they could access mainframe data. At this point, many IS managers felt threatened. The data they had worked so hard to protect and keep "clean" could now be down-loaded to anyone's PC. At first, some IS managers were reluctant to cooperate and senior managers had to step in and resolve disputes—usually siding with the user.

For organizations that moved from the control to the integration stage, *data*, not computers, were viewed as the corporate resource. Although the IS department had to acquiesce to senior management's proactive positions, it was by no means relegated to a reactive role. Because the user now had access to corporate data, new database architectures that ensured effective data definition and update procedures had to be developed. IS managers stepped in to play a decidedly proactive role by establishing effective data design and maintenance procedures. This in turn gave impetus to further applications development, because the user now had better data manipulation and analysis tools at his or her disposal.

Organizations with these user-IS department relations—relations based on cooperation—have moved into the data administration stage. Having an effective, well-managed data-base environment has become essential to the IS manager who seeks to contribute significantly to corporate strategic planning activities.

Changing Organizational Needs

As we have seen, early DP units were given what amounted to corporate carte blanche in their system development efforts. But as the cost of computing increased, so did the attention that management devoted to it. Because both the IS manager and the user had to justify costs and benefits, control systems became necessary. This necessity motivated the development of data-base management systems (DBMSs), which provide enhanced control tools for all decision-making situations.

For senior and IS management, the emphasis had shifted: Data were now viewed as a resource that had to be planned, organized, and controlled. The IS department clearly had to take an aggressive stance in the determination of policy with regard to data management. And, with the availability of commercial products in artificial intelligence, senior management can now begin to identify applications that will result in definite strategic and competitive advantages. In short, the computer is now being viewed as a competitive weapon by mature organizations.

THE MODERN INFORMATION SYSTEMS MANAGER

Our overview of the stages hypothesis, CSFs, the strategic grid, and the benefit/beneficiary matrix gave an indication of the ever-changing roles of the user and top management and their effect on the IS manager. The challenges facing the IS manager are great, and many of them are new. For the time being, experience rather than theory often serves as a guide in these uncharted areas. To be successful in the current information age, the IS manager must have the following

- An intimate knowledge of the organization's business activity.
- A sense for how technology and business can together create a competitive strategy and market advantage.
- Sensitivity to the diverse needs of professionals in the IS organization.

■ Patience in communicating with users and helping them develop realistic and clear expectations regarding the role of computers in their work.

The position of IS manager is one of considerable corporate power, influence, and opportunity. It is also one of high risk. (The turnover rate of IS managers is high; the median length of service is less than 3 years.) In the chapters that follow, we put into perspective the present course of and future possibilities for the IS manager.

CONCLUSION

The IS management models we have been discussing so far can be used by IS managers in a variety of ways. Using the stages hypothesis, the IS manager can identify the stage in which his or her organization currently lies and then determine appropriate actions with respect to such issues as planning, control, management styles, and the role of the user. A company's actual position on the strategic grid vis-à-vis where it should be relative to its industry can help the IS manager develop a strategy for change or maintenance. The CSF method provides the IS manager with a means of linking the business needs of the organization and the data/systems needs of the IS department. The IS department can identify both data that can be measured and systems that can be developed to serve as a monitoring or early-warning system and as a control device for the CSFs.

Decision-making that focuses on corporate strategy set development or the support of end-user computing (among other issues) has a conceptual basis in the models we have investigated in this chapter. Having positioned the organization with respect to these models' categories, and having assessed current and planned strategic initiatives, the IS manager is better equipped to build an appropriate management environment: to determine staff and budget planning, to develop controls and define standards, urge needed technological initiatives, and plan workable strategies. Like all models and taxonomies, those covered in this chapter are meant to serve as tools, not as inflexible descriptors or rigid rules for action. The history whose contours these tools reveal is a fast-paced and constantly evolving one, and the IS manager's toughest job is to keep pace.

DISCUSSION QUESTIONS

1. What roles might the user-manager play in the development of a new computer-based system?

2. As an IS manager in an organization familiar to you, how would you give the user a greater role in IS development? Why would you want to?

3. How would you expect the role of IS to change over the next 10 years? How would you, as an IS manager, prepare for these changes?

4. How would you describe end users with respect to their involvement in applications systems development? In your opinion, what services should be provided to them? How and by whom should these services be provided? In your response, consider users at all levels of the organization.

5. Which model of IS management most accurately reflects your perception of the approach to such management?

REFERENCES

Anthony, R. N. (1965). *Planning and Control Systems: A Framework for Analysis;* Boston: Harvard University Graduate School of Business Administration.

Bullen, Christine V., and John F. Rockart (1981). "A Primer on Critical Success Factors," Center for Information Systems Research, Working Paper 69, Cambridge, Mass.: Massachusetts Institute of Technology, Sloan School of Management.

Davis, Gordon B. (1974). *Management Information Systems: Conceptual Foundations, Structure, and Development,* New York: McGraw–Hill.

Dickson, Gary W. (1968). "Management Information—Decision Systems," *Business Horizons,* vol. 11, no. 12 (December), pp. 17–26.

Gibson, Cyrus F., and Michael Hammer (1985). "Now That the Dust Has Settled, A Clear View of the Terrain," *Indications,* vol. 2, no. 5 (July), Cambridge, Mass.: Index Group Inc..

Gorry, Anthony, and Michael S. Scott-Morton (1971). "A Framework for Management Information Systems," *Sloan Management Review,* vol. 13, no. 1 (Fall), pp. 55–70.

Keen, Peter G. W. (1980). "Decision Support Systems: A Research Perspective," Center for Information Systems Research, Working Paper 54 (March),

Cambridge, Mass.: Massachusetts Institute of Technology, Sloan School of Management.

Lucas, Henry C. (1986). *Information Systems Concepts for Management*, 3rd ed., New York: McGraw–Hill.

McFarlan, F. W., and J. L. McKenney (1983). *Corporate Information Systems Management: The Issues Facing Senior Executives*, Homewood, Ill.: Irwin.

Nolan, Richard L. (1979). "Managing the Crisis in Data Processing," *Harvard Business Review*, vol. 57, no. 2 (March-April), pp. 115–126.

Nolan, Richard L., and Cyrus F. Gibson (1974). "Managing the Four Stages of EDP Growth," *Harvard Business Review*, vol. 52, no. 1 (January-February), pp. 76–78.

Porter, Michael E. (1980). *Competitive Strategies*, New York: Free Press.

Rockart, John F. (1979). "Chief Executives Define Their Own Data Needs," *Harvard Business Review*, vol. 57, no. 2 (March-April), pp. 81–93.

Rockart, John F., and Michael Treacy (1982). "The CEO Goes On-Line," *Harvard Business Review*, vol. 60, no. 1 (January-February), pp. 82–88.

Simon, H. A. (1960). *The New Science of Management Decision*, New York: Harper & Row.

Tom, Paul L. (1987). *Managing Information as a Corporate Resource*, Glenview, Ill.: Scott, Foresman.

SUGGESTED STUDENT PROJECTS

1. Interview the IS manager in a major organization. Focus the interview on how his or her role has changed over the last several years and what the challenges are for the future.

2. Pick a company that has used computers for at least 25 years and one that has used them for 5 to 10 years. Compare and contrast the development of the IS function in each company using Nolan's stages model.

3. Interview five IS managers to determine the major issues they currently face. Compare these results with those found by Gary Dickson (*MIS Quarterly*, September 1984, pp. 135-159.)

Supplementary Reading List

Barnes, Louis B., and Mark P. Kriger (1986). The Hidden Side of Organizational Leadership," *Sloan Management Review*, vol. 28, no. 1 (Fall), pp. 15–25.

Dickson, Gary W., et al. (1984). "Key Information Systems Issues for the 1980's," *MIS Quarterly* (September), pp. 135–159.

Diebold, John (1984). "Six Issues That Will Affect the Future of Information Management," *Data Management* (July), pp. 10–14.

Drucker, Peter F. (1988). "The Coming of the New Organization," *Harvard Business Review*, vol. 68, no. 1 (January-February), pp. 45–53.

Feldman, Robert (1987). "Experts Say: Link Up Strategically, Or Die," *MIS Week*, vol. 8, no. 33, pp. 1ff.

Grant, F. J. (1987). "The Critical Success Factor That Counts," *Computerworld* (November 2), pp. 75–86.

Grayson, Ashley, and John Vornholt (1987). "The New MIS," *Computerworld* (June 1), pp. 14ff.

Hammer, Michael (1987). "Back to the Future," Computerworld (June 1), pp. 8–13.

Hammer, Michael, and Glenn E. Mangurian (1987). "The Changing Value of Communications Technology," *Sloan Management Review*, vol. 29, no. 2 (Winter), pp. 65–71.

Hartog, Curt, and Martin Herbert (1986). "1985 Opinion Survey of MIS Managers: Key Issues," *MIS Quarterly* (December), pp. 351–361.

Jenster, Per V. (1987). "Using Critical Success Factors in Planning," *Long Range Planning*, vol. 20, no. 4, pp. 102–109.

Kinkead, Michael D. (1987). "Mission Critical Systems: The Next Wave," *Mass High Tech* (March 2-15), pp. 33–34.

Lederer, Albert L., and Aubrey L. Mendelow (1987). "Information Resource Planning: Overcoming Difficulties in Identifying Top Management's Objectives," *MIS Quarterly* (September), pp. 389–399.

McFarlan, F. Warren (1981). "Portfolio Approach to Information Systems," *Harvard Business Review*, vol 59, no. 5 (September-October), pp. 142–150.

Nolan, Richard L. (1979). "Managing the Crisis in Data Processing," *Harvard Business Review*, vol. 57, no. 2 (March-April), pp. 115–126.

Raho, Louis E., et al. (1987). "Assimilating New Technology Into the Organization: An Assessment of McFarlan and McKenney's Model," *MIS Quarterly* (March), pp. 47–57.

Rockart, John F. (1982). "The Changing Role of the Information Systems Executive: A Critical Success Factors Perspective," *Sloan Management Review* (Fall), pp. 3–13.

Shank, Michael E., and Andrew C. Boynton (1985). "Critical Success Factor Analysis as a Methodology for MIS Planning," *MIS Quarterly* (June), pp. 121–129.

Withington, Frederic G. (1980). "Coping With Computer Proliferation," *Harvard Business Review*, vol. 58, no. 3 (May-June), pp. 152–164.

▫ PART II ▫

INFORMATION SYSTEMS AS A CORPORATE ENTITY

In recent years, perhaps the greatest changes in how the IS department functions, as well as in how it is perceived, have occurred at the corporate level. The IS manager, whose influence was once felt strictly on the departmental level, has been drawn into a totally new, unfamiliar, and challenging environment—that of senior management. And senior managers, like IS managers, are uneasy with this new collaboration. They recognize and accept the need to involve IS managers in strategy set development, but they have generally not been able to devise a step-by-step process to make that involvement happen.

In experiencing this important period of transition, the IS manager has been given an opportunity to carve out a new set of responsibilities. The time has come for this manager to become a major player on the senior management team, one who helps set a new agenda for the organization.

CHAPTER 3

The Role of Information Systems as a Corporate Entity

CHAPTER 4

Information Technology as a Competitive Weapon

CHAPTER 5
Strategic Information Systems Planning

CHAPTER 6
The Organizational Placement of the
Information Systems Department

CHAPTER 7
Information Systems Corporate Issues and Opportunities

SUGGESTED STUDENT PROJECTS

SUPPLEMENTARY READING LIST

three

The Role of Information Systems as a Corporate Entity

Corporate Responsibility: Three Domains

The Proactive Information Systems Manager

Resistance of Senior Management

The Information Systems Manager's Relations with
Other Managers

Major Organizational Challenges Facing the Information
Systems Manager

The Emerging Chief Information Officer

Conclusion

Discussion Questions

References

We are in the middle of a period that will be remembered as among
the most revolutionary and dynamic in the history of the industrial-
ized world: a period during which information has become of primary
importance. The challenges we face demand special and different

behavior on the part of the IS manager, who must be more creative and entrepreneurial than ever before.

The IS manager of the early 1980s could be characterized as a reactive manager, one who responded to the plans and requests from all levels of management. But things have changed so dramatically in recent years that this characterization is no longer accurate. Information-intensive organizations have come to depend on the IS manager as a proactive member of the senior management team. This shift has entailed a radical reshaping of the IS function, especially its interactions with middle and senior management. A new business partnership has been established between the IS manager and the rest of the management team.

This chapter looks at the metamorphosis of the IS department's role in the "information organization." We begin by looking at three broad areas of corporate responsibility for IS. From there we move to a discussion of the proactive IS manager; here we draw once again on the strategic grid introduced in Chapter 2. Next we turn to the issue of high-level resistance to a redefined role for IS, touching on reasons for this resistance and suggesting several strategies for involving senior managers in a necessary process of transformation. This discussion leads us to explore relations between IS and other unit managers and to investigate, in general terms, the nature and balance of power in an organization. We follow with a brief examination of the organizational challenges that IS managers must confront and then end with a look at the emerging CIO.

CORPORATE RESPONSIBILITY: THREE DOMAINS

Stuart Sinclair (1986) defines three "domains" that help organize our discussion of the corporate-level responsibilities of the IS department and the IS manager: efficiency, effectiveness, and competitiveness. The main question pertaining to the first domain is "Are we doing things right?"—that is, is the organization minimizing its unit costs for each product mix? With regard to the second domain, the important question is "Are we doing the right thing?"—that is, is the mix of products and services optimal? And the key question relevant to competitiveness, the third domain, is "Are we headed in a direction consistent with our understanding of our environment?"—that is, does the organization have an overall strategy and is it sure that this strategy is the right one?

Exhibit 3-1 coordinates these three domains with IS functions at three major organizational levels: operational, tactical, and strategic. The operational and tactical levels are discussed throughout Part III. At the strategic level, the IS manager has responsibilities in all three domains. The most challenging of the three is certainly competitiveness. Here the IS manager, as a member of the senior management team, must draw on all of his or her creative energies and insights to monitor trends and market conditions in order to identify new opportunities for the organization to pursue. This "gatekeeper" function is critical to the future survival of many organizations, especially those in information-intensive businesses. Let us look more closely at why a proactive IS manager is necessary if the modern organization is to prosper in an intensely competitive environment.

| | Organizational Level | | |
Domain	**Operational**	**Tactical**	**Strategic**
Efficiency	To reduce unit production and sales costs as much as possible To minimize turnaround times	To improve capacity planning To improve scheduling To improve inventory control and manufacturing resource planning	To optimize distribution systems
Effectiveness	To respond to all relevant inquiries	To ensure that all tasks are accomplished thoroughly	To maximize coverage of markets for sales and service
Competitiveness			To scan the competitive environment outside the firm, identifying and tracking threats and opportunities to do things differently, or to do different things and estimating the consequences of each change

EXHIBIT 3-1 The domains of information systems at three organizational levels.

THE PROACTIVE INFORMATION
SYSTEMS MANAGER

Until recently the IS manager seldom functioned in a truly proactive role at the corporate level. Rather than participating in the creation of the corporate strategic plan, the IS manager received the corporate plan along with the charge to develop an information systems plan that would help the organization, its divisions, and its departments meet their objectives. In this role the IS manager responded to initiatives taken by senior managers and was expected to do the following:

- Establish policies and procedures to facilitate the accomplishment of planning objectives.
- Acquire and allocate hardware, software, and staff resources.
- Ensure the timely delivery of systems and services needed to meet corporate goals.

Although these responsibilities are of course still integral to the IS function, they no longer completely define IS's place in the organization. To remain competitive, many organizations have discovered that they must encourage new operational relationships between IS and other units—relationships that become part of the very fabric of the organization and that may change the way it conducts its business. We will look more closely at these relationships later in this chapter.

Carol Saunders (1986) articulates this need for a radical restructuring of the IS manager's position:

> **It then becomes necessary for the Information Systems Department not only to respond to technological changes and end user needs, but to suggest ways in which IT can be used to continue and further the organization's competitive edge. Fundamental changes are required to move the Information Systems Department from IT distributors to corporate strategists. The most striking change is that the Information Systems manager no longer merely works within the framework of the organizational strategy set (i.e., mission, objective, strategy). Instead he [or she] helps develop that framework.**

On the same theme, John Rockart and Adam Crescenzi (1984) have identified a new role for senior management:

Clearly it is time for top management to get off the sidelines. Recognizing that information is a strategic resource implies a clear need to link information systems to business strategy, and, especially, to insure that business strategy is developed in the context of the new IT environment.

So we see that a new alliance must be formed at the executive level. To function well that alliance depends on the proactive as well as reactive behavior on the part of the IS manager. At the same time, senior managers are finding that they must reciprocate; they need to be open to new technologies and willing to provide a forum for their exploitation. Such changes are evolutionary. They require a well-planned and well-executed program, one that depends on the organization's intended use and control of information.

To better understand the evolution that must occur, we might recall McFarlan's strategic grid, which draws together the IS department's support and development roles (see Exhibit 2-3). Using the grid, we can get a picture of where an organization is positioned strategically and can determine whether its strategic position can or should change as a result of its current and planned use of information systems. We now return to the four categories of organizations defined by the grid, highlighting the proactive IS manager's role in each context.

The Support Category

Organizations in this category use information systems for their operational impact (i.e., cost reduction). They have not identified strategic applications, nor is it imperative that they do so. If the organization is appropriately positioned in this category, the IS manager will concentrate on maintaining a steady level of support at minimal cost. If the organization is incorrectly positioned and is missing opportunities to implement systems with high strategic value, the IS manager will need to develop initiatives to move the organization toward the turnaround category. Depending on the organization's readiness, this may require a deliberate, well-executed IS education program starting at the executive level.

The Turnaround Category

Organizations in this category have evolved from the support category as a result of proactive initiatives on the part of the IS manager, user initiatives to acquire a single-purpose system with strategic value, or industry pressures, or some combination thereof. Regardless of the strategic application, the IS manager will want to sustain the initiative by maintaining a flexible and receptive posture in seeking out additional opportunities. Joint efforts with users through R&D projects, demonstrations, dissemination of information on emerging technologies, and similar activities are appropriate.

The Factory Category

Organizations evolve into this category from the turnaround category. If this is the appropriate positioning, the IS manager should seek additional opportunities to enhance the efficiency and effectiveness of existing strategic systems. Additional IS activities should be similar to those for organizations in the support category. For organizations that should continue with the development of strategic systems but have not, the IS manager should proceed much as in the case of moving an organization out of the support category. The difference is that the organization already has an understanding of how IT can be used to its strategic benefit.

The Strategic Category

Once both the existing systems portfolio and the development systems portfolio have high strategic value, the IS manager will have moved into a leadership role regarding corporate strategy set formation. Organizations in this category have established clear competitive strategies and a strategic planning process; they treat the IS manager as a member of the executive team.

As an organization evolves from the support to the strategic category, the role of the IS manager necessarily changes from that of caretaker to that of change agent and, finally, to that of leader. Once this evolution has taken place, the following responsibilities will have been added to the role of the IS manager:

- Participation in the development of the organizational strategy set.
- Support of the business plan at corporate and departmental levels by bringing appropriate technology to the management team.
- Management of integration of appropriate technologies into the way the organization functions and even into its choice of business activity.

It would be a mistake to assume that all organizations should or even can evolve into the strategic category. Each category is characteristic of certain types of business activities. For example, well-established manufacturing-based organizations are typically found in the support category. The factory category, in contrast, typically includes service-based companies whose success in the market hinges on a few information-intensive applications but for whom the IS environment is otherwise relatively stable. The airline industry is a good example. The turnaround category normally contains organizations in transition that are developing one or more strategic systems to gain competitive advantage. Many will be organizations that are more information-based than those in the factory category. In the strategic category are found the most information-dependent organizations. Financial services industries (banks, insurance companies, and stock brokerage firms) dominate this category.

For the proactive IS manager, knowing where an organization is positioned—and where it should be positioned—is crucial. Armed with this knowledge, the IS manager can make informed decisions that are both realistic and likely to bring about genuine enhancements in the way information technologies contribute to the organization.

The strategic grid's instrumentality hinges on an important recognition: Each of its categories suggests a particular senior management "mind-set" that IS managers must accept and be prepared to work with. It will be easier, for instance, to gain approval for a bold concept if the organization is in the turnaround category than if it is in the support category, simply because of the likely attitudes and mind-set of its senior management. We turn now to this issue of mind-set and examine some of the reasons for high-level resistance to a new role for the IS manager.

RESISTANCE OF SENIOR MANAGEMENT

Yannis Bakos and Michael Treacy (1986) offer five possible explanations for the resistance of some senior managers to a more proactive role for the IS manager. One is ignorance of information technology and its potential uses and benefits. Another reason is poor communication between the IS department and the rest of the business. A third reason is a general resistance to change, of any sort, common among both IS and other personnel. The fourth and fifth reasons offered by Bakos and Treacy are lack of focus on opportunities for competitive advantage and a lack of instruments for decisively measuring the benefits of IT.

Ignorance of Information Technology and Its Potential Uses

Some of senior management's ignorance can be attributed to IS itself. Certain failures of the 1960s and 1970s left the impression that IS did not "have its act together" and could not manage effectively; this perception remains with us. Because IS departments gained a reputation for causing delay and disappointment, some senior users have been reluctant to seek out new applications of a technology that they have not yet seen as cost effective. Although many would argue that time will cure this problem, at present it is still significant.

Poor Communications Between Information Systems and Other Departments

Behaviorists might tell us that the IS professional typically dislikes meetings and would rather be an individual contributor than a team player. When this is coupled with the typical IS professional's ignorance of business activity, at least one side of the communications problem becomes clearer. (Of course, these are stereotypes, but they are not without a basis in reality.) Functional and senior managers have also contributed to the problem. Many have kept an unhealthy organizational distance from the IS department—perhaps because of reluctance to use computers or because they have not yet recognized information as a resource and systems as a strategic weapon. All these factors are probably present to some degree in the communications gap, and they need to be addressed by IS, functional, and senior managers working in concert.

General Resistance to Change

IS personnel continually advocate change on the part of other business units, but paradoxically the IS department is itself reluctant to evolve. "If it ain't broke don't fix it" and "It's worked fine for 12 years—why do I have to change it now?" are often heard whenever the threat of change seems likely. Clearly, it is human nature to react in this way, but the reaction puts a brake on needed changes.

Lack of Focus on Opportunities for Competitive Advantage

Positioning an organization to seize new opportunities requires an environment in which creative ideas flow and managers are willing to take risks. Organizations are often caught up in their current business activity and find comfort in that stability; initiative and drive may not be part of the organizational culture, at least not to the degree necessary in the information age. Managers with broad business skills (including IS) need to act boldly to seek out and support development efforts in areas of potential strategic opportunity.

Lack of Instruments to Measure Benefits

Value added is difficult to quantify or use for comparative purposes. In many cases a meaningful cost/benefit analysis for a proposed project is not available, in which case, no one except the risk-takers and entrepreneurs will be willing to move into uncharted waters. Executives must understand that the benefits from systems to improve managerial efficiency and effectiveness will almost always be largely unquantifiable. The Benefit/Beneficiary matrix can be used to address this issue; it helps managers focus on what has been done in the IT area and where emphasis may be needed.

The IS manager will have to minimize these resistances in order to operate in true partnership with corporate executives and legitimize his or her new role. For an alliance to work the IS manager must make clear that he or she is operating from a corporate perspective, with territorial interests suppressed. For the IS manager, this entails a difficult transition from a defensive and sometimes myopic viewpoint to a collaborative, far-sighted approach.

Involving Senior Management

Involving senior management in a redefinition of roles, especially if it has resisted in the past, is likely to involve more art than science. The IS manager will have to pay close attention to subtle signals from and behavior patterns of senior managers. And often the IS manager must move quickly, for the window of opportunity is generally narrow. A certain amount of risk-taking is inevitable.

Some help in this area is afforded by a model developed by Rockart and Crescenzi (1984). This model consists of three phases

1. *Phase One: Linking information systems to business management needs* Using the corporate mission and strategy statements, managers can identify the organization's CSFs. When the IS manager knows what senior management perceives as the most critical business needs, he or she can connect both the existing and planned information systems to these needs in a more direct, effective way. CSFs are a tool for gaining this knowledge (see Chapter 5).

2. *Phase Two: Developing systems priorities and gaining confidence in recommended systems* After completing phase one, the IS manager will be able to assign priorities to new systems development projects and make recommendations that are most likely to meet the organization's information and business needs. The fact that these are related to the organization's CSFs will be an important help to senior management as they review and approve the IS manager's prioritization recommendations.

3. *Phase Three: Rapid development of low-risk, managerially useful systems* Senior managers cannot always wait for 2 years for a system to become operational. Strategic initiatives are very time sensitive, and for that reason the IS department must use a methodology and a development environment that produce results quickly. Prototyping (see Chapter 16 for a detailed discussion on this development methodology) and fourth-generation languages (4GL) are the methodology and the development environment, respectively, that are best suited for the task. In time, computer-aided software engineering (CASE) methods will be sufficiently developed to be useful in further reducing systems development time.

The result of this three-phase process is that senior management becomes involved more quickly and in meaningful ways, and keeps its attention on the development process throughout. Rockart and Crescenzi contend that this three-phase process is successful for the following reasons:

- It makes a direct, fast link between IS and senior management.
- It encourages senior management to focus on those areas of the business it deems important. Thus, senior managers feel comfortable building information systems to support these areas.
- It brings about actual, not hypothetical, senior management involvement.
- IS consultants (whether in-house or external) gain significant insights into the business and become more effective as a result.
- Senior managers recognize that this process ultimately involves a lower risk than not engaging in the process at all.

The actual process that Rockart and Crescenzi suggest for involving senior management is illustrated in Exhibit 3-2. (In Chapter 5 their model will be discussed in the context of planning systems.)

Phase One: Linking information systems to the management needs of the business. Key technique: Critical success factors process

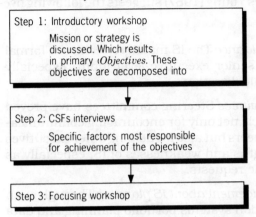

Step 1: Introductory workshop

Mission or strategy is discussed. Which results in primary *Objectives*. These objectives are decomposed into

Step 2: CSFs interviews

Specific factors most responsible for achievement of the objectives

Step 3: Focusing workshop

Phase Two: Developing systems priorities and gaining confidence in recommended systems. Key technique: Decision scenarios

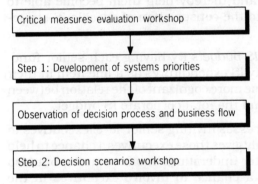

Critical measures evaluation workshop

Step 1: Development of systems priorities

Observation of decision process and business flow

Step 2: Decision scenarios workshop

Phase Three: Rapid development of low risk, managerially useful systems. Key technique: Prototype development. Implementation. Use and refinement

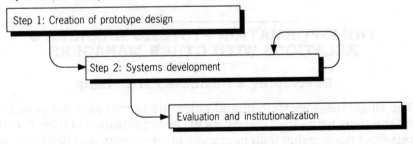

Step 1: Creation of prototype design

Step 2: Systems development

Evaluation and institutionalization

EXHIBIT 3-2 A three-phase process for senior managerial involvement in information technology.

Source: John F. Rockart and Adam D. Crescenzi, "Engaging Top management in Information technology," Journal of Systems Management, April, 1986, p. 6. © Journal of Systems Management.

There are other strategies that the IS manager can use to involve senior management. James Young (1987) suggests the following five-part program:

1. *Receiving executive guidance* The IS manager seeks out formal methods of receiving senior executive-level input, especially with respect to strategic direction.

2. *Forming steering committees* Steering committees have proved to be an excellent vehicle not only for encouraging communication among corporate peers but also for helping other executives understand the strengths and weaknesses of IS, especially as these relate to strategic requests.

3. *Educating senior management about IS planning* Through such techniques as application systems portfolio planning and data modeling, the IS executive can familiarize senior managers with IS planning concepts and thereby help them become able to contribute effectively to the construction of specific IS strategies.

4. *Developing functional IS budgets* By having each senior functional executive identify IS expenditures as a line item in their budget, each will become more cognizant of the relation between their strategic plans and the total corporate IS budget.

5. *Explaining tactical processes* Inviting senior-level executives to IS staff meetings not only gives those executives a chance to help the IS department better understand business units, but also gives the department a chance to involve executives in the tactical-level decisions faced by the IS department.

THE INFORMATION SYSTEMS MANAGER'S RELATIONS WITH OTHER MANAGERS

Developing a Business Partnership

The single message that should guide the IS manager in his or her interactions with other managers in the organization is this: *Form a business partnership with managers in other units and demonstrate to them that you really understand their business*. This message certainly implies a new role for the IS manager, who must become known less as a technician and more as a businessperson. It requires that this manager look outside the IS department toward the organization and the markets that the organization serves or might serve.

Madeline Weiss (1987) discusses the nature of the business partnership and suggests several useful activities that IS managers can undertake to improve relations not only with executives, as she suggests, but also with other managers:

- Invite other managers to IS staff meetings so that they can brief the IS staff on their activities.
- Take the initiative and suggest solutions to business problems.
- Offer workshops to help managers identify strategic IT possibilities and evaluate their competitive significance.
- Assign top analysts to a specific user area for at least 1 year so as both to learn how the area operates and to discover opportunities for creative uses of IT in that area.

Partnership and Power

If the IS manager expects to influence corporate strategy, he or she must speak from a position of power. In this regard, a major deterrent is the limited power base of most IS managers at the corporate level.

The IS department meets the criteria for high power postulated by P. J. Hickson, and coworkers (1971), whose theory on the determinants of power explains the distribution of power across an organization. The four determinants of power are:

1. *Uncertainty* Uncertainty refers to the extent to which one department copes with uncertainty for another. In many organizations, users have surrendered control over the development of applications and over the functions that information systems perform. Users thus depend on the IS department to deliver workable systems on time, to keep them up and running, and to produce timely and accurate reports. The IS department thus copes with considerable uncertainty for other operational units.

2. *Replaceability* This determinant refers to whether or not a department can be replaced easily. There are no alternatives to information systems available in the short term in most organizations; the IS department is thus not replaceable.

3. *Linkages* Linkages refer to the number of links between other departments and the department in question. The IS department accepts input from and provides output to a wide range of departments. To the extent that the services it provides are critical to the operation of user departments, IS has a large number of linkages. In information-intensive companies, user departments could operate without this linkage for only a few days.

4. *Interdependence* This determinant refers to the degree of inter-dependence between the department of interest and all other departments. In both the systems design process and informa-tion processing activity, the IS department and the user depart-ment are mutually dependent. Neither can proceed without the other.

In terms of all four determinants, the IS department would seem to rate high in power in its relationships with other departments. Henry C. Lucas, Jr. (1984) identifies three reasons: (1) the develop-ment of computer-based systems by the IS department has created operational uncertainty that only the IS department can reduce; (2) poor documentation makes it difficult to replace the IS department; (3) the IS department is highly connected to other departments. In recent surveys by Lucas (1984) and Saunders and Scamell (1986) it was concluded that the IS department rated very low with respect to power and the determinants of power. Lucas explains this somewhat surprising result by concluding that the IS department is not involved in those activities that other managers would consider of strategic importance.

The degree to which the organization is successful in its use of computing resources will be a direct function of the IS manager's success in formulating policies and procedures to appropriately channel power away from the IS department and toward users. Users need to have some sense of control over their computing activity, and the appropriate transfer of some of that control to the user will be in the best long-term interest of the organization. Application systems development is one area in which a substantial transfer of power can occur. To the extent that the IS department can move systems development activities into user areas, the power base will shift.

Some possibilities for bringing about such a transfer include:

- Allowing the user to choose which of the feasible designs will be implemented.
- Allowing the user to be project manager.
- Supporting end-user tools and training in their use so that users can do ad hoc reporting and even applications development.
- Designing systems to be run by users on their own equipment on an as-needed basis.
- Moving the organization toward a distributed computing envi-ronment.
- Allowing users to choose their own hardware/software (within reasonable bounds).

The historical development of end-user computing teaches some important lessons regarding the diffusion of IS power. End-user computing brought with it a trend toward decentralization. It reduced uncertainty, increased replacability, and reduced linkages and interdependencies; hence it reduced the IS department's power. This change was necessary; for it completed the equation that would lead to a more active role for the user and ultimately to strategic applications of IT. The danger, however, was that the power swing would be so complete that the IS department would again become a backroom operation—assuming a completely reactive role once again. The astute IS manager will not let this happen, however. For as new and improved technologies become available, the IS manager can position his or her department to be the "technology gatekeeper." The IS department should evaluate and recommend, to the organization, those technologies that can favorably impact on the organization's effectiveness, efficiency, and product/service transformation. Insofar as this is the case, the power base again shifts toward the IS department. The IS manager's objective should be to establish equilibrium with respect to the distribution of IS power across the organization.

MAJOR ORGANIZATIONAL CHALLENGES FACING THE INFORMATION SYSTEMS MANAGER

With respect to their responsibilities at the corporate or organizational level, IS managers confront many large and small challenges each day, and a good many of these challenges are unique—other managers do not have to deal with them. The top ten, discussed next in order of importance, were determined as a result of an extensive survey of IS managers reported by James Brancheau and James Wetherbe in 1987.

Integrating Information Systems and Strategic Planning

Most IS executives have not yet developed a planning process that can be integrated with the corporate strategic-planning process, despite the fact that the need to do so has been recognized by senior management. Corporate strategic planning must be business-driven rather than technology-driven; hence, a major challenge is to devise a process that minimizes the risk of missing a business opportunity because of technological ignorance. (We take up this issue in Chapter 5 and offer a possible solution.)

Gaining Competitive Advantage

Although many firms have recognized that information systems are a major strategic weapon, the IS manager has a special responsibility to spot IT-related opportunities for gaining competitive advantage—and to seize such opportunities quickly. At present, the typical IS manager's method of operation does not lend itself to innovation and quick responses.

Aiding Organizational Learning

Because organizations must learn to identify appropriate uses of computing in their operation, it is the IS manager's job to focus on helping senior managers understand how technology can make genuine, realistic contributions to the organization. This calls for determined and forceful leadership; policies and even organizational structures may need to be challenged by the IS manager.

Identifying Information Systems' Value-added Contribution

Simple cost/benefit analyses have not provided an appropriate measure of the contribution from decision support and strategic systems. Some type of value-added analysis is clearly indicated and will necessitate a closer relationship between IS and user management. The IS function must be recognized as an integral part of business activity. In concert with functional area managers, the IS manager will be better able to suggest new systems and evaluate their bottom-line impact.

Realigning Information Systems in the Organization

As we have already seen, organizational "turf" issues have arisen as a result of the trend first toward decentralization and then toward autonomous departmental computing. For some IS managers, the consequent loss of power has been difficult to accept. With the present trend toward IS as a service (replacing the notion of a monolithic IS department), IS managers must participate in a crucial realignment of IS within the organization—overcoming their sense of being threatened and working with senior management to develop collaborative relations among IS and other corporate units.

Dealing with End-User Computing

This area presents IS management with a difficult problem. How much control is needed, and how much is too much? Crucial issues are security, data integrity, systems integration, standards, and policy, which must be balanced against the need to encourage user innovations. Forcing users to circumvent an overly restrictive system of controls has negative consequences. The IS manager's job is to arrive at a balance among all the players. (Part IV discusses the issue of end-user computing, its support, and its management in detail.)

Viewing Data as a Corporate Resource

The IS manager and the organization must understand that data are a resource just as equipment, buildings, and personnel are. The organization has an investment in its data and should insist on protecting that investment and reaping profits from it. When this fact is recognized and accepted at all organizational levels, the IS manager will be in a better position to champion the exploitation of data. Part of the IS manager's task, therefore, is to make sure that everyone in the organization thinks in terms of data as a resource.

Devising an Information Architecture

Part of the problem in using data effectively is that an information architecture plan has not been adequately developed in most firms. Questions of access, data definition, and data sharing (among others) have not been answered. The IS manager has been somewhat hampered by a lack of strategic data planning as well as of expertise in the area of corporate-wide data design.

Measuring Effectiveness

The lack of reliable measures of the value of information has aggravated two problems: the need to control performance and the need to measure benefits associated with costs. Ideally, the effectiveness of a system should be measured in terms of the quality of the information that it produces. That assumes a causal relationship between information and a specific measure such as profit or return on investment. Such relationships, if they exist, have not been quantified. The same is generally true of the relationship between cost and benefit. Although cost may be easily measured, there will be many other variables confounded with the value of information, thus precluding any measure of the value of information. Both are difficult challenges facing the IS manager.

Integrating Information Technologies

The rapid emergence of "islands of technology" (factory automation and desktop publishing, for instance) has created both a managerial and a political problem for the IS manager. Organizationally, should these "islands of technology" remain separate entities, or should they be merged under the umbrella of the IS organization?

James Cash and coworkers (1988) argue that office automation, data and voice communications, and data processing should be merged and managed in an integrated fashion. Such integration is not easily accomplished, however. Each new technology should prompt a reexamination of organizational structure to find the most effective, efficient, and productive way to organize for the provision of IS services. Failure to do so, at least at the policy level, may place the organization at great risk because of the significant cost and technological complexity involved.

Merging the emerging technologies under the IS organization carries the responsibility of supporting them—a task that few IS departments are prepared to handle. To have such islands remain autonomous, however, entails various risks, including inefficiencies, duplication of effort, and waste of resources. Some judicious mix of control and autonomy is required, and it is the IS manager's job to arrive at this balance.

THE EMERGING CHIEF INFORMATION OFFICER

The original task of the IS manager was to oversee the replacement of manual systems with computer-based systems to provide information faster and more efficiently. But that task is increasingly seen as fundamentally distinct from the task of the chief information officer (CIO), who focuses primarily on creative and innovative uses of IT. Indeed, in some organizations the IS manager and the CIO are viewed as having two separate sets of responsibilities, hence as holding two separate positions. In such cases the CIO usually reports to the CEO in a staff position, although a line position (with perhaps the IS manager as a subordinate) is an alternative. In any case, the CIO is the "change agent" for new IT products, services, and processes.

Perhaps the major responsibility of the CIO is to disseminate to other managers any relevant information on the latest technology developments and to help assimilate these new technologies into the organization where appropriate. Because this responsibility ultimately affects the development of strategy, the CIO does not typically have day-to-day operational responsibilities; he or she must be free to concentrate on the broader IT issues affecting the organization and its definition of its business. The successful CIO needs to be a combination of facilitator, promoter, agitator, businessperson, innovator, and communicator—not an easy blend to find in one person. At this stage in the history of IS, they are arguably a rare breed.

CONCLUSION

The role of the IS department, and especially of the IS manager, is undergoing a total metamorphosis. The once reactive posture of the IS manager is now increasingly proactive; in certain industries the IS manager is being called on to become a member of the management team and help formulate the organization's strategic direction. Data are no longer viewed as an expense to be controlled but rather a corporate resource to be protected and invested in—and the IS manager is a major proponent of this view.

Being a technician is no longer the most important criterion for success as an IS manager. The crucial importance of developing a partnership with other executives has forced IS managers to cultivate nontechnical, truly managerial skills—and to live with a process of change.

DISCUSSION QUESTIONS

1. What specific kind of support should top management provide to the IS department if it wants IS to really be part of the corporate team?

2. In what ways can the trend toward distributed processing help or hinder the IS manager's attainment of a proactive role at the corporate level?

3. How does the strategic role of IS differ in a manufacturing as compared to a service-related environment?

4. Identify actions that can be taken by the IS department to transfer power to a user for the purpose of improving relations with that user. What are some of the potential consequences of this transfer?

5. Discuss the advantages and disadvantages of keeping separate the positions of the IS manager and CIO.

6. Data are corporate resources that are too important for major data decisions to be made within one functional area, including IS. Do you agree or disagree? What does this mean for the job title and responsibilities of a corporate data director?

REFERENCES

Bakos, J. Yannis, and Michael E. Treacy (1986). "Information Technology and Corporate Strategy: A Research Perspective," MIS *Quarterly* (June), pp. 107–119.

Brancheau, James C., and James C. Wetherbe (1987). "Key Issues in Information Systems Management," *MIS Quarterly* (March), pp. 23–45.

Cash, James, I. Jr, et. al. (1988) *Corporate Information Systems Management: Text and Cases*, 2 ed., Homewood, Il: Irwin.

Hickson, P. J., C. R. Henning, C. E. Lee, R. E. Schneck, and J. M. Pennings (1971). "Strategic Contingencies Theory of Interorganizational Powers," *Administrative Science Quarterly*, vol. 16, no. 2 (June), pp. 216–229.

Lucas, Henry C., Jr. (1984) "Organizational Power and the Information Services Department," *Communications of the ACM*, vol. 27, no. 1 (January), pp. 58–65.

Rockart, John F., and Adam D. Crescenzi (1984). "Engaging Top Management in Information Technology," *Sloan Management Review*, vol. 25, no. 4 (Summer), pp. 3–16.

Saunders, Carol Stoak (1986). "Impact of Information Technology on the Information Systems Department," *Journal of Systems Management* (April), pp. 18–24.

Saunders, Carol S., and Richard W. Scamell (1986) "Organizational Power and the Information Services Department: A Reexamination," *Communications of the ACM*, vol. 29, no. 2 (February), pp. 142–147.

Sinclair, Stuart W. (1986). "The Three Domains of Information Systems Planning," *Journal of Information Systems Planning*, vol. 3, no. 2 (Spring), pp. 8–16.

Weiss, Madeline (1987). "Transformers", *CIO*, vol. 1, no. 1, pp. 37–41.

Young, James (1987). "Ways to Win Top Brass Backing," *Computerworld* (November 4), pp. 9–10.

four

Information Technology as a Competitive Weapon

As global competition in most sectors of the economy becomes keener and as business and industry become more sophisticated in exploiting information and automation, the success and perhaps even survival of some organizations will depend on their ability to seize opportunities to use information technology as a competitive weapon. Doing so requires the integration of business planning and information-systems planning into a comprehensive strategic planning framework. Unfortunately, this integration is not widespread, in part because of the growth of what some are calling a "technology gap"—the differential between the opportunities created by information technology and its effective utilization by the organizations.

Robert Benjamin and his colleagues (1984) cite two factors that contribute to the widening of this gap. First, in recent years there has been an unprecedented increase in the functionality and improvement in the cost performance of information technology. These in effect create strategic opportunities for many organizations. Second, most senior managers have little or no experience or background in managing information technologies. Thus, they do not have an experiential base from which to draw in order to incorporate this new source of strategic opportunity into their businesses.

In this chapter we concentrate on the first factor by looking at information technology (IT) as a component of competitive strategy. We note several companies that have tried, some successfully and some unsuccessfully, to exploit IT for competitive advantage. We then discuss a conceptual model of three areas of strategic opportunity for information systems, which in turn leads us to explore how organizations assess such opportunities and what role the IS department plays in their assessment.

Our discussion of the second of Benjamin's factors—senior management's lack of experience with IT—is extended in Chapter 5, where we examine strategic IS planning systems. The focus there is on planning systems that are business driven but that incorporate opportunities to exploit IT for competitive advantage.

INFORMATION TECHNOLOGY AS A COMPONENT OF COMPETITIVE STRATEGY

According to Yannis Bakos and Michael Treacy (1986), the two major sources of an organization's competitive advantage are bargaining power and comparative efficiency. Exhibit 4-1 depicts the causal model that Bakos and Treacy use to illustrate the dynamics of competitive advantage. To date, most efforts to exploit IT for competitive advantage have focused on comparative efficiencies. IS organizations and most organizations in which IS plays a key support role, have concentrated on improving operational and managerial control. Lacking the necessary credibility and access to senior management, IS managers have not made significant contributions to the bargaining-power dimension of competitive advantage. IS managers are further hampered by insufficient understanding of the business of most organizations.

Somewhat related to the ideas of Bakos and Treacy is G. L. Parsons' (1983) identification of six general opportunity areas in which IS can make major contributions to the organization's competitive posture. The IS department can help the organization to:

1. *Increase customer switching costs.* As an example, placing terminals at the customer site and allowing them to enter orders and query order status provides a service that can only be replicated by another supplier at increased customer cost.

2. *Decrease one's switching costs against suppliers.* Somewhat the reverse of increasing customer switching cost, this involves using IT to reduce dependence on a single supplier. As

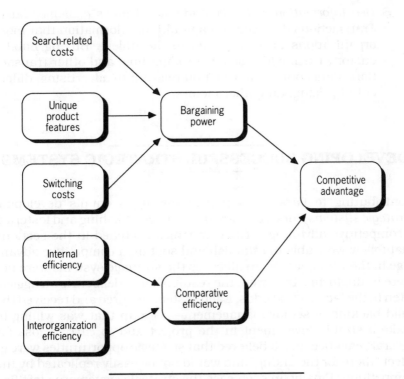

EXHIBIT 4-1 A causal model of competitive advantage.

Source: J. Yannis Bakos and Michael E. Treacy, "Information Technology and Corporate Strategy: A Research Perspective," *MIS Quarterly*, June, 1986, p. 114. Reprinted by special permission from the *MIS Quarterly*, vol. 10, no. 2, June 1986. Copyright 1986 by the Society for Information Management and the Management Information Systems Research Center at the University of Minnesota.

an example, the organization might use IT to become its own supplier.

3. *Use information technology to support product innovation for purposes of maintaining a competitive position or deterring potential product substitutes.* Increasing product quality at the same cost or decreasing cost without affecting the quality are two examples.

4. *Cooperate with selected rivals by sharing information technology resources.*

5. *Substitute information technology for labor.* This will either reduce production and/or distribution costs and hence result in lower prices or increase production volume and distribution efficiency. In any event, cost to the customer or delivery time are reduced.

6. *Use information to better understand one's customer base.* Transactions data contain a wealth of information that most organizations have not used to the fullest. Buying habits, customer demographics by product line, and other transactions data contain information relevant to advertising, differential pricing, and other factors.

DEVELOPING SUCCESSFUL STRATEGIC SYSTEMS

Contributing to Parsons' opportunities areas entails developing *strategic systems*—ones that are useful in establishing and fostering a competitive advantage. The companies sketched in the sections that follow were able to establish and sustain a competitive advantage in their businesses. In all cases the strategic systems were not mere brainstorms; they were the result of long, deliberate struggles, often in the face of great odds. Each system required and received the solid backing of senior management—a group that was willing to make a sizable investment in the project and to carry a loss for several years because it believed that strategic opportunities were in effect "there for the taking" and would not be easily replicated by the competition. Finally, in each case the strategic system was fortified by a solid and well-timed implementation plan. In many cases, success hinged on getting to the market in a timely fashion, with little margin for delay.

It is fair to say that some of these systems grew in directions not envisioned by their original developers. It was only after some time that the strategic value of the initial system became obvious within some of these organizations.

American Hospital Supply

American Hospital Supply (AHS) was one of the early pioneers in the use of computer terminals at customer locations. These terminals, which are connected to corporate computers at AHS, allow customers (i.e., hospitals) to order on-line—a capability that represents a commitment on the part of both the customers and AHS and that has had a powerful effect on the hospital supply business. It has significantly reduced the time between order placement and order delivery, has essentially eliminated one person in the vendor—customer relationship, and has given the customer more control over source of supply. Even more significantly, it has controlled a channel of distribution and placed AHS in a position of considerable strategic advantage. Others have emulated AHS's system, but the company still maintains a significant market advantage over its competitors.

American Airlines

American Airlines began developing a computerized reservation system called Semi-Automated Business Research Environment (SABRE) in the early 1960s. By the mid-1970s, the company had begun installing SABRE in travel agencies across the country; it now has more than 11,000 installations. Despite the fact that there have been several attempts to copy SABRE (several lawsuits filed by other carriers for unfair trade practices), SABRE continues to dominate the market. In fact, rather than continuing to develop their own reservations systems, many carriers now subscribe to SABRE.

It is estimated that American Airlines has spent in excess of $350 million developing SABRE. The airline did not show a profit with its system until 1983, but it has sustained its competitive advantage by continually expanding SABRE's functionality. For example, the airline spun off an office automation package for travel agencies called Agency Data Systems. SABRE now encompasses hotel reservations, car rentals, train schedules, theater tickets, and limousine rental; it even has a feature that lets travelers use the system directly.

Despite SABRE's comprehensiveness, several airlines do have their own reservations systems. American Airlines will continue to look for further enhancements to SABRE so as to maintain its role as industry leader.

Pizza Hut

In California, Pizza Hut has begun an ambitious program to revolutionize its distribution system and marketing strategies. As an experiment, it has opened a number of "pizza factories" at strategic locations throughout its trading area. These factories do not have retail facilities; they merely receive orders transmitted by computer from a central location. Once a customer's telephone order is received, it is entered into a central computer that then dispatches it to a computer at the pizza factory nearest the customer. Along with the order, the pizza factory might even receive directions for the most direct route to the customer's location. Although this represents a routine application of existing computer technology, what makes it important are the marketing implications of the transactions data processed by the computer. In the past, these data would not have been retained; however, Pizza Hut intends to use these data as input to a system that will allow them to detect trends and patterns in customer buying habits. The implications for purchasing, inventory management, pricing, and marketing are significant, and Pizza Hut stands to gain competitive advantage through better inventory management and improved customer service.

Otis Elevator

Otis Elevator is in the process of retrofitting its elevators with a computerized system that monitors operating conditions and parameters in the elevator. At the same time, the monitoring system is being installed as standard equipment in all new units. When the computer detects a potential out-of-control situation, it relays that information to the corporate system in Hartford, Connecticut, where diagnostics are generated and appropriate information forwarded to the nearest repair center. A report is then generated on the repair center's computer alerting the staff of the elevator's condition and history, the probable cause of the condition, and likely corrective action. A repairperson is dispatched to the site to repair the elevator before any accident occurs, which is a tremendous service advantage, and one that is responsible for an estimated 6% increase in maintenance-contract business.

Citicorp

Although it was not the first bank to introduce the automated teller machine (ATM), Citicorp aggressively pursued the idea of 24-hour banking only after it had installed minicomputers in its branch offices to off-load transactions from its central computer. The idea for the ATM grew out of that application, which was a cost-reduction move to process low-profit customer transactions at branch offices. As customers began to see the convenience of not having to enter the bank, ATMs gained in popularity. There are now more than 11,000 Citicorp ATMs in the United States, with locations at airports, supermarkets, and college campuses, among others.

Other regional banks and national banking networks have been forced to use ATMs to keep up with Citicorp. To maintain its lead, Citicorp is involved with networking to other ATM systems and is developing a global transaction network (GTN) to extend its services worldwide. This will pave the way for funds transfer, letters of credit, and other services to international customers.

McKesson Corporation

What started out as a pilot project for an automated ordering system grew to a sophisticated ordering, sales analysis, and inventory management system serving the majority of McKesson's 19,000 drug stores. The system generates supporting paperwork, including maps showing product locations in the warehouses to improve picking time. Through the corporation's ECONOMOST system, ordering time has been cut in half, inventories at the stores have been reduced, and profits have increased. As a result, ECONOMOST is leading the retailing industry toward a strategic redirecting of its distribution systems.

THE PITFALLS: SOME UNSUCCESSFUL STRATEGIC SYSTEMS

Not all strategic systems development efforts have resulted in success. Some have failed because they never got off the ground. Others have failed because of implementation problems late in the development cycle. And still others have failed because their proponents have not read markets or trends correctly. What follows are two instructive cases of failure.

First Boston Corporation

The Shelternet system seemed like an idea whose time had come. Shelternet was designed by First Boston Corporation to be run on a computer in a real-estate broker's office; its purpose was to help buyers locate suitable mortgages. Once the mortgage, rates, and terms were determined, the paperwork could be completed at the broker's office, thus saving the buyer a trip to the lender.

The system was operational and offered for sale to real-estate brokers. The problem was its price tag, which was higher than most brokers were willing to pay. Moreover, several local banks were not ready to accept the intrusion of the Capital Group, a New York-based firm, into their territory. Restraining orders were issued in some cases, and the product failed at the eleventh hour.

Kendall Company

Kendall, a Boston-based subsidiary of Colgate-Palmolive, is a hospital-supplies manufacturer. When the parent company decided to decentralize, Kendall followed suit and broke into seven autonomous business units. At that time, Kendall's director of management information systems (MIS) strongly believed in a centralized, mainframe-oriented MIS department. Consistent with that philosophy, hardware and software acquisitions were aimed at developing large, centralized data bases. A refocusing of senior management's attention and a new MIS director led Kendall to bring a halt to the MIS centralization plan. The shift to a decentralized network architecture with data centers in each business unit was not only costly but also put Kendall an estimated 2 years behind where it might have been.

The problem at Kendall was a lack of communication between senior management and MIS management. Had the MIS manager participated as a partner in the business-planning process, this problem would not have arisen. The MIS department was also at fault for not having tied its system plan to the general business plan.

The preceding examples are but a few of the many that describe creative applications of IT that attempt to open a strategic window of opportunity. In some cases the first company to think of an idea (American Hospital Supply, for example) established a barrier to entry for the competition (the terminal on the customer's desk) and thus established a competitive advantage. The successful applications were the direct result of innovative thinking coupled with an extensive analysis of the business environment and market situation in which the product or service would be introduced. In all cases, considerable time and effort was expended on the process.

IDENTIFYING AREAS OF STRATEGIC OPPORTUNITY FOR INFORMATION SYSTEMS

The so-called information weapon model developed by William Synnott (1987) categorizes areas within an organization where information technology may be used to establish competitive advantage. Once such an area is identified, it is senior management's responsibility to determine whether a real strategic opportunity exists. Overall corporate strategy, cost/benefit analyses, market position, comparative strengths and weaknesses, competitive forces, and other variables are all part of that determination.

As we have seen, creative thinking and a willingness to take risks are needed to identify real competitive opportunities. For the IS manager, the challenge is to be able to respond quickly. This responsiveness demands, in turn, that the IS department have in place the appropriate procedures to facilitate quick response. We will return to this topic later.

Synnott establishes three classes of what he calls information weapons (Exhibit 4-2). Under innovation he classifies those systems ("weapons") focusing on technological innovation as a weapon to establish competitive advantage. Under information he classifies those systems using information itself as a weapon. And under productivity Synnott classifies those systems that lead to cost reductions or productivity increases in production, marketing, or distribution. Each class is discussed briefly in the following sections.

Technological Innovation

Establishing competitive advantage through technological innovation requires a differentiation of an organization's products or services. For example, the IS manager might work closely with

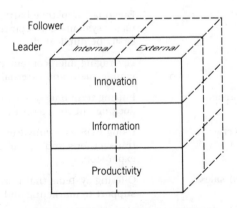

EXHIBIT 4-2 Information weapon model.

Source: The Information Weapon: Winning Customers and Markets With Technology, William R. Synnott. Copyright © 1987 by John Wiley & Sons, Inc. Reprinted by permission of John Wiley & Sons, Inc.

marketing managers to develop new products or services that use technology in ways that cannot be easily replicated by the competition. Placing terminals at customer locations is one example; although competitors could do the same, customers are not likely to install multiple vendors' terminals in their workplaces. Exhibit 4-3 provides several other examples of the use of technological innovation for competitive advantage.

Information Services

Implementing decision support systems, executive support systems, and a variety of statistical and financial reporting systems provides managers and decision-makers with a plethora of information that can help them be more effective. Otis Elevator is a good example of the use of information services to gain competitive advantage. Both

Innovation	Advantage
New products	Constantly innovating with new competitive products and services
Extended products	Leveraging old products with new competitive extensions
Substitute products	Creating competitive discontinuities through substitution
Differentiated products	Gaining advantage through unique products or added value
Super systems	Erecting competitve barriers through major systems developments that cannot easily be duplicated
Micro systems	Leveraging microcomputers for external management and external customers
Customer terminals	Putting terminals in customer spaces (locking out the competition)
Electronic delivery	Using EDS as a substitute for paper transacttions and as a means of global expansion
Computer-aided sales	Offering systems that provide compter support to marketing and sales

EXHIBIT 4-3 Specific areas of technological innovation and potential advantage.

Source: The Information Weapon: Winning Customers and Markets with Technology, William R. Synnott, Copyright © 1987 by John Wiley & Sons Inc. Reprinted by permission of John Wiley & Sons, Inc.

the historical record of a specific elevator and the nominal perform-ance characteristics of similar elevators provide service managers with information to improve the quality and timeliness of their maintenance service. This enhanced capability in turn makes Otis Elevator more competitive and more likely to win service contracts from competitors. By installing computer monitoring equipment at the time of elevator manufacture, Otis not only captures a service contract from each customer but also creates a barrier to entry by competitors. Exhibit 4-4 provides several other examples of the use of information services for competitive advantage.

Productivity-related Systems

Robotics, computer-assisted manufacturing, office automation, information centers, automated software-development tools, and programmer productivity aids are just some of the possibilities for enhancing productivity. The bottom line is a lower cost to the customer, increased quality, more timely delivery, and greater market share. A good example of this is Pizza Hut. Placing its factories closer to the customer, this company significantly reduced delivery time and delivery cost. Exhibit 4-5 provides several other examples of the use of productivity-related systems for competitive advantage.

To establish true competitive advantage through the use of information technology, the organization must meet three condi-tions (Porter, 1980). The product or service it offers must truly alter the industry structure by changing competitive relationships among the factors in the competitive forces model (buyers, suppliers, new entrants, substitute products or services, and the competition). More specifically, shifting the competitive balance toward the organi-zation requires an intimate knowledge of the industry structure and the organization's position within it. Moreover, the product or service offered must improve the organization's position in its existing businesses by bringing about cost reductions either through im-proved efficiency and effectiveness or through product differentia-tion. In some cases information may be used to create linkages between various activities associated with the production of goods or services (e.g., linking order entry to production and shipping sched-ules and giving the salesperson access to it will improve the effective-ness of customer services). Finally, new business opportunities must be created as a result of offering the product or service, which means that the organization has to extend the product or service into new and related areas to take full advantage of its innovation.

ASSESSING AREAS OF STRATEGIC OPPORTUNITY

Having seen several examples of organizations that have generated product or service enhancements capable of producing competitive advantage, we might now ask how specific areas of strategic opportunity can best be identified. Although there is no pat answer to this question, certain approaches are worth consideration. We turn now to several of them, with the caveat that they are tools, not rules.

Value-Chain Analysis

According to Michael Porter and Victor Millar (1985), competition has been affected in three vital ways by the information revolution. Industry structure has been changed, as have the rules of competition. Organizations have found ways to outperform their competitors by using information technology to create competitive advantage. Finally, organizations are finding ways to create new businesses by applying information technology to their existing operations.

Information Services	Advantage
Management support systems (MSS)	Using three classes of MSS to leverage managerial decision-making
Information brokering	Tapping into external data bases to expand the information resource
On-line information services	Selling proprietary information to customers
Information businesses	Using information as a business in and of itself
Micro information	Exploiting the extensive possibilities of internal and external micro-based information services
The PC center	Using in-house "computer stores" as a way to promote the intelligent use of business microcomputers

EXHIBIT 4-4 Specific areas of information services and potential competitive advantage.

Source: The Information Weapon: Winning Customers and Markets With Technology, William R. Synnott, Copyright © 1987 by John Wiley & sons, Inc. Reprinted by permission of John Wiley & Sons, Inc.

Value-chain analysis is a framework to explain this revolution in thinking. The value chain is essentially a division of the organization's business into technologically and economically discrete activities. In general, Porter and Millar identify nine so-called value activities (Exhibit 4-6). These activities are categorized as support activities and primary activities. Primary activities involve the creation and distribution of product and or service; whereas the support activities include the inputs to and infrastructure for primary activities. The primary activities are linked as in a chain, and each adds value to the product (with an accompanying cost for that value added). By examining this chain, the organization can identify ways to lower its costs, establish product differentiation, or change its competitive scope. The result will be the creation of competitive

Productivity-related System Area	Advantage
Technology investment	Using the level of investment in technology is the real measure of management's commitment
Management productivity	Applying computing power directly to managerial work in order to leverage management
Operations productivity	Employing methods and techniques for increasing operational effectiveness for less cost
Office productivity	Aiming office automation initiatives at white-collar workers at all levels of the organization
Data processing resources	Deriving productivity benefits from economy-of-scale computing
Systems resources	Attacking the software development bottleneck
Communications resources	Developing options for optimizing communications services at least cost
Productivity through leveraged resources	Using existing resources to offer new customer resources
Productivity as a by-product	Gaining productivity benefits as a by-product of innovation
Productivity from competitive scope	Achieving productivity increases from market expansion or contraction

EXHIBIT 4-5 Specific areas of productivity-related systems and potential competitive advantage.

Source: The Information Weapon: Winning Customers and Markets With Technology, William R. Synnott, Copyright © 1987 by John Wiley & Sons, Inc. Reprinted by permission of John Wiley & Sons, Inc.

SUPORT ACTIVITIES	Firm infrastructure	Planning models					
	Human resource management	Automated personnel scheduling					
	Technology development	Computer-aided design	Electronic market research				
	Procurement	On-line procurement of parts					
		Automated warehouse	Flexible manufacturing	Automated order processing	Telemarketing Remote terminals for salespersons	Remote servicing of equipment Computer scheduling and routing of repair trucks	
		Inbound logistics	Operations	Outbound logistics	Marketing and sales	Service	
		PRIMARY ACTIVITIES					MARGIN

EXHIBIT 4-6 Information technology permeates the value chain.

Source: Reprinted by permission of the *Harvard Business Review*. An exhibit from "How Information Gives You Competitive Advantage" by Michael E. Porter and Victor E. Millar (July-August 1985).

advantage. Using this chain, Porter and Millar suggest five steps that organizations can take to exploit the strategic opportunities that information technology creates.

Assess Information Intensity Organizations need to assess the information intensity of each link in their value chains in order to identify strategic opportunities. Higher intensity implies greater opportunity; if the customers or suppliers with whom the organization deals are highly dependent on information or if the product is mainly information-related, strategic opportunity is likely. Assessing information intensity can uncover areas of business activity for which an investment in information technology may be necessary.

Determine the Role of Information Technology in the Industry Structure The organization needs to know how competitive pressures might arise from buyers, suppliers, and competitors, and how it might be affected by information technology. New strategies may be needed to retain industry position or improve it if any of these pressures materialize.

Identify and Rank the Ways in Which Information Technology Can Create Competitive Advantage The organization must know how particular links of the value chain might be affected by information technology. If those links that can be affected represent high cost or critical areas of business activity, then they are areas in which the IS manager should focus his or her efforts. The resulting effect must also be anticipated, for it might be a change in industry structure, the value chain, or the market position of the organization's products and services. Some consideration must be given to the possibility that the effect may be different than envisioned and may actually have a negative outcome for the organization.

Investigate How Information Technology Might Spawn New Businesses Excess computer capacity or corporate data bases may provide opportunities for spin-off businesses. Porter and Millar suggest that organizations answer the following three questions

1. What information generated (or potentially generated) by the business could be sold?

2. What information-processing capacity exists internally to start a new business?

3. Does information technology make it feasible to produce new items related to the organization's current products?

Develop a Plan for Taking Advantage of Information Technology To take advantage of strategic opportunities that information technology presents requires a plan that assigns priorities to the strategic investments that the organization needs to make. This decision making should not be the sole province of the IS department. In fact, the process should be business driven, not technology driven.

Porter and Millar conclude their discussion of value chain analysis with the following worthy statement:

> **The importance of the information revolution is not in dispute. The question is not whether information technology will have a significant impact on a company's competitive position; rather the question is when and how this impact will strike. Companies that anticipate the power of information technology will be in control of events. Companies that do not respond will be forced to accept changes that others initiate and will find themselves at a competitive disadvantage.**

Value-chain analysis is a useful planning tool for organizations in the support or factory category of the strategic grid we encountered in Chapter 2. The value chain will help such organizations identify areas in which productivity improvements might be made. It may also point the IS manager toward certain system enhancements or even new technologies that the organization should acquire.

The Competitive Forces Model

The value chain can be expanded outside the organization to incorporate suppliers' and buyers' value chains (Porter, 1980). Organizations in the strategic or turnaround categories or in any of the domain 3 cells of the benefit/beneficiary matrix (see Chapter 2) might examine the linkages between the supplier/buyer value chains. There may be ways to use the technology to create information linkages and hence establish competitive advantage. A more descriptive model of the relationships among these value chains is the value system shown in Exhibit 4-7.

Competitive advantages are "certain abilities or combinations of abilities, that the superior performer possess uniquely or to a greater degree than any of its competitors." (Wiseman, 1988). To establish competitive advantage, the organization must look for product/service differentiation as well as linkages among buyers, suppliers, competitors, and substitute products. Five competitive forces operate on the organization in this value system (Exhibit 4-8). Each force is briefly discussed next.

Threat of New Entrants   New entrants to an industry may cause reduced margins by lowering prices. Smaller market share may also result as new entrants jockey for position in the market. In some cases the market may actually expand, and market saturation may not occur. To protect themselves from such threats, organizations already in the market may attempt to create technological barriers to the entry of new competitors.

Rivalry Among Existing Firms   If one or more of the competitors in an industry discovers a technological opportunity to improve its position, rivalry in the form of retaliation and countermoves by other organizations will intensify. Lower prices, improved quality, and faster service are likely to result. Although customers may be better off in the short run, the long-run effects may be to reduce margins and hence weaken the industry.

Threat of Substitute Products   New information technologies have certainly brought more opportunities in the way of price/ performance improvements through substitute products. Organizations need to be particularly sensitive to the substitution of computerized products for their human counterparts. The replacement of tellers with ATMs is a good example. Those banks that first installed ATMs gained an advantage over the competition; however, that advantage was not sustainable. Banks are now forced to install ATMs to remain competitive. ATMs were initially an offensive strategy, but have now become a defensive strategy.

Bargaining Power of Buyers   Buyers exert considerable influence on an industry by competing against one another, by forcing prices down, and by bargaining for service and quality improvements.

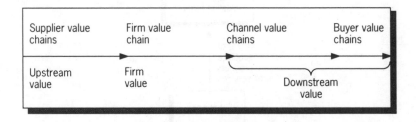

EXHIBIT 4-7 The value system.

Buyers tend to be in a position of strength if they account for a large portion of one organization's sales, if the product they purchase represents a large portion of their fixed costs or purchases, if the products they purchase are standard, if they face few switching costs, and if they are a threat to vertical integration or are already producing some of the products they purchase from suppliers. To parry the buyer's threat, a company might look for ways to increase the buyer's switching costs, might preselect buyers who are not in a position to pose a threat, and finally might look for ways to provide differentiated products or services to one of the large buyer groups.

Bargaining Power of Suppliers Suppliers that have differentiated products or are not threatened by substitute products are in a powerful position relative to their competitors. If a particular industry is not a major part of a supplier's business, the supplier can exert power over that industry in the form of price increases and/or quality decreases.

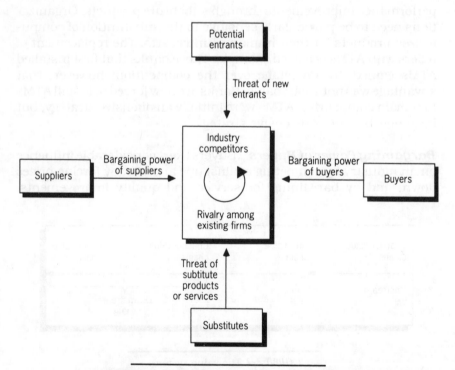

EXHIBIT 4-8 Five forces driving industry competition.

Source: Michael E. Porter, *Competitive Strategy, Techniques for Analyzing Industries and Competition*, New York: Free Press, 1980, p. 4. Reprinted with permission of The Free Press, a division of Macmillan, Inc. Copyright © 1980 by The Free Press.

Porter suggests three generic strategies from which an organization might choose in order to establish competitive advantage. For each one, he identifies the potential impact of IS as it relates to corporate strategy. The first strategy is to be the low-cost producer. In terms of this strategy, IS permits major reductions in support staff as well as better use of manufacturing facilities, significant inventory and accounts receivable reductions, and better use of materials through reduction of wastage.

The second strategy is to offer a unique, differentiated product. Here IS can become a significant component of product cost and hence a differentiating feature. IS can also affect product development life-cycle times (CAD/CAM provides this advantage). Moreover, IS can make customization possible and can improve customer service and need satisfaction, all of which can be built into the pricing decision.

The third strategy is to develop systems to identify and meet the needs of specialized markets. In terms of this strategy, IS can facilitate the identification of market niches through analyses of corporate or industry sales data bases.

Porter identifies two fundamental risks associated with these generic strategies: failure to attain or sustain competitive advantage and the erosion of this advantage as a result of industry evolution. The IS manager can be instrumental in reducing each of these risks. Maintaining competitive advantage is an ongoing IS planning responsibility for organizations in the turnaround, factory, and strategic categories. Reducing the second risk is more difficult and may involve joint efforts between IS and functional management to seek ways to further differentiate the organization's product or service.

CONCLUSION

In *A Passion For Excellence* (1985), Tom Peters and Nancy Austin list among the essential ingredients for organizational success, the necessity of constantly innovating and looking for ways to improve customer service. In all the examples given earlier, innovation is a key ingredient. Although the product or service enhancements undertaken are not all sophisticated in their use of computer technology, they are extremely effective in terms of exploiting strategic opportunities.

Regardless of the type of business, there are countless opportunities for IS managers to initiate creative IT applications that can lead to competitive advantages. In service- or information-based organizations, such opportunities will typically exist at the strategic and tactical levels; in manufacturing industries these opportunities are usually found at the tactical and operational levels. No matter what the business, however, the challenge is identical: to think imaginatively about ways in which information technology can position the organization to be an industry leader.

DISCUSSION QUESTIONS

1. Are all opportunities for competitive advantage strategic in nature?

2. Does offering access to SABRE to the individual traveler create competitive advantage for American Airlines? Why or why not? Do you see any potential problems resulting from this offering?

3. Discuss the First Boston and Kendall examples of strategic system initiatives that failed by commenting on Porter's three conditions for the establishment of competitive advantage.

4. In an employee-owned firm consisting of an airline, a hotel chain, and a reservation system, the (pilot-dominated) ownership tried to promote the reservation system to support the airline. What do you think?

REFERENCES

Bakos, J. Yannis, and Michael E. Treacy (1986). "Information Technology and Corporate Strategy: A Research Perspective," *MIS Quarterly* (June), pp. 107–119.

Benjamin, Robert I., John F. Rockart, Michael S. Scott-Morton, and John Wyman (1984). "Information Technology: A Strategic Opportunity," *Sloan Management Review*, vol. 25, no. 3 (Spring), pp. 3–10.

Parsons, G. L. (1983). "Information Technology: A New Competitive Weapon," *Sloan Management Review*, vol. 25, no. 1 (Fall), pp. 3–14.

Peters, Tom, and Nancy Austin (1985). *A Passion for Excellence*, New York: Random House.

Porter, Michael E. (1980). *Competitive Strategy*, New York: Free Press.

Porter, Michael E., and Victor E. Millar (1985). "How Information Gives You Competitive Advantage," *Harvard Business Review* (July-August), pp. 149–160.

Synnott, William R. (1987). *The Information Weapon: Winning Customers and Markets with Technology*, New York: Wiley.

Wiseman, Charles (1988) *Strategic Information Systems*, Homewood, Il: Irwin.

five

□

Strategic Information Systems Planning

The Planning Challenge

Three Levels of Planning

Information Systems Planning Methodologies

Extending the Critical Success Factors Methodology

The Business Systems Planning Methodology

An Integrated Strategic Information Systems Planning Process

Conclusion

Discussion Questions

References

Meaningful IS planning is one of the most difficult managerial functions for the IS manager, although it ranks high in importance in the eyes of most experienced IS managers. Of course, it can be argued that IS planning is a waste of time. The competitive environment seems to change without rhyme or reason; technology races ahead in dozens of directions (some uncharted); system vendors come and go; and the global economy shifts dramatically in response to unstable balances of payments, fluctuating exchange-rates, and the vagaries of international stock markets. Things change rapidly and in a seemingly random fashion, rendering most plans obsolete even before they are completed. Yet one can counter that IS plans are written to be changed as circumstances change and, if prepared in that light, are both useful and necessary.

This book takes the position that organizations should implement a planning process that incorporates IS and business planning. In some organizations the role of the IS department in this relationship will be entirely reactive; in others, the relationship will be integrated and the IS department will play both a reactive and a proactive role.

To be effective, the IS planning process must take into account the organization's present use of information technology (IT). As we have seen several times, the strategic grid (discussed in detail in Chapters 2 and 3) is helpful in assessing this use. An organization may be correctly positioned with regard to its use of IT, so the IS planning process may need to be merely supportive of the overall business plan. However, if the organization is not using IT appropriately, the planning process will have to focus on change and on new applications.

We examine these and related issues in this chapter, which begins with a general overview of the planning process and of three basic levels of planning. Next, the chapter explores several IS planning methodologies. We conclude with a discussion of a new model for the strategic IS planning process. It is designed to fully integrate business and IS planning in any organization.

THE PLANNING CHALLENGE

IS planning has undergone a significant metamorphosis during the 30-year history of commercial information processing. Until recently it was appropriate for an IS manager to react to the corporate business plan by developing an IS plan to support the organization in achieving its plan objectives. That is no longer sufficient; many organizations are now expecting the IS manager to participate in the formation of business strategies. Therefore, the IS department has a dual planning responsibility: first to help define the business activity and then to define precisely how IS will assist in this activity. We will return to this dual responsibility at the end of this chapter; but at this point, the essential questions we face are whether the planning process should be business driven or technology driven and, furthermore, whether it should be top-down or bottom-up. Ideally, the planning process should be business driven; however, there is a risk that senior managers, who are not technologically literate, may overlook significant opportunities for the strategic use of IT if the process is overly business driven. In contrast, if it is technology driven, there is the risk that an IS manager, who is not sufficiently aware of the business itself, might also miss such opportunities.

The ideal corporate environment for planning is to have top managers (including the IS manager) who are sophisticated in their understanding of both business and technology. As an alternative, having an IS manager as an accepted member of the senior management team decreases the risk of missing strategic IT-related opportunities. In any event, organizations should look for planning methodologies that provide a forum for the IS manager to contribute actively to the formation of the business plan.

Defining a workable IS planning framework is difficult. Much depends on whether the organization uses IT extensively for competitive advantage or simply in a support role. Timing is also a critical factor. It would be a mistake, for example, to impose a fixed planning horizon on every functional area of the organization, just as it would be a mistake to assume that each functional department or division is at the same stage of IT development.

The question of top-down versus bottom-up planning is an important one. Using a top-down framework, senior management sets the business direction for the organization and assigns priorities for new initiatives, empowering each business-unit head (including the IS manager) to determine the needed systems and resources to accomplish the goals of the business plan. This framework helps structure the planning activities of middle-level managers, supervisors, and nonmanagement professionals, but it may pose a threat to creativity. A bottom-up framework, in contrast, gives individual managers an opportunity to develop new ideas and new project initiatives that will at least be reviewed at higher organizational levels. To the extent that further efficiencies and productivity enhancements are possible, the bottom-up framework is more likely to unearth them at lower levels of the organization.

THREE LEVELS OF PLANNING

IS planning takes place at three distinct levels in the organization: strategic, tactical, and operational. Exhibit 5-1 shows how these levels are "stacked." The following sections discuss each one briefly. A simplified way of looking at these levels is that at the strategic level we are concerned with what will be done; at the tactical level, with how it will be done; and at the operational level, with who will do it and when. Envisioning IS planning as a hierarchic construct helps us focus on the relationship between corporate strategic plans and the most fundamental tactical and operational activities undertaken by the IS department. Furthermore, knowing that relationship gives the IS staff a basis for making prioritization decisions for the projects and activities for which they are responsible. In the rest of this chapter we examine strategic-level IS planning, saving for Part III our discussion of the tactical and operational levels.

Strategic Information Systems Planning

Strategic IS planning increasingly entails the participation of the IS manager in the general business-planning exercise. That is, the IS manager is not only asked to develop specific systems to implement corporate strategy but is also expected to participate in the actual development of that strategy. Strategic planning has two principle dimensions:

- **Strategy development,** in which the external environment is monitored and strategic information is gathered, and
- **Strategy implementation,** in which appropriate systems are designed and implemented to generate the information and computer support needed to accomplish strategic goals.

The implementation dimension has typically involved IS in a reactive role, and for this activity there are well-developed methodologies

EXHIBIT 5-1 Levels of IS planning.

(Rockart, 1979; IBM, 1984). With regard to a framework for involving the IS department in corporate strategy development, however, not much is available.

Tactical and Operational Information Systems Planning

Once the goals and objectives of IS are clearly understood and priorities have been assigned, it becomes the responsibility of middle-level IS managers to decide how to accomplish these goals and objectives.

A number of projects to accomplish these goals and objectives will have been defined as part of the strategic planning process. There will be three types of projects to consider. The first type will address problem areas where performance is below normal. Shipping, scheduling, and billing errors, delays in order fulfillment, production errors, increases in refunds and returned products from customers, system failures, delays in project completion, and larger than normal budget variances are typical problems to be dealt with. The second type of project will involve system maintenance. Increases or changes in business activity will often necessitate changes to existing application systems. These changes may be very minor (increasing file size to accommodate increased customer base) or major (system integration resulting from a buy out or merger). The third type of project will be new systems development. These will arise in response to a number of plan activities such as new products or services, the addition of new information system applications, and the incorporation of new information technologies into organizational operations. Middle-level managers will have to consider all three types of projects concurrently as they plan, prioritize, schedule, budget resources, and determine the appropriate control guidelines to accomplish them.

Monitoring resource use at the project level is the main task at the operational level of IS management. This task consists mostly of supervising the establishment, control, and variance reporting of the "who and when" aspects of ongoing operations. These are discussed in more detail in Part III.

INFORMATION SYSTEMS PLANNING METHODOLOGIES

Having identified the three levels at which IS planning occurs, we now examine various strategic IS planning methods. In this discussion we assume that a no-planning option is not viable. Exhibit 5-2 does include this option, however, along with the four others—stand-alone planning, reactive planning, linked planning, and integrated planning.

Stand-alone Planning

Organizations practicing stand-alone planning may generate a business plan and a systems plan but make no attempt to coordinate the two. Such organizations are usually found in the support category. Senior management is engaged in business planning but may be unaware of any uses of computing and/or information with potential strategic benefits.

The IS department in such organizations is in a reactive mode, and its planning activity is limited almost exclusively to budget planning. If the organization is missing strategic opportunities to use IT, it will be largely the responsibility of the IS manager to bring this problem to the attention of senior management (on the assumption, of course, that the IS manager perceives the problem). Education and demon-

Type of Planning	Description	Degree of Integration
1. No planning	No formal planning takes place, either business or information systems.	No plan
2. Stand - alone planning	The company may have a business plan or an information systems plan, but not both.	Business or system plan
3. Reactive planning	A business plan is prepared and the information systems function reacts to it – a traditional passive systems role.	Business plan ▷ System plan
4. Linked planning	Business planning is "interfaced" with information systems planning. Systems resources are matched against business needs.	Business plan / System plan
5. Integrated planning	Business and information systems planning occur simultaneously and interactively. They are indistiguishable.	Business or system plan

EXHIBIT 5-2 The planning spectrum.

Source: The Information Weapon: Winning Customers and Markets With Technology, William R. Synnott, Copyright © 1987 by John Wiley & Sons, Inc. Reprinted by permission of John Wiely & Sons, Inc.

stration programs for senior managers may be helpful in moving the organization from stand-alone planning to another option.

Reactive Planning

Reactive planning is the type most often used in modern organizations. A business plan is generated (without the direct input of the IS manager) and passed down to the IS department. The IS department is then responsible for generating a systems plan to support the business plan. In this process the IS department assumes a completely passive role.

Linked Planning

Organizations in the turnaround category and strategic categories often use planning systems that take into account information technology and how it can help meet certain business needs. Such organizations are in a "change mode" regarding strategic systems. As we will see shortly, critical success factors (CSFs) may be used effectively by such organizations' IS managers to help define information needs and to match systems resources against overall business needs.

Integrated Planning

Having business planning and systems planning occur simultaneously requires that the IS manager participate actively in the formation of the corporate business plan. In addition, functional business managers must also participate actively in IS strategic plan formation, especially with regard to assigning priorities, allocating resources, and making technology investment decisions. Fully integrated planning requires an IS manager who understands the business function and business managers who understand the value and role of IS. Few organizations can boast of such expertise.

EXTENDING THE CRITICAL SUCCESSS FACTORS METHODOLOGY

To be more useful to the strategic IS planning effort, the CSF method presented in Chapter 2 has been extended to include three distinct "critical sets" (Henderson et al., 1987). Exhibit 5-3 presents a planning approach that is based on this extended CSF approach and that conforms to the linked planning option discussed earlier. Each critical set contributes to what is referred to as a strategic data model in the extended CSF methodology.

The first set is the critical information set (CIS), which is the output from the CSF method and which becomes input to the design of the management information system (MIS). The second is the critical assumption set (CAS). CSFs are based on assumptions regarding the conditions that exist or might exist in markets of interest to the organization, and as these assumptions change, so might the CSFs. An executive support system (ESS) to monitor these assumptions is desirable, and the CAS is such an entity. The dotted line in Exhibit 5-3 represents feedback (e.g., changes in assumptions) to business

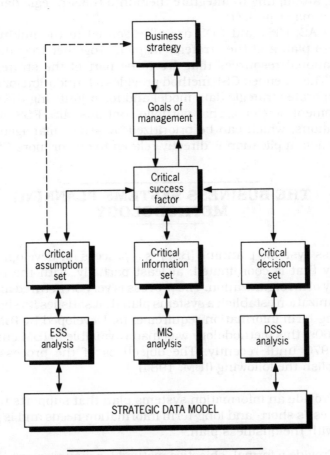

EXHIBIT 5-3 The extended CSF methodology.

Source: Reprinted from Journal of Management Information Systems, vol. 4, no. 1, 1987 by permission of M. E. Sharpe, Inc., Armonk, NY.

strategy development. ESS analyses are generally undertaken outside the traditional IS planning framework. ESS data are usually highly aggregated and often change slowly, and therefore developing data modeling to incorporate them is not a trivial problem.

The third set is the critical decision set (CDS). Related to each CSF are one or more decisions that must be made to ensure the successful performance of activities associated with that CSF. Each of these decisions requires some input. The CDS is such input; it corresponds to the decision support systems (DSS) that may be developed. The earliest DSS were developed in an end-user computing environment as stand-alone applications. Many were done independently of any consideration of existing data dictionaries, naming conventions, or established design principles. For that reason, attempting to integrate them into the strategic data model will be a major project.

The CAS, CIS, and CDS are all essential to the linking of the business plan and the strategic IS plan. Together they define the informational resources that are to be part of the strategic data model. The extended CSF method provides a foundation for defining the corporate strategic data model and for prioritizing the systems development portfolio. That portfolio contains MIS, ESS, and DSS applications, which can be prioritized by senior management because each application is directly related to one or more CSFs.

THE BUSINESS SYSTEMS PLANNING METHODOLOGY

Business systems planning (BSP) is a process for developing an IS strategy that is coordinated, at least partially, with the business strategy of an organization. The process is very structured and helps an organization establish a systems plan that satisfies its short-term and long-term information requirements. Developed by IBM in the late 1960s, this methodology was made available to IBM customers from 1970 until recently. The objectives of the process are to accomplish the following (IBM, 1984)

1. Provide an information systems plan that supports the business's short- and long-term information needs and is integral with the business plan.

2. Provide a formal, objective method for management to establish information systems priorities without regard to provincial interests.

3. Provide for the development of systems that have a long life, protecting the systems investment, because these systems are based on the business processes that are generally unaffected by organizational changes.

4. Provide that the data processing resources are managed for the most efficient and effective support of the business goals.

5. Increase executive confidence that high-return, major information systems will be produced.

6. Improve relationships between the information systems department and users by providing for systems that are responsive to user requirements and priorities.

7. Identify data as a corporate resource that should be planned, managed, and controlled in order to be used effectively by everyone.

BSP consists of both top-down planning and bottom-up design and implementation. In Exhibit 5-4, *business processes* consist of the activities that make up the value chain, and these in turn define the *business data* requirements of the organization. Both the *business processes* and *business data* are identified through extensive interviews and discussion of the business plan. The planning phase is complete once the *information architecture*, best suited to meet the needs of managers at all levels in the organization, has been determined. The output of this step will be a definition of current system resources, the identification of additional resources that will be needed, and a prioritization scheme. The design and development phase begins with the *information architecture* phase and includes the development and modification of both new and existing data bases. This analysis is needed so that new computer applications can be defined. The *applications* step consists of the definition of specific projects to be undertaken, development priorities, functional specifications, and, finally, system implementation. To complete the BSP methodology, the new applications support *business processes*, which in turn contribute to *business objectives*.

BSP is a planning approach that is more appropriate for organizations in the support or factory categories. Its strengths include the following:

- It involves senior management.
- It enhances communications among personnel at all levels of the organization (user, user management, senior management, and IS management).

- It sensitizes senior management to the costs, benefits, and capabilities of information systems.
- Being highly structured, it can be replicated and compared year to year.
- It is well-documented.
- It provides goals for the IS department around which an implementation plan can be structured.

Its weaknesses are that it is difficult to implement, is highly dependent on the interviewer's skills, and risks missing competitive opportunities. According to James Martin (1982) its major weakness is that its output is often not connected to existing data bases and systems, thus increasing the communication problem with IS personnel and preventing the development of a specific IS plan.

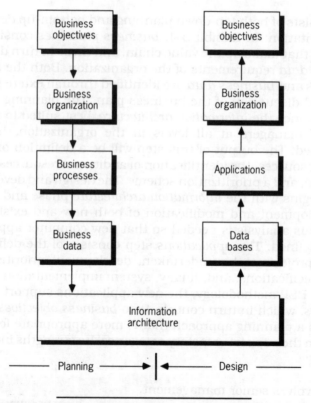

EXHIBIT 5-4 Top-down analysis with bottom-up implementation.

Source: Reprinted by permission from *Information Systems Planning Guide* © 1984 by International Business Machines Corporation.

AN INTEGRATED STRATEGIC INFORMATION SYSTEMS PLANNING PROCESS

Planning is a way of guaranteeing and maintaining a competitive advantage. Organizations that understand this also understand the importance of fully integrating IS planning at the senior-management and departmental levels. The IS department plays a dual planning role, as the model we now present illustrates. One role is proactive and involves the IS department in strategy set formation at the corporate level and application systems initiatives at the departmental level. The other role is reactive and involves the IS department as a support service to implement systems that help corporate officers and functional business units meet their planning objectives.

The model consists of five steps, each of which is discussed in detail in the following sections. Exhibit 5-5 illustrates the model.

Step 1: Environmental Analysis

Initiation of the environmental analysis is largely the responsibility of the IS manager. In this step, both internal and external factors affecting the organization's use of IT are documented. Internal factors measure and define the organization's use of IT and potential changes or increases in that use. Documenting internal factors may entail locating the organization on the strategic grid in order to gain a better understanding of which planning methodology would be consistent with the organizational climate (i.e., the degree of formality or informality, level of detail, planning horizon, etc., that would be appropriate). The readiness of the IS staff to assimilate new technologies and trends also needs to be documented; it may be necessary for the IS manager to consider trade-offs between long-range staff development and the timely hiring of professionals with the requisite skills.

Analysis of the external factors entails consideration of the organization's competitive position with respect to IT. This analysis includes an assessment of how IT has affected and can affect the industry as well as the organization itself. A traditional analysis of strengths, weaknesses, opportunities, and threats (SWOT analysis) common to strategic business planning will often be part of this exercise. Value-chain and value-systems analyses are also useful. The IT trends that can be identified may suggest new strategic opportunities for the organization.

Environmental analysis is a proactive activity initiated and conducted by the IS department. Its resulting series of reports are input to planning meetings both at the corporate level for business planning and at the departmental level for departmental planning. The environmental analysis also provides information to help the IS department in its own planning activity. Trends and uses of IT may suggest to the IS department a number of changes that should be made in its data-base architecture to improve efficiency and/or effectiveness. As envisioned here, the environmental analysis is not a once a year exercise but rather a continual process that generates a steady stream of information on specific environmental issues. It

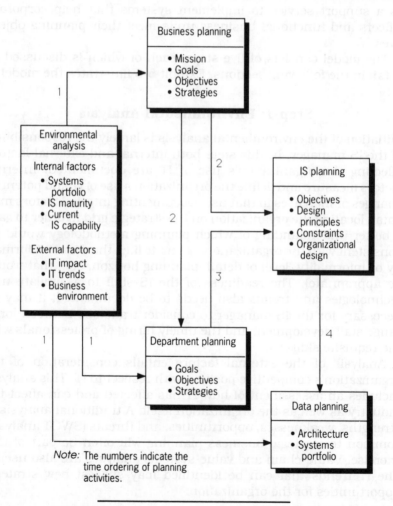

Note: The numbers indicate the time ordering of planning activities.

EXHIBIT 5-5 An integrated strategic IS planning model.

is the responsibility of the IS manager to see that such information is appropriately directed throughout the organization.

Step 2: Business Planning

Using the information gleaned from the environmental analysis, the organization determines if it can use IT to make a significant change in the way it interacts with its markets. It might learn that it can gain competitive advantage by changing the markets in which it is doing business. The output of this process will be a new or revised strategy set (mission, goals, objectives, and strategies) that will serve as input to all departments (including the IS department) for their planning. Each department translates this corporate strategy set into its own departmental strategy set.

Step 3: Business Unit and Department Planning

The environmental analysis might also suggest to the organization that it should look for internal applications of IT to improve the way that it currently conducts its business. Both this information and the corporate strategy set are the basic input data that business units and the functional-area departments will use to generate their strategic plans. As at the corporate-level, three types of projects may result (problem resolution, system maintenance, and new systems). Each can appear in unit and departmental plans and will become input to the IS strategic planning process. Value-chain analysis (see Chapter 4) will often be used by the units and departments to identify areas of opportunity for competitive advantage.

Step 4: Development of the Strategic Information Systems Plan

The IS department, acting reactively, translates the corporate, business unit and departmental strategy sets into a strategic IS plan. Tools that might also be used to develop the strategic IS plan are the BSP framework, the strategy set-transformation approach (King, 1978), and the ends/means analysis (Wetherbe and Davis, 1982). Refer to the cited references for details.

Step 5: Data Planning

Once the IS plan is in place, data-planning activity can begin. One approach is to define the information architecture (part of the BSP methodology discussed earlier) along with a portfolio of development projects (the *application* step of the BSP methodology). Data flow analysis and information flow techniques may also be used.

The final step for the IS department is to prepare the necessary inputs to the budget-planning process. This topic is taken up in Part III.

CONCLUSION

Strategic IS planning in modern organizations runs the gamut from wholly separate from business planning to tightly integrated with that planning. At present, organizations in the support and factory categories of the strategic grid can successfully use the BSP method, and those in the turnaround and strategic categories might use an extended CSF method. However, a generalized method for fully integrating corporate strategic planning with IS strategic planning is not yet available.

A new planning model incorporating the dual nature of the IS department's planning role has been suggested here. It involves the IS manager's participation in corporate strategy set formation and development of IT initiatives as well as of systems to help specific business units achieve their objectives.

DISCUSSION QUESTIONS

1. As IS manager, how would you reconcile the individual efforts of users to develop their own strategic information systems with the efforts of top management to develop a corporate strategic system? What kinds of problems and issues do you see emanating from such independent user actions?

2. As IS manager, who from your organization would you involve in IS planning, and how?

3. As IS manager, how would you support user departments during business planning?

4. Why do you think the business systems planning methodology is difficult to implement and how does its use open the organization to the possibility of missing competitive opportunities?

REFERENCES

Henderson, John C., John F. Rockart, and John G. Sifonis (1987). "Integrating Management Support Systems into Strategic Information Systems Planning," *Journal of Management Information Systems*, vol. 4, no. 1 (Summer), pp. 5–24.

IBM Corporation (1984). *Business Systems Planning: Information Systems Planning Guide*, 4th ed., pub. no. GE20-0527-4.

King, W. R. (1978). "Strategic Planning for Management Information Systems, *MIS Quarterly*, vol. 2, pp. 27–37.

Martin, James (1982). *Strategic Data-Planning Methodologies*, (Englewood Cliffs, N.J.: Prentice-Hall).

Rockart, John F. (1979). "Chief Executives Define Their Own Data Needs," *Harvard Business Review*, vol. 57, no. 2 (March-April), pp. 81–92.

Wetherbe, J. C., and G. B. Davis (1982). "Strategic MIS Planning Through Ends/Means Analysis," MIS Research Center Working Paper, University of Minnesota, Minneapolis.

six

□

The Organizational Placement of the Information Systems Department

IS departments have adopted diverse organizational structures and alignments as a result of historical evolution, accident, planned change, or the pressures of corporate culture—forms that may or may not be appropriate for a given organization. The rapid transition toward an end-user-oriented environment has rekindled the issue of whether the department should be centralized or decentralized—in short, it has begged the question of the IS department's position or alignment within the corporate structure. Moreover, the reporting responsibilities of the IS manager in a context in which autonomous uses of information technology are dispersed throughout the organization are not clearcut. This fact, too, raises the question of structure and alignment.

These and related issues are the focus of this chapter. We begin this chapter by tracing the evolution of the IS department's location in the organizational structure; to do so, we revisit the stages hypothesis (Nolan and Gibson, 1974; Nolan 1979) discussed in Chapter 2. Next, we look at typical organizational placements for the IS department. We then take up the question of which structural options make best use of the IS department—that is, which options best position the department to contribute significantly and consistently to the organization's competitive arsenal. We look at centralized and decentralized structures for the IS department. Finally, we explore reporting relationships, with special emphasis on CEO styles of work and their effect on the IS manager.

HISTORICAL TRENDS IN INFORMATION SYSTEMS ORGANIZATIONAL STRUCTURE

The Initiation Stage

Because the first commercial computer applications were usually in the accounting area, the data-processing staff normally reported to the head of the accounting department. As providers of a service, the data-processing staff had to worry about ensuring the timely delivery of correct reports to the accounting department and responding to application development requests from them. Moreover, the data-processing supervisor had to deal with only a single technology (batch processing on a single mainframe). From an organizational standpoint, life was fairly simple.

The Contagion Stage

As other functional managers became aware of the potential benefits of IS applications in their areas, it became necessary for the data-processing supervisor to establish relationships with other departments and implement procedures regarding the allocation of production time and development support. Policies had to be developed to accommodate the needs of these new users. At the same time, the accounting department saw its control of computing resources erode as others began to contend for computing time and programming resources. The data-processing supervisor was often under great pressure from his or her old boss to play favorites and give the accounting department preferred treatment.

Many departments were able to convince senior management that their needs were very different from those of the accounting department and that it was in the organization's best interest to let them establish their own computing resources. This pressure was quite effective. The data-processing supervisor, who reported directly to the head of the accounting department, did not fully understand the needs of users in other departments and was not, in any case, in a position to meet them. Letting other units establish their own computing facilities was a means of avoiding a confrontation with the accounting department and letting everyone get on with their own business. This laissez-faire management approach was more expedient than well thought out.

As the number of requests for applications continued to grow, it became necessary for data processing to form its own department to serve users who could not justify their own equipment and staff. This new department was typically located on the same organizational level as its user groups.

The Control Stage

The unbridled growth of computer use was inevitably noticed by senior managers, who temporarily brought a halt to rapidly increasing expenditures for computing resources by making the data-processing manager (by now known in many organizations as the IS manager) responsible for implementing controls and cost/benefit measures. This was unfamiliar territory for the IS manager, who had never before needed to learn cost/benefit analysis techniques, to estimate systems development times, or to establish monitoring and control procedures. Senior management began looking at the IS department as it would any other service department in the organization. In so doing, they evaluated the IS department using tried and true cost-justification criteria. The IS manager, who had previously been protected from such close scrutiny, was now competing on the same turf as other middle managers; it was strange turf, with new and strange rules. The power and politics of the management team had to become part of the IS manager's tool kit.

The IS manager had been promising systems for literally anything users requested. As monitoring and control systems went into place, however, it became evident how poorly managed the IS department was. Excessively late, over-budget projects were the rule rather than the exception. As we have seen, the typically poor management skills of the IS manager (remember they were "techies") and the department's failure to deliver on promised systems resulted in a serious loss of credibility and user confidence.

The Integration and Data Administration Stages

As computer applications became more sophisticated and IS took on a more visible role in business affairs, many organizations recognized that they would have to use their computing resources more efficiently and effectively. This meant that the IS manager needed a broader corporate perspective so as to be able to assist functional managers actively in their search for ways to use information technology to good advantage. A new kind of relationship began to develop between the IS and other functional managers. The immediate result was that the IS manager had an opportunity to regain user confidence and to be treated and received as an equal among functional managers. At the same time, however, pockets of computer applications began to spring up independently of the IS department. These "islands of technology" (CAD/CAM, desktop publishing, word-processing centers, robotics, etc.) presented (and still present) a difficult organizational structure issue for the IS manager, who had to define the department's position regarding their operation. In many cases the professionals responsible for various islands of technology knew more than the IS staff did about the use of the technology, so centralizing such islands under the IS department might prove detrimental. From a senior management perspective, there was no clear-cut solution, so the IS manager was on his or her own to recommend and defend a particular organizational decision.

The Maturity Stage

At present, organizational use of information technology has moved beyond the organization itself and into the marketplace. Relationships with customers and suppliers are heavily affected. In fact, the IS manager may be called on to establish working relationships with customers and suppliers so that the organization may retain its competitive position. Few if any organizations have reached the maturity stage—a point at which information technology is fully integrated in the organization at every level and the IS manager is a full-fledged member of the senior management team.

INFORMATION SYSTEMS AND ORGANIZATIONAL STRUCTURES: THE CURRENT SITUATION

Having traced the historical evolution of IS department's placement in the organizational structure, we see that both the breadth and depth of the IS manager's responsibilities have changed dramatically since the data-processing days. The hardware environment has evolved from single-batch to remote-batch to terminals, micros, distributed and networked systems; software applications have evolved from simple accounting to control systems to decision-making systems; and special-purpose uses (as reflected by the islands of technology) have also emerged. In addition, organizations no longer rely heavily on skilled programmers; users can and are doing their own applications development work independent of the IS programming staff. Thus, the IS manager now has a wide range of technologies to plan for and control, and he or she must make crucial resource-allocation decisions.

The organizational reach of the IS manager's job has also undergone major changes. Senior managers expect a greater corporate-level contribution from the IS manager and have raised the IS manager to a higher position in the organization. This has created what at least one author, Darrell Owen (1986), has called an "elevation gap." As Owen explains, this gap gives rise to several concerns. The most immediate is that the expectations of senior management are raised, and the IS manager is not always prepared to meet those heightened expectations. Another concern is that because the IS manager is increasingly drawn into corporate issues, he or she has less time to spend actually managing the IS department's operations. In those IS departments that need a lot of attention from the IS manager, there will be problems. As new technologies are added, the department ends up supporting those new technologies without the necessary degree of managerial control. Exhibit 6-1 graphically illustrates this elevation gap.

David Whieldon (1981) makes several useful observations regarding developments that are affecting the IS department's position in the organizational structure. His insights are summarized here.

1. *Applications development is increasingly passing into the hands of users* This trend has become so strong that developing applications systems is often considered a responsibility of end-user departments, many of which have amassed a good deal of computing power.

2. *Satisfying users has become more difficult as major projects grow complex, requiring months and even years to complete, while smaller projects suffer from neglect.* The very sophisticated "super systems" are multifunctional and often involve ill-defined needs. These systems require significant development effort. They tend to hold the attention and involvement of top management at the expense of less strategic and smaller systems.

3. *The division between systems analysis and programming is increasingly proving unworkable, and more comprehensive functions may have to be devised.* The linear systems development life cycle is frequently inappropriate and is being replaced with a variety of adaptive and cyclical methodologies such as prototyping (see Chapter 16). These newer methodologies often merge analysis and programming in an evolutionary cycle. In addition to such methodological changes, the use of fourth- and fifth-generation tools further blurs the design phase of the development process. With these new tools, users specify what is to be done, not how it is to be done; as a result, both the logical and (to some extent) the physical design phases have become at least partially imbedded in the software. The challenge that has not yet been fully addressed is to revise systems development methods to be compatible with the nonprocedural languages.

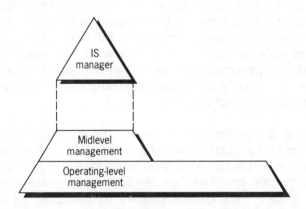

EXHIBIT 6-1 Technologically expanded organization.

Source: Darrell E. Owen, "Information Systems Organization-Keeping Pace with the Pressures," *Sloan Management Review*, vol. 27, no. 3, Spring, 1986, p. 64. Reprinted by permission of the publisher.

4. *MIS/DP personnel, by nature and by training, sometimes have difficulty communicating and working harmoniously with users.* The common perception of the IS professional in many organizations is that he or she would rather not go to meetings and would rather write instructions than verbally explain them. Users, on the other hand, are seen as a virtual mirror image of the IS professional: they take comfort in verbal explanations and prefer not to struggle with reading and deciphering often cryptic documents. In their view, meetings are productive and generally not a waste of time. Some stereotyping is inevitable here, but the potential for clashes of style is nonetheless real when the two types work together on a systems development project, as many organizations have learned from experience.

5. *Assignments may not provide sufficient interest, motivation, or advancement opportunities to keep IS personnel content, productive, and eager to remain in the organization.* Because systems development has migrated into user departments, many IS departments have had to downsize their systems and programming groups. In some cases the IS department is beginning to take on the appearance of a utility environment rather than the design and development environment it once was. Development efforts that remain in the IS department tend to focus on corporate-level projects or so-called super systems, neither of which typically sustain the interest and motivation of programmers or analysts in the manner to which they grew accustomed during the days of the large, centralized IS department.

6. *Program maintenance and similar chores in the organization are often slighted by IS personnel.* Program maintenance has never been a sought-after assignment in most IS departments. Because users are able to take care of cosmetic changes that occur frequently, the programmer's maintenance chores tend to be of the "bug-chasing" variety more than anything else—a situation that frustrates many programmers.

In diverse industries and contexts, these trends are having a marked effect on organizational structure and the placement of the IS department within the structure. New forms of organizations, and perhaps even new positions, are needed; present structures do not serve the needs of the organization effectively and are not likely to do so in the future.

We turn now to several structural possibilities and examine their effects on the IS department's efforts to enhance the organization's competitive posture. Clearly, major decisions regarding structure face senior management and, by implication, IS management. The following sections present factors that need to be considered by those decision makers whose task is to position the IS department appropriately within their organizations. In Chapter 11 we look inside the IS department itself and consider various structures for the functional elements that comprise the department.

ORGANIZATIONAL STRUCTURE: SOME BASIC CHOICES

A Centralized Structure

A centralized IS department manages all corporate computing activities from a single office. This does not imply (as was once true) that all processing takes place at one location. It is entirely possible that under a centralized structure the IS department may have several remote computing facilities that depend on one or more processors for their computing power. Large networks of processors and terminals can be part of a centralized structure as can stand-alone processors.

A centralized organizational structure is therefore defined as one in which the following hold true:

- One line manager is directly responsible for all IS issues (standards, policy, procedure, communications, and security).
- There are defined corporatewide procedures and controls for systems analysis, design, and programming practices.
- Data administration is under the control of one office.

Centralized organizational structures do offer a number of advantages. Certain corporate-level reports serve as consolidations of divisional—and even departmental—level financial and operating activities and are therefore easier to generate in centralized as compared to decentralized organizations. Standardized data items and summary rules aid in report preparation and interpretation. Problems with incompatible hardware and software and communications tend to disappear under a centralized structure; having to write bridge software and conversion software is very costly and problematic and is avoided in a centralized situation.

Centralization also provides more staffing options and opportunities for career advancement than do other forms of organization. It is easier to hire and keep talented people because there is greater specialization, career advancement, and project variety in a centralized as compared to a decentralized setting. Staff turnover and

shortages are easier to absorb, too. Finally, better resource allocation and control systems are possible, and economies of scale as well
as greater leverage with vendors result from a centralized organizational structure. More productive use of resources is a likely benefit
of these economies of scale.

A Decentralized Structure

In a decentralized organizational structure, information processing
occurs at several sites that are managed independently. Each of
these sites functions in the same way as the centralized organization
just described. A decentralized organizational structure is thus
defined as one in which the following hold true:

- Several processors function independently of one another,
  perhaps under different sets of standards and operating procedures.
- Each unit may have its own analysis and design procedures and
  controls.
- Special-purpose data bases, data administration, and applications are in place at each unit.

The decentralized organizational structure has a number of advantages. Having the development staff closer to users means that the
staff has greater access to product-specific knowledge and can thus
provide a higher level of expertise in application development (and
probably a higher degree of user satisfaction as a result). The
development staff tends to be more responsive to user needs and to
avoid the conflict over resources that crop up in centralized organizations. Enhanced responsiveness means that production work can
be scheduled for single user groups rather than across units with
differing priorities. For cost control and cost-benefit purposes, a
decentralized organization is typically better; users are more sensitive to cost considerations because they deal with these costs in their
project proposals and feasibility studies. The likely result is a more
productive use and allocation of resources as well as users who are
more sensitive to these issues. (Users' profitability is at stake, and
therefore they are more likely to pay attention to costs than they
would in a centralized organization.)

Which Structure Is Best?

The answer is predictable: There is no best organizational structure.
As it turns out, usually some hybrid of the two is appropriate. For

example, operations may be centralized, but systems and programming may be decentralized. The reverse is also practiced, especially in companies that are geographically dispersed. And operations and programming may be centralized but systems decentralized. This is likely to occur in larger, more computer-mature organizations. Applications definition and systems analysis may be done by analysts reporting to functional business managers.

There are, however, some useful guidelines for choosing the appropriate structure. A centralized structure is usually best suited in situations where IS is heavily used by senior management. Organization-wide functions, such as payroll and most accounting functions, are best served by a centralized system. Not all user departments will have sufficient need for computing to be able to justify their own staff and facilities; these, too, are best centralized.

A decentralized structure is best suited for organizations that have unique or specialized needs. When applications require very rapid response time or development support, their development is best decentralized to the appropriate department. There may be cases where particular user applications are unique and the demand for computing power is sufficiently large that the department or division can justify its own computing facility to support that single application (Exhibit 6-2). Decentralization makes sense in such cases.

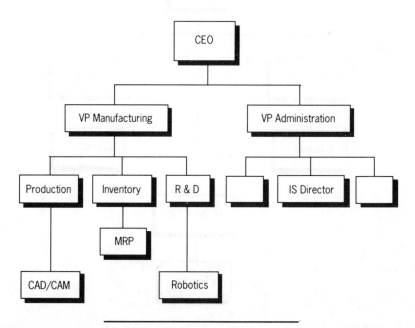

EXHIBIT 6-2 Decentralization of information systems in a manufacturing division.

Multidivisional organizations, those with several independent subsidiaries, or those that are geographically dispersed also tend to profit from a decentralized structure. Exhibit 6-3 is an example of a multidivisional company with major IS functions in each division.

The answer to which IS organizational structure to adopt can also be found by examining the organization's strategic plan. As Arthur Thompson and A. J. Strickland III (1986) point out, strategy implementation involves every unit asking itself "What is required for us to implement our part of the overall strategic plan?" This includes an examination of the organizational structure and alignment relevant to the organization's chosen strategy. Thompson and Strickland identify a five-sequence procedure for fitting structure to strategy:

1. Pinpoint the key functions and tasks requisite for successful strategy execution.
2. Reflect on how the strategy-critical functions and organizational units relate to those that are routine and to those that provide staff support.

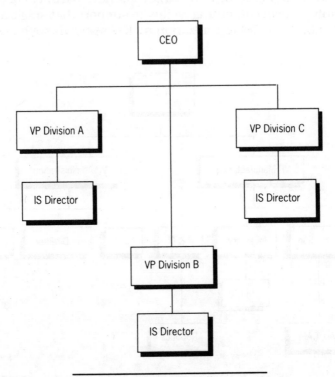

EXHIBIT 6-3 Information systems decentralized across geographically dispersed divisions.

3. Make strategy-critical business units and functions the main organizational building blocks.
4. Determine the degrees of authority needed to manage each organizational unit, bearing in mind both the benefits and the costs of decentralized decision making.
5. Provide for coordination among various organizational units.

Although these refer to the organization as a whole, there are very definite guidelines for the IS department. For example, project teams or task forces may be formed around strategy-critical functions or business units. Identifying the CSFs associated with strategic functions and tasks may suggest new or revised applications systems as well as development and investment priorities.

Aligning the Information Systems Department in the Organizational Structure

Regardless of the organizational structure, certain reporting relationships between the IS manager and senior managers need to be defined. Exhibit 6-4 illustrates an organization in which the IS manager reports to a vice president. In this organization all four vice presidents are significant IS users. Having the IS manager report to a major user opens up the possibility that resources and priorities may not be equitably assigned; the IS manager may feel pressure to meet the needs of the user to whom he or she reports. In such cases it would make good sense for the IS manager to report at a level above

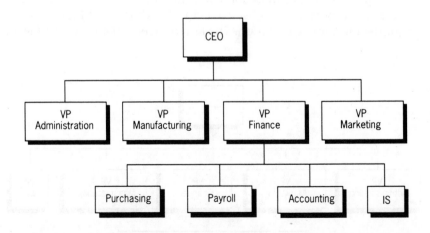

EXHIBIT 6-4 Information systems centralized at the vice-presidential level.

that of the highest major user. Exhibits 6-5 and 6-6 illustrate two viable alternatives. In Exhibit 6-5 the IS manager reports at a level above the highest user—in this case to the CEO. Often the IS manager holds the title of vice president in such organizational structures. Exhibit 6-6 has the IS manager reporting to a steering committee that in turn reports to the CEO, who often chairs the steering committee meetings. The title of director is usually given the IS manager in these organizational structures.

When the IS manager reports above the level of the highest active user, the possibility of bias toward users at the level at which IS reports tends to be defused. The manager to whom the IS manager reports will not have a vested interest in the decision and can therefore be expected to evaluate the alternatives on their own merits. Moreover, the IS manager tends to acquire some leverage when dealing with tough issues and decisions. It is important that senior managers locate the IS department in a position on the organizational chart that gives it a wide purview and some real clout in dealing with others. The IS manager must have perceived power when trying to establish relationships with other managers across the organization.

In a centralized organizational structure, the IS manager should not report to a major user. In such reporting relationships, IS managers would feel constant pressure to compromise their autonomy; moreover, they would worry about whether a favorable decision toward the unit to which they report would be viewed as biased. The manager to whom the IS manager reports would also be in a difficult position; the issue of conflict of interest would be continually present.

The appropriate organizational alignment is therefore to have the IS manager report at a level at least equal to that of the highest-level major user in the organization. The IS manager must report to a level

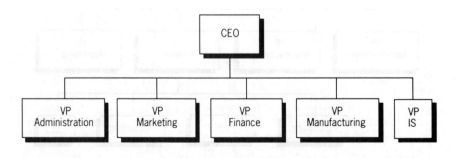

EXHIBIT 6-5 Information systems centralized at the chief executive level.

that is high enough so that the user community will not perceive any conflict of interest. Reporting high in the organization has another benefit, too: the IS manager has a broader view of the organization and is in a position to make better-informed decisions regarding the organization's use of computing technologies. The IS manager's decisions are likely to be better simply because this manager will have a wider constituency to take into account when weighing the benefits and costs of various alternatives. (All this is, of course, predicated on the assumption that functional managers and senior executives pursue corporate instead of parochial interests.)

The Steering Committee

Richard Nolan has been cited as suggesting that the IS manager should not report directly to the CEO (Lasden, 1980). He argues that the CEO cannot devote enough time to the IS manager. However, the CEO can be clearly involved through the steering committee, a mechanism for bringing IS into the corporate strategic planning process. Generally, a steering committee will function as a board of directors for the IS department. As such, its basic responsibilities will be to establish priorities, control expenses, and make policy decisions. Nolan (1982) offers the following list of five main responsibilities for the steering committee:

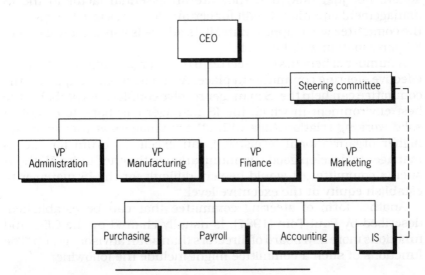

EXHIBIT 6-6 Information systems centralized at the vice-presidential level and reporting to a steering committee chaired by the CEO.

1. *Direction-setting*: Working on linking corporate strategy with IS strategy, with planning as the key activity.
2. *Rationing*: Approving the allocation of resources within the IS department.
3. *Structuring*: Dealing with how the IS function interacts with the rest of the organization and resolving the issue of centralization versus decentralization.
4. *Staffing*: Making decisions related to IS personnel through a consultation-and-approval process; selecting the CIO.
5. *Evaluating*: Establishing performance measures for the department and ensuring that they are met.

Because the steering committee can be a critical link between the IS manager and the rest of the organization, the IS manager should urge that such an entity be created if one is not already in place. Some consideration must be given, however, to the degree of authority that the IS manager will surrender to a steering committee. Generally the steering committee's role should be limited to an advisory one. Giving such a committee management responsibility means that the IS manager will have as many bosses as there are members of the steering committee. Of course, the problem with giving the steering committee a purely advisory responsibility is that it might view its role as purely cosmetic and not take it seriously. The IS manager must be sensitive to this issue and assure the members (through action, not just talk) that they are an essential factor in the IS management equation. Credit for certain decisions must be given to the committee when appropriate. If its advice is continually ignored, its participation will diminish.

A number of benefits can accrue to the IS organization that has an effective steering committee in place. As a "court of last appeal," the committee can help the IS manager resolve conflicts. As probably the best environment in which the IS manager can hope to establish solid working relationships with other managers at the same and higher organizational levels, it is an excellent forum for the IS manager to develop good communication with other units. Without such a committee, it would be very difficult for the IS manager to establish equity at the executive level.

Another form of steering committee that can be established, described by Paul Tom (1987), is usually chaired by the CEO and functions more as a board of directors than as an advisory group. The functions of such a committee might include the following:

1. Determining appropriate levels of expenditure and capability for the IS department based on the organization's strategic and tactical plans.
2. Approving specific proposals for the acquisition of major hardware and software.
3. Approving long- and short-range IS plans.
4. Determining whether specific projects are to be undertaken on the basis of criteria such as expected return on investment, business value to the organization, effect on competitive position, effect on internal organization, and conformity with corporate plans.
5. Determining project priorities.
6. Reviewing and approving cost-allocation methods.
7. Reviewing project progress.
8. At specific decision points, determining whether projects should be continued or abandoned.
9. Resolving territorial and political conflicts arising from new systems.

To be effective, any type of steering committee must be run in an orderly and professional manner. The CEO should chair the committee, thus reinforcing its importance to the other senior managers. Because the membership will be chosen from among senior managers, it is important that these individual's time be protected. This suggests that the meetings must have a very specific agenda, with clear and concise information distributed ahead of time and definite start and stop times. At such meetings the IS manager must avoid jargon and present only information that is relevant to the business decision being considered. For most IS managers this environment is difficult. For many, however, it offers the only chance to create the executive-level partnership that effective strategic planning requires.

In working with senior management to align the IS department appropriately within the organization structure, the IS manager faces one important conundrum. On the one hand, if senior executives do not understand the trade-offs of various alternatives, they may make decisions that are questionable or even counterproductive. On the other hand, in trying to address their confusion, the IS manager may put them into a state of what Tom has called "analysis paralysis"—when senior managers become involved in so much detail at such a low level that they lose sight of the decision they have been asked to make and either fail to make it or postpone making it until doing so is fruitless. Negotiating the currents between treacherous shores is no small task.

REPORTING TO THE CEO

A situation in which the IS manager reports directly to the CEO of an organization may come about as the result of careful and deliberate planning or it may simply be an accident of history. It may also be the result of a decision that was correct at some point in the organization's history but is no longer appropriate. In any case, although reporting to the CEO carries a certain status, it also entails meeting certain implicit expectations, handling certain kinds of corporate political issues, and understanding certain behavioral dimensions. The risks are high; the job security is low. For the successful IS manager, however, the rewards to both the organization and the individual are great.

John Rockart offers the following thoughts on when it makes sense to have the IS manager report to the CEO (Lasden, 1980):

- When the CEO is analytically minded and wants to use IT to manage the organization.
- When the IS manager is managerially as well as technically skilled.
- When the IS department has developed to the point where it is considered a true management resource.

In this reporting relationship, the IS manager must realize that the CEO will be evaluating him or her with the same yardstick used for other senior managers reporting at this level. If the IS manager is continually sensitive to the bottom-line impact of decisions, has good business sense, can communicate effectively, and—most importantly—can self-govern, he or she will survive. Herbert Halbrecht contends that most IS managers cannot survive in this type of environment (Lasden, 1980). Being a technician is fundamentally irrelevant; what is needed is a business leader who happens to have, as the tools of his or her trade, information technology.

For organizations that do elevate IS to the top, there are several noteworthy hazards. When the CEO gets involved in IS development details, he or she may impose a perspective that will subvert the primary purpose of a system, rendering it less effective for the actual user. In addition, IS managers who enjoy easy access to the CEO may be less inclined to build real consensus among users and the result may be a dangerous buildup of resentment. Furthermore, a busy CEO who is given a direct role in making decisions about IS may be distracted often enough to keep the IS department perpetually in limbo.

For any manager who has access to the top, effective communications with subordinates becomes more difficult; people invariably do not speak to such a manager as freely as to those with less elevated connections. Nonetheless, some CEOs, such as Terrance Hanold (president of Pillsbury in the late 1960s and early 1970s), have IS managers report directly to them, on the reasoning that other managers will grasp the importance of IS and be more likely to use it (Lasden, 1980).

CEO Styles and the Reporting Relationship

One way of approaching the issue of reporting to a CEO is to characterize the CEO's working style and then devise strategies for dealing with that style. For the purposes of this discussion, six types of CEOs and their styles can be identified (see Exhibit 6-7). Each is briefly discussed in the sections that follow.

The Well-Informed and Action-oriented CEO The IS manager must work hard just to keep up with this executive. This reporting relationship is exhilarating but risky for the IS manager. Because the CEO has anticipated the need for a particular application system and probably completed some of the preliminary work, it is crucial that the IS manager be well-prepared for every meeting with the CEO. Phone calls from the CEO at unexpected times are the norm; this CEO has a great demand for precise, in-depth knowledge, makes decisions quickly, and does not tolerate errors. In instances in which the CEO is wrong in his or her assessments of IT, responsibility still rests with the IS manager. Because this CEO is such a strong executive, it is difficult for the IS manager to gain control of the IS function. Obviously, a strong IS manager is needed to balance the relationship.

The Well-Informed CEO This executive is hesitant to let the IS department become too integrated for fear that the organization may become technology driven. The strategy for the IS manager is to approach each problem from a business perspective rather than a technological one. The IS manager must convince the CEO that he or she is a businessperson first. This means having an intimate understanding of business activities, issues, and opportunities.

The Partially Informed, Action-oriented CEO   The IS manager is competing with other business unit and functional managers for this CEO's approval of his or her requests. This is new turf for the IS manager, who must have a good sense of the business and the bottom-line impact of IS proposals, for that is the criterion against which proposals are evaluated by this CEO. Proposals based on more efficient, productive usage of resources carry no weight unless they are backed up by hard-dollar estimates of their bottom-line impact.

The Partially Informed, Delegative CEO   The partially informed, delegative CEO is the most common type of executive with whom the IS manager interacts. The reporting relationship with such a CEO encounters obstacles as a result of the CEO's delegation of IS activities to subordinates. Initially, the IS manager might achieve

Type	Characteristics
Well-informed, action-oriented	Understands IS in both concept and application. Is an aggressive and determined leader who knows what needs to be done with respect to IS. Required no selling and has probably completed some of the preliminary work that the IS manager is accustomed to doing.
Well-informed	Although understanding IS, is hesitant to let the IS department become a visible factor in corporate strategy development.
Partially informed, action-oriented	Needs to be convinced by the IS manager. Once convinced, is a strong supporter.
Partially informed, delegative	Is well-insulated from the IS manager. Concerned about costs, failures, and risk; derives a sense of safety in being insulated from IS even while understanding the benefits.
Disinterested, action-oriented	Has chosen mostly out of ignorance and/or fear to ignore IS; fears some relinquishing of control to a technology that is not understood.
Disinterested	Indifferent, unwilling to make a decision unless necessary. Threatened by a change.

EXHIBIT 6-7 A taxonomy of CEO types.

success by looking for opportunities to work through the second-line managers to whom the CEO tends to delegate responsibility. Earning their respect and confidence can eventually lead to gaining the attention of the CEO.

The Disinterested, Action-oriented CEO The IS manager needs to convince this executive of the benefits and value of IT. Once convinced, he or she is as ardent a supporter as any well-informed counterpart. An intermediary is usually needed; this may be a senior manager who has the ear of the CEO, a social acquaintance, or another CEO whom this one admires and respects. In any case, the IS manager is not likely to be successful with a direct frontal assault, even if he or she could enter this CEO's office freely. The IS manager will have to cultivate a business relationship with someone whom the CEO trusts and let that person open the door to further opportunities—essentially a version of the "Trojan horse" strategy.

The Disinterested CEO The best way for the IS manager to handle this type is to work with other senior managers and avoid dealing directly with this CEO. To depend on this CEO is risky. This CEO will not make a decision unless absolutely forced to do so. The CEO's strategy is to wait and hope that only one alternative remains among the many he or she currently faces. If interaction cannot be avoided, then looking for another job may be the best strategy for the IS manager.

CONCLUSION

Organizational structure is an important variable in the definition of the IS manager's role. Corporate-level planning and strategy development, the need to support end-user computing, and the emergence of islands of technology, are among the major factors that must be taken into account when attempting to align the IS department in a particular organizational structure. Efforts to sustain a strong centralized structure may be futile, as current trends point toward decentralization as the preferred form. Regardless of the structure chosen, the IS manager must inevitably interact with certain senior managers and/or the CEO. Here, human-relations and political skills are more valuable than technical ones, and they dictate the ultimate success of the IS manager in positioning his or her department effectively and appropriately within the organizational structure.

DISCUSSION QUESTIONS

1. If senior management is too premature in elevating the IS manager to a peer relationship, what problems might result in an organization that has not reached a level of stability and maturity with respect to IS?

2. For each of the CEO types, develop a reporting strategy for the IS manager who reports to them.

3. Identify some of the difficulties encountered by the IS department that is making a transition from a centralized to a decentralized organizational structure.

4. How instrumental should the IS manager be in determining the organizational structure?

REFERENCES

Lasden, Martin (1980). "Should MIS Report to the President?" *Computer Decisions* (August), pp. 54–65.

Nolan, Richard L. (1979). "Managing the Crisis in Data Processing," *Harvard Business Review*, vol. 57, no. 2 (March-April), pp. 115–126.

Nolan, R. (1982). "Managing Information Systems by Committee," *Harvard Business Review*, vol. 60, no. 4 (July-August), pp. 72–79.

Nolan, Richard L., and Cyrus F. Gibson (1979). "Managing the Four Stages of EDP Growth," *Harvard Business Review*, vol. 52, no. 1 (January–February), pp. 76–78.

Owen, Darrell E. (1986). "Information Systems Organizations—Keeping Pace with the Pressures," *Sloan Management Review*, vol. 27, no. 3 (Spring), pp. 59–68.

Thompson, Arthur A., Jr., and A. J. Strickland III (1986). *Strategy Formulation and Implementation*, 3 ed. (Plano, Texas: Business Publications, Inc.).

Tom, Paul (1987). *Managing Information as a Corporate Resource*, (Glenview, Ill.: Scott, Foresman).

Wiseman, Charles (1988) *Strategic Information Systems*, (Homewood, IL: Irwin).

Whieldon, David (1981). "Organizing MIS/DP to Meet the New Challenges," *Computer Decisions* (October), pp. 156–176.

seven

Information Systems Corporate Issues and Opportunities

Decentralization of Systems Development Activity

Strategic Planning

Organizational Structure

The Information-Based Organization

Preparing for the Future

Conclusion

Discussion Questions

References

As we move toward the year 2000, three major trends confront IS managers as they attempt to define their department's roles and responsibilities in an ever-changing, highly competitive business environment:

- The continuing movement of systems development activity from the IS department to user departments, which necessitates a restructuring of relationships.

- The evolution of the process of corporate strategic planning to one that fully integrates information technology.
- The evolution of the corporate organizational structure from a hierarchical structure toward a "flatter" one.

These trends are clear; what is not clear are the actions IS departments should take to best prepare themselves for the coming business environment. In this chapter we explore each of these trends and identify specific issues that IS managers and senior management face as they try to position the IS function to best serve the organization.

DECENTRALIZATION OF SYSTEMS DEVELOPMENT ACTIVITY

Users are methodically assuming certain responsibilities that were once the exclusive domain of the IS department. In earlier chapters we identified the causal sequence that has led to this change: the backlog of user requests followed by the advent of the microcomputer, user-friendly data-base management systems, and communication linkages to mainframes.

We are now experiencing an increasingly rapid shift of operational activity to the end user. In fact, end-user computing is estimated to account for more than half the computing cycles used (Benjamin, 1982). Some users, having become quite experienced in applications development, are beginning to train others on their staff, both with and without the support of IS. The tasks for the IS manager are to determine what computing activities can and cannot be decentralized and to anticipate problems that may result from independent actions by users. Those problems can be grouped under the areas of control, standards, and integration.

Control-related Problems

Too little control of computing resources leads to unproductive use of those resources and can also create severe integration problems in the future; too much control forces users to find ways to circumvent established procedures. Because growing numbers of users are moving ahead with applications development with or without the blessing of the IS department, it is in the best interest of the IS department to implement controls that users will see as beneficial.

Involving the user in the establishment of these controls improves the likelihood of compliance. The purpose of controls should be perceived as not to constrain the user but rather to define the environment in which computing activity will take place. If controls are so perceived, the IS department will have an opportunity to plan and implement appropriate computing strategies for the organization.

Standards-related Problems

The issue of the need for standards in hardware and software acquisition has held the attention of IS management for several years. However, although hardware/software standards can confine the user to a supportable set of applications, the standards problem is far from resolved. As users continue to develop their own applications, standards will also be needed in such areas as documentation, systems development procedures, systems testing, data security, and data integrity. Such standards will be difficult to implement and even more difficult to enforce.

One tactic would be to demonstrate to user management the problems that will result if there are no standards, as well as the benefits that can accrue to user departments and the organization when such standards are in place. User management must form an "enforcement partnership" with IS management, and IS management has the responsibility to see that this happens by recruiting user managers to help draft a set of enforceable standards. In fact, involving user management as a principle architect of such standards may be essential to a successful program. A primary benefit of these standards to the IS department is that the problem of systems integration will be mitigated.

Integration-related Problems

To meet senior managers expectations for increasingly strategic uses of computing, the applications development portfolio must be integrated with the existing systems portfolio, to which both IS and end-user departments contribute. Because user-developed systems can be important to the organization's competitive position, shared data and systems integration becomes crucial.

While decentralization continues, there is a need to begin working toward a different type of centralization. Data integration and systems integration cannot occur unless hardware and software are interconnected. This leads to two developments. First, centralization occurs at the network level as the IS department becomes a utility responsible for providing hardware interconnectivity. Second, the IS department searches for organizational structures that will encourage and support the development of integrated applications. Robert Benjamin (1982) argues that this requires incorporating a number of software improvements, such as reusable code, data-base administration and management, systems development environment, structuring methodologies, design languages, end-user languages, use of software packages, and implementation of shared systems. As an example, IS management, in cooperation with user management, could institute design walk-throughs, the approval of systems documentation, and validation of successful system tests before placing a user-developed system in production. Having such checkpoints in place ensures conformance with agreed to standards and keeps the IS department informed of user ideas that may have further strategic value.

STRATEGIC PLANNING

Ideally, a strategic planning process that incorporates IT for competitive advantage should be business driven. That is, the needs of the business for new products, new markets, and new distribution channels should determine the IT requirements of the organization. However, the present level of computer fluency in the functional business departments is such that for the next several years the IS department must play a principle role in strategy set development in order for the organization to incorporate competitive uses of the technology. The difficulty in using IT to establish competitive advantage is that most IS managers do not understand the business environment sufficiently to advise senior management, and business-function managers do not understand the technology sufficiently to recognize IT-related opportunities for competitive advantage.

In time, business-function managers will become more computer fluent, IS management will become more business fluent, and the problem of a shared language will be somewhat lessened. It will not be solved, however, until a fully integrated strategic planning process is developed for general use. In the meantime, how should the IS manager proceed?

The IS manager can take two tacks. The first is to form a technology support group (Exhibit 7-1). This group would monitor not only emerging technologies for possible use by the organization but also those technologies currently being used. The technology support group would consist of persons with business acumen as well as considerable computer fluency. Its objective would be to explore ways to use IT to the organization's advantage. One way of accomplishing this would be through the issuance of "white papers" or "position papers" that would present, in lay terms, an assessment of emerging or existing technologies with potential strategic value or that would suggest strategic opportunities to senior, departmental, or IS management.

If it is not possible for the IS manager to form such a group, a fallback position would be for the IS department to issue similar position papers as input to organization-wide strategic planning activities. In either case, the IS manager is taking a proactive position with obvious payoffs for the organization. The challenge to the organization is to evaluate IT in terms of its value to the organization's competitive position and then act swiftly.

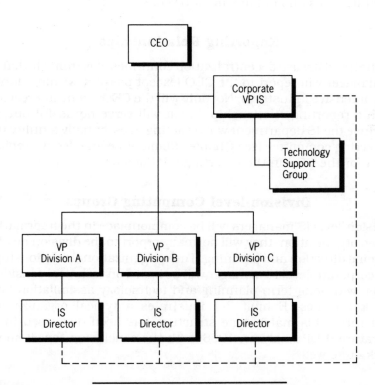

EXHIBIT 7-1 The location of the technology support group in an organization with division-level IS managers and a corporate-level vice president.

ORGANIZATIONAL STRUCTURE

As we have seen, the IS department is undergoing an organizational metamorphosis whose outcome is not clear. The responsibilities for traditional IS services and support are being split—some remain centralized and others become decentralized. The responsibilities that have remained centralized include management of wide-area networks, data-center operations, development of corporate-wide systems, education, standards, planning, quality assurance, security, and hardware/software architecture. The responsibilities that are becoming decentralized include systems development, operations, local-area networks, and end-user support. For IS managers, who choose to be reactive, this split is difficult to deal with. For others who take a proactive position, the challenge is to determine which IS-related responsibilities should be centralized and which decentralized, and how this should be decided and implemented. What does this split mean in the context of overall organizational structure? Several issues and options must be considered.

Reporting Relationships

As the trend toward decentralization continues, it is unlikely that the IS manager will report to the CEO (except possibly within information-intensive industries). Not only will the CEO not be interested in such a reporting relationship, but it will serve no useful purpose because the IS department will be acting in essentially a utility role. A steering committee (see Chapter 6) might be an effective replacement for the CEO in the reporting relationship.

Division-level Computing Groups

Division-level IS managers will be commonplace in the information-based organization; they will normally report to the division head for ongoing direction and planning. Their organizational relationship to the corporate-level IS manager will be based on technical considerations, with long-term planning and technology assimilation being the key issues. Exhibit 7-1 illustrates a typical organizational structure. This matrix-type structure has been discussed in the literature (EDP Analyzer, 1986) with the conclusion that it should work quite well.

The Corporate-Level Information Systems Department

Organizations may choose to form IS departments that function at the corporate-level in a staff capacity. In addition to certain centralized responsibilities, such corporate-level IS departments will concentrate on strategic and technical planning. Playing a staff role, the IS manager of a corporate-level department will be more involved in corporate-wide education, standards setting, and the steering committee. Guidance of the IS function across the organization, rather than controlling it, will be the emphasis; in this light, the technology support group would be assigned to the corporate-level IS department.

The corporate-level IS manager will probably function as the CIO and will carry a vice-presidential title. IT policy and strategy development are this person's major responsibilities, along with linking of corporate and IS strategy. This position may or may not include IS management duties.

New Technologies

J. I. Cash and P. L. McLeod (1985) recommend the formation of an emerging technology group that would function much as a traditional R&D group. Its primary responsibility would be to identify innovative and strategically valuable IT areas and to follow up with whatever implementation strategy is appropriate. Such a group would call on others in the organization to assist in determining new technologies' applicability to current or forecasted business activity. Obviously, there needs to be a symbiotic relationship between this group and the functional business units. Many experimental projects would have to involve both group members and functional business personnel, with project managers coming from either group.

The technology support group is essentially a variant of Cash and McLeod's group. It carries the same responsibilities regarding new technologies as well as additional responsibilities regarding existing technology.

Management Control

Underlying the evolution of the IS department as described in Nolan's stages model is an evolution in the management accounting structure of the IS department. James Cash et. al. (1988) defines the evolutionary stages as unallocated cost center, allocated cost center, profit center, and investment center. The unallocated cost center is typical of stage 1 and 2 organizations. The rationale is to create as few barriers and as many incentives as possible to encourage use of the computing resources. In stage 3 the proliferation of user requests resulted in establishing the IS department as an allocated cost center. Users were charged for services so as to "keep them honest" in their requests. Cash et. al. identify several issues, including competitive pricing, effects on innovation and R&D functions, charge-back concepts and pricing process, and maintenance versus development charges.

Organizations in stages 4 and beyond frequently establish the IS department as a profit center. Here IS must learn to function as a business within a business. They must market their services internally and be price competitive with outside agencies vying for the same customer. In many cases the profit-center concept leads to external markets, as pointed out by William Synnott (1987).

The near future will see yet another change as the IS department is established as an investment center. Much of the IS expenditure for hardware and software will be evaluated on an ROI basis. Indeed, even the prioritization of projects in the development portfolio will be determined from an ROI perspective.

THE INFORMATION-BASED ORGANIZATION

Peter Drucker (1988) makes the following assertion: "to remain competitive—maybe even to survive—they [businesses] will have to convert themselves into information-based organizations, and fairly quickly." Drucker argues that as businesses learn to use information more effectively and efficiently for diagnosis and decision making, several layers of management will no longer be needed. There is already evidence of this flattening in organizations as several layers of management are being deleted. As this metamorphosis takes place, the "knowledge worker" emerges as critical to the actual performance of the organization's work. Drucker foresees the emergence of task-focused teams, with functional departments transformed into enforcers of standards and trainers of specialists. To function effectively, the information-based organization will require the following:

- Common objectives that translate directly into action plans.
- Specific action items that clearly state management's performance expectations.
- A thorough understanding by all personnel of their responsibility to move information both up and down in the organization.

These requirements suggest a total evolution of the present command-and-control structure inherited from the industrial age to what would appear to be a looser structure entailing a federation of task forces, each with the requisite specialist skills. In Drucker's opinion, this new structure brings with it a new set of management problems—in particular, issues of reward and recognition, of purpose, and of management structure.

Because reward and recognition will not be attached to a management hierarchy, other methods of crediting individual performance will have to be found. The problem is not easy to solve because of the strong attachment that professionals have to promotion as the only visible sign of accomplishment. Basic attitudes regarding management and title will have to be changed. This new corporate environment will have to provide individuals with a clear sense of self-worth and accomplishment. Some possibilities may be profit-and-loss responsibility for the project they manage or recognition of successful project completion by reassignment (somewhat similar to the military tour of duty). Job title is another means to differentiate the experience and accomplishment of the individual. Hierarchies such as junior analyst, analyst, lead analyst, and senior analyst can be used.

In addition, senior management will have to help the loosely coupled federation of task forces acquire a view of the organization as a whole so that senior specialists, managers, and line workers share a common sense of purpose. Finally, a new senior management structure will have to be defined. Should task-force managers eventually become the senior management team or will a separate structure of senior specialists exist in conjunction with some type of task-force structure? It is not clear from Drucker's writing exactly how the senior management team will be recruited. If they come from the ranks of the task-force managers, then some type of development program will be needed to prepare them for senior management roles. Drucker expects this to be the most difficult management issue for the information organization.

PREPARING FOR THE FUTURE

In preparing for the 1990s and beyond, the IS manager has many balls to juggle, many choices to make, and many opportunities to pursue. John Kirkley (1988) points to the following as the most important rules for the IS manager to bear in mind. These rules focus the manager on the future, and they apply to information-centered organizations in any industry:

1. The IS manager should understand the needs of the business and remember that the IS department exists to support corporate financial and strategic goals.
2. The IS manager should maintain a corporate view of systems and should always look for ways to integrate systems, counsel sophisticated users, and support user-based applications development.
3. The IS manager should work toward fully integrating IS planning with corporate strategic planning.
4. The IS manager should ensure that control of data resources is returned to the IS department.
5. The IS manager should build sound working relationships with all users.
6. The IS manager should establish and maintain a strong information center to help educate users but more importantly to build solid contact with the user.

CONCLUSION

Information-age organizations are at the threshold of exciting new opportunities in their use of computers and information. Taking advantage of these opportunities will not be the result of divine inspiration or accidental discoveries. Rather, it will be the result of deliberate planning, penetrating analyses of business activities and competitive position, close evaluation of alternatives, and decisive action. Implementation planning and execution may be the only thing that differentiates the winners from the losers. That is, the separation between success and failure may be very fragile.

DISCUSSION QUESTIONS

1. Discuss the role and responsibility of the IS department in Drucker's information-age organization.
2. Propose a management structures for Drucker's information-age organization and identify the major challenges for the IS manager in this organization.

3. Identify the major management issues associated with the evolution of the IS organization to the combined centralized/decentralized structure.

REFERENCES

———(1986). "Organizing for the 1990s," *EDP Analyzer*, vol. 24, no. 12, pp. 1–11.

Benjamin, Robert I. (1982). "Information Technology in the 1990s: A Long Range Planning Scenario," *MIS Quarterly* (June), pp. 11–31.

Cash, James I., Jr., et. al. (1988). *Corporate Information Systems Management: Text and Cases*, 2 ed., (Homewood, IL: Irwin).

Cash, J. I., Jr., and P. L. McLeod (1985). "Managing the Introduction of Information Systems Technology in Strategically Dependent Companies," *Journal of Management Information Systems* (Spring), pp. 5–23.

Drucker, Peter (1988). "The Coming of the New Organization," *Harvard Business Review*, vol. 66, no. 1 (January-February), pp. 45–53.

Kirkley, John (1988). "The Restructuring of MIS: Business Strategies Take Hold," *Computerworld* (March 21), pp. 79ff.

Synnott, William R. (1987) *The Information Weapon*, (New York, NY: Wiley).

SUGGESTED STUDENT PROJECTS

1. Pick an industry and trace the use of IT for competitive advantage for firms in that industry.

2. Pick a company and identify the specific forces (buyer, supplier, substitutes, new entrants, rivalry) with respect to the uses of IT. Comment on the strength and stability of these forces. Suggest ways that IT may be used to parry competitive thrusts or alter competitive balance.

3. Pick a company. Investigate and comment on the involvement of IS in corporate planning and on the IS planning process.

4. Discuss the value chain for an organization familiar to you. Identify areas of potential competitive advantage.

Supplementary Reading List

————(1985). "Information Power: How Companies Are Using New Technology to Gain Competitive Edge," *Business Week* (October 14), pp. 108–114.

————(1986). "Organizing for the 1990s," *EDP Analyzer*, vol. 24, no. 12 (December), pp. 1–16.

————(1987). "In Search of a Strategic Edge," *Computerworld* (June 29), pp. 73ff.

————(1987). "Rockart Exhorts Line To Lead," *Computerworld* (July 27), pp. 59ff.

————(1987). "The Role of Business Systems Groups," *EDP Analyzer*, vol. 25, no. 8 (August), pp. 1–16.

————(1988). "Diebold Exec Notes MIS Expectancy Gap," *Management Information Systems Week* (January 4), p. 34.

Ackerman, Robert F. (1987). "IRM Planning—A Practical Necessity," *Journal of Systems Management* (September), pp. 27–31.

Allen, Leilani (1987). "How Companies Plan," *Computerworld* (September 21), pp. 97ff.

Alper, Alan (1987). "Five Who Honed Strategic Edge," *Computerworld* (June 1), pp. 87ff.

Ansoff, H. Igor (1987). "Strategic Management of Technology," *Journal of Business Strategy* vol. 7 (Winter), pp. 28–39.

Bakos, J. Yannis, and Michael E. Treacy (1986). "Information Technology and Corporate Strategy: A Research Perspective," *MIS Quarterly* (June), pp. 107–119.

Benjamin, Robert I. (1982). "Information Technology in the 1990s: A Long Range Planning Scenario," *MIS Quarterly* (June), pp. 11–31.

Benjamin, Robert I., et al. (1985). "Changing Role of the Corporate Information Systems Officer," *MIS Quarterly* (September), pp. 177–188.

Blackwell, David J. (1987). "Who Needs a CIO?" *CIO*, vol. 1, no. 2 (November-December), pp. 56–57.

Blair, John (1987). "Not Again! The Messy Business of Planning," *Computerworld* (November 30), pp. 69–76.

Boynton, Andrew C., and Robert W. Zmud (1987). "Information Technology Planning in the 1990's: Practice and Research," *MIS Quarterly* (March), pp. 59–71.

Brancheau, James C., and James C. Wetherbe (1987). "Key Issues in Information Systems Management," *MIS Quarterly* (March), pp. 23–45.

Breath, Cynthia Mathis, and Blake Ives (1986). "Competitive Information Systems in Support of Pricing," *MIS Quarterly* (March), pp. 85–93.

Briggs, George, and David Coursey (1987). "New MIS Structure is Seen Evolving," *Management Information Systems Week* (July 20), p. 35.

Buchanan, Jack R., and Richard G. Linowes (1980). "Making Distributed Data Processing Work," *Harvard Business Review*, vol. 58, no. 5 (September-October), pp. 143–161.

Buday, Robert S. (1987). "Quicksand—What Kills Strategic Systems," *Information Week* (May 11), pp. 24–28.

Buday, Robert S. (1987). "The Strategic Use of Information: Seizing the Competitive Edge," *Information Week* (May 26), pp. 26–62.

Corbin, Darrell S. (1988). "Strategic IRM Plan: User Involvement Spells Success," *Journal of Systems Management*, vol. 39, no. 5 (May), pp. 12–16.

Daniel, Evelyn (1983). "Information Resources and Organizational Structure," *Journal of the American Society for Information Science* vol. 34, no. 3, pp. 222–228.

Dearden, John (1987). "The Withering Away of the IS Organization," *Sloan Management Review*, vol. 28, no. 4 (Summer), pp. 87–91.

Demb, Ada Barbara (1975). "Centralized versus Decentralized Computer Systems: A New Approach to Organizational Impacts," Center for Information Systems Research, CISR Report 12, Massachusetts Institute of Technology, Cambridge, Mass.

Donovan, John J. (1988). "Beyond Chief Information Officer to Network Manager," *Harvard Business Review*, vol. 66, no. 5 (September–October), pp. 134–140.

Eisen, Jerrold (1988). "How to Grab an Exec's Attention," *Computerworld* (September 26), p. 19.

Er, M. C. (1987). "The Impact of Information Technology on Organizations," *Journal of Systems Management* (April), pp. 32–36.

Ferreira, Joseph, and James F. Collins, Jr. (1979). "The Changing Role of the MIS Executive," *Datamation*, pp. 26ff.

Fisher, Marsha Johnston (1987). "Push to Set Corp. Goals, MIS Urged," *MIS Week*, vol. 8, no. 40 (October 8), pp. 1ff.

Forcht, Karen A., et al. (1987). "Emerging Roles of the MIS Professional: Technocrat or Change Agent?" *Journal of Systems Management*, vol. 38, no. 11, pp. 10–18.

Gerrity, Thomas P. (1984). "The Role of the CEO in Managing Information Technology," *Information Strategy: The Executive's Journal*, Fall, pp. 4–8.

Gillin, Paul (1983). "Exec Urges Plan to Align DP, Business Strategies," *Computerworld* (October 24), p. 14.

Gray, Daniel H. (1986). "Uses and Misuses of Strategic Planning," *Harvard Business Review*, vol. 64, no. 1 (January–February), pp. 89–97.

Henderson, John C., and John Sifonis (1988). "The Value of Strategic IS Planning: Understanding Consistency, Validity, and IS Markets," *MIS Quarterly* (December), pp. 187–200.

Henderson, John C., et al. (1987). "Integrating Management Support Systems into Strategic Information Systems Planning," *Journal of Management Information Systems*, vol. 4, no. 1, pp. 5–24.

Ives, Blake, and Gerard P. Learmonth (1984). "The Information System as a Competitive Weapon," *Communications of the ACM*, vol. 27, no. 12, pp. 1193–1201.

Johnston, H. Russell, and Shelley R. Carrico (1988). "Developing Capabilities to Use Information Strategically," *MIS Quarterly* (March), pp. 37–48.

Johnston, H. Russell, and Michael R. Vitale (1988). "Creating Competitive Advantage With Interorganizational Information Systems," *MIS Quarterly* (June), pp. 153–166.

Kanter, Jerome (1986). "The Role of Senior Management in MIS," *Journal of Systems Management* (April), pp. 10–17.

Kanter, Jerry (1988). "Information Literacy for the CEO," *Journal of Information Systems Management*, vol. 5, no. 5 (Winter), pp. 52–57.

Kerr, James M. (1987). "Corporate Data Models Flourish from the Bottom Up," *Computerworld* (May 11), pp. 71 ff.

King, William R., and T. S. Raghunathan (1987). "How Strategic Is Information Systems Planning?" *Datamation* (November 15), pp. 133–137.

King, William R., and Ananth Srinivasan (1981). "The Evolution of Information Systems Planning, Development and Evaluation," Working Paper Series WP-447, Graduate School of Business, University of Pittsburgh, Pittsburgh.

Kirkley, John (1988). "The Restructuring of MIS: Business Strategies Take Hold," *Computerworld* (March 21), pp. 79–93.

Kline, Randall R. (1988). "The Art of Planning: Lessons from History," *Journal of Systems Management* (April), pp. 22–25.

LaBelle, Antoinette, and H. Edward Nyce (1987). "Whither the IT Organization?" *Sloan Management Review*, vol. 28, no. 4 (Summer), pp. 75–85.

Lasden, Martin (1980). "Should MIS Report to the President?" *Computer Decisions* (August), pp. 54–65.

Lasden, Martin (1981). "Long-Range Planning: Curse or Blessing?" *Computer Decisions* (February), pp. 101ff.

Lederer, Albert L., and Andrew G. Putnam (1987). "Bridging the Gap: Connecting Systems Objectives to Business Strategy with BSP," *Journal of Information Systems Management*, vol. 4, no. 3 (Summer), pp. 40-46.

Lederer, Albert L., and Vijay Sethi (1988). "The Implementation of Strategic Information Systems Planning Methodologies," *MIS Quarterly* (September), pp. 445-461.

Leifer, Richard (1988). "Matching Computer-Based Information Systems with Organizational Structures," *MIS Quarterly*, vol. 12, no. 1 (March), pp. 63-73.

Lucas, Henry C. Jr. (1984). "Organizational Power and the Information Services Department," *Communications of the ACM*, vol. 27, no. 1, pp. 58-65.

Lucas, Henry C., Jr., and Jon A. Turner (1982). "A Corporate Strategy for the Control of Information Processing," *Sloan Management Review*, vol. 23, no. 3 (Spring), pp. 25-36.

Malina, Debbie (1987). "The Making of the CIO," *Mass High Tech* (July 6-19), pp. 19ff.

Mallach, Efrem (1988). "Working Backward to Strategic Planning," *Computerworld* (April 18), pp. 19ff.

Mandell, Mel (1987). "The CIO: Myth or Reality?" *Computer Decisions* (March 23), pp. 66-71.

Markus, M. Lynne (1983). "Power, Politics, and MIS Implementation," *Communications of the ACM*, vol. 26, no. 6, (June), pp. 430-444.

Markus, Lynne, and Niels Bjorn-Andersen (1987). "Power over Users: Its Exercise by System Professionals," *Communications of the ACM*, vol. 30, no. 1 (June), pp. 498-504.

Martin, Josh (1981). "Choosing a Management Style," *Computer Decisions* (December), pp. 79ff.

McClelland, Sam (1987). "The Consultative Style of Management," *Information Management* (January-February), pp. 12-13.

Miller, Howard W. (1988). "Developing Information Technology Strategies," *Journal of Systems Management* (September), pp. 28-35.

Millman, Zeeva, and Jon Hartwick (1987). "The Impact of Automated Office Systems on Middle Managers and Their Work," *MIS Quarterly* (December), pp. 479-491.

Miron, Michael, et al. (1988). "The Myths and Realities of Competitive Advantage," *Datamation* (October 1), pp. 71-82.

Moccardi, Sal (1988). "Otis Elevator Dispatches Peace of Mind," *Inbound/ Outbound* (August), pp. 20-28.

Moskowitz, Robert (1986). "Strategic Systems Planning Shifts to Data-Oriented Approach," *Computerworld* (May 12), pp. 109-119.

Nolan, Richard L. (1982). "Managing Information Systems by Committee," *Harvard Business Review* vol. 60, no. 4 (July-August), pp. 72–79.

Nolan, Richard L., and Thomas R. Mantz (1987). "Getting Execs up to Speed," *Computerworld* (April 13), pp 85ff.

Oliva, Terence A., et al. (1987). "Selecting Competitive Tactics: Try a Strategy Map," *Sloan Management Review*, vol. 28, no. 1 (Spring), pp. 5–15.

O'Riordan, P. Declan (1987). "The CIO: MIS Makes Its Move into the Executive Suite," *Journal of Information Systems Management* (Summer), pp. 54–56.

Owen, Darrell E. (1986). "Information Systems Organizations—Keeping Pace with the Pressures," *Sloan Management Review*, vol. 27, no. 3 (Spring), pp. 59–68.

Parsons, Gregory L. (1983). "Information Technology: A New Competitive Weapon," *Sloan Management Review*, vol. 25, no. 1 (Fall), pp. 3–13.

Potter, Doug (1987). "Long-Range Systems Planning," *Datamation* (May 15), pp. 113–116.

Power, Daniel J. (1983). "The Impact of Information Management on the Organization: Two Scenarios," *MIS Quarterly* (September), pp. 13–20.

Radding, Alan (1987). "Are You a Corporate Officer or a Consultant?" *Computerworld* (April 13), pp. 75–77.

Rennie, Robert J. (1988). "Client Centered Management," *Journal of Systems Management* (September), pp. 11–13.

Rifkin, Glenn (1986). "Training for MIS," Computerworld, July 28, pp. 43–58.

Rifkin, Glenn, and Mitch Betts (1988). "Strategic Systems Plans Gone Awry," *Computerworld* (March 14), pp. 1, 104–105.

Rouse, Robert A., and Curt Hartog (1988). "The New MIS Professional—Part 1," *Journal of Systems Management* (May), pp. 6–10.

Schultz, David I. (1986). "Strategic Information Systems Planning Sharpens Competitive Edge," *Data Management* (June), pp. 20–38.

Shore, Edwin B. (1983). "Reshaping the IS Organization," *MIS Quarterly* (December), pp. 11–17.

Sinclair, Stuart W. (1986). "The Three Domains of Information Systems Planning," *Journal of Information Systems Management*, vol. 3, no. 2 (Spring), pp. 8–16.

Stokes, Stewart (1986). "Competency Planning Leads Managers Through Tough Terrain," *Computerworld* (July 28), pp. 50–51.

Strassmann, Paul A. (1980). "The Office of the Future: Information Management for the New Age," *Technology Review*, vol. 82, no. 3 (December/January), pp. 54–65.

Sullivan, Cornelius H, Jr., and Charles E. Yates (1988). "Reasoning by Analogy—A Tool for Business Planning," *Sloan Management Review*, vol. 29, no. 3 (Spring), pp. 55–60.

Synnott, William R. (1987). "The Emerging Chief Information Officer," *Information Management Review*, vol. 3, no. 1, pp. 21–35.

Szewczak, Edward J. (1988). "Exploratory Results of a Factor Analysis of Strategic Information: Implications for Strategic Systems Planning," *Journal of Management Information Systems*, vol. 5, no. 2 (Fall), pp. 83–97.

Targowski, Andrew S. (1988). "Systems Planning for the Enterprise-wide Information Management Complex: The Architectural Approach," *Journal of Management Information Systems*, vol. 5, no. 2 (Fall), pp. 23–37.

Walter, William (1988). "Seeking Secrets of SIS Success," *Computerworld* (October 10), p. 21.

Ward, John M. (1987). "Integrating Information Systems into Business Strategies," *Long Range Planning*, vol. 20 (June), pp. 19–29.

Warner, Timothy N. (1987). "Information Technology as a Competitive Burden," *Sloan Management Review*, vol. 29, no. 1 (Fall), pp. 55–61.

Weiner, Michael, and John Girvin (1985). "Chief Information Officer—Does Your Company Need One?" *Computerworld/In Depth* (May 13), pp. ID2–ID5.

Weiss, Madeline (1986). "Creating a Management Development Program for MIS," *Computerworld* (July 28), pp. 52–53.

Weiszmann, Carol (1987). "Cloning Skills for Planning," Computerworld (October 19), pp. S1ff.

Whieldon, David, (1981). "Organizing MIS/DP to Meet the New Challenges," *Computer Decisions* (October), pp. 156–176.

Williamson, Mickey (1987). "A Manager For All Seasons," *Computerworld* (June 1), pp. 25–27.

Withington, Frederic (1987). "How to Succeed in the CIO Business," *Computerworld* (March 2), p. 17.

Young, Jim (1987). "Ways to Win Top Brass Back," *Computerworld/ Focus* (November 4), pp. 9–10.

Young, Jim (1988). "In the Hands of Laymen," *Computerworld/Focus* (November 2), p. 6.

Young, Lawrence F. (1984). "The Information System as a Corporate Strategic Weapon," Information Strategy: *The Executive Journal* (Fall), pp. 21–25.

Zachmann, William F. (1988). "Centralization vs. Decentralization: Finding the Appropriate Balance," *InfoWorld*, p. 68.

Zmud, Robert W. (1984). "Design Alternatives for Organizing Systems Activities," *MIS Quarterly* (June), pp. 93.

Part III

INFORMATION SYSTEMS AS A FUNCTIONAL ENTITY

Because many interesting and challenging professional opportunities await IS managers at the corporate level, it is tempting for such managers to focus much of their energy on pursuing these opportunities. Yet the IS manager cannot afford to become so involved in corporate issues that he or she neglects the crucial responsibility of managing the many elements of the IS department. Indeed, acceptance at the corporate level frequently hinges on a sound track record with regard to departmental management.

Running an IS department is not an easy task even for IS managers with considerable experience. The IS arena is changing significantly, and new approaches are required so that the maximum benefits of the IS resource may be delivered to the organization. With the increasing complexity of IS comes a rising need for increased professionalism and for solid, basic managerial skills. It is therefore important for the aspiring IS manager to be able to identify the more important issues of today's IS department and understand selected management approaches appropriate for coping with the new circumstances.

CHAPTER 8

Duties of the Information Systems Department

CHAPTER 9

The Elements of Information Systems Department
Management

CHAPTER 10

Functional Challenges and the Information
Systems Manager

CHAPTER 11

Organizing the Information Systems Department

CHAPTER 12

Information Systems Personnel Management

CHAPTER 13

Information Systems Development Methodologies
and Projects

CHAPTER 14

Information Systems as a Functional Entity: Issues
and Opportunities

SUGGESTED STUDENT PROJECTS

SUPPLEMENTARY READING LIST

eight

□

Duties of the Information Systems Department

External Influences on the Information Systems Department

Internal Influences

Proactive or Reactive Responses: Two Dilemmas

The Information Systems Department's
Functional Responsibilities

Compromise and Consistency: Striking the Balance

Conclusion

Discussion Questions

References

Although it is undeniably important to ensure the integration of business and technical goals at the highest corporate levels, the IS manager who does only this is little more than a consultant. In fact, the IS manager faces a broader challenge: In addition to consolidating the IS-executive relationship, the IS manager must command a thorough knowledge of the IS department itself—the services it can provide, the means of delivering these services, and the general role of the department in advancing corporate goals.

For some IS managers, keeping in mind this difference in orientation—corporate versus departmental—is difficult. The challenge does not reduce simply to developing objectives at the corporate level and then turning to the department to carry them out. Rather, the challenge is to maintain a dual or "stereo" vision of corporate opportunities and needs in tandem with departmental capabilities.

This chapter begins by looking at certain external and internal influences on the IS department. We then move to an examination of the department's functional responsibilities, which are broadly characterized as technical, futurist, and innovative. Next, we discuss two responses of the IS department to its environment: proactive and reactive. The chapter ends with a look at compromise and consistency as the twin demands felt by modern IS departments.

EXTERNAL INFLUENCES ON THE INFORMATION SYSTEMS DEPARTMENT

The IS department is a business in that numerous external influences act on and modify its effectiveness. These influences are schematized in Exhibit 8-1 and are similar to the structure of this text.

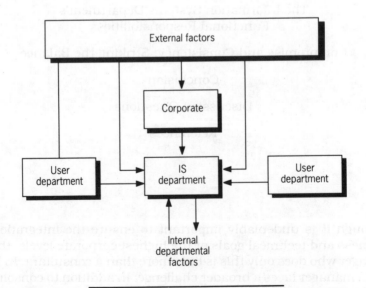

EXHIBIT 8-1 External and internal influences on the IS department.

The first step in expanding the field of vision of the department is to acknowledge the significance of external influences. The second is to identify each influence and its potential effects. Only then can responses—both proactive and reactive—be considered.

Business Environment

The IS department confronts a variety of influences that lie outside the corporate boundaries but nonetheless constrain or enhance the activities of the department. Among these are the following

- Technological developments
- Required systems practices (generally accepted accounting principles, government regulations)
- Vendor-related issues
- Specialized industry systems practices
- Employment conditions
- Economic conditions
- Actions of competitors and customers
- Standard business practices (e.g., contractual, ethical)

Some of these influences may be allowed for in the corporate planning process. Whether they are or not, however, the IS department must be able to identify the impact of each and to take appropriate action. This may entail responding to a situation that has already developed (such as a highly competitive vendor climate that encourages price negotiation) or taking proactive steps (such as avoiding long-term vendor contracts and relationships in anticipation of such a climate). Although not every condition of the business environment can be forecast, and some provide no opening for departmental initiatives, it should be observed that the creative IS department seldom permits itself to be victimized by external circumstances; many constructive avenues are open in even the difficult situations.

Intracorporate Relations

Strong and active relationships with key user departments exert a major influence on the IS department's activities and, ultimately, on its effectiveness. The IS manager's role is to develop a personal rapport with the heads of user departments. Because senior IS professionals interact closely with senior users during major projects, they are well positioned to convey the proper sense of support to user executives. Of course, the same supportive attitude should be displayed toward all users; otherwise, senior executives may feel that the IS department is being manipulative. It is important to remember that user executives' attitudes about IS support are based largely on reports from subordinates who may be quite sensitive to discrepancies in support. Consequentially, these executives may not be comfortable trusting an IS department's systems and programming group to install a new system because of a negative reputation earned from poor support of system maintenance. The IS manager must therefore either ensure consistently satisfactory support or educate users as to true IS performance issues.

W. J. Cecchi (1988) observes that such initiatives as performance/capacity monitoring can effectively prevent problems with intracorporate relations. Reactive approaches, Cecchi contends, cannot guarantee long-term problem prevention. Exhibit 8-2 illustrates both proactive and reactive approaches. Clearly, maintaining good intracorporate relations involves not just facilitating a general exchange of information but, more importantly, carefully choosing the right things to communicate and the appropriate format in which to communicate them. The way in which an IS department establishes and demonstrates leadership will decide its effectiveness; but whatever the method, relations based on trust must evolve. Trust does not exist where the IS department is perceived as trying to build an empire, as treating users condescendingly, as viewing any user (however obscure) as unimportant, or as preempting users' responsibility for their own areas. Trust is also unlikely to flourish if the IS department opts for passive, subservient relations with users. Those unfamiliar with information technology are usually not aware of the opportunities that automation presents or, conversely, of the restrictions that accompany its proper use. If an IS department simply waits to react, users may either unnecessarily confront serious problems or miss opportunities to save money or improve performance.

INTERNAL INFLUENCES

Within the IS department, certain activities must be undertaken if the department is to deliver the anticipated benefits of IS to other business units. These required activities influence both the department's structure and its posture with respect to the rest of the organization. The department's most obvious responsibility—to carry out tasks specified by authorized users—clearly requires a reactive posture. Once systems and procedures are in place, the department reacts on an ongoing basis to various user departments'

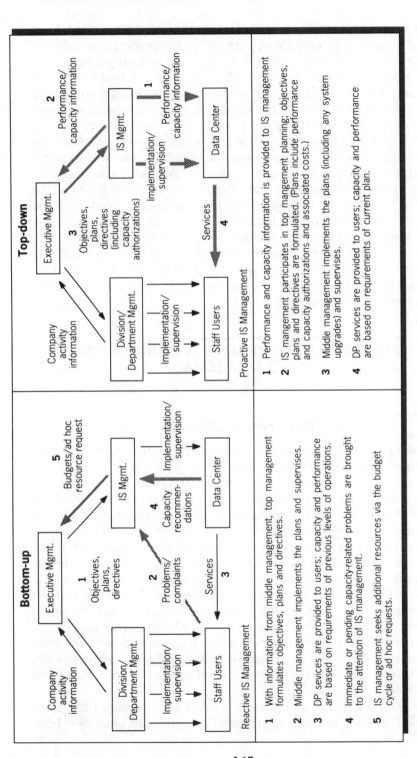

EXHIBIT 8-2 Proactive and reactive management approaches.

Source: W. J. Ceechi, "The Proper Role for Performance Management." Reprinted with permission from the March 1988 issue of *Infosystems* magazine. Copyright © 1988, Hitchcock Publishing Co., All rights reserved.

requests for the operation and maintenance of the systems. Even though such tasks contain opportunities for proactive responses, the department is essentially responding to external prompts.

In addition, there are some IS departmental tasks that are normally spelled out only in the form of broad, ongoing responsibilities and that heavily influence the ways in which design, development and operation duties are carried out. For example, all data must be accurate and reliable, systems should operate efficiently and lend themselves to growth and modification, and both systems and data must be robust and protected. Although the degree to which these and similar basic, implicit responsibilities must be fulfilled will vary depending on the IS department's plans and the corporate environment, the IS manager must ensure that such tasks are attended to in a routine manner—regardless of users' interest or desire for them. For instance, controls, flexibility, and fail-safe features must be built into all systems, even if users object because they are paying for the effort, they are in a hurry, or they are unwilling to support extra complexity.

PROACTIVE OR REACTIVE RESPONSES: TWO DILEMMAS

The Service Dilemma

Attempting to play its role, the IS department encounters a fundamental paradox. The overt mission of the department is to perform technical duties required by others—that is, to act as a service department responsible for meeting the needs of other business units. However, the IS department is also responsible for the organization's appropriate and strategic use of technology; it must lead efforts to maximize returns on technical investments. Naturally, these two responsibilities can be in conflict. In some cases, meeting corporate obligations may mean undermining commitments to supporting certain users' wishes. In other cases, the need to support technology that is easy and popular with users may involve a temporary lapse in corporate-level duties. Although user and corporate needs often can be simultaneously satisfied with creative compromises, the real challenge to the IS manager is to consistently satisfy both through the use of a combination of leadership and service postures.

An example showing that each mode has an appropriate place draws a contrast between operational and strategic activities. Initiating sudden changes at the operational level has two flaws: It does not allow for mental or physical adaptation, and it places the burden of evaluation, reaction, and planning on operational management personnel. Although occasionally operational changes must be sudden and unexpected, there are better ways to implement change. Ideally, major introductions of technology should be made at the strategic level, where adequate planning and coordination can occur and where room can be made for any necessary preparatory activities such as education and analysis. Once subordinates are involved, major operational issues have been addressed and broad commitments have been made. Although revisions will occur, the key decision of acceptance or rejection of proposed changes have been made by those who are responsible. When change is accelerated, care must be exercised to ensure uniform organizational acceptance. Even when low-level users openly advocate the adoption of a new system, senior managers must be approached in such a way that they too will support the necessary changes. Sometimes this is done through the user chain of command, sometimes by the IS department, and sometimes by both. Exhibit 8-3 shows various ways in which the dual roles of providing leadership and service can be segregated so that the IS manager can pay careful attention to both.

The Cost-Control Dilemma

Just as there is a potential conflict between the service and leadership roles that the IS department must fulfill simultaneously, so

	Leadership	Service
By level of activity	Strategic Some tactical	Some tactical Operational
By strategic grid	Strategic/ turnaround	Factory/support
By project life cycle	Development/ implementation	Operation/ maintenance
By job type	IS management	IS professional
By various circumstances	Weak user	Strong user
	IS in power position	IS without power position

EXHIBIT 8-3 Ways of segregating leadership and service.

there is a conflict in the responsibilities of the department with regard to controlling costs while promoting change. On the one hand, the IS department is expected to make the most efficient use of authorized resources: Some changes are clearly trivial and unnecessary, and there must be some safety valve to prevent frenzied change. In many cases this means limiting the use of an IS resource (either personnel or machine time). Most IS departments employ some form of resource rationing, and IS managers look for fair ways to say no in order to maintain the department's supportive image. On the other hand, if things are accomplished, it is difficult to gain approval for—much less explain—projects that involve changing areas that are not problems or introducing new programs, particularly if these projects are seen as the department's idea. Yet a crucial element of the department's responsibility is to identify new opportunities for appropriate use of technology.

Senior management usually has a very clear cut view of this dilemma: The IS department should make changes that make financial sense and avoid those that do not. In strict environments this may mean performing cost/benefit analyses; in others, value-added analyses or estimations of intangible benefits are sufficient. Certainly, the IS department would like to convey an image of rationality in its decision making, but doing so is not simple. Sometimes unrequired changes can be made by users to appear financially important, especially if there is no serious accountability or if benefits cannot be measured. The IS department is usually in no position to question users' spurious claims regarding systems. More typically, important changes may not lend themselves to financial measurement and payback. This is often true of programs that the IS department would like to promote.

Ultimately, regardless of how quantified the process is, someone is certain to disagree with IS resource-allocation decisions. For the IS manager, the task is to ensure that senior management generally agrees that IS resources are directed in cost-effective and cost-controlled ways and that users generally feel that system projects are necessary and valuable. Often processes or institutions such as charge back, senior management steering committees, and detailed planning and budgeting efforts help achieve the right balance, as they permit general corporate input into IS resource-allocation decision making. In companies where the IS manager has a more autonomous role in determining and deploying IS resources, decisions must be consistent with corporate strategies and corporate circumstances should be examined for unrecognized IS-related opportunities.

The IS department can afford to be more proactive with users when working within a strategic time frame but perhaps less so when in an operational mode. Variation will depend on the organizational level; an IS department manager is likely to initiate user service-level agreements, whereas operators are likely to react to existing service-level agreements. The issue in question will also govern the degree of proactivity or reactivity: A strategic system is more likely to receive the independent attentions of the IS department than is a low-leverage accounting system. All these factors must be weighed. Exhibit 8-4 indicates possible proactive and reactive responses at a range of levels.

Level	Proactive	Reactive
External	Establish vendor program Target technical opportunities Promote activity in professional societies	Evaluate announcements of new technology React to competitors' uses of competitive technology
Corporate	Participate in strategic planning Provide executive training	Take budget-reduction action Justify staffing levels
User	Monitor user serviece levels Provide user education and orientation programs	Investigate complaints about system performance Act on maintenance requests
Internal	Institute increased controls and measurement Institute internal cross-training program	Respond to turnover problem with improved benefits Undertake emergency equipment repairs

EXHIBIT 8-4 Possible proactive and reactive responses at various levels.

THE INFORMATION SYSTEMS DEPARTMENT'S FUNCTIONAL RESPONSIBILITIES

The functional responsibilities of the IS department are both diverse and extensive, much more so than has traditionally been assumed. Exhibit 8-5 illustrates this diversity by showing, through an analysis of time usage done by Gary Dickson and James Wetherbe (1985), the wide range of intra- and extra- organizational participants with whom the IS manager must deal. (A large percentage of time is spent dealing with people within the IS department.) Exhibit 8-6 shows the varied areas of work handled by the IS manager; as the exhibit shows, considerable time is devoted to general management and to industry-related applications.

As the various dimensions of the department's functional responsibilities are evaluated, it is appropriate to consider the levels of proficiency required of the IS manager and selected managerial subordinates. Because certain skills such as personnel management or financial analysis are more or less mandatory in any organization, IS managers are responsible for providing them to the IS department on their own or through others. Ultimately, IS managers shoulder the responsibility for meeting corporate expecta-

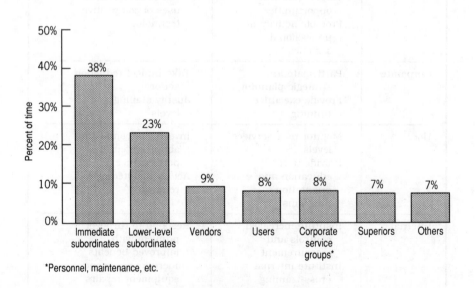

*Personnel, maintenance, etc.

EXHIBIT 8-5 Time spent by IS executives with other organizational participants.

Source: Gary Dickson and James Wetherbe, *The Management of Information Systems*, New York: McGraw-Hill, 1985, p. 9. Reprinted with permission.

tions of the department, for discharging their own duties, and for supervising their staff.

Technical Responsibility

The most widely accepted and understood functional responsibility of the IS department is its technical responsibility. In fact, too much is made of this area, and often other areas receive insufficient attention. Unless IS professionals appreciate the fact that technology must have practical applications, they may become arrogant about their specialized knowledge yet unable to apply it effectively. IS departments that try to force the latest technology down the throats of the organization are not exercising appropriate technical responsibility.

Selecting Appropriate Technology The IS department must be aware of available commercial technology and its costs, uses, and compatibility with existing technology. Here, a knowledge of vendors is more useful than an understanding of electronics. Naturally, technical competence is important; for instance, when laser-based optical data storage was first introduced, technical professionals knew that optical media could not be rerecorded as could magnetic

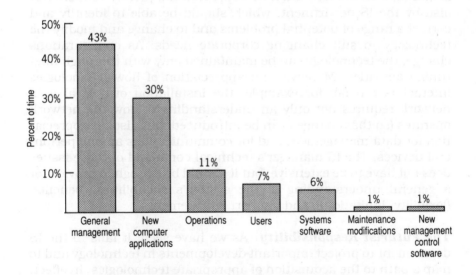

EXHIBIT 8-6 Time spent by IS executives on different areas.

Source: Gary Dickson and James Wetherbe, *The Management of Information Systems*, New York: McGraw-Hill, 1985, p. 9. Reprinted with permission.

media and were thus inappropriate for some applications. An understanding of technology permits astute IS professionals to understand the limitations as well as the growth potential of technical developments. Those who understood the benefits of data-base management systems, for example, positioned their organizations to take advantage of them early; in some smaller organizations, IS professionals waited to see that applications software houses were supporting certain data-base management systems and that hardware was powerful enough to handle the overhead before committing to these systems. In either case, IS professionals must know what to look for and to gather enough cost/benefit information to make a good business decision regarding forays into new technical areas.

Devising Appropriate Applications As important as it is to know and understand technology, appreciating how it can be applied is ultimately more vital. Ensuring both the presence of a need and the availability of a certain technology to satisfy it is crucial if wasteful or pointless investments are to be avoided. To this end, it is useful for IS professionals to develop networks within their industries and to become aware of how various technologies can work in real-world scenarios.

Providing for Adequate Maintenance and Modification Once acquired, a technology must be supported not just by vendors but also by the IS department, which should be able to identify and correct a range of potential problems and to change and modify the technology to suit changing corporate needs. As configurations change, the technology can be maintained only with thorough fine-tuning activities. Moreover, an appreciation of how technologies interact is crucial; for example, the installation of a local area network requires not only an understanding of how the network operates (so that changes can be introduced) but also an appreciation for data management and for communications among peripheral devices. The IS manager's technical command of these issues does not have to be extensive, but it should be enough to provide for a general understanding of the system's capabilities, benefits, flexibility, limitations, and support requirements.

The Futurist Responsibility As we have seen, it falls to the IS department to project important developments in technology and to map a path to the acquisition of appropriate technologies. In effect, the department serves as a corporate futurist.

The IS strategic plan guides decision making and helps the manager determine the correct timing of new acquisitions or other strategically relevant actions. If a certain new computer technology is right around the corner, in the judgment of the department, the manager may decide that it makes sense to lease rather than purchase a computer required immediately. If integrated voice/data communication offers strong benefits, perhaps it is prudent for the organization to align itself with a vendor likely to provide an integrated solution. Or if the manager believes that an industry standard (such as ISDN) will be adopted, he or she may decide to choose a vendor currently committed to that standard.

Maintaining constant vigil over the technical arena is the price of accepting the responsibility of acting as corporate futurist. IS managers usually rely on professional periodicals and writings for summary assessments of developing technologies. Although such prognoses must constantly be brought up to date, a past example of such a forecast identifies 10 technologies worth watching (Gantz, 1987):

1. *Software-defined Networks (SDN)*: This technology will allow user equipment to communicate more flexibly, and with greater intelligence and control, with other equipment.

2. *Local Area Networks (LANs)*: The ability of localized devices to communicate with each other will expand as more functionality is added and interfacing is made easier. User work will change to take advantage of the greater capabilities.

3. *Graphics*: The graphics capabilities of laser printers and desktop publishing will allow expansions to many new applications and locations.

4. *Compact Disk/Read-only Memory (CD/ROM)*: Associated with optical disk storage, this technology increases the volume and speed of retrieval for on-line access from the megabyte (millions) to the gigabyte (billions) range. This may strain the ability to communicate, but it opens the realm of image storage.

5. *Personal Computer/Facsimile*: Another technology that may break barriers to digital image management, this allows personalized telecopying.

6. *Fast Packet*: This will allow packet switching to compete with T1 line speed, reduce price performance, and support large, diverse networks.

7. *T4/DS4 Transmission and Switching*: This offers extremely high transmission speeds, well beyond those of T1.

8. *Real-Time Computing:* Transaction networking and factory automation are just two applications that are increasing and need high-performance, high-reliability response time.

9. *Electronic Data Interchange (EDI):* The trend has been established to allow direct communication of computers operated by different companies. This will be essential in some areas in order to place orders for products and services, coordinate shipment and receipt, manage accounts, and so on. Standards are evolving that will allow general participation in this movement.

10. *Pay-Phone Networking:* Private pay-phone operations will provide a variety of services.

The technologies just cited as worth watching are very communications weighted. The knowledgeable IS manager might want to include some additional ones that proceed from other technical areas

- Multiprocessor computing: Improvements in how many computers can work together on the same problem will not only expand the horizon of supercomputing but will also enlarge the quantities and kinds of problems with which computers can deal.
- Optical disk data storage and retrieval: This technology may find ways to deal with the update problem and will greatly expand the storage capacity, speed of retrieval, and reliability of data storage while at the same time reducing the cost. It will also provide a medium most conducive to image storage as well as voice, data, and document storage.
- Image processing: The ability to recognize images and integrate that information into traditional data-processing activities will result from hardware and software breakthroughs (array processing, for instance) and standards for controlled integration with other technologies.
- Document management: The ability to store, transmit, and process integrated document information consistently and in tandem with other data processing will depend on the adoption of standards and the subsequent expansion of appropriate software.
- Radio communication: For localized communication (within a mile or two) the use of high-frequency, low-power broadcasting can replace hard-wiring costs and allow portability and flexibil-

ity for full-function LANs. Ultimately, the capability exists for cellular LANs as well.

The attention given these and other emerging technologies will depend to a large degree on the opportunities each presents for an individual company. Projecting the success or failure of each is not enough. The timing of introductions of new capabilities, their compatibility with current technologies, vendor reactions, costs, and other variables all must be taken into account if the company is to position itself appropriately and to select, apply, and manage new technology.

Industry Knowledge

To know how technology can best be applied, it is essential to understand the context in which it is to be used. Fortunately, much of the information processing requirements of a particular organization can be understood by examining the industry to which it belongs. A bank, for example, will have processing needs very different from those of a manufacturer but very like those of another bank. The alert IS professional will appreciate the particular requirements of the industry in question and will ensure at least a basic level of support before contemplating modifications, alterations, or additions.

Traditional Approaches   Often IS professionals are hired from competing or similar organizations because they offer industry-specific experience. Even veterans of one company learn to focus on industrywide automation trends and tend to concentrate on standardized application areas. Knowledge of one or more effective industry-specific solutions to a given IS-related problem is of great value to a company that does not want to reinvent the wheel or to risk failure because of inexperience.

Of course, this knowledge is not gained solely from prior experience. A strong educational program consisting of industry seminars, vendor orientations, and site visits can bring an inquisitive IS professional up to educational par with his or her veteran counterparts. In fact, a too-heavy reliance on experience can be detrimental as it may prevent the professional from looking at an application problem in a fresh way or even considering a more flexible implementation of a traditional solution. Still, conventional wisdom says that it is better to start with an appreciation for traditional and proven methods than to try to master new application areas without the benefit of this baseline awareness.

Responsibility for Innovation   Despite the natural inducements for companies within the same industries to use similar technical solutions, competitive pressure will always cause corporations to look for newer, more efficient solutions as a way to outperform their competitors. Because the major responsibility for innovation rests with senior management and the IS planning process, it is easy for the IS rank and file to ignore it. However, the IS manager should ensure that IS professionals never bypass an opportunity for devising functional improvements. Even major systems ideas often originate with the insights of those who work closely with applications. Furthermore, opportunities for new and creative applications also come in small packages. Details such as the format and content of a customer invoice can lead to competitive advantages for companies that are alert to these subtleties.

Adopting new ideas requires a degree of prudence. To put it in terms of an old adage: "Be not the first by which the new is tried, nor yet the last to set the old aside." Too innovative an approach may entail a multitude of bugs and problems to be worked out. However, waiting too long can cause organizations to forfeit the chance to reap early benefits. The IS manager must steer a course between the two extremes, one that is appropriate to the circumstances and the organization.

Management

The skills of technology and industry knowledge are merely tools that professionals use to perform services. The skill of deploying these tools is the third and perhaps most important part of the IS department skill set. The management task not only sets the process whereby the various talents are used but is responsible for determining what exactly is to be done. Proper management is critical because even the proper industry and technical skills improperly applied can result in an inefficient process, inexact solutions, inadequate resources, or failure. However, because management skills alone are insufficient, the IS manager is further challenged to use management, industry, and technical skills in a harmonious balance.

COMPROMISE AND CONSISTENCY: STRIKING THE BALANCE

In describing the task of programming, Gerald Weinberg (1971) identified four virtues of a program (meeting specifications, meeting a schedule, being adaptable, and being efficient) and pointed out the trade-offs that programmers must make to balance these elements. Similar compromises must be forged at the systems level, and even more complex trade-offs occur at higher organizational levels.

At the departmental level there are trade-offs between doing things quickly and doing things precisely, and between products that are full-featured and those that are efficient. Differing departmental activities must be emphasized in the correct measures and at the correct time to achieve optimal results. One possible analogy is a sports team with various players who have differing assignments but who all contribute to the success of the team. IS too has its diverse roles as exemplified by the basic job differences shown in Exhibit 8-7. This comparison reminds us of the need for harmony among diverse functions, cooperation made more difficult by the time phased sequencing of activities and the designed conflict of goals necessary as checks and balances.

Another analogy to IS development is the building of a complex customized structure such as a subway system. Here, the user has some obvious needs that can be described in varying levels of detail. Meeting the user's needs requires detailed planning, integration of tasks, and the application of many different specialized technologies.

Job Elements	Major Divisions of the IS Department		
	Systems and Programming	Operations	Technical Support
Education	BS	AS/high school	BS/MS
Task guidelines	Variable	Highly structured	Very loose
Work schedule	Partially structured	Rigid	Unstructured
Task complexity	Moderate with variety	Simple but repetitive	Extreme but nonrepetitive
Social needs	Moderate	Very little	None
Task/business need relationship	Direct strategic and tactical relationship	Direct immediate relationship	Very indirect

EXHIBIT 8-7 Job requirements of the major functional areas of the IS department.

Once the system development is underway, the changes that the user can make become more limited and more expensive. After the system is completed, it is turned over to a different group of people to operate—a group that requires high reliability and ease of use. Delivering these services depends in turn on a third group of specialists who maintain, replace, and make changes to the mechanical parts of the system. Changes can be made by the original group of builders: The cost and impact of these changes will depend on their nature and on the degree of integration. Naturally, the group responsible for operating the subway can be negatively affected by any disruptions. However, to serve the user and to keep the system running, some changes will be necessary. Like the IS manager, someone or some function must be in a position to orchestrate the timing of various functions and balance the activities of each group with an interest in the subway system.

Analogies such as these are useful to permit conceptualization of complex IS departmental processes. By understanding the basics of how the whole mechanism performs, it becomes easier to appreciate the purpose of the unique niche occupied by each IS department entity. The follow discussion introduces the major IS department entities and their salient characteristics.

Introducing Change: Systems and Programming

The IS group responsible for building elaborate structures that respond to user needs is the systems and programming group or function. This group must be able to respond to specific requests for support or to analyze a problem situation to determine possible solutions. Like any builder, this group is required to display inventiveness in solving problems but cannot let its creativity eclipse the goal of constructing products that satisfy specific needs. Elegant, unused solutions are a failure; the customer may not always be right but is always the customer, and so must be satisfied.

Because this same group is responsible for system changes, it will try to identify or anticipate them in the system design. Changes or extensions to a system can be made easier if the original blueprints allow for them. However, systems and programming's first goal is to meet immediate objectives within schedule and budget.

Maintaining Routines: Operations

The group required to operate the products built by systems and programming is also driven by the requirement to satisfy the customer. The operations group or function may be perceived as offering a different service because it typically makes systems available to users in a timely, reliable, and accurate manner. The ability to do this rests not only on the operations group's own performance but also on the ease of use designed into the system by the builder. It is at this level that early, general design decisions are seen as providing flexibility or obstacles to operations.

Specific, agreed-on levels of performance are necessary if operations is to meet its responsibility. If the performance target is constantly changed by users, operations cannot be assured of meeting it. Similarly, if the environment changes, operations must reassess the resources it is working with before determining how to meet users' needs. This is why operations is very demanding of systems and programming. The original product may be attractive to systems and programming because of its user-oriented features, cost and schedule, elegance, and so forth; but operations is more interested in whether it will hold up under heavy use and perform accurately. Moreover, once a system is proven usable, operations is most effective if no changes are made to it. Systems and Programming, however, must make changes to satisfy the user, to maintain system usefulness, and just to keep busy. A real conflict can develop if these functions are not properly orchestrated.

Lobbying for Obscure Details: Technical Support

The building and operating of systems both have the advantage of being visible and readily understood activities. Users generally see the benefits inherent in these tasks. What they sometimes lose sight of, however, is the fact that systems rest on complex technology, and behind the scenes someone must keep that technology in working order. The group responsible for this in the IS department is technical support. This group's duties are broad and affect systems and programming and operations in various ways. The technical support staff selects the hardware, software, and communications technology with which systems are to be built. They guide the ways in which the system will be used by advising analysts and programmers on design and programming alternatives that take advantage of the hardware and software on which applications will run. Technical support is also responsible for ensuring that the technology is maintained in proper order and performs well. This means that technical support is concerned with how efficiently systems and programming designs the system as well as how operations runs it. Technical support wants to be allowed to maintain the technology in top working order. Naturally, the operations group may have some difficulty with the many changes that might affect it; thus, another conflict may arise.

Championing the Nontraditional: Information Centers and More

The role and relationships of the previous three groups or functions are well understood within the IS department. In many cases, the interlocking activities that help define the relationships are reasonably well established by processes and tradition. As technology advances, new methods offer solutions to old problems—problems that may have been poorly addressed by the functions just described. Although a new approach may carry the promise of success, there must be a way to deliver its benefits in concert with traditional IS services and functions. Although systems and programming may not design user services, this group knows user needs and can help with the success of new data-access projects. Similarly, operations must support new methods even though this group may vie with operations for control of some systems. And new approaches rely heavily on technical support even though this group usually remains hidden from users.

Obviously, nontraditional functions, such as office automation, voice communications, and end-user computing (EUC), must find a comfortable, supportive home within the IS department; however, those who champion new approaches must be realistic about their importance. There is as much to be learned from traditional methods regarding data accuracy and protection, or integrity of design, as from ad hoc reporting, "what-if" analysis, prototyping, and similar new functions.

CONCLUSION

Managing an IS department requires an awareness of and sensitivity to a variety of dimensions. Along with the different focuses of corporate-level personnel, IS department personnel, and users, there are also the very different demands and possibilities of technology, applications, and management. For any given situation, both proactive and reactive approaches can be used. This complexity can be confusing.

If IS management were only a matter of compartmentalizing and categorizing each problem or decision, it would be an easy task indeed. But even the most carefully defined IS tasks contain the various dimensions we have encountered. IS management therefore addresses a rich interrelation of elements that play on one another and cannot be realistically isolated. Only by maintaining a truly global perspective can the IS manager hope to direct the IS department as a functional entity in a thorough and effective way.

DISCUSSION QUESTIONS

1. What factors might affect the attention an IS manager gives to external influences as opposed to internal ones?

2. What kind of background will provide an IS manager with a sound combination of technical, application, and management skills? What might a traditional career path neglect?

3. How would IS managers divide their attention among systems and programming, operations, technical support, and other departmental functions?

4. What are some of the consequences for the IS department of fluctuating conditions in the business environment? How might the IS manager avoid or limit their effects?

5. What are some specific actions an IS manager might take to provide corporate leadership that will not jeopardize a supportive image?

6. How can today's IS manager stay current on new technology? To what extent must the IS manager understand technical details?

7. What factors would lead you as IS manager to chose a strategy of pioneering new industry applications versus a more conservative approach? Describe some of the risks of pioneering.

8. Is it appropriate to determine areas where IS managers should strengthen their skills by analyzing where today's IS managers typically spend their time?

9. Which of the ways of categorizing leadership behavior and service behavior as contrasted in Exhibit 8-3 seems most appropriate to you? Why?

10. Of the examples of proactive and reactive behaviors shown in Exhibit 8-4, what steps can be taken to anticipate the listed reactions? What reactions might have to take place for each proactive example not performed?

REFERENCES

Cecchi, W. J. (1988). "The Proper Role for Performance Management," *Infosystems* (March), pp. 45–46.

Dickson, G., and J. Wetherbe (1985). *The Management of Information Systems* (New York: McGraw–Hill), p. 9.

Freedman, David H. (1987). "Harvard MBA's Could Be Hazardous to IS Managers," *Infosystems*, vol. 33, no. 9 (September), pp 26–28.

Gantz, John (1987). "10 Technologies Worth Watching," *Telecommunication Products & Technology*, vol. 5, no. 9 (September), pp. 58–60.

Weinberg, Gerald M. (1971). *The Psychology of Computer Programming* (New York: Van Nostrand Reinhold), pp. 15–26.

Young, Jim (1987), "Industry Merger Fever," *Computerworld-Focus*, vol. 21, no. 32A, (August 12), p 8.

nine

The Elements of Information Systems Department Management

Planning

Organizing

Staffing

Directing

Controlling

Conclusion

Discussion Questions

References

All management involves certain discrete functions. Regardless of the specialized or nonroutine activities that managers find themselves performing, they are nonetheless responsible for these functions on a daily basis. Exhibit 9-1 is one framework for viewing IS department management (Lucas and Turner, 1982). It shows the interrelationship of functions; each must be addressed if effective and supportive information processing is to be provided to the organization. We have chosen to build our discussion around the management functions derived from the Lucas and Turner framework:

- Planning
- Organizing
- Staffing
- Directing (applications and operations)
- Charging and controlling.

Directing is discussed generically here; its special role in applications and operations will be covered in Chapter 10. Similarly, equipment management will be discussed in Chapters 10 and 14 as a specialized managerial skill. The options available in organizing the IS department are significant enough to deserve the isolated explanation provided in Chapter 11. Likewise staffing is explored separately in Chapter 12 because of its interrelationship to many other personnel issues.

Exhibit 9-2 presents some of the issues related to each management function and identifies actions and alternatives available to the IS manager dealing with each issue. In this chapter we look at the five

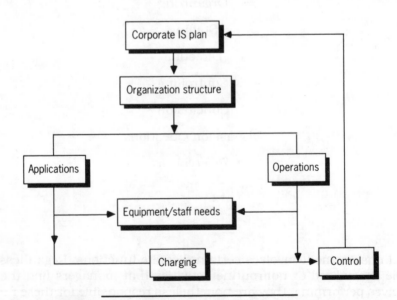

EXHIBIT 9-1 A framework for managing the IS department.

Source: Reprinted from "A Corporate Strategy for the Control of Information Processing," by Henry C. Lucas, Jr. and Jon A. Turner, *Sloan Management Review*, Spring 1982, p. 30, by permission of the publisher. Copyright © 1982 by Sloan Management Review Association. All rights reserved.

functions of management and many of the questions they raise and the alternative course of action they suggest.

PLANNING

Planning is the essential orchestration of the activities of the IS department. Planning unifies diverse activities, providing a "road map" for the undertaking of complex tasks that must be well coordinated, accomplished over extended time frames, and inclusive of many people.

Planning is perhaps the most critical function in IS department management because it sets up all the others. Any IS plan, be it a high-level document or a small project plan, is the basis for communications among various IS department functions. Individual work plans permit IS managers to identify tasks and delegate them to specific department members. Plan reviews ensure commonality of goals and consistency of timing, and project plans enable IS managers to avoid duplication of resources, cost overruns, and other problems. A project plan may be as simple as a GANTT chart providing information on such areas as task identity, task responsibility, and project start and end times, or based on a more sophisticated PERT technique that might include such features as assignment of support resources, task dependencies, critical path identification, and cost itemization by task (see Exhibit 9-3). Still more advanced planning tools allow resource scheduling across projects, which prevents the overcommitting of a critical resource or unnecessary idle time. Of course, all such planning techniques provide the opportunity for actual-to-plan comparisons.

Responding To Corporate-level Input

As we have seen, planning sets the direction for the IS department's activities. It must also ensure that corporate and IS directions are consistent. The typical IS department business plan might contain the following

- Statement of departmental mission
- Statements of strategy and philosophy
- Critical success factors analysis
- Major multiyear project activities
- High-level financial analysis
- Growth projections

I. Corporate MIS Plan	*Issue*	*Recommendation*
	Mechanism	Operational plan: 1 year; Longer-term plan: 3-5 years; Technology assessment; Link to organization plan; Separate IS planning officer
	Involvement	User and management input
	Contents and format	Applications needs; Operations needs; Implications for staff and equipment
	Priorities	Senior-level committee to choose applications areas
	Reporting	Annual report of MIS tied to plan
II. Organization Structure	*Issue*	*Alternative*
	Type	Centralized, distributed, decentralizd for operations and analysis/design
	Evaluation	Criteria: Service levels; Cost responsiveness; Flexibility; History of organization
	Control	Balance local autonomy with corporate needs
III. New Applications	*Issue*	*Recommendation*
	Generate new ideas	From plan; also, procedures for requests
	Package	Evaluate: functional fit to needs
	Selection	Multicriteria scoring models
	Development	Extensive user input; Management involvement setting goals; Reviewing system
	Change	Preparing organization to manage and cope with change
	Conflict	Ways to use conflict constructively

IV. Operations	Issue	Recommendation
	Measurement	Develop user-oriented measures
	Evaluation	Administer regular evaluations including variety of measures

V. Equipment/staff Needs	Issue	Recommendation
	Evaluation and choice criteria	Develop evaluation methodology
	Compatibility among vendors	Establish vendor compatibility policy
	Technological assessment	Factor likely technology changes into decisions

VI. Charging	Issue	Alternative
	To charge	Yes or no; Advantages and disadvantages
	Charging mechanism	Full or partial charge out: Accounting techniques

VII. Control	Issue	Recommendation
	Overall evaluation	Compare results to plan
	Frequent feedback	Monitor progress on systems development projects; Conduct user surveys as discussed under operations

EXHIBIT 9-2 Management alternatives for each IS management element.

Source: Reprinted from "A Corporte Strategy for the Control of Information Processing," by Henry C. Lucas, Jr. and Jon A. Turner, Sloan Management Review, Spring 1982, p. 31, by permission of the publisher. copyright © 1982 by Sloan Management Review Association. All rights reserved.

Such elements have a carefully defined relationship (as highlighted in Exhibit 9-4) around which any planning process is built. This relationship must be reinforced through the planning process itself. An iterative approach (such as the one indicated in Exhibit 9-5) is a means of uniting broad guidelines in the details of the plan.

Other, more detailed planning activities are a natural follow-on to the IS business plan; they become extensions of that plan and typically result in "subplans" that support the IS strategic plan. Richard Nolan (1982) illustrates this fact in his description of the

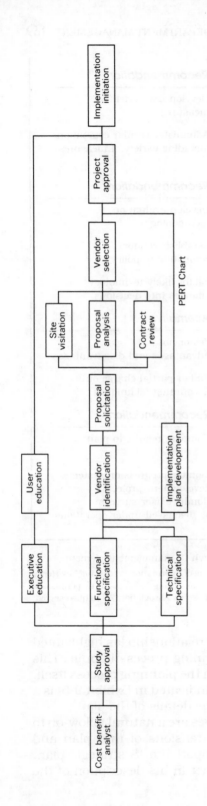

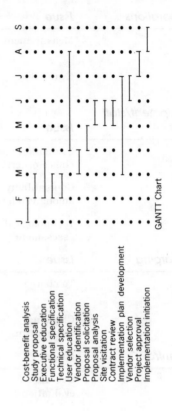

EXHIBIT 9-3 Two planning methods for a software acquisition project.

PERT Chart

GANTT Chart

Cost-benefit analysis
Study proposal
Executive education
Functional specification
Technical specification
User education
Vendor identification
Proposal solicitation
Proposal analysis
Site visitation
Contract review
Implementation plan development
Vendor selection
Project approval
Implementation initiation

planning and control of computer architecture as shown in Exhibit 9-6. Detailed plans are developed in response not only to the broad IS business plan but also to selected parts of the corporate business plan and functional department plans. Planning can also be used proactively by detailing IS department direction and scheduling preparation for some anticipated event. Some of these pieces must be developed by appropriate departmental groups responding to higher-level goals. For example, systems and programming develops hiring plans on the basis of the major multiyear project activity plan. Training plans are based on hiring plans as well as on other proposed events such as planned technology introductions, and development programs. These dependent or secondary plans usually require several iterations before they are adequate and cohesive.

Developing a business plan is a process in which all IS department managers participate. It may involve informal discussions around a table or may be structured so that each planned activity has its own

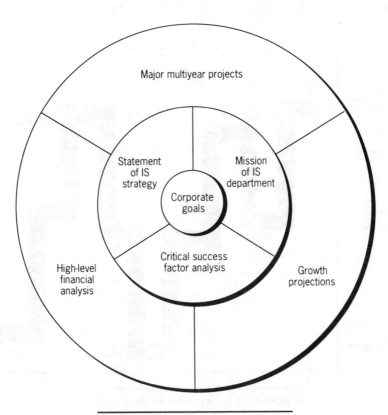

EXHIBIT 9-4 Elements of a typical IS business plan.

formatted documentation. However undertaken, this process helps ensure that future-year plans are supportable and generally free of surprises. As the IS business plan takes shape and generates secondary plans, upcoming-year activities begin to be specified in some detail. Greater detail normally translates to specific expenses and capital needs, which, of course, lead to the IS department's annual budget. One means of planning for budget preparation is the matrix technique shown in Exhibit 9-7. Project activities appear along one axis and support elements along the other. (Overhead costs, such as managers' salaries, are identified as a separate internal program or allocated across several areas.)

Ensuring Successful Information Systems Department Planning

Beyond the mechanics of constructing a business plan are general rules of thumb that should be followed. Mark Klein (1987) has outlined seven keys to successful IS planning:

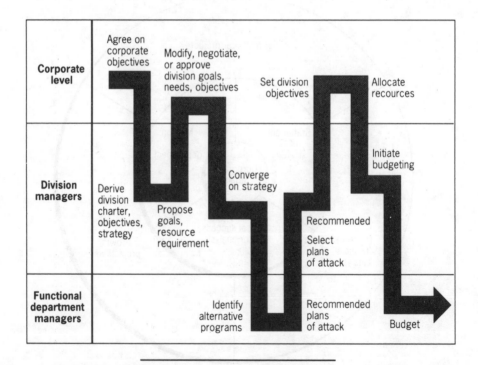

EXHIBIT 9-5 A corporate planning cycle.

Source: Howard Frank, "Developing Strategic Plans," *TPT/Networking Management*, Pennwell Publishing, Westford, MA. Copyright April 1988, pp. 34–38.

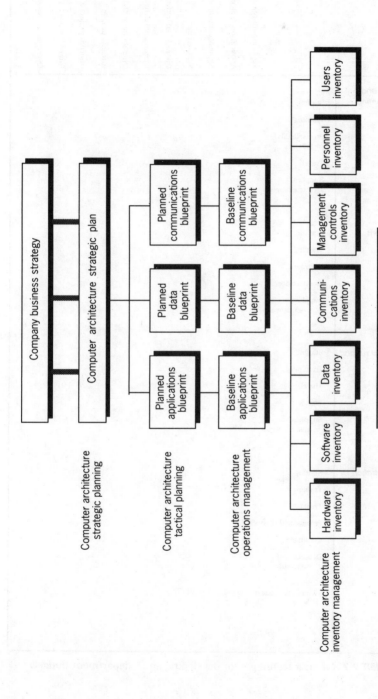

EXHIBIT 9-6 Computer architecture planning and control.

Source: Richard L. Nolan, "Building the Company's Computer Architecture Strategic Plan," *Stage by Stage,* vol. 2, no. 4, p. 3. Copyright 1981, Nolan, Norton & Co., Lexington, MA. All rights reserved. Reprinted with permission.

	Application project 1	Application project 2	Application project 3	Maintenance	Operational activity 1	Operational activity 2	Operational activity 3	Internal project 1	Internal project 2	Internal project 3	Overhead activity	Total
Systems and programming												
Staffing												
Training												
Professional Services												
Travel												
Supplies, miscellaneous												
Operations												
Staffing												
Training												
Hardware												
Maintenance												
Supplies, miscellaneous												
Technical support												
Staffing												
Training												
Travel												
Software												
Supplies, miscellaneous												
Administration												
Staffing												
Training												
Travel												
Professional services												
Contingency												
Depreciation, overhead												
Supplies, miscellaneous												
Total												

EXHIBIT 9-7 A matrix technique for developing an IS department budget.

1. *Prepare a map for the future.* The plan must lead the way to productive and profitable uses of technology and thus must be actionable and manageable.

2. *Balance technology push with demand pull.* A plan that is too technology driven or too driven exclusively by user demand will not work.

3. *Determine true requirements.* Analyzing critical success factors (see Chapter 2) can help reduce shortsightedness in business requirements.

4. *Executive sponsorship.* IS department planning must be conducted with the authorization, involvement, and understanding of senior management.

5. *Build on existing investments.* Plan future investments on the technical foundations of the past, wherever possible.

6. *Develop the plan to an appropriate level of detail.* Too much detail is a common failing of most plans. Issues should be kept at a broad level in order to be useful in the anticipated executive dialogue.

7. *Undertake transition planning.* IS managers should not plan only end-user projects but should also include projects to improve the IS infrastructure including plans for new policies, standards, procedures, tools, and support concepts.

Developing the Information Systems Department Budget

A well-developed budget establishes a clear link between expenditures and anticipated benefits. IS department budgeting is properly governed by the corporate budget process. Therefore, project spending recommendations must be closely related to project benefits so that senior management can immediately grasp the business returns expected from each expenditure and so that cost-cutting decisions can be made in the areas of least impact.

A carefully evolved budget does not allow spending on visible user systems at the expense of essential underlying support for such areas as hardware, software, and support services. Project plans that address all levels of support, both direct and indirect, help to overcome this problem and therefore are a fundamental component of the IS budget. At least two other areas of expense must also be budgeted: ongoing operations and department administration. The latter includes activities ranging from refurbishment of office facilities to improvements in the security program. Normally these expenses consist of numerous minor expenditures and/or do not follow the discrete life cycle of a given project. For this reason they are often accounted for in the budget by lump-sum budgeting or expense estimations by category.

If the corporate budgeting method can be adjusted, IS managers might aggregate various categories of expense in diverse accounts. They might also request allowances for the segregation of periodic maintenance fees from one-time repair costs. In addition, they might investigate the possibility of spreading charges across appropriate time periods. In some environments, project budgets separate from operational budgets are convenient and efficient. Time-period comparisons (e.g., the current month compared to the same month in the previous year) may make sense in stable environments but will not in organizations undergoing rapid change; for these, standard budget projection reports are more appropriate, ideally including projections of the many fixed expenses that the IS department typically incurs.

Some Practical Planning Concerns

How Much Planning Is Enough? As the individual ultimately responsible for departmental productivity, the IS manager must determine how much planning effort is needed. Too little will certainly jeopardize productivity and even the appropriateness of certain undertakings. Too much will leave insufficient time and resources for actual work. Planning is, as we all know, only a means to an end. The IS department usually is not measured solely on the basis of the quality of its plans.

Determining the proper level of planning is an element of overall business strategy. The Japanese typically devote two-thirds of a project to the planning phase. Because this heavy concentration on planning provides for enormous attention to detail, projects are typically implemented reasonably efficiently. Americans, in contrast, usually spend only one-third of the project period on planning; two-thirds is devoted to more dynamic and spontaneous implementation. Interestingly enough, neither method seems fundamentally faster or more accurate. Each has its advocates. To Americans, the Japanese method appears overly cautious, meticulous, and lacking in flexibility. To the Japanese, the American method seems out of control, risk prone, and rambunctious.

Where large teams are involved and where the task is especially complex, an extra focus on planning seems to have its benefits. Where the goals are firmly fixed, detailed plans also have their place.

However, where flexibility is required and where creativity and powers of invention are called on, too much planning can be a detriment. (One of the advantages of a technique such as prototyping, which we will encounter in Chapter 13, is that it avoids this complexity.) When the tasks are more easily divisible, when there is less dependency on intercorporate communications, and when there is a premium on proceeding on the basis of clear work plans, lengthy planning may be superfluous. Of course, claiming that the proper degree of planning is circumstantial sidesteps the problem: it leaves the hard project-by-project planning decisions to the judgment of the IS manager.

Who Plans Projects?   Ideally, the eventual project manager should prepare the initial project plan. For several reasons, however, this can be difficult. It may be unclear who will manage the project, because many projects begin to be planned far in advance of formal activation. Even if the appointee is known, this person could be involved in another assignment. In any event, the IS manager might not think it appropriate to invest too much of this person's time in preliminary planning, especially if he or she has not been previously involved in formulating the project concept.

Of course, it is not always easy for the project manager to come on board after the planning process is over and to implement unfamiliar plans with conviction and enthusiasm. To circumvent this problem, the project plan often is left in a broad and general state until a transition can be made and the project manager is ready and able to refine the plan. (Of course, this requires a somewhat flexible schedule and a corporate attitude that allows for adjustments.)

Making Multiyear Commitments   For the largest projects, project planning extends over several years and requires task scheduling and financial commitments that also span this period. Unfortunately, businesses tend to avoid expense commitments beyond the current fiscal year and currently conservative accounting methods discourage the capitalization of large projects. Thus, the project manager is at the whim of corporate budgetary approval processes. Carefully coordinated project activity may be deferred in midstream because of funding problems. More likely, the project manager may be expected to accelerate or defer the work plan merely to accommodate financial conditions. The realistic IS manager knows that often an IS project is subordinated to corporate financial health.

Planning Accuracy   Although everyone understands that a plan is an educated estimate, many plans require a high degree of accuracy because so much rests on them. The IS manager faces a difficult question: Should a margin of error be included and, if so, how much? Many agree that some safety factor should be included in estimates of project timing, staffing, spending needs to account for potential risks. At the same time, the manager is held accountable for a prudent and responsible use of resources and is pressured to minimize resource needs. Some managers can, under the right conditions, scientifically derive the right balance by identifying all likely risks and the statistically correct level of needed resources. Unhappily, not all projects or all risks lend themselves to such quantification.

Experimental Funding   With so much attention on user support, prior approval, and so forth, it is easy to lose sight of the need to permit IS departments to undertake research and development. IS departments can make use of the freedom to explore by acquiring new technologies on a trial basis; trying new methods of management, development, or control; and studying new applications areas.

Of course, prophesying the specific benefits to be derived from such endeavors is impossible. In fact, IS departments cannot foresee a year in advance which R&D areas are to be explored. Nonetheless, a modest and predetermined level of R&D funding has the potential for generating substantial long-term paybacks. For example, IS departments that initiated data dictionary projects expecting only improvements in internal efficiency were later rewarded by the much more powerful benefits of a corporate information custodial tool. Not every chief executive appreciates this kind of opportunity, however. It is the IS manager's job to explain the need for R&D funding to senior management.

Ongoing Cost Estimations   Every IS project must be justified on the basis of two kinds of costs: one time, which are the most immediate and visible kind and which are easily planned for, and ongoing costs, that must be factored in to offset benefits in the financial analysis. The straightforward task is to consider both kinds of costs during the project investigation phase; the difficult task is to ensure that these costs are not forgotten during implementation. For example, if eventual computer-operations support and programmer maintenance are needed for a new computer system, not only must these be provided at the appropriate time, but the ongoing nature of such support must be understood at the point of approval of the project so that later support resource approval will have a specific, clearly understood basis.

ORGANIZING

A key IS manager duty is organizing groups' activities so as to ensure efficiency. By identifying tasks and responsibilities and combining similar activities, IS managers avoid such unnecessary barriers as ineffective communication and conflicting duties. Organizing is a fundamental means of integrating the performance of the IS department, and it can strongly influence the nature of IS products. Chapter 11 is devoted to a detailed examination of IS organizational issues.

When considering organizational structures, a balance must be struck between two contrary directions. On the one hand, the more specialized a group is, the more effectively it can accomplish specific goals. On the other hand, too many subunits contribute to inefficiency in several ways. First, some diversity in the tasks people perform daily is known to contribute to job enrichment and challenge. Moreover, specialization may create groups too small to work effectively and lacking backup or a solid group process. Management skills are not easily bred in an overly compartmentalized environment. Specialization also tends to create many small units that experience ongoing communication difficulties. Finally, if many organizational components are to be orchestrated, multiple organizational levels and an attendant management structure are necessary. The resultant overhead costs can significantly hamper organizational flexibility, responsiveness, and efficiency.

Building Around Existing Skills

In most business settings, and particularly in IS organizations, an organizational structure is already in place, even if it is only an informal one. One common means of organizing is to pair functional groups' skills with specific tasks. For example, the technical support group may have responsibility for office equipment (such as telephones, copiers, and word processors) because its skills are effective in meeting this responsibility. However, another school of thought holds that organizational structures should be designed without consideration for existing people and skills; no organization can depend on the same people forever, and tailoring too much to existing talents may make it hard to identify talents that are needed but currently absent. The responsibility for decisions that strike a balance between these two extremes rests with the IS manager.

Building Job Content

The job is the basic building block of the organization. Deciding what goes into each discrete job is a significant organizational decision, one that is guided by an implicit philosophy. One of these is the choice between a manager and a "doer." For example, intermediate-level departmental positions could consist of pure management duties or could include other functional duties, depending on how the IS manager thinks about this mix. In some companies the concept of worker/manager is deemed appropriate at certain (but not all) levels. Project managers, for example, might be expected to perform systems-analysis functions. In other companies the reigning philosophy is that managing is a specialized, full-time job; functional work is delegated to skilled workers.

Another fundamental job-content choice is between specialization and generalization. Many organizations feel that a generalist strategy, whereby there is enough functional variety in each group to challenge and develop diverse skills in employees, provides more flexibility and helps employees to advance. Others counter that such a strategy prevents the acquisition of comprehensive knowledge in particular areas and inhibits individual progress on the learning curve. The debate turns, of course, on productivity—and here the numbers argue both ways. Exhibit 9-8 contrasts the generalized versus the specialized approach to organizational structure in the IS department.

Timing the Organizational Changes

IS managers face the tricky problem of deciding how often to adjust the organizational structure of their departments. Adjusting too seldom invites the frustration and inefficiency that goes hand in hand with an inappropriate framework. Yet adjusting too frequently is even more detrimental. New organizational structures are intimidating to some employees. During the adjustment period, work will be done slowly and cautiously. Another disadvantage of too many organizational changes is that employees' reliance on a formal structure will disappear. If someone is not sure how a task should be accomplished or knows that the organizational frame in which it is to be accomplished might soon change, this person may begin relying on informal systems. This tendency can make an organization very personality dependent.

Obviously, the extent of the organizational change is an important criterion. For instance, reassigning minor responsibility for document distribution is less disruptive than restructuring the whole user request-handling process. Moreover, the climate in which adjustments take place also influences the nature and quantity of organizational changes. A security-conscious environment may reject changes of too threatening a nature.

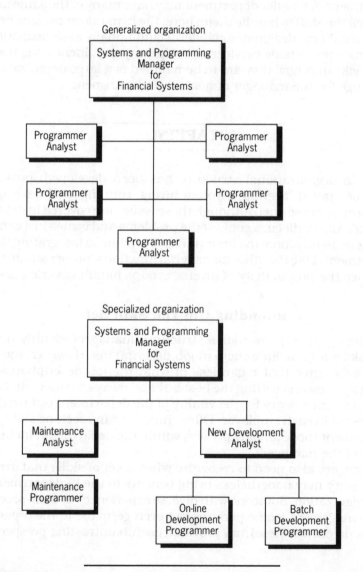

EXHIBIT 9-8 Specialized versus generalized organization of the IS department.

Size Constraints

It goes without saying that the organizing function is affected by the size of the IS department. What may not be as obvious is that a larger organization does not simply have more people to put into organizational boxes; it also has additional tasks that have to be formalized. Identifying, justifying the need for, and assigning these tasks is a major organizational challenge facing the manager of a large IS department. A smaller department may have many of the same tasks but lack the staff to handle them; here, the IS manager assigns broad responsibilities, designates collateral (additionally assigned) duties, and procures outside services to bridge any gap. Identifying necessary tasks and how they are to be handled is a large organizational challenge for the manager of a small IS department.

STAFFING

Once an organizational structure has been developed, positions must be staffed. Staffing involves hiring, training, and developing appropriate personnel. Although these issues are covered in detail in Chapter 12, we discuss some of the problems and issues in a general way here, to reenforce the importance of staffing in integrating the IS department. Like the other managerial functions, proper staffing can enhance the productivity of diverse groups handling varied tasks.

Rounding Out the Skill Set

In defining the organization's structure, managers identify necessary skills and include them in job descriptions. However, most IS managers agree that regardless of what the job description says, filling a job means getting the best but not always a perfect fit. Some talents are necessary for the vitality of the department but need not be present in each employee. Often, hiring means seeking skills that supplement those already present within the department, including those of the manager.

Managers also need to recognize when a set of skills that are not mandatory may nonetheless bring benefits to the IS department or the organization. Someone with diverse experiences in data-processing management (some perhaps not even germane to the organization's current business) may provide a useful contrasting perspective.

Hiring for Teamwork

No amount of job specification can guarantee the much-needed chemistry among IS department members. Much depends on personal goals. Even the internal promotion of a person who has been an ideal team member can upset the balance if this person's newly sparked ambition makes him or her less cooperative. One factor in building a team is to plan for diversity in roles. No group can easily accommodate too many informal leaders, visionaries, rule enforcers, or followers. Each team needs an assortment of qualities.

Hiring from Inside or Outside

New positions or vacancies are filled either from inside the department or organization or from outside. Each source of personnel has its strong and weak points, and a balance is needed. Although a person hired from within has not done the job before, he or she does bring a proven track record and strong knowledge of the organization and (it is hoped) its systems. In contrast, an outside hire will not have an "institutional memory" but is more likely to bring fresh ideas and new approaches. Depending on their background, outside hires also may elicit a higher degree of respect, at least initially, from those who will depend on them. (Of course, this respect may be counterbalanced by some resentment from peers or those with aspirations for the job.) And too much outside hiring exerts a negative effect on the manager's ability to motivate employees or to retain veteran employees.

<u>DIRECTING</u>

Once departmental goals are spelled out and the right people are in place with clear, interlocking responsibilities, it is time for IS department specialists to do their assigned work. As this work proceeds, the IS manager must direct all activities. Directing is a management function that is powerfully affected by decision-making styles and practices. The quality and appropriateness of a manager's directing hinges on two factors: how he or she delegates authority and how he or she makes decisions.

Delegation

Delegation is the deliberate assignment to others of authority and control in specific contexts. A major part of the IS manager's job is to delegate tasks and spell out appropriate boundaries. For example, authority may be delegated to a project manager to commit financial and human resources to the project within certain approved bounds. The IS manager retains control of decision making; he or she is in effect the "court of appeals" for unpopular decisions. Although authority can be delegated, responsibility cannot. The senior manager will always be responsible for the consequences of subordinates' actions and decisions.

Decision-making

Within the technical discipline of IS, the decision-making responsibilities of IS managers are ambiguous. It is true that senior managers are often not as technically current or sophisticated as their more specialized subordinates. However, IS managers typically have considerable familiarity with technical issues, are capable of understanding those issues, and are likely to have made important technical decisions before. More importantly, they understand the business context of decision-making and can look broadly at this context.

One of the most difficult decisions facing the IS manager is determining those IS projects that need departmental backing at the executive level. Although user projects may be chosen by users or other senior executives (with possible input from the IS manager), deciding on internal projects is the responsibility of the IS manager, who must justify the necessary resources. The problem is that many internal projects are important, and most have sponsors who feel that they are critical. Ultimately, the IS manager must perform a cost-benefit analysis or other value measurement to decide which ones have payback. For those projects proposed on a "must-do" basis, the IS manager must test the long-term necessity of each one and decide if any are deferable. The manager must also test project proposals to determine if there are cheaper alternatives.

IS managers are caught in the middle of two camps. Sometimes businesses inappropriately overlook long-term problems that immediate investment would avoid. In such cases the IS manager should be a persuasive but objective advocate for the professional position of the IS department's technical personnel. Just as often, though, the manager will see that the right decision is the one that is less technically rigorous. Here the manager must not only influence the decision making but must also explain the final decision to the IS professionals so that they are able to accept and support it.

Decision-making Styles   Many IS managers take their cues on decision-making styles from their staff. By evaluating the staff carefully, a manager can determine which styles are the most effective. A range can be successful; the choice hinges on the situation. Exercising executive privilege with respect to technical decisions—for example, overriding the judgments of personnel with far more technical expertise—is an ill-advised decision-making style. Leaving major decisions to subordinates who are not ready for the pressure of responsibility or for attendant political problems is another example: the manager with such a laissez-faire style fails to direct such employees appropriately and effectively. In such situations the IS manager must be highly conscious of options in his or her decision-making behavior.

Consistency is a prerequisite for effective decision-making. If the IS manager makes decisions arbitrarily, staff members will have trouble knowing how to act or react. The best decision-making styles are supportive, which means that the manager makes it clear who is to assume certain responsibilities—including that of decision making itself. If the chosen decision-maker is the IS manager, then his or her decisions should be timely, clearly communicated, and readily seen as appropriate. If the decision making is left to a subordinate, that person's decision should be supported in all but the most severe circumstances. If it must be overruled, extra effort should go into reestablishing the employee's confidence in his or her decision-making skills.

Because IS-related decisions are frequently influenced by diverse factors, decision making is sometimes undertaken by a group that may not actually make decisions but can contribute strongly to them. Facing a decision on the choice of technology, the IS manager often promotes discussions with his or her staff on the merits and flaws of various options. In formal environments a study team may be commissioned to collect and analyze information and make a recommendation. Even though the IS manager makes the ultimate decision, the staff contributes important information on which the final choice is based. Such participation not only helps improve the quality of departmental decisions but also can plant support for final managerial decisions. (This participatory process should not, however, reenforce strong ownership of any one option by a staff member, a situation that can engender hostility toward an unfavorable decision.)

Developing Decision-making in Others Delegation is the first, crucial step in helping subordinates develop their decision-making skills. It is important for the IS manager to review decisions with subordinates and to identify those that were especially sound, those not as strong as they could have been, and, of course, those that were arbitrary or brought about problems. In encouraging subordinates' decision-making, managers sometimes overlook the options of doing nothing or of waiting, as well as many other less obvious but effective alternatives, such as role-playing or mentoring. Moreover political and business-context factors, unforseen contingencies, and various long-term issues are frequently overlooked or minimized by inexperienced managers who tend to fix on immediate, obvious questions or issues when they delegate decision-making. Experienced managers know that many decisions, especially long-term ones, are formed by diverse, interrelated issues.

The most important component of effective decision-making is confidence. This can be built and protected only by encouraging managers and professionals to make careful choices and then stand behind them. IS managers must give their employees support; if they do not, they jeopardize subordinates' confidence in their decisions. Of course, in doing so, managers must be willing to accept the consequences of faulty decision making by subordinates.

Techniques for Decision-Making   One straightforward decision-making technique is to use comparisons. IS managers frequently look to other similar IS departments to review comparable decisions and their results. Peer environments are an important source of data. As long as the basis for the eventual decision is spelled out in advance, the comparative process can help in surfacing important factors and establishing the right decision.

Management by objectives (MBO) is another methodology helpful to managers attempting to specify who is to decide what. With this technique a manager and subordinate mutually agree on departmental and individual goals that support and are consistent with stated plans. Although MBO is a planning and control-oriented technique, it does spell out areas in which subordinates should make important decisions. As such, it encourages participative decision making and allows close coordination between manager and subordinate. Ground rules for maintaining a common direction for all departmental decisions can be specified at the same time that objectives are agreed on, thus giving both decision maker and supervisor a sense of order.

Maintaining a Corporate Focus   Part of directing involves recognizing functional issues influenced by corporate plans and policies and making decisions in terms of this link. This is far more complicated than simply keeping the organization's interests in mind; the interests of the IS department's staff must be considered and accommodated. The task becomes one of making and encouraging decisions that are in the best interests of both the department and the organization and selecting effective compromises when conflict becomes inevitable.

Communicating

Communicating is a crucial function with major implications for the overall direction of IS departmental activity. The manager's task is to ensure that internal information, such as applications knowledge and technical plans, is disseminated both within the department and to those users and managers whose jobs depend on the timely and accurate receipt of such information. Communicating thus refers to the distribution not just of computer reports but also of project status information, systems functionality data, IS resource information, and similar topics that depend more on human than on machine delivery. Moreover, professionals within the IS department also need information from users, senior management, vendors, and others external to the department. And even within the department, different functions need to be coordinated—to communicate. Good communication is not important only because it can guarantee the success of a particular product, but also because employees' sense of organizational identity and belonging depends on knowing what is going on beyond them.

Written Communication Written communication has the advantage of being permanent, self-documenting, and readily referenced, if not always precise. This is true of paper or electronic documents, such as electronic mail. However, written communication does not lend itself effectively to two-way exchanges and requires extra effort for the sender.

Written communication can be either scheduled or unscheduled. Examples of scheduled communication are project status reports or department project completion reports produced once a month. Occasionally these are formatted like project documentation, to make their preparation easier and to aid the reader in understanding them. Because many technical professionals either do not express themselves well in writing or prefer not to spend their time writing, formatted documents or prompt-driven on-line tools and other scheduled, formal communications ease the process of document preparation for the technical professional.

Unscheduled documents are produced as needed to elicit a decision, inform others about a project's status, document developments, and so on. Managers need to know when such communication is appropriate and when it may be extraneous or cause more harm than good. Technical professionals tend to underuse unscheduled communication and may be made uncomfortable if asked to use it consistently.

Meetings The telephone permits exchanges between two (sometimes more) people and is a standard, well-understood fixture in the modern office. An outgrowth of telephones, voice messaging is used much as is a written document but eases the burden of preparation. However, because IS communication frequently involves a number of people and because dialogues are desirable, group gatherings are normally required. Traditionally such gatherings are physical, although technology allows other approaches (such as telephone conference calls or video teleconferencing).

In the IS department the use of periodic staff meetings and department meetings can ensure that information is passed consistently and in such a way as to improve departmental coordination. Yet such meetings, which involve peers and highlight issues of professional interest, are too often viewed as tedious and unproductive. Meetings with groups of outsiders have a worse reputation. The problem is that many meetings tend to be of secondary importance to IS professionals and of critical importance to system users. During the initial stages of a project, IS team members need user input to understand the specifications to which they are to build. This gathering of data normally occurs fairly quickly; the process has become very procedural. After this, meetings are usually held to keep all team members (mostly the users) informed. Users tend to depend upon meetings as the only way of staying in touch with IS activities; IS professionals tend to look on them as an unnecessary interruption of their important work. Moreover, users are frequently more skilled at participating in meetings than are IS professionals.

The task for the IS or project manager is to keep communications flowing without burdening the technical professionals. Written communication helps, but it does not allow for satisfying feedback. One approach is to appoint a delegate to represent the IS department in meetings with users. This offers the advantages of releasing several professionals from an obligation to spend their time in meetings. However, users may feel that their input in such a forum is not receiving adequate response. A typical problem is that it is difficult to respond to user input during the system construction phase because the IS department's latitude is limited by commitment to a set design. Nevertheless, user frustration during the early stages of a project can seriously influence user reactions to the final results. Communicating with users is thus a delicate and critical task.

How Much Is Too Much?   As we have seen, IS professionals often have an aversion to communication because they do not see it as an important part of their job. For them, the main goals are designing, constructing, implementing, and operating systems. They recognize that communication plays a role in accomplishing these goals, but they tend to feel that it is overdone.

They may, in fact, be right—especially in light of the number of meetings held regardless of whether there is anything to discuss. Clearly, communicating time takes away from work time. And sometimes meetings and memos are used to exercise unnecessary influence, to satisfy curiosity, or merely to cover the fact that a project is in a phase where some team members have very little to do.

IS managers should not let the demands of communication needlessly drain the efficiency of the department. However, they must at the same time remain sensitive to the real need for adequate communication.

Communications in Place of Progress   In an environment that places a premium on consensus decision making, strong disagreements or impasses can be stressful. It is sometimes easier to take ambiguous action rather than unpleasant but direct action that will break the deadlock. This is especially true in terms of interaction with users. IS professionals in situations of conflict frequently call a meeting, solicit extraneous data, or write summarizing memos in the vague hope that such stalling actions will somehow break the logjam.

This is not what communicating is about. Communication can be used effectively in such circumstances, but only if those involved are prepared to work toward a genuine resolution of conflict. A memo to a common executive asking for a verdict, or a meeting ,or a presentation with a clear goal of changing someone's mind or proposing a compromise are examples of productive communication efforts. For IS professionals who do not understand that consistent communicating can be a productive use of their time, the IS manager's role is to provide appropriate instruction and to serve as a good example.

Secrecy and Communication   Open communication of information has the obvious advantage of providing a sense of participation and belonging. Unfortunately, openness is not always possible. Many times it is unwise to announce plans that may involve sensitive business decisions or secrets before those plans are to be implemented. Once certain plans are approved, it may be necessary to avoid spreading news of them any further than required. IS professionals may have to learn to live without continual full disclosures from senior management.

The IS manager who seeks to be more of an insider must learn what can be appropriately and safely communicated so as to keep certain key department members prepared for certain eventualities. In potential merger situations, for instance, technical analysis and business-systems evaluation are increasingly recognized as pivotal tasks and those professionals responsible for these tasks must learn how to be privy to confidential information without revealing it.

CONTROLLING

The IS manager monitors and controls the output of the department not so much by overseeing work but by evaluating key outputs measured at predetermined points. To know what to measure and what measurements indicate good or bad performance, objectives must be established. Different performance objectives are required for different processes, beginning with major departmental efforts and eventually extending to individual performance. Establishing performance objectives means that three kinds of goals be defined: project, operational, and internal. These are briefly discussed next.

1. *Project Goals* Each project has unique goals. Although spending and human-resource-usage goals can be defined, it is the project's functional specifications—an extended version of the statement of project objectives—that are measured directly. These specifications constitute a user description of the end product.

Estimates of compliance with functional specifications are necessarily subjective based, as they sometimes are on judgmental assessment of compliance with inexact needs. Nonetheless, project specifications are one of the most important yardsticks against which performance is measured.

2. *Operational Goals* Once production systems are constructed and installed, the IS department usually has responsibility for operating them. The department's performance is then measured on the basis of the timeliness and precision with which these systems are operated. Minimizing the number of abnormal end of jobs (abends) or restarts is the performance objective in a run or batch environment.

Project goals tend to be satisfied once and are somewhat adjustable; operational goals tend to be repetitive and inflexible because users depend on the system to do their jobs. For on-line systems, operational goals are systems availability (according to some predetermined goal) and solid performance (e.g., solid response time or even machine utilization below a certain threshold). With all systems, reports and data updates as well as data accuracy are important operational goals.

3. *Internal Goals* To maintain a general level of service and ensure that general support exists, many internal programs and activities are required. For example, because users require protected data, a program of backup and recovery is necessary. Other examples include supporting operating system software, network management, and administration and management of technology so as to comply with needs for documentation, structured techniques, and technical approvals. To ensure protection against risks, to guarantee completeness, and to deliver user products in a controlled manner, the IS department must perform such tasks even when users do not understand or even agree to them.

The Input/Output Equation

Taken as a whole, IS can be seen as a series of processes to which inputs in the form of resources are applied to achieve the desired output or benefits. Controlling entails choosing which inputs and outputs can be measured most easily and accurately and which are most appropriate for a particular environment.

One approach to controlling is to set performance goals for the results of IS department efforts and to try to minimize the inputs necessary to achieve these goals. Inputs are easily measured; they include capital expenditures, operating expenses, staffing, and usage of hardware and software.

Another approach to controlling is to establish inputs through some budgeting or project-approval process and then to concentrate on maximizing output. As output, certain services, report compliance, data accuracy, and so forth are reasonably straightforward to measure; unfortunately, however, these outputs tend to be nonnegotiable and in these areas it is best to try to minimize inputs. New programs or systems offer real opportunities to improve output. The measurements here tend to be more subjective, and the benefits usually come long after the investment input. For this reason, the task of measuring overall output is accomplished at a strategic level and undertaken periodically on a companywide basis. (A systems audit will usually accomplish this.)

For more immediate measurements of output, other tools are used to gauge objectively the levels of support. One tool is a user satisfaction survey, which not only gives an overall (though superficial) view of the IS department's effectiveness but also can point to specific areas that need improvement or at least more attention. A more formal method is the user service contract, a specific, point-by-point agreement with each user area that is drawn up before the performance period and that everyone signs. It itemizes quantifiable outputs that the IS department is to provide and that will then be measured. The contract process is very detailed but lays out the rules fairly and in advance.

If input can be quantified and output identified (even subjectively), then one might wonder whether efficiency can be measured, as it is the ratio of output to input. Surprisingly, efficiency is not the best indication of the IS department's performance. Ignoring the difficulties that differing units of measure cause, there are several reasons why attempts to measure efficiency may not work. First, finding a basis of comparison is difficult. Year-to-year comparisons of input\output ratios may be appropriate, but there is no way to factor in extraneous environmental factors. An important problem is the fact that current outputs or benefits come from previous inputs or investments. The ratio during one period does not necessarily reflect a causal relationship. In fact, efficiency measures during any single period can be misleading, as it is always possible to maximize short-term efficiency by incurring long term costs.

Probably the most important reason for not measuring efficiency is that most organizations do not try to optimize the efficiency of their IS departments. The most efficient level might be well beyond what a company can afford or well below what it might need. The goal is rather to minimize input for a given mandatory level of output and/ or to maximize output for a given limited level of input. (As it turns out, the results of doing either fall within a confined range.) In short, the IS manager's focus needs to be effectiveness, not efficiency: that is, how well the IS department is serving the organization.

Key Information Systems Performance Measures

A helpful and increasingly more common measurement approach is to view the IS department as a full-function company. Just as financial analysts use ratios to determine the health of a company, so the IS manager can use selected measurements appropriate to each function to determine the performance of the IS department in general. David Norton (1981) suggests just such an approach and employs specific measurements, as shown in Exhibit 9-9. The ratios of personnel to hardware and software costs, repair/maintenance to hardware costs, education and training to personnel costs, supervisor to worker costs, and so forth may prove equally meaningful. In environments where IS departments bill for their services, performance might even be measured in terms of department profitability. Collectively, such figures constitute an "annual report" on the IS department and yield meaningful trend data when compared from year to year.

Charging

Charge back is a commonly used method of developing a common denominator for inputs and outputs and for building a framework for user/IS department cooperation. With charge back, every element of service—from the cost of a report to an hour of programmer time—is quantified and "sold" to users. Charge back is somewhat different from cost allocation or cost spreading, as it provides users with freedom of choice. It also lends itself to joint planning by users and the IS department, makes conformance easy to measure, and allows for comparisons to other resource alternatives, such as outside services. The manner in which charge back is used should be dictated by the strategic position of the information technology, the stage of IS development, and the level of the CIO development (McKinnon and Kallman, 1987). Exhibit 9-10 illustrates the kind of charge back appropriate for each state.

Charge back has certain potential drawbacks, however. Once resources have been scheduled in response to user plans, the IS department's latitude to make changes and especially to add services is limited in the short run. The method is very procedural and, like any accounting procedure, somewhat elaborate. The costs developed, especially for computer resources, are not immediately understood by laypeople. Above all, charge back presents some real strategic dilemmas for IS management, primarily because it puts IS-related decision making and cost justification squarely in the hands of the user. (There are strong arguments for and against this. Some suggest that the propriety of charge back is dependent on the IS development stage of F.W. McFarlan (see Chapter 2), i.e., turnaround/no charge back, support/charge back, etc.) Consequentially, the IS department should ensure that individual beneficiaries take responsibility for resource use but should not try to "pass the buck" to users for the justification of companywide programs. Depending on how overhead is spread out and rates computed (e.g., based on full or partial utilization), costs users ultimately incur can be made to appear generous or onerous. Bearing this in mind, IS

Perspective	Typical Measures

Marketing

The marketing perspective enables us to focus on the most difficult question: How well are we doing when viewed through the eyes of our customers? Information needed for measurement is botained through normal market research techniques including customer surveys, consumer panels, and statistical analysis.

Market Segments. The overall market must be divided into specific segments.

Market Penetration. The current use of information systems can be contrasted with their potential in specific areas. In studies we have found that leading-edge DP organizations achieve market penetrations of up to 70%. Trailing-edge organizations, on the other hand, have been found as low as 10%.

Strategic Alignment. Critical success variables tell us which market segments are most important to the success of the overall business. Strategic alignment demonstrates the extent to which our penetration matches the important segments. We should see penetration of at least 70% in a critical success segment.

Customer Satisfaction. User surveys (generally administered with questionnaires) measure the perceptions of our customers concerning the quality of service. To be of value, specific criteria such as timeliness, accuracy, and reliability should be evaluated. Such surveys frequently identify problems in specific market segments with specific systems.

Financial

The way in which an organization spends money reflects its underlying structure. Financial analysts discovered long ago that appropriately constructed financial ratios can provide insight into the

Cost Growth Index. The rate of growth in data-processing costs should be normalized to the growth rate of the overall organization. An index greater than 1.0 indicates that data processing is growing faster than the overall business. This enlightens us as to which stage the organization is in and the likely set of management issues it is facing.

Maintenance Norms. The ratio of maintenance costs to production costs allows us to ascertain the levels being spent on maintenance. Most organizations average around 0.4 across their portfolio. Rarely, higher levels are found. Lower levels, however, are frequently found, indicating that maintenance is being neglected.

relative health of its underlying structure. Information for these measures is generally found in the financial management system.

Labor Intensity. The ratio of production labor costs to equipment costs demonstrates the labor or capital intensity of the production environment. The ratio normally averages about 1.0 with well-run organizations ranging from 0.7 to 1.2 depending on the industry.

Drop-down Ratio. Development dollars that are being spent this year should result in production dollars being spent next year, and in the the years to come. Our experience indicates that this ratio should be approximately 0.5. This measure provides us with a high-level indicator of the productivity of development efforts.

Engineering

The engineering perspective allows us to examine the quality of the product from a technical viewpoint. The tools of the product engineer are generally based on detailed statistical analysis of various product characteristics.

Portfolio Life Cycle. Computer systems, like any other product, have a life cycle. Nolan, Norton & Company research has found that well-designed systems require approximately 2 years to "burn in" after they become operational. After 6 years, even a well-maintained system begins to deteriorate. Generally, the system should be considered for redesign after 8 years. These patterns should be reflected in an organization's portfolio.

Maintenance Profiles. Statistical profiles showing the levels of maintenance required by individual systems help identify specific problems. General trends can be observed when systems are classified by age, technology, etc.

Manufacturing

The computer room is the manufacturing department of data processing. Our main concern here is the efficiencyand service levels with which this resource is used. Generally, data are drawn from special-purpose systems within computer operations.

Response Time. The average response time of an online system during peak demand, or the on-time delivery rate for batch systems, provides an indication of how well user requirements are being satisfied.

Capacity Utilization. The degree to which capacity is utilized during peak periods provides a high-level measure of the need for future expansion.

Personnel

The DP human resource is in short supply and is extremely mobile. Companies must make a major commitment to attracting and retaining this resource. Information regarding performance measures in this area is obtained from special-purpose systems or studies conducted by the personnel department.

Staff Turnover. The annual turnover rate of staff professionals provides an indicator of the security of this resource. Industry turnover rates average approximately 28%. Observing internal trends is much more meaningful than comparing one company with another.

Salary Competitiveness. Through special studies, the average salary paid for a given job can be indexed to those offered by competitors. Such a measure allows management to ensure that this variable is being consciously managed.

Training Allocation. Examining a ratio demonstrating the percentage of available time devoted to professional training and develpment can determine whether the training allocation is adequate.

EXHIBIT 9-9 The annual report: A program of key performance measures.

Source: David Norton, "If You Can Measure It You Can Manage It," Stage by Stage vol. 3, no. 3, Fall 1981], p. 3. Copyright 1981 Nolan, Norton & Co., Lexington, MA. All rights reserved. Reprinted with permission.

managers could steer user decisions. For example, batch systems can be made to appear unattractive when compared to on-line systems, and development projects can seem to be very costly when compared to end-user computing.

A more fundamental argument against charge back is that charging for in-house services is intrinsically discouraging, so much so as to diminish IS resource usage. If this is true, one approach would be to implement selective charge back. Operational costs could be charged but development costs maintained as a corporate expense. (Of course, this assumes that charge back is not being implemented as an "off-the-books" program and that costs are actually being charged to user budgets.)

With a charge-back system in place, an organization has the option of choosing to measure the IS department on the basis of either cost efficiency or service responsiveness. If the latter basis is chosen, the IS department might be treated as a cost center, and its short-term savings are passed on as reduced rates to users. Budget overruns would increase the rates to users, but all requested services

4 Flexible Price Charge Back
Strategic, mature, proactive.
Prices set to influence resource
consumption and maximize benefits
at low levels of management.

3 Standard Cost Charge Back
Turnaround, integration, coalescence.
Future costs are fixed to give users
more control in budgeting and tracking
DP expenses.

2 Average Cost Charge Back
Factory, control, coalescence. Prices
are based on past usage and costs
creating fluctuations beyond user
control. User is charged "hard-money."

1 Allocation Charge Back
Support, initiation, reactive. Prices are
set to educate high level users about
DP costs, "soft-money" charge.

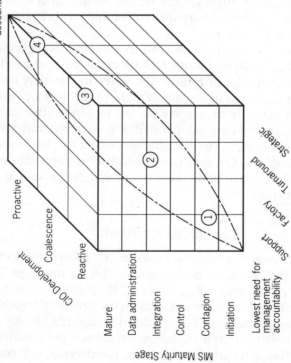

EXHIBIT 9-10 Relating chargeback systems to computer environments.

Source: William P. McKinnon and Ernest A. Kallman. "Mapping Chargeback Systems to Organizational Environments." *MIS Quarterly* vol. 11. no. 1. March. 1987. p. 13. Reprinted by special permission. Copyright 1987 by the Society for Information Management and the Management Information Systems Research Center at the University of Minnesota.

would be provided. In contrast, an IS profit center reflects savings as its own efficiencies and answers for excessive spending. The profit-center option offers a businesslike challenge to the IS manager, but many organizations feel that quality of service and long-term benefits might suffer if the IS manager is encouraged to put department profits ahead of service.

Quality Assurance Programs

To control the quality of systems developed for operational use or any program allowing for the manipulation of important corporate information, a separate, specialized quality assurance (QA) program is implemented. Usually this program is administered by persons who work closely with a systems-development methodology (described in Chapter 13) to provide a focus for, emphasis on, and/or enforcement of systems accuracy, reliability, and integrity. QA personnel create a comprehensive standards manual that guides project team members through the development process. The QA group also makes sure that various project approvals are gained in time and in the right order.

QA groups can play an important role in managing separate review processes so that disagreements can be resolved and productive compromises struck, if appropriate. QA staff can also play the same role in the important area of testing. Whether they develop thorough test criteria or actually run tests so as to stress the proposed systems, QA personnel can independently guarantee that products work according to design. Finally, after a product has been accepted and implemented, the QA group can conduct a postevaluation to ensure that the promised benefits of the project have been achieved at the specified costs.

Trends in Control

Apart from implementing controls that directly govern and indirectly influence specific levels of performance, the IS manager is also accountable for reviewing the effects of IS support in a broader context. Unlike detailed performance reviews for which benchmarks can be developed, meaningful generalized standards are difficult to establish. One method that introduces this generic perspective is the extended use of budget comparisons (expressed as ratios of company revenues). Usually some allowance is made for industry variations. Exhibits 9-11 and 9-12 are examples of such comparisons.

As the exhibits show, there are clear differences among industries that are explainable by the ways in which various industries use IS.

EXHIBIT 9-11 Budget summary and comparison.

	1987				1988			
Industry	IS as a Percentage of Revenue	IS Budget ($M)	Revenue	Profits	IS as a Percentage of Revenue	IS Budget ($M)	Revenue	Profits
Banking and finance	4.5	$3904.4	$86968.2	$4867.4	0.5[a]	$4,512	$902,488[a]	$(2,263)
Electronics	3.7	4839.8	131274.4	8121.4	4.0	5,836	145,909	11,668
Food and beverage	1.6	1657.1		6282.8	1.6	1,819	113,675	6,784
Health care and pharmaceutical	0.6	270.6	48789.5	4043.6	1.1	576	52,248	5,004
Industrial and automotive	2.7	7432.4	273394.5	10490.5	2.7	7,748	286,950	12,804
Insurance	1.7	1678.5	100115.5	5182.4	2.2	2,653	120,597	6,309
Metal and metal products	1.1	495.0	45083.3	-1572.7	1.2	622	51,849	1,275
Petroleum and Petrochemicals	1.3	3312.3	261975.1	10324.1	1.3	3,842	295,537	5,647
Process	1.6	1572.8	99029.9	5167.7	1.7	1,912	112,446	6,272
Retail	0.2	327.7	167211.4	3917.9	0.4	670	167,499	4,768
Transportation	1.3	712.7	54994.5	89.5	1.3	757	58,210	2,762
Utilities	1.0	1189.0	121687.4	10172.5	2.0	2,526	121,278	12,269
Total	1.8	27392.3	1494858.0	67087.1	1.9[b]	33,473[c]	1,531,198	73,299

[a] Assets rather than revenues are indicated in the banking and finance category.

[b] Based on revenue and budget totals from all industry sectors other than banking and finance.

[c] Includes the banking and finance expenditures.

Note: Each category represents 10 large companies in that industry.

Source: Excerpted from *Datamation*, September 1, 1987, copyright © 1987 by Cahners Publishing Company.

199

Industry	1987				1988			
	Hardware	Software	Personnel	Overhead	Hardware	Software	Personnel	Overhead
Banking and finance	31	17	49	3	32	7	47	14
Electronics	29	10	50	11	28	9	50	13
Food and beverage	37	13	40	10	35	14	40	11
Health care and pharmaceutical	25	11	55	9	30	10	51	9
Industrial and automotive	42	8	43	7	43	7	43	7
Insurance	36	9	48	7	36	11	44	9
Metal and metal products	31	9	52	8	28	9	54	9
Petroleum and petrochemicals	34	9	46	11	34	11	47	8
Process	40	12	38	10	36	9	41	14
Retail	40	10	42	8	39	11	40	10
Transportation	35	10	50	5	32	7	50	11
Utilities	22	17	54	7	26	8	53	13
Total	34	11	47	8	33	9	47	11

EXHIBIT 9-12 Distribution of IS funds as a percentage of total expenditures.

Note: Each cateegory represents 10 large companies in that industry consistent from year to year.

Source: Excerpted from *Datamation*, September 1, 1987. Copyright © 1987 by Cahners Publishing Company.

Banking and finance use large amounts of information technology, relative to their revenues, to manage their extensive asset bases and provide customer service in a competitive environment. Electronics, largely computer companies, by virtue of being newly developed, practice what they preach and use information technology in sophisticated ways. Retail, in contrast, tends to spend comparatively little on its central operations as compared to the large revenues it generates; much of its technology is decentralized at separate stores. The numbers underlying these percentages can reveal other typical practices, some of which Exhibit 9-12 highlights. The food and beverage industry's high spending on packaged software as compared to the utilities industries' high personnel costs is a function of the need of the latter to customize many applications. The industrial and automotive industry spends heavily on hardware driven by heavy use of supercomputers for modeling new designs and manufacturing technologies such as computer-aided design (CAD) and high speed local area networks on factory floors.

Changes are instructive in that they highlight trends to be aware of. Although all industries seem generally to be increasing their investments in IS, the insurance industries increase is especially strong and seems to be directed heavily toward software with disproportionate increases in personnel. This might indicate a change in a personnel-biased pattern traditionally associated with the insurance industry and IS.

Obviously, isolated companies will differ on the basis of their growth experience, relative financial health, and corporate philosophy, but these trends are useful benchmarks. The IS manager should appreciate when variations from trend information represents a conscious and healthy corporate decision or an arbitrary or unhealthy deviation and be prepared to influence any necessary and appropriate changes.

Some Practical Concerns

There are many ways to control performance, and sound managerial judgment is a prerequisite for IS managers who choose and implement controls. For controls to work effectively and nondisruptively, they have to be well known and understood. The best results are gained if controls are consistently used over several years so that project managers and other professionals know what to expect from them. Sometimes special situations call for customized controls, and as circumstances change, controls may need to be altered. Periodic adjustments and changes are certainly appropriate; however, controls should not be seen as a throttle that can be quickly or carelessly used for fine-tuning. Annual spending cycles can be distorted if project spending approvals and budgetary guidelines are constantly revised.

IS project managers should be delegated enough authority to deal with surprises, conflicts in guidance, and other management-related issues. Although controls give structure and help guide an activity to its conclusion, they can also rob it of spontaneity, saddle it with costly overhead, and stifle potential creativity and shortcuts—all of which argues against too many controls on project managers.

The control function is the feedback loop into the management process that can trigger adjustments to plans, realignment of departmental organization, new staffing actions, increased communications, or even alterations to the control process itself. Managers need to review controls with an eye toward taking any corrective action that the controls seem to strongly suggest or prompt. In other words, controls are not merely a means of restricting what can or should be done; they are also—and equally importantly—a catalyst for action and change.

CONCLUSION

IS departments face a difficult challenge: to deliver as many benefits as possible from the array of information technology currently available. This challenge cannot be met without well-defined management skills. Only if activities are integrated through the managerial functions of planning, organizing, staffing, directing, and controlling will a positive outcome for specific projects (or even ongoing general operations) be possible.

The successful IS manager not only performs each managerial function well but also has an ability to assess new situations and know which function or combination of functions needs to be applied. This is a complex task—and one that is certain not to get any easier.

DISCUSSION QUESTIONS

1. How might an IS-related problem be analyzed to determine which management function might be exercised to achieve an appropriate solution?

2. What might some of the ratios mentioned in the discussion of department planning indicate to an observer?

3. Does the relative importance of the functions of management change for different stages of Nolan's and Gibson's stages of growth (see Chapter 2)?

4. What percentage of time should the IS manager devote to each of the functions of management? Should the total equal 100%?

5. Might other duties of the IS manager exist that make management functions less important than normal? What might some of these be?

6. What dangers exist in comparing a single company to the industry averages identified in Exhibits 9-11 and 9-12?

7. What methods might the IS manager use to cast departmental controls in a positive and motivating light?

8. Can communication technology have a productive or clarifying effect on the quantity or quality of IS professionals' communications?

9. What makes management of the IS activity different from management of other corporate areas—engineering, for instance?

REFERENCES

Klein, Mark M. (1987). "The Diebold Report: Seven Keys to Successful IS Planning," *Infosystems* (March), p. 58.

Lucas, Henry C., Jr., and Jon A. Turner (1982). "A Corporate Strategy for the Control of Information Processing," *Sloan Management Review* (Spring), pp. 25–36.

McKinnon, William P., and Ernest A. Kallman (1987). "Mapping Chargeback Systems to Organizational Environments," *MIS Quarterly* (March), pp. 5–19.

Nolan, Richard L. (1982). "Building the Company's Computer Architecture Strategic Plan," *Stage by Stage* (Nolan, Norton & Company, Lexington, MA), vol. 2, No. 4, p. 3.

Norton, David P. (1981). "The Annual Report: A Program of Key Performance Measures," "If You Can Measure It You Can Manage It," *Stage by Stage* (Nolan, Norton & Company, Lexington, MA), vol. 1, no. 3, p. 3.

"Industry by Industry IS Survey" (1988). *Datamation* (November 1), pp. 4–40.

ten

□

Functional Challenges and the Information Systems Manager

Challenges for Systems and Programming

Challenges for Operations

Challenges for Technical Support

Islands of Technology

General Functional Responsibilities

Conclusion

Discussion Questions

References

IS tasks and, consequently, IS departmental functions break down into the following areas:

- Systems and programming
- Operations
- Technical support

- Islands of technology
- General responsibilities

Certain specific challenges affect the management of each functional area. In this chapter we identify these challenges along with various industry trends and popular approaches to managing each area. We conclude with a look at general functional responsibilities.

CHALLENGES FOR SYSTEMS AND PROGRAMMING

Systems and programming, the group responsible for building an organization's information systems, is usually the most visible and "glamorous" part of the IS department. The following sections highlight some important systems and programming management options and call attention to specific management-related difficulties.

Analysis Versus Programming

Identifying systemic solutions to problems and technically constructing these solutions are such different tasks that they have traditionally been assigned to two different jobs, that of the analyst and that of the programmer. As applications development technology becomes less specialized and inaccessible and as the wisdom of putting the tools of solution in the problem solver's hand becomes more apparent, it is common to see a merger of these jobs—both to provide job enrichment and (in small environments, at least) to address an economic necessity. However, the original practice of separating analytical from programming tasks is still followed, especially in larger organizations. (In some cases analysis and programming are being moved back to the user, a phenomenon we discuss in Part IV). Different aspects of the development process are emphasized by the differing alignments of jobs and tasks, as Exhibit 10-1 shows.

In most environments the choice of organization of this functional area usually has been established by past practices. However, an awareness of how differing approaches work will benefit the IS manager who wants to get the most from a chosen strategy. In one environment, it may make sense to segregate the duties into two different jobs; in another environment merging them into one job type is preferable. When a chosen strategy has outlived its usefulness, the IS manager may choose to alter the strategy. However, as with any fundamental change in jobs and duties it should be undertaken with care and the expectation of a long transition period to fully effect the change.

Development Versus Maintenance

If the systems and programming area is seen as the glamorous side of the IS department, the development area is generally seen as the attractive, high-visibility side of systems and programming. Because developers build or install new systems and usually tackle broader business-systems design issues, many IS professionals believe that the development area offers greater latitude for practicing skills and more visibility for results. Curiously this greater latitude may tolerate lower skill levels than maintenance because it permits the builder to avoid areas of complexity in the design.

The tasks undertaken by the maintenance area differ from those in development for these reasons:

- They are smaller in size when measured in dollars.
- They are smaller in size when measured in repair time.
- They are limited to changing existing applications and/or
- To correcting system misfunctions.

Maintenance tasks usually require an intimate knowledge of applications, a facility for patching (usually old) technology, creativity in devising shortcut methods, and an ability to work quickly and under pressure to handle emergencies.

Development tasks, in contrast, call for longer-range vision and the ability to create (not to change), to communicate with a wide range of people, to work on long-term tasks, to train, and to consider broad alternatives. It is difficult for one person or group to handle

Analysts and Programmers	Analysts/Programmers
Promotes special technical skill concentration	More potential communication problems
Increased specialized efficiencies	Increased flexibility
Job conforms to specialized skills	Positioned for early consideration of technology
Allows segregation of duties	Streamlined Development

EXHIBIT 10-1 A comparison of job/task assignments in the systems and programming area.

both kinds of tasks, but splitting them up requires close communication between the groups (e.g., maintenance must not only understand new systems but should also have a say regarding the ease or difficulty in maintaining a prospective system).

It is a fairly consistent practice to assign junior systems and programming personnel to maintenance and more senior professionals to development. This ignores the fact that junior staff can often work more effectively in the more unconstrained technical environment of new systems, and senior professionals tend to be able to work quickly and creatively and to possess the sound knowledge of existing applications needed in maintenance. (maintenance is less tolerant of learning curves and early career mistakes than is development.) Reversing this traditional pattern would require extraordinary salesmanship on the part of the IS manager and a rebalancing of the relative emphasis placed on each function.

Project Management Versus Functional Caretaking

In a systems and programming area where development accounts for the bulk of available resources, it is not unusual for developmental activities to typify departmental practices—for instance, cost-benefit analyses, separate general and detail design steps, segregated testing, formal user sign-offs, and training steps. These project related activities rely heavily on written work, process controls, communication, attention to procedures, and committee decision making. (Such features could very easily be applied across the board to all systems and programming activity for the sake of consistency and convenience.)

In contrast, a department that is maintenance-oriented usually exhibits markedly different traits, often resembling a caretaker. There are few delay-causing approvals; decision making occurs at a lower level of management; there is less emphasis on elegance and more technical skills as opposed to application skills; and working relationships with operations are close.

Make Versus Buy Decisions

An analyst faced with a problem to be solved through a new application is often confronted with the question of whether the application system should be built or purchased. In some situations there is no commercial alternative; for other applications (such as payroll or general ledger) systems are so standardized and generally available that building one would be viewed as largely unnecessary. However, as the marketplace offers a wider variety of products in selected vertical markets and as the pressure to install systems quickly becomes more pronounced, buying software is increasingly becoming an option. The most common question asked is whether the purchased or "canned" software will match closely enough the needs of the new system. One rule of thumb says that purchased software is adequate if it matches 80% of the overall features that users specify. Ten percent could then be provided by special additional programming, and the final 10% could be deferred. This is a very generalized and judgmental approach; more sophisticated analysis would segregate "must-have" from "nice-to-have" features so that a purchased package could be assessed with respect to essential features.

Other factors must be considered when deciding whether to purchase or build a system. (Some of these factors are given in Exhibit 10-2.) Because managers in different environments tend to have their own opinion about the relative merits of each option, it is not unusual to find that IS departments gravitate toward either "mostly purchase" or "mostly make" positions in order to standardize on skills, project management methods, technical software management procedures, and other elements.

Advantages of Building	Advantages of Buying
All requirements can be met	The system can be cheaper
A better understanding of the systems can be gained	The purchaser can inspect the systems before buying
Efficiency can be improved	The system can be installed quickly
System changes are controlled	The system is already documented
The builder can select the technology	There are other user to check with
There are more opportunities for staff development	Some maintenance is provided
There is greater confidentiality	There are extra features
	Personnel with systems experience can be hired
	The vendor can provide functional expertise

EXHIBIT 10-2 Buying or building software: The advantages of each.

Many users prefer to start evaluating software packages as soon as the IS project is begun. This has two disadvantages. Not only are some users likely to fall under the spell of a vendor's sales pitch before the decision-making process is complete, but users are also likely to avoid taking responsibility for developing unbiased requirements that serve as the basis for technical specifications. If requirements are established after too much "window-shopping," they may become an unrealistic amalgamation of every vendor's feature or a condensed version of a single vendor's product. However, if packages are assessed too late in the cycle, user requirements may be locked in.

Another timing problem concerns gaining financial approval, which is often needed early in the project. Although a make/buy decision or package-selection decision is premature at this stage, certain cost figures are needed. A decision must not be forced; it is wiser to provide a tentative budget based on the most likely or most costly scenario until firm cost figures can be provided. Some enlightened IS project control procedures actually force this iterative cost-analysis process.

Buying Software

Buying software is more complex than might first be imagined. In addition to the actual functioning of the software product, other issues affect its viability and long-term prospects.

The choice of vendor is critical. The vendor should be reputable and financially strong enough to ensure ongoing support to the product. The vendor's staff should have knowledge of and familiarity with the product area. Evaluating vendor services is an important part of the selection decision. The product should be backed by services for which the department has a predetermined need, such as hot-line repair services, documentation, telephone help services, or ongoing product enhancement plans. These should be specified in the product contract along with payment expectations and timing requirements. The area of product enhancement should be of special interest, as the department may prefer that the product not be changed too much or that it be changed in specified ways. As much as practical, such details should be specified in the contractual agreement.

Many IS departments undertake a formal product evaluation. Vendor demonstrations of product functionality are insufficient; discussions with other clients of product performance and vendor services can give insights into actual operational performance.

The request-for-proposal (RFP) process is a technique for formal evaluations. The RFP itemizes a comprehensive list of needs to which qualified vendors formally respond. The process is costly but also more scientific, more thorough, and (some would say) more fair. In some environments (such as government agencies) the RFP process is required; others use it for major decisions or to test the seriousness of vendor interest.

When acquiring software, the IS manager occasionally is given the opportunity to perform "beta site testing." If the department is shopping for new or upgraded features, it may find them just ready to be released by a vendor. If these features are deemed very important, the vendor may sanction the product's use in a beta site mode—that is, a test mode using a real-life subject (the IS department) that understands that everything may not be perfect. By serving as a kind of "guinea pig," the department is able to test the preannounced products and may in fact receive some extra attention from the vendor, who will want to know of and fix any problems.

After a final decision and selection are made, the IS manager must perform the critical step of negotiating a relationship with the vendor. The department must determine that the vendor will not declare bankruptcy, is legally bound to make its product work, and has actual users for the product. The department must also identify its recourse if the product does not work as advertised; must decide on valid reasons for canceling the contract; and must pose a myriad of questions concerning various unreasonably bleak circumstances. Agreement to these points forms the basis for a good relationship.

Trends in Software Technology

The IS manager should be aware of trends in software technology that can enhance the productivity, flexibility, or reliability of the systems and programming area. Some salient trends are discussed in the sections that follow.

Fourth-Generation Languages   The trend in programming languages has been toward easier, more convenient, and more feature-rich versions. The smart IS manager knows that productivity is the key criterion for evaluating a new language, which is why the latest wave of commercial languages holds so much promise. They provide for simplified, Englishlike instructions and summarized operations. These new languages are referred to as fourth-generation languages because they represent a radical change from instruction-oriented languages (third-generation) to nonprocedurally based languages.

Purists may not like the lack of elegance, dependence on data base management systems, or machine inefficiencies of these languages. However, if IS departments do not migrate to them, users will, for these languages are becoming easy enough to master that some users are able to develop their own applications using fourth-generation languages. (The fuller implications of this trend are explored in Chapter 16.) The advantages that IS departments seek with fourth-generation languages include

- Productivity improvements
- Backlog reduction
- Data integrity
- Application integration
- Broader usability
- Top-down design potential
- Flexibility
- Portability
- Enhanced security
- Decision support advantages

These benefits are not unanimously accepted, however. Some professionals perceive the following disadvantages:

- Questionable productivity
- High software costs
- Professional resistance
- Unproven image
- Hardware inefficiencies
- Insufficient functionality
- Loss of data integrity without universal approach
- Documentation difficulties
- Lack of opportunity to initiate acquisition

There is little question that fourth-generation languages will be the basis for the majority of future computing. What is in doubt is how the IS department's use of this technology will evolve. With fourth-generation languages come tough questions for the IS manager. Does the role of the data base administrator change as data access and authorization become more a part of the technology? Does security become more distributed as users become aware of fourth-generation languages? Are typical testing processes valid if applications can be changed so easily? Are typical systems and programming job delineations still valid? Where will the technology take us?

Application Generators and Program Generators   As an alternative to powerful software that monopolizes machine time, some productivity software is structured to turn broad programmer requirements into efficient computer instructions in a translation process. These generators (so-called because they generate machine-efficient instructions) come in two flavors. Application generators produce computer instructions directly each time they are run (Waldrop, 1982). Program generators produce program code such as Cobol (Stewart, 1982), and the programs are then compiled, linked, and executed.

There are advantages to each. Program generators obviously produce code that can be modified, integrated, or transported. Application generators, in contrast, are used more directly and thus are easier to use. Each can be used as prototype generators.

Artificial Intelligence and Expert Systems The technology surrounding these new areas is new and evolving, and the management process surrounding it is similarly undeveloped. As in the early days of computing, the cult of expertise regarding artificial intelligence (AI) and expert systems is populated by a few mavens who, given their special knowledge or experience, have monopolized these areas of development. Projects typically remain small and not easily replicated. Because individual creativity cannot be delegated, these development projects tend to be lengthy and not responsive to time pressures. In many cases, solutions tend to evolve as systems are repeatedly changed and modified. As expert systems become a bigger part of organizations, ways to use this technology more effectively, such as the development of expert systems shells, are being introduced.

Applications Software The following applications software features can be anticipated:

- On-line documentation
- User-generated reports
- More global integration
- In-stream training features
- Environmental mobility
- Integrated applications text/graphics.
- Integration with other technologies (e.g., image, voice recognition)

Eventually these capabilities will become generic to the technology rather than specific parts of an application.

Forfeiting the Analytical Mandate

As greater emphasis is placed on new technology, many IS departments are not keeping up their systems (or methods) analysis skills.
Although a system is obviously more than computer programs (and
should include work flows, activity analysis, delineation of responsibilities, forms design, and more), the consolidation of analyst/
programmer jobs and increased user input into system design have
diminished the objectivity and comprehensiveness that used to be
the hallmark of the IS department. Some would claim that the old
practice of thorough systems analysis is cumbersome and of little
value, given the current base of automation use. In most IS organizations, however, traditional systems analysis is undertaken for
fewer and fewer projects (Young, 1987).

CHALLENGES FOR OPERATIONS

The responsibilities of the operations area are typically very different
from those of other functional areas and can include

- Providing around-the-clock systems coverage
- Meeting critical timetables
- Ensuring accuracy and consistency
- Dealing with less-trained, less-technical staff than are found in
  the rest of the IS department
- Undertaking mechanical and repetitive tasks
- Serving as a focal point for user service
- Managing a larger budget than other IS department functional
  areas owing to hardware, maintenance, people, and other
  expenses
- Performing diversified tasks

Trends in Operational Jobs

In structuring operations, the IS manager should be aware of certain
trends that are slowly reducing the diversity of operational jobs.
These trends affect data entry, production, and support in particular.

Data-Entry Trends Traditionally, information to be stored or
processed has been entered by a special data entry unit or section (in
some cases contract services) that uses techniques such as batch-
ing, verification, and special edit and update runs to ensure accurate
input. This specialized section reporting to operations is becoming

less common, however, now that users are entering the data themselves via on-line systems. A certain amount of editing is appropriately imbedded in on-line applications; however, structured controls such as verification are largely disappearing and are being replaced by more knowledgeable users and more forgiving systems. In some applications, scanning provides a technical means of avoiding manual input. As a consequence, data-entry units are destined to become obsolete and operations will need to use more automated techniques to ensure the input of accurate information.

Production Trends The production unit has traditionally performed such tasks as

- Input control and setup
- Console operations
- Distribution control
- Scheduling

These functions, too, are under siege by modern systems. When jobs can be run directly by users, there is no need to input control information, set up the job control language (JCL), execute the job, or even on occasion distribute the report. Obviously, not every system can accommodate such automation. The technology, the system design, and the nature of the application all need to be favorable. For example, in some applications where timing (general ledger, sales reporting, etc.) or control (payroll, accounts payable, etc.) is needed, operations is still the area of choice to provide a traditional separation of duties and independent, reliable control of execution.

Support Trends A wealth of ancillary duties have arisen around operations, and these too will change as applications evolve. Tape libraries, for example, will play lesser roles in checking out volumes for application runs as more information is contained on line. However, as the quantity of data to be catalogued and backed up increases, and until technology allows all data to be maintained on line, the importance of easily handled magnetic media will ensure that tape libraries are a key operations responsibility.

Problem resolution used to be the exclusive domain of more technical IS departments. The advent of better problem-resolution tools and the importance of more rapid response to on-line problems have expanded the role of operations in identifying, diagnosing, and resolving problems. All signs point to a healthy continuation of this trend. Problem resolution usually requires separate persons with specially developed skills, but it also demands additional knowledge and greater flexibility and responsibility from the computer operator.

Statistical and technical reporting have been traditionally required of operations by the rest of the IS department so that machine performance can be assessed and evaluated. As more EUC takes place and as the use of technology comes under closer scrutiny, charge back or cost-of-use reporting becomes even more significant. More than just running the reports, this activity is of great importance, as rates must be determined and rules for costing developed (regarding who pays for reruns, for example).

Hardware Management

After the cost of personnel, the cost of acquiring hardware is the largest with which the IS department must contend. Hardware maintenance is yet another large cost. Moreover, the management of hardware directly affects service levels and even the environment itself. As Exhibit 10-3 shows, different constituencies have particular interests in certain facets of hardware management. Thus, this management becomes a balancing act for Operations as this group

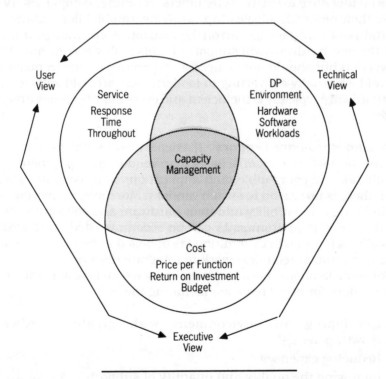

EXHIBIT 10-3 Various constituencies of hardware management and their interests.

Source: Jerry L. Rosenberg, "Capacity Planning as a Business Process," *Mainframe Journal*, May/June, 1988, p. 12. Reprinted with permission of the author.

seeks to improve certain areas without adversely affecting elements of other areas.

The actual selection of hardware has a strong influence on the work climate, systems, skills, and so forth that characterize an IS department. For this reason, IS professionals often describe their experiences or current situations by using brand descriptors ("I have always worked in an IBM shop," or "Their software is targeted for a DEC environment.") This usage demonstrates more than brand awareness, as the hardware and its vendor influence so many other elements of operations.

Selecting New Hardware   IS departments rarely have the opportunity to decide what brand of hardware they want. Only once every 4 or 5 years do IS departments face the need to replace an outmoded technology. Even then, there is much incentive to retain as much of the applications system as can be salvaged in order to control costs. Even for transportable languages such as COBOL, there are many differences from one machine to another that necessitate considerable testing and modification.

As an incentive to existing customers, computer companies try to make their new technologies "upwardly migratable" (for instance, if a certain software package ran on their old hardware, they guarantee that the new hardware will support it). This ability is convenient for conversion but should not be used as an excuse for the IS manager to avoid eventually converting to modern software. Old software on new hardware typically is inefficient and eventually becomes unsupported.

Choosing Hardware Vendors   If a department's staff is trained in the use of hardware from a particular vendor, all equipment and peripherals are compatible, and applications and users are stabilized, there is no reason to switch vendors. Moreover, many vendors are building compatibility into their hardware and software so that multiple vendor environments can be accommodated more easily. This allows for growth by addition (as opposed to replacement) and for a minimum of technical work to integrate devices.

For some IS shops, however, it makes sense to look at completely new vendors for other reasons, including these:

- Developing an environment with greater hardware growth potential
- Reducing expenses
- Improving the quality and quantity of support
- Creating an environment with better machine performance

- Developing an environment with more specialized application
- Enlarging the pool of trained people
- Acquiring more stable products
- Working with a vendor with greater financial stability

Various other factors should be considered when assessing differences in hardware vendors. One of the most important is the hardware architecture and the underlying strategy. Some vendors have committed to networked structures, others to common operating systems, and some to redundant fail-safe processing; still others seek compatibility with other vendors. Another factor that can be important if the department cannot build all its applications is the availability of applications software. Additionally, the kind of systems software available for a certain vendor (usually from the vendor itself) is a factor that must be investigated.

Assessing Hardware Performance   There are two fundamental approaches to acquiring hardware: supporting a specific application and supporting general corporate operations. Acquisitions governed by the former approach are usually undertaken through an RFP-type process whose key determinants are support of specific software or support of a specific volume and kind of processing. This is the kind of acquisition to which people are referring when they say that "the hardware decision is secondary to the software decision." The hardware itself becomes more important when selecting for general, relatively unspecified series of applications. Then the specifications can concentrate on issues of support, price, architecture, and so on.

At some point in the comparison of different pieces of hardware, it becomes necessary to use a common performance yardstick. Unfortunately, measurement of hardware performance is more an art than a science. The early unit of millions of instructions per second (MIPS) is one way to quantify a computer's output, but it indicates little about productivity because a computer's software may be using instructions inefficiently or its other necessary hardware elements may be inadequate. Even given equal amounts of memory, channel speeds, and so forth, one system can spend extra time housekeeping as compared to another. Scientific computers use "flops" (floating point instructions per second) as a more meaningful unit of measure. Other new developments in computing make traditional measures less meaningful. Reduced instruction-set computers (RISC) are designed to accommodate the fact that many confined tasks, especially in scientific computing, can be done without the wealth of instruction types that other systems use. Scientific computers need to execute more instructions to accomplish a task but can process them so much faster that increased throughput results.

Hardware performance goes beyond the CPU speed. The channel speed, read/write/seek speed of the disk drives and tape drives, and other peripheral features such as cache memory all contribute to overall performance. And this does not include the characteristics of the system software (multitasking methodology, data-management features, communication methods, and more). No wonder that after reviewing these traits, studying intangible factors, hearing vendor pitches, visiting different users to compare results, and reading professional evaluations, IS managers are still sometimes reduced to flipping a coin.

Several additional factors should also be considered. There are comprehensive statistics published on the mean time to failure of different devices. These statistics become less meaningful if vendors provide protections such as backup processors or alternate routing. Moreover, the ease of repair and accessibility of parts make even down-time comparisons complicated. IBM coined an acronym, RAS (for Reliability, Availability, and Serviceability), that is an attempt to cover this area. Some IS managers are already thinking of the future when one or more upgrades might be needed to keep pace with corporate growth. But the IS manager must always separate those upgrade opportunities that are currently available from those that are merely a vendor's promise of things to come.

A final concern is any differences in functionality that may become important to the decision as vendor offers begin to seem the same. Until that day when hardware becomes a true commodity, functions such as restartability, systems access, and even physical issues such as power use, air-conditioning requirements, space needs, cabling and chilled water requirements are still important.

The potential integration of devices is an especially difficult issue for the IS manager to deal with. At a certain level, all computers can communicate. It is even possible, with clever applications design, to "integrate" two systems through a crude tape or communications interface. However, this is usually not what is needed by environments looking to integrate separate systems. The ability to communicate on a logical level by running similar communications protocols is just one of the many functions that allow a vendor to describe its offering and that of another vendor as integrated. The advantages of integration will differ from department to department. It may be appropriate to support two or more vendors permanently, especially if one vendor is meeting a specialized application or hardware need. Integration could still be useful if a jump from one vendor to another is too big to make all at once, and vendor compatibility could allow migration over a longer period of time.

Maintaining Hardware   Maintenance of hardware is a basic part of every Operations area's responsibilities. It is usually accomplished largely by outside vendors through the following arrangements:

- By a primary vendor on a fixed-fee contract basis
- By a primary vendor on a time-and-material (T&M) basis
- By a primary vendor on a fixed-fee basis for prime-time coverage on a T&M at other times
- By a third party on a fixed-fee basis
- By a third party on a T&M basis
- By paying a fixed fee to a third party who pays the T&M bills of the prime vendor
- By contracting for selected components to be kept on site
- By contracting for a minimum amount of preventive maintenance

Some vendors demand that if others maintain equipment or if third-party features are added to their equipment, they must reinspect the equipment at the owner's expense before they will maintain it. In evaluating a vendor's maintenance capabilities, it is wise to consider location of the local office, location of spare-parts inventories, the number of repairpeople and the number of sites they must maintain, the average years of experience per repairperson, the average response time per call, and problem-call procedures.

Managing the Facilities   Ideally, the operations manager should have an engineering mentality. As equipment acquisitions are being planned, the manager should perform calculations to ensure that there is sufficient cooling in BTUs (air-conditioned or chilled water), enough power in kilovolts, enough space in square feet (including room to open equipment panels), and sufficient proximity of other equipment so that no component will violate its maximum distance allowances for communication restrictions. To accommodate the considerable cabling, a raised floor usually must be installed. Obviously, much of this is eliminated with smaller systems; indeed, some small systems are installed like any other piece of office equipment.

Depending on the difficulty of pulling wires throughout the facilities, extra wires might be installed for future terminals or devices if such a move is deemed prudent. An Operations manager with a sharp pencil and little patience with minutiae might propose a more advanced and convenient wiring scheme or perhaps a local area network (LAN) for current and future convenience, cost control, and technical positioning. Yet another feature that a cautious Operations manager might recommend is an uninterruptable power system (UPS) to protect a large operation in the event of brownouts, power spikes, or even power outages. Although expensive, such systems are worth the investment in large operations.

Dealing with Change and Testing

Operations is responsible for the reliable, accurate performance of all corporate information systems. Operations areas have a reputation for opposing change; for instance, with user-run systems they are concerned about controls on the introduction of unreviewed data into the data base. The role of operations is not to oppose change in general but to be rightly skeptical of untested ideas.

In testing new systems, operations is likely not to look at the "goodies" as a user might but to try to find weaknesses and problems. When this attitude of skepticism is manifested during times of high excitement or in a climate of urgency for systems and programming, the operations area's criticisms or recommendations may not be perceived as constructive. During such periods the IS manager might be able to prevent permanent damage to intrafunctional relations by invoking high-level decision-making authority.

The Cost of Controls

A diligent operations department will seek to protect against every infringement and guard against every possible "bug." Beyond those protections designed in at the beginning of a system, other controls are added to correct any subsequent error and infraction. The IS manager must question this overcompensation and balance the cost of the control with the cost of the possible error. A good example of this is the tendency to back up files repeatedly to avoid time-consuming restores should a program cancel. If backing up an extra time for a daily job takes 1 hour more per night, whereas recovering to the same point (using older back-up files, logs, reruns) in the event of a problem takes 7 hours, then it should be obvious that unless the job in question fails once a week or more that it would save total computer time to not do that extra backup. (This assumes that you could use the extra 1 hour a day *and* that you can tolerate a 7-hour restore in the event of a problem.) The IS manager's guidance is often needed to determine the degree of required control, so that the costs of protection are kept proportionate to their value.

Trends in Operations Management

Fault-Tolerant Computing   On-line systems are becoming more integral to the operation of many businesses (financial transactions, order-taking systems, dispatch systems, airline reservations, and so on). With this comes a growing need for guaranteed systems availability. In addition to designing applications to be robust, certain hardware vendors are delivering systems that have "fail-proof" designs that use intelligent systems software, redundant hardware, and parallel processing to keep working even when some system parts fail. These systems are typically specialized around transaction systems. Although they represent much more expensive solutions to application problems, as system downtime becomes increasingly unacceptable for many businesses, these systems become worth the investment.

Lights-out Operations   With increasing on-line systems and the need for continual access, around-the-clock operations are fairly common. However, the job of overseeing the system for long periods of time is a tedious one. In remote locations an operator might not have alternative work to fill in lull periods. To relieve this problem and to save on attendant costs, certain businesses are seeking to clean up their systems and automate the monitoring, error-handling, and recovery process to the point where an operator is not necessary. Although previously operations managers have loaded discretionary chores into this otherwise idle time, lights-out operations remove all manual chores from a computer room for a specified time period. Essential problem-related tasks can be handled by centrally located operators. Many technical advancements will be required before single sites can cleanly handle lights-out operations.

Remote Diagnostics   As a result of advanced hardware design, problem diagnosis and resolution have evolved to the point where phone lines are used for interactive diagnostics. Hardware and software vendors use remote diagnostics to save costly, time-consuming trips to client sites. Remote diagnostics also open the possibility of the vendor's making direct changes and modifications on user software. As broad as the service possibilities are, questions regarding user security and confidentiality are equally wide-ranging.

Help Desk   As the function responsible for receiving input and requests for scheduling support, for providing terminals and perhaps other equipment, and for delivering reports and data, operations is questioned often on systems functionality, data definition, and applications capability, even though knowledge of these areas is more concentrated in other functional branches of the IS department. One response to the increasing need for user support is the "help desk," a dedicated group of professionals responsible for screening all calls for assistance and either routing them to the right area or finding answers personally. Thus, questions of a technical or applications nature would be handled by the appropriate specialist, whereas queries for report accuracy or terminal "repairs" could be handled directly by operations.

The goals of the help desk are to serve as a clearinghouse and to minimize bureaucracy. The concept of the help desk is predicated on the belief that as more new users are introduced to the systems, the department's IS clients will not have a strong appreciation for the complexities of IS and should not be forced to deal with them. (Many help-desk referrals could be to the information center or some other user self-help facility.)

Although other functions are sometimes designated as the help-desk home, operations is the most popular location, for several reasons:

- Operations typically receives the first phone call from many users anyway.
- Operations is staffed for long hours.
- Operations provides services in a manner that is reasonably uncluttered by red tape.
- Operations is in a position to track user requests through problem resolution.
- Operations is frequently the group that answers most queries.
- Many queries must be responded to quickly by operations.

CHALLENGES FOR TECHNICAL SUPPORT

Technical support, as defined in Chapter 8, has long been the Cinderella of IS, forced to labor in obscurity while the two sisters (systems and programming and operations) receive more attention. Historically, as systems software became more complex, technical support's role grew even more arcane and obscure. Recently, however, several trends have reduced the distance between the company and technical support, bringing this function out of the closet.

- Vendors are realizing that systems software maintenance should not be too complex; simplicity of design and ease of administration must be built into systems software.
- With the growth in systems software, more systems specialization is necessary. No longer are systems programmers alone sufficient; IS shops large enough to support them require communications analysts, data-base technicians, and even specialists for various products.
- Most importantly, some of these specialties are becoming important to users, and the technical support specialist is being required to play a more visible role in the user-support process. These responsibilities place technical support professionals closer to users and alter their role in relation to other IS functional areas.

Accommodating Technical Complexity

As just mentioned, one way in which vendors are handling increasing complexity is by simplifying the software interface. Although doing so usually reduces users' understanding of a product and may also reduce some flexibility, these losses are compensated for by growing software functionality. The remaining rigidity is one of the IS department's costs of working at a higher level of productivity.

As software becomes more comprehensive, technical support must be more procedure driven to accommodate and keep track of different types of changes. Moreover, testing of these changes must be more isolated and somewhat more inventive, as the possible problems increase geometrically with the complexity of the environment (e.g., the expanding amount of software to maintain, pieces of the operating system, performance tools, utilities). A parallel problem is managing the growing systems libraries where programs, systems procedures (procs), macros, and so on are stored.

Managing Performance Fine-tuning systems to perform optimally is one of the thankless jobs of technical support—a job that demands care, ingenuity, and attention to detail. The enemies of fine-tuning include

- Changing hardware configuration
- Changing applications
- Changing technology
- Increased complexity
- Quickly or poorly written programs
- Evolving, inconsistent environments

- Increased functionality
- Routine operating system repair and maintenance

Technical support is always held accountable for system performance, but there are always advocates of the above-mentioned constraints that oppose the preventative measures that technical support might propose. IS managers can rarely accomplish sound system performance without making sacrifices in other areas.

Managing the Network   Managing the network used to be a largely clerical activity involving authorizing the installation of another terminal and then keeping track of the terminal number, user authorization, and other details. Currently, network management is expanding rapidly. The diversity of devices and the wealth of applications on the network means that network access involves more than simply determining what terminal number to assign. Moreover, the network itself needs attention to expand capacity, provide reliable routing, integrate various functions, and incorporate new and promising technologies. When diverse types of transmission information are involved (as shown in Exhibit 10-4), this task becomes even more complex and important. With increasing functionality available, issues of security and application access are entering the realm of network management.

One technique that is receiving considerable attention is network planning; a process that anticipates with adequately defined capacity the growing traffic needs inferred from projected information and operational activity. This allows the communication management function to prevent head-on collisions between evolving technology, new and improving applications, and the ever-increasing demand for

Type	Examples
Voice	Person-to-person communications
Data	Computerized business data
Text	Office, publications, reports
Graphics	Blueprints, schematics
Image	Facsimile
Video	Television

EXHIBIT 10-4 Modes of information transmission.

access. It also capitalizes on the opportunity to share projected capacities among technologies (voice or data) or applications.

Managing the Data

Ever since information was stored on magnetic media, it has been technical support's duty to manage that data. Typically, the task been accomplished by a data-base administrator (DBA) who controls the use of a data-base management system as well as data stored outside this data management software. Because the DBA initially worked predominately with packaged software, many see this role as still largely technical (e.g., maintaining the software, optimizing CPU performance, managing disk utilization, developing backup/restore procedures). Some environments, however, have responded to the growing trend of information resources management (IRM), data integration, broader data access, and so forth by making the DBA's job (or a like function) more managerial. In this mode the DBA concentrates more on data-dictionary management, data access, data organization, and information planning. This has been carried so far in some organizations that the DBA is no longer a member of technical support. Ultimately, both aspects of the DBA's role must be addressed.

Data Positioning In its broad managerial aspect, the DBA role involves dealing with the translation of data into information and the conceptual positioning of this information within an organization. Different organizational levels have needs for different information, accessed differently, as shown in Exhibit 10-5. Each category of information has its own set of characteristics that describe the input and output needs of various users. Exhibit 10-6 shows how these characteristics change based on the target audience. The IS department, usually represented by the DBA, is responsible for directing the design of systems, selection of tools, and management of data to achieve the appropriate results.

Ownership versus Custodianship Two views of data ownership dramatically affect the approach that a DBA takes toward data management. According to the first view, individual pieces of data are owned by individual functions that are responsible for their definition, maintenance, accuracy, and so forth. This clearly establishes these responsibilities and leaves the DBA with more custodial duties. As needs for data access and disposition arise, the DBA usually must involve the data owners. This theory easily covers personally created data and has the advantage of maximizing owner attention to data-related duties.

The second view holds that even at the data element level, data are a corporate resource and belong to everyone. Although responsibilities to enter, review, and correct data are assigned to departments or individuals, a central function such as the DBA normally makes these determinations along with that of who has a "need to know" in order to assign data access capabilities. Even with the usual escalation and management approval provisions, the DBA's authority is usually greater than it is according to the first view. The choice depends on the organization's emphasis on data security, decentralization, and need for general data access, as well as on the stature of the IS department and the DBA.

Selecting Data Structures One of the DBA's important duties is determining how data should be organized. Obviously, a critical time for doing this is at the point when a data-base management system is selected; here, the needs for hierarchical, network, or other structures can be assessed. Even after this event, however, decisions must periodically be made as to how data relationships should be represented under the chosen structures or whether certain data belongs under such a structure at all. Moreover, the DBA may see the

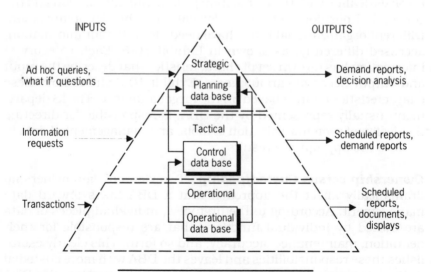

EXHIBIT 10-5 Information needs by organizational level.

Source: Fred R. McFadden and Jeffrey A. Hoffer, *Data Base Management*, Glencove, IL: Benjamin/Cummings, 1985.

need for alternative structures to meet selected needs or as a platform for migration. Thus, a relational data base may be chosen to supplement a traditional data structure in order to support some EUC functions and for future applications.

Whatever the technology, the DBA role cannot be overemphasized, for it subtly determines the usability of data. Even those organizations astute enough to appreciate the significance of data structure issues cannot afford to frequently fund complex and disruptive data-restructuring projects. Mistakes made in one instance will be paid for repeatedly.

Data Integrity In a like manner, the meaningfulness of data is strongly affected by decisions regarding how data are related, defined, and maintained. Moreover data accuracy and renovation responsibilities must be fulfilled regularly. Many of these assignments and decisions rightly occur in systems and programming projects, which means that project leaders, analysts, and even programmers are instrumental in deciding issues of data integrity. The DBA must make sure that technical support retains responsibility for guidelines and standards in this area as well as selected review responsibility. (The days where this could be enforced through necessary control of centralized software are disappearing.)

Information Characteristics	Operational Control	Management Control	Strategic Planning
Source	Largely internal ⟶		External
Scope	Well defined, narrow ⟶		Very wide
Level of aggregation	Detailed ⟶		Aggregate
Time horizon	Historical ⟶		Future
Currency	Highly current ⟶		Quite old
Required accuracy	High ⟶		Low
Frequency of use	Very frequent ⟶		Infrequent

EXHIBIT 10-6 Information requirements by decision category.

Source: Reprinted from "A Framework for Mangement Information Systems," by Anthony Gorry and Michael S. Scott-Morton, *Sloan Management Review*, Fall 1971, p. 59, by permission of the publisher. Copyright © 1971 by Sloan Management Review Association. All rights reserved.

Providing for Data Security

Because it sets up access to most software and systems, technical support often ends up with security responsibilities by default. Because security can mean data access, application or function access, or network access, technical support is in a good position to orchestrate all three areas. It is often difficult, however, for a highly skilled function such as technical support to take over a very procedural, even clerical, duty such as security.

Of course, there are more substantial aspects of this duty. Often, providing completely flexible control over who can get at what from where is too sophisticated a task for many security environments, and some compromises must be struck. Also, a continuing challenge is to not let security procedures or systems overhead get in the way of user-friendly efficient systems use. This is particularly difficult in today's EUC environment. Access requests may arise spontaneously; access needs may be one-time and are more individual than departmental; intended use may not be clearly known; and access needs may even extend into the personal files of others. This does not even consider the nonsecurity issues of maintaining data currency and ensuring proper data definition. Security in such a setting can be very complicated.

One helpful capability is the provision of granular security, which allows access to less confidential portions of the data base without jeopardizing the confidentiality of sensitive portions. For example, a department manager could access the personnel records of people in that department without being able to see similar records of others. This access could be restricted to appropriate portions of the record without disclosing personal data. Granular security even allows access to summary data (such as the average salary of all corporate employees at a certain level) without giving any specific information on any individual. Such a system requires even more security management effort but conforms more closely to the growing needs of modern corporate computing.

Another difficult trade-off that must be determined when managing security is how much protection to invest in. There are clear costs to installing, operating, and maintaining data security that must be kept commensurate with the risks of loss or compromise of important information. Determining the value of information and the degree to which protection is necessary is ultimately a management responsibility. In administering a data security program, the IS department is often put in the unfortunate position of independently deciding on security measures due to company indifference or compromising with resistent user(s) at inappropriate levels.

Providing Strategic Leadership

Technical support is often seen as a supporting cast in the more exciting drama of IS. Yet without adequate resources for managing systems software and adequate time for and attention to the necessary controls, an organization's technical systems will suffer through declining performance, limited or decreased functionality, and the risk of serious failure. Not only will excessive amounts be spent on unnecessary hardware, but the increasing tangle of applications will defy maintenance and threaten established functions. Computing is one area where "an ounce of prevention is worth a pound of cure," holds true, as the cost of correcting negligence is way out of proportion to the cost of avoiding it in the first place.

Technical support's attention is also important in the area of strategic positioning, although its effects may not be easily discernable. As we have seen, the final IS strategic plan is a melding of a variety of ideas, inputs, and concerns, and technical support's role complicates this. Technical support represents the emerging technologies, products, and features that a company should consider, and it makes clear that accommodating new "guiding technologies" requires careful positioning years in advance. Technical support also isolates "supporting technologies" required to carry out strategic plans and details a program for acquiring or bolstering these areas of technology. In some cases, delays or costs (or both) can be shown to entail unexpected disadvantages.

Technical support is usually omitted as an important player in strategic planning because technology is all too often seen as a simple and secondary hurdle to be overcome in the course of meeting business objectives. Technical forecasts are by nature speculative and frequently arcane and complicated—too much so for some pragmatic senior manager. For these reasons, Technical support and the sponsoring IS manager usually have a difficult time as they lobby for inclusion of new technology in corporate and even IS department plans.

ISLANDS OF TECHNOLOGY

The term "islands of technology" is frequently used to describe the establishment, usually in isolation, of a specialized solution for a particular area or problem. Several factors have accelerated the trend toward islands of technology. Technology itself has opened the door, first with micro- and minicomputers (which can be devoted to a selected use) and later with specialized software and devices to meet singular needs. The push toward decentralization and entrepreneurship in organizations has also helped move computer acquisition decisions to user departments, allowing them to acquire stand-alone solutions sometimes without the knowledge or approval of the IS department. Competitive needs have dictated much of this trend.

Finally, users have developed their skills so as to be ready to assimilate necessary new technology. No longer easily intimidated, users are increasingly computer literate, aggressive professionals who know their needs and are no longer satisfied with inadequate or no solutions. For them, islands of technology are a highly positive new development.

Examples of Islands of Technology

Office Automation   From its simple beginnings in word processing, office automation has expanded to become a complex part of the modern office environment. It can include

- Word processing (stand-alone, shared logic, or networked systems)
- Electronic mail
- Copy/image management and/or image transmission
- Records management
- Integrated voice communications
- Video conferencing
- Miscellaneous automated functions (e.g., travel services, room and equipment reservations)

This list certainly varies, of course, from organization to organization.

It is instructive to consider the differences between automated systems and what we think of as traditional information systems. The former must be simpler and less complicated to use but, in the case of word processing, more responsive. Access in many cases is more casual and sporadic but available to a much larger clientele. Originally, integration of the many elements was not as important as simplifying systems access to standard and easily used equipment. Recently, integration of various elements—word processing and electronic mail, for instance—has become more important now that the separate elements have established themselves. Other disparities between office automation systems and IS include some differences in vendors, dissimilar work procedures and measurements, different job types, and different business roles.

In pioneering office automation, many industry experts have made much of statistics that indicate that equipment investments per person in office environments are vastly less than those per worker in agriculture and blue-collar environments where productivity is measurably higher. Productivity comparisons are complicated, but what seems to be clear is that capital investment for white-collar workers is catching up to that of blue-collar workers (Exhibit 10-7). (Average per capita investment for farm workers is even higher.) Stephen S. Roach (1988) interprets this as follows: "American businesses seem utterly convinced that the answer to the white-collar productivity quandary lies in ever greater amounts of information-processing technology." Of course, there are historical reasons for the differing levels of investment, and in general this figure has as much to do with employment levels as it does investment levels. For this reason, not every business environment is moving toward more per capita automation. Business for which office and clerical activities are critical to the organizational mission are selectively investing. Many companies are more prudent, buying office equipment only when isolated investments make sense and when selected functions can be economically automated. The broad assumption that greater investment in information technology will make white-collar workers more productive must be examined for each environment individually and implemented discerningly.

One difficulty in achieving office automation is that it belongs, in a sense, to everyone; no single department typically cost-justifies or installs it. Because it usually applies to the company at large, ownership (including maintenance and administration of the system) can be hard to determine.

	Average per Capita Investment	
	1980a	*1987b*
Blue-collar worker	$24,000	$22,700
White-collar worker	$3,000	$9,200

a Electronic Business, February 1980, pp. 52, 65.
b Roach, Stephen S. (1988). White Collar Productivity: A Glimmer of Hope, (New York: Morgan Stanley), September 16, p. 15.

EXHIBIT 10-7 Equipment investment by industry sector.

Computer Integrated Manufacturing   Computer-integrated manufacturing (CIM) is another island of technology. Unlike office automation, ownership of this application is usually more focused. Moreover, CIM is a very visible and high-payback application, concentrated as it is on a high-cost and critical part of the business. CIM itself is an accumulation of smaller units of automation. Some of the elements of CIM include

- Work-flow control (bar codes, laser scanning, etc.)
- Material control (automated material-handling systems, etc.)
- Process control (numerical machine control)
- Production planning and scheduling
- Robotics
- Computer-aided design/computer-aided manufacturing (CAD/CAM)

These and other elements of CIM require special knowledge of manufacturing, material handling, distribution, and so on. For this reason, and because CIM applications are very nonstandardized, CIM systems usually are heavily sponsored by an internal engineering group or rely heavily on outside specialized consulting. Many vendors can be involved, and integrating them is a real challenge, as no clearly accepted standard such as the manufacturing automation protocol (MAP) has become popular. One important integration challenge that must be faced is how to include mainframe data and transactions within the CIM environment.

Desktop Publishing   As laser printing and flexible software come together, the tools to prepare simple typeset and visually stimulating documents have become cheap enough to be acquired by many companies—and even departments. In-house preparation of price lists, assembly instructions, newsletters, product documentation, and a variety of other materials is becoming cheaper, faster, and more versatile. Moreover, the multiple steps involved in typesetting are avoided and errors are reduced. Such tools as personal workstations are easily available and immediately useful for copywriters, layout artists, and even graphic artists. However, the average company still relies on outside services for sophisticated processes or products such as three-color printing, printing on nonstandard stock, die cuts, and perfect binding.

Computer-Aided Software Engineering   It is only natural that with the application of technology to so many tasks, a similar application would be developed with respect to IS tasks. This is indeed happening under the guise of computer-aided software engineering (CASE). We have seen how tools such as program generators, applications generators, and fourth-generation languages have streamlined the task of building technical solutions. CASE attempts to make the complicated and cumbersome process of design and analysis more compact and manageable. It involves automating data design and application flowcharting, integrating data dictionary input, and performing systems modeling. The exciting claim of CASE tools is that they speed up the design and analysis process while simplifying abstract ideas and improving design quality by allowing more participation. Ultimately, CASE products promise to integrate highly productive languages so as to compress the whole system-implementation process and to allow highly flexible prototyping to take place.

Integration Options

The role of IS in the management of islands of technology is by no means clear. In some environments, because of past opposition or perceived lack of expertise, the IS department is not even responsible for the strategic identification of such efforts. Even where the department has been an early champion, the degree to which it guides and leads an independent automation effort is controversial, pitting IS technicians against user technical experts and even executive against executive. On the one hand, the IS department's leadership and input can provide much help to users. Important issues such as data protection, documentation, procedurization, and testing have been pioneered by IS. Also, the department can make sure that technology, systems, and data are capable of being integrated—if not immediately, then down the road. On the other hand, all these helpful guidelines tend to be seen as restrictions by those who ultimately own the systems. Users increasingly lobby for more autonomy, freedom from compliance with corporate standards, less emphasis on future integration, and more emphasis on current effectiveness. For these reasons, many sponsors of islands of technology have opted for low or no integration, freedom to pick any vendor, and minimal interference. Even CASE, an island within IS, suffers from the fact that many of its available products are stand-alone and PC-based.

Users' reactions are largely justified, in light of the IS department's past tendency to want to control rather than assist where possible. The challenge for the IS department is to overcome the image (and sometimes the fact) of being unreasonably dominating and to be perceived as a facilitator of users' best interests. Then the department can guide user behavior or integration efforts, directing them toward the best interests of the company at large.

Addressing Selected Responsibilities

Certain issues of responsibility must be addressed before investing in islands of technology. If additional jobs are generated, where should they report and what types of jobs should they be—user or IS oriented? Where will security be handled? Who will plan disaster recovery and documentation control? Will data management and network management be handled as an IS responsibility? Will hardware and software be acquired using standardized acquisition procedures? Where will the equipment physically reside? Each of these questions must be answered in such a way as to ensure efficiency, protect the organization, and aid user progress.

It should be apparent that the IS department can share heavy responsibility for an island of technology without actually owning the application portion. A more sensitive responsibility, one defined more in practice than through formal procedures, is planning and migration. The user undoubtedly has ambitions for the future application of a particular type of automation. Helping the user to realize these ambitions and introducing other corporate opportunities are clearly tasks that fall within the IS department's scope of responsibility. However, they must be accomplished by involving others—and the department's and user's perceptions of when the timing is right for integration may be very different.

GENERAL FUNCTIONAL RESPONSIBILITIES

Many responsibilities of the IS department do not fall into easily defined functional categories. They consist of activities that affect traditionally defined areas in variable ways. Some of the more common and more important of these responsibilities are discussed in the sections that follow.

Vendor Relations

It is a poor IS manager who does not recognize the important role that vendors play in helping the manager achieve departmental goals. Vendors should not be taken for granted, overlooked for the contributions they can make, or factored carelessly into department strategies.

Strategies for Using Consultants One of the most flexible types of vendor is the consultant. Whether they are individuals or firms, consultants can advise, provide objective evaluations, or actually perform selected tasks. Herman Holtz (1985) identifies consultant roles ranging from totally task oriented to totally process oriented (see Exhibit 10-8). Any role that combines both elements must be thought out very carefully. For instance, responsibility for a problem solution may cause a consultant's coordination of a participative process to be heavy-handed and nonproductive. The consultant's level can range from directive to nondirective, as Exhibit 10-9 shows. How much of a given activity is allotted to the consultant helps define the consultant's place in the problem-solving process. Regardless of the consultant's capacity, work may be charged on a fee basis (one price for the specified service) or on a time and materials basis (an hourly rate plus expenses).

A major reason to seek a consultant's help is to supply specific, necessary skills or experience not available in-house. If one-time guidance is appropriate, a one-time fee may provide the needed input. If the consultant's assistance is to be extensive, it is wise to specify the exact role and the amount of help needed even when being charged on a time and materials basis. If the offered skill is of ongoing consequence, acquisition of the necessary skill by the in-house staff may be prudent. One way to accomplish this is through a training relationship with the consultant.

Another major advantage of consultants is their objectivity. If a controversial decision is being faced or an unpopular action must be determined, a consultant can demonstrate objectivity and a methodical approach in the face of resentment or skepticism. If a decision is not foregone, a consultant can help clarify factors that can aid professionals in making up their minds. Even when there are several opposed camps, consultants can function effectively as tie-breakers if they are chosen fairly and everyone recognizes their expertise.

For organizations with much work and too few resources, consultants can assist in or even take over a task. If an entire project is being turned over to the consultant, a fixed price may ease the IS manager's mind about "fee churning." In contrast, if the consultant is just another pair of hands under the direction of corporate supervision, pay-as-you-go pricing is more typical. The latter arrangement avoids the need to specify the "deliverable" in contractual detail. However, the IS manager should be sensitive to the possibility that detailed specifications are being avoided because the company has not yet decided what it wants. No project should be undertaken with too vague and ambiguous a charter—and especially not if consultants are involved.

	Consultant as Process Facilitator
Consultant as Technical Expert	

Task Orientation	Process Orientation

Role Characteristics

Task	Process
1. *Problem Verification:* By "expert" evaluation and collection of data.	1. *Problem Verification:* By "problem sensing" and facilitating a clear articulation that includes attitudes and feelings.
2. *Problem Solving:* Provides ideas and opinions, designs research for data, and develops solution for the client-system.	2. *Problem Solving:* Works on the problem-solving capability of the system, improves problem - solving process, and facilitates creativity.
3. *Feedback:* Presents research data with "expert" interpretations.	3. *Feedback:* Provides meaningful data, facilitates assimulation of data, and allows for client interpretation.
4. *Utilization of Research:* Makes specific and concrete recommendations based on data.	4. *Utilization of Research:* Develops client use of data and facilitates action by client based on learning.
5. *Relationship to Client:* Objective, detached, and task oriented. Connection is short - term and problem - oriented.	5. *Relationship to Client:* Personal, involved, and process oriented. Connection is long - term and system- oriented.
6. *Involvement:* Primarily with the problem to be solved.	6. *Involvement:* Primarily with people and groups in the organization.
7. *Systems Approach:* Concern is with implications of the problem for other parts of the organization.	7. *Systems Approach:* Concern is for collaborative relationships and exchange of resources among parts of the organization.

EXHIBIT 10-8 Range of consultative roles.

Source: Herman Holtz, *Using Consultants Successfully*, Westport, CT: Quorum Books, 1985, p. 59.

Objective Observer | **Process Counselor** | **Fact Finder** | **Identifier of Alternatives and Linker to Resources** | **Joint Problem Solver** | **Trainer/Educator** | **Information Specialist** | **Advocate**

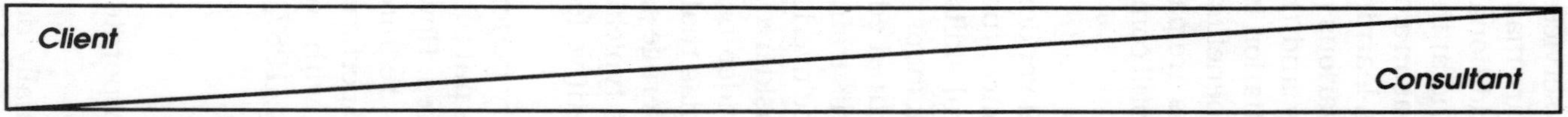

Level of Consultant Activity in Problem Solving

Directive

Objective Observer	Process Counselor	Fact Finder	Identifier of Alternatives and Linker to Resources	Joint Problem Solver	Trainer/Educator	Information Specialist	Advocate
						Regards links and provides policy or practice decisions	Proposes guidelines persuades, or directs in the problem-solving process
				Offers alternatives and participates in decisions	Trains client		
		Gathers data and stimulates thinking	Identifies alternatives and resources for client and helps assess consequences				
Raises questions for reflection	Observes problem-solving process and raises issues mirroring feedback						

Nondirective

Client

Consultant

EXHIBIT 10-9 Multiple roles of the consultant.

Source: Herman Holtz, *Using Consultants Successfully,* Westport, CT: Quorum Books. 1985. p. 61.

Products Versus Services   Some vendors provide a product, such as hardware or software, and simultaneously offer services of which the IS manager should be aware, including hardware maintenance, software hotline services, training resources, or additional features or functions. Even vendors whose help seems to end at the sale are able to impart much useful information. (For this reason alone, many IS managers engage in constant window-shopping, learning what is on the market and the strengths and weaknesses of various products.)

For more sophisticated products, the company and the vendor enter into contractual agreements. Contract negotiation is the time during which to ask about any extra services and benefits, as those can be made part of the agreement. (Such requests are particularly effective if timed to occur while several vendors are still competing for the contract.)

Training   One of the most important services that vendors provide is training: training on how to use new products, conceptual training (including education on future technology), general skills training, and more. Training occurs through hands-on workshops, in off-site classes, via self-study material, or via less-structured educational opportunities such as user conferences. Some of this training is free or included in other vendor fees and should not be overlooked.

Specialized training vendors should also be considered. Whether classroom instruction, seminar format, or on-site video-based training, this teaching is devoid of salesmanship and bias that might be present from a prime vendor. If specialized coverage is needed, consultants or even local colleges and universities typically accommodate customized IS training needs for a competitive fee.

Programs for Vendor Relations   The satisfactory performance of a vendor is seldom accidental, as the better vendors put considerable effort into delivering required products and services. However, it is important for the IS manager to specify what is required and to monitor performance levels so as to guarantee solid performance and continuing attention. Vendor-relations programs with some of the following features may help to ensure this (Young, 1987)

- Periodic meetings to review activity
- Written itemizations of expected deliverables
- Annual sharing of appropriate portions of Corporate plans
- Periodic reviews of contract provisions
- Annual performance evaluations (if not formally done by the vendor)

- Periodic visits to client and vendor sites
- Documentation of unsatisfactory performance or issues o concern
- Documentation of exemplary or highly satisfactory performance

The vendor is not merely another employee, yet many of the same issues apply with regard to good relations. Vendor and company must have a shared understanding of their roles. Specific objectives must be mutually understood, performance must be monitored, and evaluations must be shared.

The EDP Audit

With the growing dependence on IS services, there is commensurate interest on the part of business owners and senior management in controls and protections to ensure the accuracy and continuity of business processes. As Exhibit 10-10 shows, auditing the areas of concern through the use of a structured, carefully defined process is an important way of maintaining control (Porter and Perry, 1984). Auditing can include observation, verification of reported activities, validation of procedures through testing, and evaluation of operations in general, with recommendations for additions, changes, and improvements. There are three organizational levels from which the EDP audit might originate. Each is discussed briefly next.

Quality Assurance Function of the IS Department   IS managers try to develop departmental activities that to an extent are self-policing. This means that appropriate checks and balances and departmental standards are developed and IS products are inspected for compliance with original specifications and the general standards. With the increase in the amount and importance of these activities, however, a position independent of other IS functions and responsible for quality assurance is being created within many IS departments. Although the responsibilities of this position may vary, they might include

- Establishing IS department rules for project specifications
- Establishing rules for project approval
- Establishing general systems standards
- Ensuring appropriate approvals on each project
- Establishing systems documentation requirements
- Ensuring compliance with documentation standards
- Establishing rules for systems testing

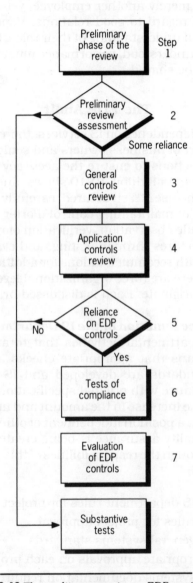

EXHIBIT 10-10 The audit process in an EDP environment.

Source: W. Thomas Porter and William E. Perry, *EDP Controls and Auditing*, 4th ed., Boston: Kent, 1984, p. 2.

- Monitoring or conducting systems tests
- Identifying design requirements for systems protection
- Identifying the required components of a disaster recovery plan
- Testing the disaster recovery plan
- Managing the process of moving the project into production
- Postevaluation of completed projects to determine if functional objectives have been met
- Coordinating all external audits

Two schools of thought exist on the role of quality assurance (QA). One maintains that to monitor the rules of the auditing process, QA should not be a participant in that process. For example, how can QA judge fairly if testing has been done, if QA is conducting the testing? Another school of thought counters that QA is best equipped to conduct impartial auditing activities because it knows the rules. The choice of viewpoint is complicated where project activities cannot be separated easily from project controls and tests for quality. And it becomes a moot point when IS departments are compelled to decide duties on the basis of practical considerations such as staffing limitations or project productivity.

One of the more formidable arguments against having QA participate in project activity is that doing so jeopardizes some of the respect that separation from other professionals provides. Above all, QA's rulings and decisions must be respected or IS professionals will lose their appreciation for the value of rules and procedures.

Corporate-level Auditors Companies have long maintained auditors on their payroll to make independent (albeit internal) assessments of financial risk and exposure. It is becoming increasingly important to extend this review process to IS areas. Doing so eliminates the possible conflict of interest that QA might be faced with in an audit situation. [Corporate-level auditors actually provide relief only to certain QA area, as only the largest environments can afford to have corporate-level personnel who specialize in and can concentrate on IS systems. Historically, it has been someone with a background in assessing controls but with no foundation in technology. Therefore, issues such as basic data protection can be addressed easily at the corporate level, but more intricate issues (change control or library access security, for instance) must be left to the more knowledgeable and involved personnel in quality assurance.]

One responsibility that is typically elevated to the corporate level is that of major system postevaluations. Some feel that if the IS department measures the value of its own work, even via independent personnel, a certain prejudice might be at work. Moreover, corporate auditors are more likely to adopt a broader corporate perspective and to be able to criticize both the IS department and user. One weakness of many system appraisal programs at the corporate level is lack of up-front involvement. At the time of major project approval, benefits and costs must be spelled out in such a way that they can be measured and schedules provided for indicated achievements. Doing so clarifies how and when the evaluation should be made. The timing should be far enough from the date of project completion to measure permanent change but before other factors can erode the effects of the system. One year is not atypical.

These measurements of improvements, be they of expense levels, head count, or inventory levels, should not only be tangible and noncontroversial but should factor out other influences such as change of business volumes. Unexpected but serendipitous benefits should be identified, just as unexpected costs would be. The result of this analysis is a report card on the project as well as a set of recommendations for other associated actions, for future changes to the project processes, or (typically) both.

External Auditors   A typical view is that outside evaluators are enemies of the best interests of the IS department. Many companies view internal review programs as protection against outside auditor criticism. A more receptive attitude will reveal that outside auditors can supply fresh vantages from which to view system protections. Their advisory power can help gain approval for actions that the IS department has been futilely recommending. External auditors can look at new areas, test areas that the department does not have the resources to address, and offer a highly professional report card. To gain these advantages, of course, the IS manager must avoid playing an adversarial role.

Auditors identify risks and point out how to reduce them. If every auditor's concern were eliminated, IS departments would drown in controls. It is up to the IS manager to measure the likelihood of risk and the cost of protection. It is simply not cost effective to protect against all possible eventualities. The IS manager's crucial job is to decide if and how to avoid them.

Administrative Services   The IS department runs not only on technology and mainstream skills but also through many ancillary activities, as we have seen. The IS manager must ensure that support elements are available in a manner conducive to long-term productivity, which certainly means being able to identify and appreciate the need for standard and specialized assistance. Some common forms of assistance are examined next.

Administrative Assistance At some level, secretarial help must be considered, and the debate in this area is over how much personal support IS professionals should receive. One extreme says that the IS department should pioneer the use of office automation tools and can limit its needs for secretarial help by using voice and electronic messaging systems, document storage and retrieval systems, and other automated systems. Adversaries of this approach claim that a professional is too highly paid to spend time typing or filing; assistance should be available for these tasks.

Future technology may resolve this argument, but for now both extremes (and everything in between) can be found. It is enough to know that IS departments tend to adopt one position or the other, either of which suggests much about other practices and behaviors.

Document and Library Services Here, too, technology may be providing an answer to a need. Where paper documentation is required in abundance, specialists in documentation are often assigned to the task, thus freeing up programmers and analysts to perform more technical duties. Even where systems are on line, user instructions and documentation might be written by a technical writer who can offer clear communication to users.

In larger environments, the libraries of applications and systems software documentation (not to mention project documentation, vendor literature, professional subscription services, books, and magazines) represent an overwhelming and often uncontrolled resource. Not simply as a convenience to IS professionals but by way of controlling access and protecting this body of knowledge, a company might provide a library complete with librarian(s) in its IS department. Like a regular library, this might encompass meeting rooms, visual aids, research services, and other features.

Training The practice within large environments of having internal training resources is deemed either a luxury associated with size or a necessity brought about by the complex demands of many projects and many people. If the IS manager is pragmatic, he or she might observe that in-house training is a cost-effective way to accomplish something that every shop must deal with—training of IS professionals and keeping them up to date. There was a time when companies allowed IS professionals to become obsolete, but most environments now know that this causes system obsolescence and personnel turnover.

In-house training, even that which uses professionally prepared media, rests on the recognition that technically competent and good teachers are rare. Although some companies may rotate people through teaching positions, these persons must have the talent to convey their knowledge to others. Training needs must also be anticipated so that material is ready when needed. Testing, refresher courses, research work, transfer courses (commercially available seminars, trade shows, etc.), courses for rounding—all the trappings of an academic environment have found their way into in-house IS training programs.

Large size is not a prerequisite of dedicated training resources. Even modest IS shops have found that a training coordinator is valuable to plan education, develop individual training plans, administer the program, keep training records, determine the best-quality training, and generally get the most mileage out of a training budget.

Planning/Budgeting/Financial Support As the work load for the IS manager grows, it may be prudent to concentrate some of the more specialized managerial tasks in a separate position, to relieve some of the work load and to dedicate focused skills on important duties. Planning, budgeting, or financial support (capital requests, buying and selling equipment, etc.) can be provided, or some other area (such as technology research) can be singled out. The choice of area(s) where support is useful normally depends on the department's priorities and/or areas that the IS manager is unable to address effectively. Because the provider of support is usually a single individual or at best a small staff, this is an excellent position for a technical professional without well-developed skills or for an IS manager in training.

CONCLUSION

Each function in IS has specialized characteristics and makes special contributions to the IS team effort. The IS manager must have a well-developed appreciation for these. In addition, each function raises certain alternatives among which the IS manager must choose in order to assemble a cohesive department supportive of the organizational mission. Subordinate managers within the department may well have highly sophisticated insights and supply valuable opinions and judgments. However, many decisions improving the performance of one function come at the cost of performance of another function; therefore, it is the IS manager who is ultimately responsible for putting the team together and making it work.

DISCUSSION QUESTIONS

1. How much knowledge of the individual functional areas of the department must an IS manager have?

2. What actions might be taken or techniques used by the IS manager to promote cooperation and teamwork among the different IS functions?

3. Is complete compatibility of the IS functions an important goal for the IS manager?

4. Should completely independent islands of technology be addressed in the IS business plan? Why or why not?

5. To what extent will strategies for islands of technology (regarding centralization, guidance, etc.) be consistent for all islands within a company, and to what extent will they differ from island to island?

6. What instances exist where the general IS manager responsibilities of planning or budgeting belong at a higher (corporate) or a lower (IS functional) level?

7. Compared the role of technical support today with what you think it will be 10 years from now. Will it be more or less important, larger or smaller, more or less complicated?

8. Who should pay for purchased applications software, the IS department or the user? Why? What are the advantages and disadvantages of each option? What factors affect this decision?

9. What is the future of the programming task? Who will do it, and where will they work?

10. How might the attitudes of operations and quality assurance differ regarding controls? Who is in a better position to determine the right level of protection?

REFERENCES

Holtz, Herman (1985). *Using Consultants Successfully* (Westport, CT: Quorum Books), pp. 59-61.

Jenkins, A. M. (1983). "Prototyping: A Methodology for the Design and

Development of Application Systems" (Indiana University, Division of Research, School of Business, April).

Porter, W. Thomas, and William E. Perry (1984). *EDP Controls and Auditing*, 4th ed. (Boston: Kent).

Roach, Stephen S. (1988). "White-Collar Productivity: A Glimmer of Hope?" (New York: Morgan Stanley, September 16), pp. 1-17.

Stewart G. (1982). "Program Generators," *Popular Computing* (September), pp. 112-122.

Waldrop, J. (1982). "Application Generators: A Case Study," *Proceedings of the 1982 National Computer Conference* (Reston, VA: AFIPS Press) pp. 351-358.

Young, Jim (1987). "Vendor Support: You Don't Know What You've Got 'til It's Gone," *Computerworld-Focus*, vol. 21, no. 09A (March 4), p. 6.

Young, Jim (1987). "Methods Analysis Revisited," *Computerworld-Focus*, vol. 21, no. 27A (July 8) p. 8.

eleven

□

Organizing the Information Systems Department

The way in which the IS manager organizes IS functions and resources defines departmental relationships and establishes (or at least suggests) hierarchies. Organizational structures can have positive and stimulating effects as well as debilitating ones—all of which must be understood. Moreover, the IS manager must be aware of special concerns that relate to making transitions between two structures.

What holds true at the corporate level also applies at the departmental level. Just as reporting relationships of the IS department as a corporate entity can have a powerful effect on the organization as a whole, so reporting relationships and the distribution of duties within the IS department can play a crucial part in the department's performance.

This chapter begins with a brief overview of organizational practices and their evolution. After examining some of the hazards of not planning for organizational structure, we proceed to look at variations in structure and the relationship of specific structures and goals. Next, we move to technology and organizational structure—a complex relationship.

The chapter then investigates organizational strategy. We discuss several possible alignment schemes, the centralization/decentralization issue, and options for support structures. After examining a few variations on typical organizational strategies, we end with a consideration of the ramifications of organizational change and ways to manage that change.

THE EVOLUTION OF ORGANIZATIONAL PRACTICES

Organizational practices have been influenced over the years by several factors, including

- Technical improvements
- The extent of automation in companies
- The size of automation projects
- The role of users in automation

When programmers knew all the technology and did all the analyses, the IS department's structure was simple; in essence, it consisted of a single large grouping of generic programmers and another large grouping of operators with common skills. But as systems and technology became more complicated, individual jobs became more distinctive and skill-dense. Within the large groupings, programmers became distinct from analysts; specialization by application, technology, or activity began; and operators became distinct from one another on the basis of their specialized duties. Project growth eventually meant more responsibility, and technical advancement added to the richness of the job mix. It became necessary to establish new units in the IS department: technical support, administrative services, even quality assurance units sprang up. IS departments became comparatively large and highly structured.

Although all this was consistent with the evolving size and intricacy of the IS department's duties, the evolving structure was not responsive enough to meet competitive and service needs. Some user departments set up their own IS operations to support their stand-alone computing needs in order to be rid of an onerous dependence on the central IS department.

Today, efforts are slowly being made to locate the best ways of streamlining and simplifying automation. Help-desk functions are created to minimize any departmental bureaucracy that stands in the way of user assistance. Information centers, through sophisticated technology, are similarly trying to meet user needs without complicating things by involving too many layers of the organization.

The result of this streamlining approach is the containment of systems and programming responsibilities and minimized growth pressure. Other technologies make less necessary separate groupings of analysts and programmers, programmers and some technicians, and professionals and some service functions. Information centers have become a kind of competitive challenge as traditional applications development methods and operational performance are seen as needing improvements in turnaround and usefulness. These trends have forced the IS department to consider organizational simplification and attendant job reformulations. And along with these trends are the ever-spreading scope of the department's mandate and growing corporate expectations.

THE HAZARDS OF UNPLANNED EVOLUTION

Some IS departments have not recognized the importance of deliberate and methodical determinations of organizational structure. Others, although appreciating that organization is important, have been handicapped by events that have thwarted their plans for developing viable organizational structures. In both cases, the existing organizational structure has obtained its form randomly rather than as a result of a careful construction.

The effects of random structuring can be serious. A critical senior analyst might threaten to quit, for instance, unless he can report directly to the IS manager. If his request is granted (as many organizations would chose to do), systems and programming would not be a self-contained unit but would have duties that were split out for the person independently reporting to the IS manager. The manager would then be likely to be involved in the task of balancing applications development-support efforts between two locations.

Another hypothetical example is the departure of the operations manager. Because of a budget squeeze, this managerial position is not filled; instead, the operations supervisor, the data-center services supervisor, and the data-entry supervisor all report to the IS manager. Over time this situation becomes institutionalized and a more cohesive structure is never reestablished. Or (using this same example) suppose that to cover for a vacant data-center managerial position, the IS manager transfers all hardware acquisition, contract, and maintenance responsibilities to the technical support manager. Even if the data-center manager's job is refilled, it might be easier to leave the transferred duties in the technical support area rather than move them again. Thus, job content becomes determined by convenience or tradition, not appropriateness of duties and tasks.

Of course, job content must be varied somewhat to accommodate diverse talents and interests. But many organizations are held hostage to shifts of responsibility as skill-related factors change or as IS department members launch successful campaigns to take over attractive areas without appreciating the implications for the organization as a whole. If resource shortages exist, they can be rebalanced. If skills are missing, they can be developed or acquired. And if interest is lacking, it can be instilled or at least encouraged through the use of MBO techniques. None of this can happen instantaneously, however, and patience is necessary. Organizational structures are meant to provide some degree of stability; thus, taking the time to create an appropriate structure is important.

Changes to the structure need to be balanced with practical and immediate concerns and must not be indiscriminate. In a situation where obstacles to a supportive organizational structure exist, the IS manager needs to consider whether a new organizational strategy—one that is more cautious, more long term, or perhaps even more drastic—is needed.

DIFFERENCES IN ORGANIZATIONAL STRUCTURES

Because different organizational structures emphasize different aspects of the department and nurture important departmental programs, it is natural that IS departments would want to chose structures that highlight certain strengths and concentrate on achieving certain goals. It is an important duty of the IS manager to determine what strengths should be emphasized and what department goals to enhance through the use of organizational structures. Organizational variety in turn results from real differences in the corporate environments in which various IS departments must function. Sheer size, for example, can permit levels of specialization that are simply not cost effective in a smaller environment. With larger major units such as systems and programming and operations, a greater variety of support services can be justified on the basis of greater economies of scale.

Large organizations do not necessarily opt for unified groupings of skills and services, however. Many large IS shops are designed around the principle of general-purpose groups of autonomous, decentralized functions. Such decisions are typically determined by the overall corporate organizational strategy. In cases where a company is practicing decentralization, compressed management structure, broad span of control, and so on, it is appropriate (not to mention more effective) for the IS department's organization to resemble that of the larger entity.

Antoinette La Belle and H. Edward Nyce (1987) have observed that the degree of compatibility between corporate control of policy and resources and decentralized control of information-related functions is a measure of an organization's equilibrium. Conversely, incompatibility indicates destabilizing organizational behaviors, as shown in Exhibit 11-1. Still, quite different philosophies can be effective, providing policy and resource control and information-processing control are kept consistent.

DELIBERATE STRUCTURES AND SPECIFIC GOALS

In *Strategy and Structure*, Alfred Chandler (1962) articulated what is now a maxim of organizational theory: structure follows strategy. In a specific reference to IS, Robert Zmud (1984) proposed that organizational design be chosen to encourage work behaviors that are consistent with the task environment (see Exhibit 11-2). For instance, the area of technology management might best be served by a matrix-alignment structure (see Exhibit 11-8) to spread skill specialization to several sources, whereas a functional approach might be advisable for internal auditing where specialization by selected areas might work best. Variation can be expected in process and coordination as well. (Exhibit 11-3 shows this variation across IS subunits.)

For IS departments that have clear priorities, specific organizational structures are highly effective. For instance, the goal of completing a major application development project might be met by setting up the major project development team as a separate organizational unit, with the project manager reporting to the IS manager. This structure would last only as long as the project, although for projects of sufficient length it might be useful to isolate the project effort to allow management and staff to concentrate on this single important task. Another reason for organizational segregation is task uniqueness. A systems and programming group might determine that its maintenance activity is sufficiently different from major project activity to warrant a separate subunit to handle it.

Tasks might be organizationally combined for the opposite reason: to highlight job similarities and promote coordination. Responsibility for data-base administration might be assigned to technical support to ensure that operating systems software changes are

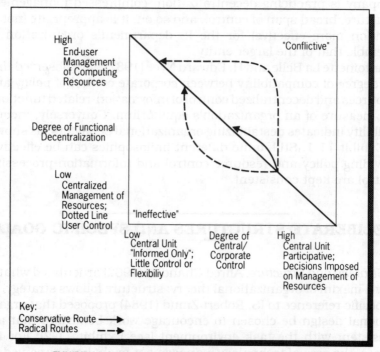

EXHIBIT 11-1 Equilibrium in IS organizational structures.

Source: Antoinette La Belle and H. Edward Nyce, "Whither the IT Organization," *Sloan Management Review*, vol. 29, no. 4, Summer, 1987, p. 79. Reprinted by permission of the publisher. Coyright 1987 by the Sloan Management Review Association. All rights reserved.

orchestrated and that the technical resources of vendors, machine time, and so forth are shared.

Other reasons for effecting an organizational change include development of a person or a function, positioning of common duties for efficiency, grouping of like tasks to improve quality. It is crucial, however, for the IS manager to be able to point first to the corporate or IS departmental goal to be achieved and then to the organizational change that will support it. Having a clear business-driven goal protects the IS manager from being held hostage to outside circumstances or acting on capricious, technology-driven urges. Moreover

Design Alternative	Task Environment	Work Behaviors
Structural		
Functional	Stable Routine	Efficiency Consistency Reliability
Product	Dynamic Segmented market	Effectiveness Rapid response
Matrix	Turbulent	Effectiveness Flexibility
Process		
Mechanistic	Simple Stable	Efficiency Dependability
Organic	Complex Dynamic	Effectiveness Adaptability
Coordination		
Formal	Stable Routine Independent tasks	Consistency Reliability
Informal	Dynamic Uncertainty Interdependent tasks	Adaptability Rapid response Cooperation

EXHIBIT 11-2 The interrelationship of organizational design, task environment, and work behaviors.

Source: Robert W. Zmud, "Design Alternatives for Organizing Information Systems Activities," *MIS Quarterly* June, 1984, p. 84. Reprinted by special permission. Coyright 1984 by the Society for Information Management and the Management Information Systems Research Center at the University of Minnesota.

Information Systems Subunit	Structure	Process	Coordination	Other Issues
Delivery system	Product Some functional	Mechanistic	Formal Some informal	
Systems development	Functional	Mechanistic Some organic	Informal Some formal	Multiple Dynamic
Support center	Matrix	Organic	Informal (external) Formal (internal)	Overlapped Dynamic
Information center	Functional Product	Organic	Informal	Overlapped Disintegrating
Research and development	Product	Organic	Informal	Isolated
Technology diffusion	Matrix	Organic	Informal	Dynamic Disintegrating Overlapped
Planning	Functional Some product	Organic	Informal (internal) Formal (external)	Dynamic Overlapped Umbrella Disintegrating
Internal auditing	Functional	Mechanistic	Formal	Overlapped Umbrella
Administration	Functional	Mechanistic	Formal	

EXHIBIT 11-3 Some prototypical organizational designs.

Source: Robert W. Zmud. "Design Alternatives for Organizing Information Systems Activities." *MIS Quarterly* June, 1984. p. 88. Reprinted by special permission. Copyright 1984 by the Society for Information Management and the Management Information Systems Research Center at the University of Minnesota.

it provides something specific against which to measure the success of the reorganization effort. Although these improvements may be slow to materialize, the IS manager should know that benefits from organizational improvements tend to be pervasive and long lasting.

TECHNOLOGY AND STRUCTURE

Technology tends to have contradictory organizational impacts. We have seen, for instance, how improved programming technology has had a simplifying and consolidating influence on the organizational unit responsible for programming. At the same time, however, new programming technology has made it possible to distribute the programming task throughout the organization, often as a secondary duty of a less technical job or even of a user.

New technologies frequently add responsibilities to existing jobs and then, as they become more important, spin off to become separate functions. This was the case with communications software, which first was handled by systems programmers and later required the creation of a new position, that of communications analyst. Other IS organizational elements that have come into being and evolved as a result of technological developments are the information center, telecommunications, and various R&D groups appropriate to large environments.

Futurists claim that many specialized groups devoted to the maintenance of new technologies are short lived and that eventually these technologies will become self-managing. This may yet happen; however, the following often-made predictions show no immediate signs of occurring:

- Elimination of programming as a human task; English–language-like machine instructions.
- Elimination of computer operators; systems that execute jobs on the basis of user requests and automatic backups.
- Elimination of system programming; self-tuning and remote maintenance by vendors.

However, to the degree that the IS manager observes trends such as these occurring or can make such prophesies take place, organizational structures must be adjusted to accommodate them.

The IS manager must anticipate how technology can be used to make the IS department organization more efficient. This may requires him or her to recognize when labor intensive tasks can be automated. Likewise, when new technologies are acquired by the corporation, the IS manager must often make organizational adjustments to be able to support it. Responses to both call for a realistic, even cautionary attitude by the IS manager, an attitude often cultivated by experience.

INFORMATION SYSTEMS DEPARTMENT ORGANIZATIONAL STRATEGIES

Apart from reacting to the influence of corporate organizational strategy, IS managers can select organizational options that facilitate distinctive strategy appropriate to the IS department. These options may derive from the IS strategic plan, the skills and experience of IS personnel, the professional preferences of those personnel, and other sources. The following are some common organizational schemes.

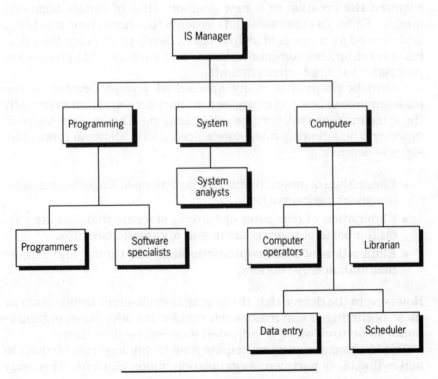

EXHIBIT 11-4 A functional alignment.

Alternative Alignments

Within IS departments, individual jobs can be grouped in similar ways based on three different alignments: functional, project, and matrix. Each is briefly described in the following sections.

Functional Alignment   With this alignment, personnel are grouped by what they know. For example, programmers are separated from analysts, system programmer duties are grouped by software product, or systems and programming staff are grouped by the technologies they work with. (see Exhibit 11-4).

Functional alignment was the earliest and remains the most common of organizational structures. Its advantages and disadvantages are listed in Exhibit 11-5.

Project Alignment   IS personnel can also be grouped by the tasks they perform, regardless of the skills required. For example, operators can have broad responsibilities for running several computers or pieces of equipment. The task of systems and programming professionals might be divided between maintenance or large projects. Task alignment can either broaden or restrict the variety of work in comparison to skill alignment. Exhibit 11-6 illustrates one popular way in which IS professionals' work responsibilities are compartmentalized.

This approach is more typically found in large organizations where such a method helps keep attention focused on many important

Advantages	Disadvantages
Everybody understands his or her tasks	The IS manager spends too much time on problems arising between organizational elements
The structure confers stability	Training and development opportunities are poor
There is a greater opportunity for the development of specialized skills	There is a higher risk of project failure
This structure provides a system of checks and balances	Communication within the departement is more difficult
Standardization within a functional area is possible	

EXHIBIT 11-5 Advantages and disadvantages of functional alignment.

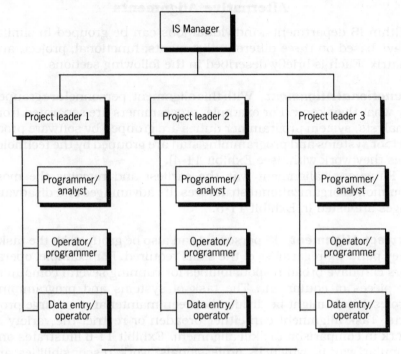

EXHIBIT 11-6 A project alignment.

Advantages	Disadvantages
Everyone understands the work of the department	The structure is not highly stable
This structure is highly receptive to new ideas	This structure demands continuous management attention
This structure offers greater adaptability	There are few opportunities to develop special skills
There is a shorter chain of command, which makes each person more visible	This structure offers no clear career path
The structure provides for better cost control	

EXHIBIT 11-7 Advantages and disadvantages of project organization.

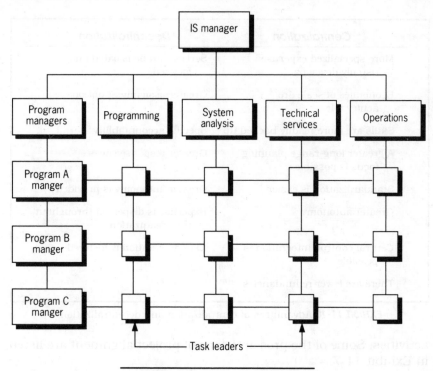

EXHIBIT 11-8 A matrix alignment.

Advantages	Disadvantages
Better assessment of an individual's skills and professional development	Success is highly dependent on the interaction between the functional manager and the project manager
Better utilization of specialized skills	Project management is more difficult because the project manager does not have line responsibility
Highly flexible and adaptable to changing environments	Greater potential for political difficulties
	Some communication problems may result because of dual reporting

EXHIBIT 11-9 Advantages and disadvantages of a matrix organization.

Centralization	Decentralization
More specialized expertise usually develops	Service can be isolated and focused
Economies of scale are achievable	Greater assignment options
Skills are more readily backed up	Specific accountability
A greater long-range planning focus is possible	Greater responsiveness
Standardization is easier	Greater autonomy is provided
Greater autonomy	Expertise is dispersed throughout the organization
Central control/integration is possible	Experimentation is fostered
There are fewer redundancies	

EXHIBIT 11-10 Advantages of centralization and decentralization.

activities. Some of the pros and cons of project alignment are listed in Exhibit 11-7.

A variation on this alignment is the service alignment. Jobs can be organized by the group to which a service is being provided. Systems and programming is often segregated into groups conforming to user departments (manufacturing, marketing, etc). In certain large companies the entire IS department (including operations and technical support) is aligned in such a manner; only IS service and support groups such as training administration or quality assurance might remain centrally grouped, and these units provide services to functional support groups while the IS manager coordinates as the common boss.

Matrix Alignment   This structure is a hybrid that simultaneously accommodates functional and project approaches. According to this alignment, units maintain a dual allegiance: one to a functional group and the other to a project group (see Exhibit 11-8). As one might suspect from an environment with parallel lines of authority, managing can be complex and fraught with bureaucracy.

A large, dynamic organization that prizes flexibility would be likely to use a matrix alignment. This approach has the advantages and disadvantages described in Exhibit 11-9.

Centralized Versus Decentralized Organizational Structures

A major factor in structuring the IS department is the issue of centralization. For example, Operations can either be grouped centrally (as is traditional) or be decentralized (i.e., with its people and equipment divided into groups that support a functional division). The choice of approach depends on the IS manager's perception of the relative advantages illustrated in Exhibit 11-10.

Decentralization Schemes According to John Rockart and colleagues (1978), there are three major dimensions to be considered in any discussion of centralization or decentralization: systems management, systems operations, and systems development. Each can be positioned with an independent degree of centralization or decentralization, as Exhibit 11-11 illustrates.

In general, organizations tend to have more centralized operations and less centralized development activities. Management and control activities are so varied that wide differences are seen in practice from company to company. Jack Buchanan and Richard Linowes (1980) have refined the three-dimensional view by specifying that development and operations have an execution component as well as a

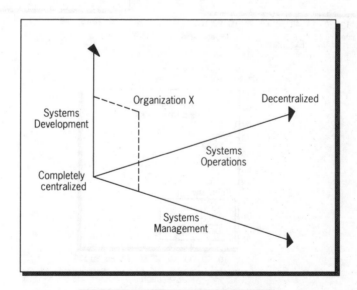

EXHIBIT 11-11 Dimensions of decentralization/centralization.

Source: John F. Rockart, et al., "The Management of Distributed Processing," Center for Information Systems Research, Massachusetts Institute of Technology, December 1978, CISR 39, p. 6.

control (management) component that might be centralized or decentralized separately. Thus, a company might allow functional units to determine their own computer use or project activity (i.e., decentralized execution) but have highly uniform and structured standards or budget restrictions (i.e., centralized control). Other permutations are also conceivable. Using Buchanan's schematic (altered for a presentation), Thomas H. Johnson of Nolan, Norton & Company has revealed patterns that differ from industry to industry (Exhibit 11-12). Even though the breadth or height of each square illustrates the amount of variation that exists between companies in

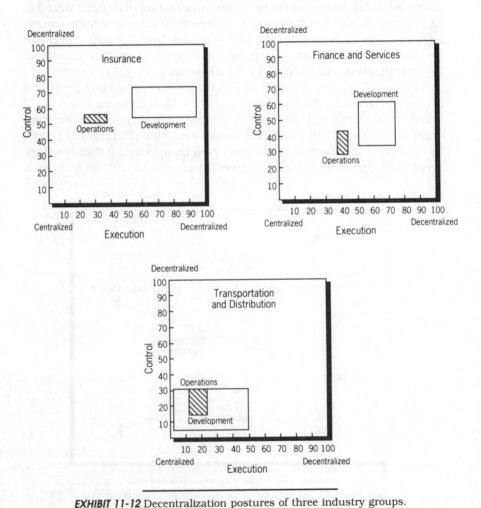

EXHIBIT 11-12 Decentralization postures of three industry groups.

Source: Thomas H. Johnson, presentation entitled "Characterization of Distributed Data Processing," Nolan, Norton & Co., Lexington, MA, 1982.

that industry, it is the general contrast in patterns from industry to industry that stand out.

Centralization or Decentralization of Tasks to be Executed   Within areas as complex as management, development, and operations, individual elements may be treated differently. For instance, the use of an IS product might be decentralized whereas security authorization could remain centralized. Buchanan and Linowes illustrate the probable pattern of decentralized versus centralized tasks to be executed in the data-processing unit (Exhibit 11-13). This pattern varies from unit to unit. Manufacturing, for example, could have a system configuration that is more decentralized than that of accounting.

Organizational Options for Support Functions

The degree to which support services are emphasized relative to the major IS functions to which they provide assistance is an organizational question with implications for how power is distributed to line managers, staff managers, and ultimately the IS manager. The training function can serve as an example. When the duties and attendant resources of training belong to line managers of systems and programming, operations, and so on, there is a greater latitude and autonomy for each group than if training were provided by a separate group under a training manager. If training support comes from a separate organizational unit it could mean less control for each line manager but with possible service benefits that come from economies of scale. If the training manager of this separate unit reports directly to the IS manager, not only are this manager and other line managers nominal peers, but the IS manager is in a position to become more involved in deciding on training resource deployment and thus to exercise more detailed control. The same analogy can be extended to quality assurance and other support areas.

This method of gaining (or, conversely, distributing) control might be consistently applied to all internal support functions. Or it might be used selectively to emphasize or de-emphasize a selected function. For instance, IS managers might have the data-base administrator report directly to them as a way of devoting attention to and exercising control over data administration services.

EXECUTION

Hardware operation
The user prepares source documents and manages data entry through terminals to DP center.

Telecommunications
The user specifies the volume and scheduling requirements for communications through his or her configuration of terminals.

Systems programming
The user only uses the DP center's operating system, compilers and utilities.

Application system maintainance.
The user both documents and assists in diagnosing system errors.

Data-base administration
The user determines his data requirements and develops a logical data-base design.

Applications programming
The user assigns some internal personnel to participate in the programming team.

Systems analysis
The user is quite involved in most analysis work, including some program-level system design.

System documentation
The user develops his own manuals and shares in writing program design specifications.

User training
The user alone is responsible for all internal training activities.

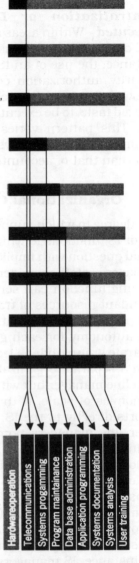

■ Decentralized

▨ Centralized

EXHIBIT 11-13 Patterns of task centralization and decentralization in the DP unit.

Source: Reprinted by permission of the *Harvard Business Review*. An exhibit from "Making Distributed Data Processing Work" by Jack R. Buchanan and Richard G. Linowes September-October, 1980. Copyright © 1980 by the President and Fellows of Harvard College; all rights reserved.

Some Variations on Information Systems Departmental Organizational Strategy

Often IS managers will alter the traditional approaches used by most IS departments in order to meet some special need. Because organization is such a fundamental tool, nontraditional approaches elicit much controversy. Many feel that the following techniques have little use within IS; however, the IS manager should be aware of them.

Dual Reporting Structures   We have seen that the matrix alignment has the weakness of requiring dual leadership. Some organizations go further and design divided responsibilities into selected jobs. For example, an EDP auditor might report to the controller but answer to the IS manager on issues of standards, techniques, machine use, and other areas. The manager of IS planning might work for the IS manager but have a dotted-line responsibility to the vice president for strategic planning. Such arrangements are dictated by the nature of a job (or combination of jobs) that one person might hold, the cultural climate, the evolutionary nature of the job, and/or the persons involved.

Temporary Organizational Structures   Because changing an organizational structure is such a major process, it is usually done infrequently. Moreover, because organizational structures are usually intended to supply a sense of stability, it is typical to provide these structures with a degree of permanence. Nevertheless, some IS managers will announce temporary organizational moves. A task group may be staffed with full-time members assigned only for the duration of a project. Often the future assignments of these professionals will depend on the outcome of the project. Of course, any uncertainty of future assignment will influence individual performances; perhaps negatively if the inevitable stress is not well managed or perhaps positively if future possibilities can serve as a motivator.

THE RAMIFICATIONS OF ORGANIZATIONAL CHANGE

Organizational adjustments should not be undertaken without careful analysis of the diverse effects they may have. Although an organizational change can bring about many competitive advantages for the department and the company as a whole, it can have equally negative repercussions. Benefits in one area may entail problems in another area. The decision to proceed can be made intelligently only if all the ramifications are considered and anticipated.

Emphasizing Efficiency and Enhancing Job Content

Departmental efficiency is an important element to be promoted through reorganization. Decentralization is sometimes undertaken if it will allow a particular unit to work more quickly or accurately by being closer to the units in need of its services. Allowing a unit to thus specialize in a selected aspect of a service might also improve efficiency. However, it is just as possible that centralization, with its concentration of skills, greater synergy, and better control, will allow the unit to generate more output using the same number of people. Careful judgments must be made.

As crucial as efficiency to the department is the content of particular jobs. By packaging responsibilities correctly, superfluous communications can be eliminated and shared duties combined. Group cohesion and teamwork can be built into job content. The resulting task depth, scope, and challenge can improve job satisfaction, and in general focus the application of employees' energies, reduce turnover, improve morale, and attract qualified new employees.

Increasing Career Opportunities

The desirability of jobs and job groups created by the proper organizational structures attracts junior employees and qualified outsiders alike. To take advantage of internal resources, a pyramid of progressively more demanding jobs must be skillfully assembled. Jobs must be organized in such a way as to use less senior job skills as a base on which to build the requirements for higher-level positions. Making the structure consistent with efficiency and overall corporate needs is not always easy.

Sophisticated career structures will not only use senior skill needs to create advancement opportunities within IS department functional units but take advantage of potential advancement opportunities in other IS functional units or departments other than IS.

Improving the Organization's Intraindustry Competitive Posture

It is not unusual for organizational solutions to be similar in similar industries. When environments and tasks are alike, it makes sense that common solutions will be found. For this reason, many organizations tend to emulate one another in their structure. This is perpetuated by industry IS professionals who move between corporations and replicate organizational structures with which they are familiar.

This can be a mistake if a decision on the organizational structure is reached by default or as a result of habit rather than rigorous assessment. A unique organizational approach may provide distinct competitive advantages. (Making intercompany migration of IS professionals less convenient may be one of these advantages.) To the extent that corporate strategies of different companies within an industry are different, so the IS department organizations should reflect these differences.

MANAGING ORGANIZATIONAL CHANGE

As we have seen, organizational structures are manifestations of corporate objectives, both strategic and tactical. No one should think about changing an organizational structure without first analyzing the general corporate situation. Reorganizing may not be the only way to improve or respond to a particular situation. In fact, because it is a tool of major and lasting impact, it should be used only when other measures have been exhausted.

Planning for Change

Structural change needs to be planned for, not undertaken to remedy an immediate problem. It is best viewed as a component of a strategic vision.

A key consideration in any decision to undertake organizational change is staff. The IS manager must be able to determine the skills that a new structure will necessitate and to assess the qualities of existing staff (or of applicants for unfilled positions). To arrive at a popular, effective reorganization, most IS managers tend to build their new organizational structures around people already on board. From a business standpoint this provides the advantage of employee familiarity with the corporate culture, as well as known, demonstrated sets of skills. To the extent that different positions represent an attractive advancement, reorganization can be considered a personnel benefit.

Reorganizations are fraught with political peril. For instance, a benefit to one IS department member may be viewed more negatively by a competing member of your staff. IS managers should relieve staff anxiety about structural change by eliminating doubt and trepidation whenever possible. Avoiding "lingering announcements" is one way to do this; demonstrating career opportunities inherent in a new structure is another.

Evolutionary and Revolutionary Approaches to Change

In considering the approach to be taken in any restructuring situation, one important issue to determine is whether to make quick, dramatic changes or to introduce smaller, less traumatic adjustments. Depending on the circumstances, either might be appropriate.

A dramatic, radical change will achieve the ultimate structural objective immediately. It might also convey a message of urgency and decisiveness to the affected staff. In contrast, an evolutionary approach might involve making several small adjustments over a period of time to achieve the same structure. This approach is less likely to cause stress and turmoil, but may lead to more uncertainty. It would, however, allow a more methodical adjustment by the staff to new roles and responsibilities. Should the new direction have a major element of risk, an evolutionary approach can allow for the testing and graceful reversal of a plan that just does not work. Similarly, small but important changes can be made along the way. Received wisdom suggests that major realignments can be effectively undertaken only infrequently. Smaller changes, in contrast, can take place more frequently.

CONCLUSION

Every business has to deal with the issue of structure. This issue is of additional importance to IS because there are a variety of factors for which an organizational structure position must account. As technology evolves, the role of IS within the company requires ongoing consideration, as do the careers of IS professionals. Peoples' effectiveness changes with time as do the specific IS goals within the corporation.

The nature of organizations is such that required changes to remote parts of the organizational structure can affect the entire structure. It is this insidious, yet essential, character of organizational structures that requires IS managers to be ever vigilant for negative repercussions from or opportunities for improvement to the IS organizational structure.

DISCUSSION QUESTIONS

1. How should the organizational structure be addressed in the planning process? Should the IS manager depend on the

corporate personnel department for help in organizational planning?

2. With the growing popularity of distributed systems, is it appropriate that IS departments evolve to a more decentralized structure? Why?

3. Do you believe that different parts of the IS department can be organized along different lines as Robert Zmud suggests? What are some potential difficulties of this approach?

4. What is a reasonable estimate of frequency for major reorganizations of the IS department? What factors might affect this timing?

5. What conflicts could the use of both centralized and decentralized approaches in a single organization cause?

6. Give some examples of how IS department organizational structure could reinforce IS department strategy.

7. Name some advantages and disadvantages of temporary organizational structures.

8. Identify some possible symptoms of an IS organization that might cause the IS manager to consider reorganization.

REFERENCES

Buchanan, Jack R., and Richard G. Linowes (1980). "Making Distributed Data Processing Work," *Harvard Business Review*, vol. 58, no. 5 (September-October), pp. 143-161.

Chandler, Alfred (1962). *Strategy and Structure* (Cambridge, MA: MIT Press), p. 113.

La Belle, Antoinette, and H. Edward Nyce (1987). "SMR Forum: Whither the IS Organization," *Sloan Management Review* (Summer), pp. 75-85.

Rockart, John F., Christine V. Bullen, and John N. Kogan (1978). "The Management of Distributed Processing," Center for Information Systems Research, Massachusetts Institute of Technology, Cambridge, MA, CISR 39 (December).

Young, Jim (1987). "Who Reports to Whom," *Computerworld Focus*, vol. 21, no. 40A (October 7).

Zmud, Robert W. (1984). "Design Alternatives for Organizing Information Systems Activities," *MIS Quarterly* (June), p. 93.

twelve

□

Information Systems Personnel Management

Information Systems and Other Professionals:
Differences and Similarities

The Information Systems Professional and the Environment

The Information Systems Professional as Part of a Group

Elements of Information Systems Personnel Management

Conclusion

Discussion Questions

References

People have always been the most important asset of the IS department. From the beginning it has been obvious that computer hardware and software are only as useful as the people charged with deploying them. However, changes in the IS area promise to make this fact even more dramatic. The total cost of running an IS department is increasingly dominated by personnel costs as hardware/software costs decrease in relative terms. IS challenges are less and less a function of complicated, highly specialized technical

270

issues as sophisticated products become more turnkey in nature—and more available to the general population, whose familiarity with (and even training on) new equipment can be influenced by IS personnel. Diagnosing IS-related situations, identifying opportunities, creating appropriate user-friendly technology and selling it to prospective users, and effectively supporting the technology are new tasks that will test the skills of IS personnel in diverse ways.

Unhappily, the IS management field has a history of insensitivity (bordering at times, on contempt) toward personnel issues. Moreover, for reasons not confined to a lack of skills on the part of the IS manager, IS professionals have not always proved themselves to be effective when deviating from duties of a traditional (i.e., largely technocratic) nature. One complexity that has stymied many IS managers is the need for management that recognizes not just individuals and their strengths and weaknesses, but also the relationship of individuals and tasks. This "situational management" calls for deft managerial responses, as Exhibit 12-1 suggests.

To craft personnel policies that meet the needs of IS professionals, the IS manager must know a good deal about this person we call the IS professional: what motivates or deters him or her, what his or her task-related behaviors are, and how constructive behaviors can be encouraged. In addition, the IS manager needs to understand IS group dynamics—not because they are radically different from other group dynamics, but because certain subtle and important characteristics of IS group dynamics guide manager's specialized treatment of IS personnel.

We begin this chapter by looking at some of the similarities and differences between IS and other professionals, including users and managers. Next, we discuss the IS professional's relationship with

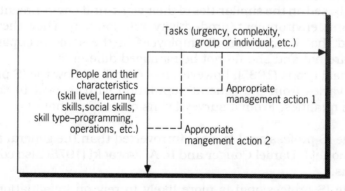

EXHIBIT 12-1 Situational management

the corporate environment in which he or she works. We then proceed to examine IS personnel as group workers; here we touch on team building and matching congruent styles. The elements of IS personnel management are our final focus: job analysis, employee selection, task assignment, motivation and corrective action, and employee development.

INFORMATION SYSTEMS AND OTHER PROFESSIONALS: DIFFERENCES AND SIMILARITIES

Gerald Weinberg (1971) has suggested that there are behavioral differences in IS professionals that distinguish them from other workers. To Weinberg these differences are meaningful and important. Many IS managers have thought it important to recognize and understand this "IS type" personality. Other observers, such as Brett Middleton (1988), do not necessarily agree. They might say that the similarities between IS and other workers are more important than any differences that may exist. Moreover, most of what is often pointed to as unique characteristic behavior belongs to a set of selected behavioral variations that are not unique to or even concentrated in the IS profession. Finally, these observers argue that certain noticeable differences are determined by the work and not the persons performing it. This viewpoint would suggest, for instance, that all programmers are not necessarily detail-oriented personalities but simply appear that way because their work requires considerable attention to detail.

Similarly, after field research, Thomas W. Ferratt and Larry E. Short (1988) concluded that IS people are no different than non-IS people based on the similarities of their work-unit environments and work-unit environment/productivity relationship. They therefore inferred that IS and non-IS employees at the same occupational levels are not and should not be managed differently.

Michael Lyons (1985), however, has described how the IS professional varies from the general population with respect to several diverse qualities. From a survey Lyons concluded that

- The IS professional is more introverted than the general population. [J. Daniel Couger and R. A. Zawacki (1978) also confirm this.]
- The IS professional is more likely to rely on imagination and creativity than on seeing things in a practical, realistic way.

- The IS professional is much more likely to make decisions on a logical basis rather than on the basis of personal values or feelings.
- The IS professional functions in a more orderly, controlled fashion than the average person, who is likely to be more flexible and adaptive.

Of course, Lyon's sampling contained diverse IS professionals and contradictory traits were observed. However, the general pattern was clear. In addition to these qualities, Weinberg observed that IS professionals are much more rewarded than others by the nature of their job, were less deferential to legitimate authority, and might be driven by goals of exactness that transcended simple business requirements. Many of these traits are manifestations of the qualities that Lyons observed.

In looking to characterize the behaviors of professionals, we tend to use models that group behaviors into convenient and meaningful classes. An exceedingly simple model derives from academia, where students sometimes broadly categorize one another as "poets" or "engineers." The distinction to which these labels refer—between the judgmental/subjective and the scientific/tangible—has influenced the current stereotype of the IS professional as inhumanly mechanical.

A more thoughtful delineation is that of left-brain/right-brain individuals. Right-brain activity or thinking tends toward the aesthetic, the subjective, and the artistic, whereas left-brain activity and thought are usually quantitative, logical, and precise. Although each of us relies on both kinds, the proportions do vary. The IS professional might be accused of being left-brain-dominated, although many emerging IS activities, such as user relations, are undoubtedly right-brain related. Chapter 19 will look at other implications of this dichotomy.

Yet another popular model separates people into two types, A and B, on the basis of internal motivations. The Type A individual is a high-energy, frequently high-stress, compulsive performer. Indeed performance for this person is usually more important than any social benefits of work. Salespeople are often used as examples of this driven personality. Type B individuals, in contrast, are more content with their surroundings and their role; their relations with others do not seem to affect their job satisfaction. Perhaps surprisingly, the Type B personality is the one most often cited as consistent with the image of the technologist.

Information Systems Professionals Compared to Users

There are obvious, natural differences between users and IS professionals. Kate Kaiser and Robert Bostrom (1982) characterize this gap as shown in Exhibit 12-2. They suggest that the barriers these differences present might be overcome by more forgiving technologic interfaces that would permit structured input and management by IS personnel and flexible output as needed by user personnel. The Kaiser and Bostrom study goes on to show great similarities between IS professionals and the users who work with them on projects. Closer examination reveals that these IS professional-like users may be atypical and unlike those users who are not involved in actual IS projects. If this is the case, it indicates that the real communications gap is occurring within the ranks of users: That is, the disenfranchised end-user can be the ultimate cause of systems failure.

Information Systems Professionals Compared to Managers

Similar conflicts in personality type can be read into the popularly noted differences between IS professionals and managers. The manager is usually perceived as being responsive to and respectful of authority, willing to work through other people, and very sensitive to achievements. IS professionals are perceived as being more respectful of knowledge than of authority, driven by the objective of correctness and precision, and less concerned about personal relationships. Within these and other perceptions lie the possible

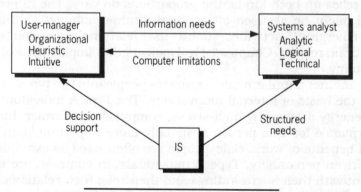

EXHIBIT 12-2 IS professionals and users: closing the gap.

Source: Kate M. Kaiser and Robert P. Bostrom, "Personality Characteristics of MIS Project Teams: An Empirical Study and Action-Research Design," *MIS Quarterly*, December 1982, p. 44. Reprinted by special permission. Copyright 1984 by the Society for Information Management and the Management Information Systems Research Center at the University of Minnesota.

sources of many a manager-IS professional impasse. Both can be firm in their beliefs and egocentric in their reaction to conflict; which can lead to a performance deadlock when strong personalities draw on differing value systems. Even if we believe that such stereotypes are not the rule, their occasional occurrence is still a formula for problems.

Some observers point out that there are enough similarities between IS professionals and managers to lay a common ground for good relations and work habits. Of course duplication of skills can create conflict, and gaps in skill mixes may cause problems. Often, persons with opposing skills, such as a talker and a listener, form the best team. Within the IS department, the following contrasts can be found:

- Conceptual–Practical
- People-oriented–Technically oriented
- Control-oriented–Change-oriented
- Qualitative–Quantitative
- Abstraction-oriented–Detail-oriented

Any supervisor/subordinate tandem must bring a mixture of skills that suggest an efficient way of dividing up the tasks. Naturally, a team is stronger when one person's strengths cover for another's weaknesses. Exhibit 12-3 is an exercise in varying traits. It is instructive to imagine pairs of situations in which each group of traits can work effectively both in conjunction with and in opposition to each other.

THE INFORMATION SYSTEMS PROFESSIONAL AND THE ENVIRONMENT

Differing personality types must not only interact constructively (as much as the work relationship requires) but must also fit the business climate and the tasks at hand. As we all know from experience, different personalities adapt differently to different tasks. This is one reason why some programmers enjoy maintenance programming and others do not. Although many people can and do perform two disparate tasks, most people display a predilection toward one kind or the other. (The ambidextrous IS professional, for example, is rare.) Clearly, the manager best serves the department by aligning individual affinities and tasks, even generic ones such as administrative paperwork, which nearly every IS worker must perform in some measure.

The individual's fit with the broader dimensions of the work climate should also be considered. Much can be inferred about a particular work environment by examining the industry of which the company is a part. It is usually supposed that a banking environment is fairly cautious and conservative; an insurance company is specialized, methodical, and procedural; and a high-technology environment is more innovative and adventurous. Although these

	My Boss's Style	My Style is Like/Unlike
Is the boss a listener (prefers to hear and talk) or a reader (prefers to read and write) when it comes to discussing ideas, problems, or plans with you?		
Is the boss a preparer (prefers to plan and organize extensively before meetings or presentations) or an ad libber (prefers to do only minimal preparation and would rather work very informally)?		
Is the boss a doer (prefers to decide quickly on action steps and implement them) or a planner (prefers to analyze, review, and plan in detail first before taking action)?		
Is the boss an exciter (tends to be very energetic, enthusiastic, and expressive) or a stabilizer (tends to be more subdued calm, and shows little emotion)?		
Is the boss a teacher (prefers to give out step-by-step instructions and coach in detail) or a resource (prefers to give only general guidelines then be available for help if needed)?		

EXHIBIT 12-3 Hypothetical supervisor/subordinate styles.

patterns are not universal, they do occur often enough to suggest that certain professionals will fit better in banking than in high-technology firms.

Corporate philosophy is a more variable determinant of the work climate and one that makes each climate unique. Even the normally staid climate of a banking firm can be agitated by a management philosophy that encourages aggressive risk taking. Conversely, a usually free-wheeling firm can be "repersonalized" by managerial guidance toward coordination, consensus, and prudence.

Of course, no situation will be ideally tailored to any one professional. The constant changes in modern work environments cloud the issue of worker–climate fit even further. Regardless of the circumstances, IS professionals must display tolerance, flexibility, and the ability to decide which possible areas of conflict can be accommodated and which can be handled by selected adjustments to behavior. Insight into their own motivations will assist each IS professional make wise evaluations in the event of conflicts with the work climate.

THE INFORMATION SYSTEMS PROFESSIONAL AS PART OF A GROUP

As we have seen, the right mix of contrasting skills can balance approaches to a problem, decrease the risk of inferior solutions, and strengthen compromise decisions. Of course, strengths and weaknesses of the manager must match those of his or her subordinates if a truly effective team is to be built. The IS manager who thinks in broad terms might lend a useful perspective to team members driven by the urgency of immediate results. It is less likely that a manager obsessed with immediacy will have a productive relationship with subordinates who prefer a meticulous, methodical work process.

A strong team results when key success factors are reinforced by selected skills. If user involvement and participation is especially essential to a particular project, many if not all the project team members should have strong interpersonal and communications skills. The mix of those who lean toward formal communications and organized meetings and those who are more comfortable communicating by walking around can, of course, vary, but if the team is generally oriented toward good rapport with users, it is likely to be effective.

ELEMENTS OF INFORMATION SYSTEMS PERSONNEL MANAGEMENT

Just as computer systems have a life cycle that starts with justification and definition and proceeds through development and implementation to ongoing maintenance, so can the management of IS personnel be divided into certain sequential components. Every employee starts by applying for a position or role, proceeds to being selected to fit that position or role, and goes on to improve and be further developed for subsequent roles. Along the way, managers exercise control by rewarding and motivating desirable performance and identifying and correcting poor performance. The cycle of IS personnel management is characterized by certain ongoing tasks for which the manager is responsible—tasks in the areas of job analysis, selecting new employees, assigning work, and motivating and developing employees. These areas are discussed in the sections that follow.

Job Analysis

There are many approaches to establishing and structuring jobs. One approach is to use methods-analysis techniques to identify and group like tasks into units of work that can then become positions. Where these tasks are elements of a complex process, the technique can also involve relating one group of tasks to another to provide effective job integration. Technology can be useful in suggesting how job tasks should be grouped, or the job-structuring approach might be guided by conceptual strategies such as specialization or generalization, flexibility or specificity, tight supervision or autonomy, and so forth.

Each job must, of course, be capable of being performed. It should be a desirable function, and it should be environmentally consistent and not overly clerical if peer positions are more cerebral. Nor should it be narrowly focused if all other jobs are broad in their orientation.

Along with performance-oriented considerations, technical considerations, and strategic issues, "people issues" are a big factor in job design. The number of interactions will indicate the approximate portion of the job that will be spent in communications. The IS manager will want to ensure this remains in a reasonable range. The nature of the relationship must also be known. A service role, a directive role, and an advisory role will each place a different skill demand on the ultimate incumbent. However, each identified relationship will have a varied combination of interaction types, which will in turn require a variety of interpersonal skills for the job.

Employee Selection

Turnover No discussion of IS job selection should begin without confronting the occupational fact of high turnover rates. Especially for scarce skills, the IS manager is faced with frequent replacement hiring, long periods of job vacancy, evaluation of few qualified (and only a few more marginally qualified) candidates, trying to select candidates that will be comparatively stable, and attempting to remove causes of turnover.

Some experts claim that turnover is inevitable because IS professional are always looking for challenge and greater opportunities. They will therefore always be restless, especially when career structures, job markets, and measures of professional success are designed to encourage movement. Others argue that turnover is largely induced by poor management practices and an attitude that expects people to leave and be replaced.

Jack Baroudi (1985) conducted a study of turnover and its organizational causes and concluded that much turnover was caused by role conflict and role ambiguity, not a little of which was introduced by specific management action—clumsy department or project reorganizations, unclear role definitions and reporting responsibilities, and vague work priorities. A recent interview of IS professionals in *Computerworld* (February 8, 1988) cited several other causes of employee dissatisfaction, including

- Ineffective or poor management
- Lack of advancement or career growth
- Not enough staff or overly heavy work load
- Lack of resources or poor or obsolete equipment
- Lack of communication with management

Certainly, not all this is avoidable; however, it is clear that IS management could do a far better job of working with IS professionals and removing some of the causes of turnover.

A less common but real scenario is the problem of low turnover. Unless there is some flow of less productive and/or frustrated staff from an IS department, performance problems build up. To avoid stagnation, Richard Nolan (1981) points out that there is a healthy level of turnover that is commensurate with the size of the department, as shown in Exhibit 12-4.

Hiring: Inside Versus Outside For the straightforward case of an existing job that needs to be filled, the IS manager is often faced with a fundamental choice: to promote or retrain an existing employee or to hire a new person. Each option has advantages and disadvantages, as Exhibit 12-5 shows.

When hiring from the outside, the IS manager confronts many sources for acquiring candidates:

- Search firms
- Company recruiters
- Direct advertising
- Colleges and universities
- Job fairs
- Cooperative education/training programs and internships
- Employee referrals or walk-ins
- Competitors

Each method tends to attract a different kind of candidate; therefore, most companies are selective about the methods they choose to use. However, so as not to become too homogeneous, most IS departments acquire candidates from a variety of sources and fill openings through internal and external channels.

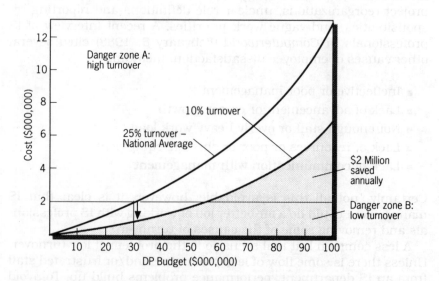

EXHIBIT 12-4 The cost of computer professional turnover in DP departments.

Source: Richard L. Nolan, "Managing the Human Resource," *Stage by Stage* vol. 2, no. 2, 1981, p. 2. Copyright 1981 by Nolan, Norton & Co. All rights reserved. Reprinted with permission.

Credentials and Potential Some managers tend to be very literal about job specifications and insist on finding candidates whose years of experience, education, work exposure, and so forth are exactly as specified. This approach is popular within the IS field, as the need for technical compatibility usually requires that candidates' backgrounds be carefully assessed against specific technical requirements. But what tends to be left out by this approach are factors that are harder to verify, hence somewhat subjective: communication skills, intellectual depth, flexibility, urgency, and so on. Managers can determine the presence of these factors using their own common sense and insight. Some managers make a special effort to emphasize the importance of such intangibles in the selection process. However, because these areas are less easily verified than specific credentials, many IS managers tend to rely exclusively on finding a good "fit" with an objective hiring profile.

Hiring from Inside	Hiring from Outside
Advantages	
Encourages general loyalty	Allows for wider selection and deeper skill set possible
Builds on proprietary skills	Adds variety to existing skill set
Lowers recruiting costs	Skill training is not required
Controls transition for employee and employer	Brings fresh ideas
Disadvantages	
Generates new opening	May involve expensive skills
No experience in new job	May cause internal resentment
Develops inbreeding	Chemistry may not be right
Requires more in-house training	Provides no detailed knowledge of employee's work history
Does not bring new ideas	May involve costly or lengthy hiring process; right candidate may not exist
	More likely to lose new hire

EXHIBIT 12-5 A comparison of internal and external hiring.

It is becoming increasingly common for managers to dismiss some of the usual hiring "tickets," such as educational degree, work experience, and years of specific technical experience, and to hire employees who possess a strong industry knowledge, good business skills, a high energy level, and other similar qualities. The logic of such an approach is that because the IS field is changing and advancing, it is more important to find employees who can fit into the future environment that it is to attract employees strictly on the basis of current needs.

Task Assignments

Once an employee is on board, the manager's ongoing responsibility is to assign work so as to maintain productivity and get the most out of the employee. Assigned tasks should be used to offer variety, challenge, novelty, and (most importantly) career development opportunity for the IS professional. Extra assignments that add interest to a job without overburdening the employee can also be created. Tasks such as researching new technologies, training other professionals, briefing users or managers, and preparing documentation can be useful pieces of work and can help expand the staff's talents.

Job rotation is one extreme means of providing task variety. This technique can revitalize employees who are bored and is especially useful in removing barriers between departmental units. Paul Licker (1985) cites the benefits of an especially dramatic form of this practice, IS-user job rotation. The key advantage here is improved interactions, although other benefits are recognized as well. Placing IS knowledge in user hands and user knowledge in IS hands forces the kinds of questions and eventual understanding that are needed if the boundaries of effective computerization are to keep expanding. Exhibit 12-6 not only shows how Licker feels this solution to IS-user interaction is an improvement to other traditional ways, but itemizes the comparative strengths of alternative methods of promoting this intracompany interaction.

One of the tools that the IS manager has to work with is the ability to build the job to include task variety. This need not simply accommodate the tasks to be accomplished but can be organized to accommodate the working habits, style, and behavioral characteristics of the person to be doing the work. (For permanent jobs, of course, this has the disadvantage of being slightly "out of focus" every time there is a staffing change). One of the tough choices an IS manager must make is how much should the job (or even the task) be structured to accommodate the individual and how much should you select the individual to fit the job. Often too much insistence on the latter concludes with current staff being inadequate and outside hiring being required to find the right behavioral skills. IS professional are quick to appreciate when specific technical skills are needed but often are not as accepting of the fact that behavioral skills that they may not possess are required.

Motivation

Keeping IS professionals positive and focused requires a set of agreed-on behavioral and performance objectives, a consistent means of assessing actual compliance with those objectives, and a process of reviewing performance and mutually determining a future

Dimension of MIS-Company Interaction			
Forms of MIS - Company Interaction	Interpene - tration	Joint Effort	Understand - ability
Classic DP units	Low	Low	Low
Classic DP units with systems analysts	Medium	Low	Medium
Classic DP units with computer services representatives	Medium	Medium	Medium
Classic DP units with systems analysts with prototyping	Medium	High	High
Information center	Low	Medium	Medium
End-user software	Low	Low	High
Multidisciplinary task units	Medium	High	High
Job rotation	High	High	High

EXHIBIT 12-6 Forms of MIS-company interaction.

Source: Paul S. Licker, "Breaking Down the Wall: MIS-User Job Rotation," Journal of Information Systems Management, vol. 2, no. 2, Spring, 1985, p. 11. Copyright 1985 Warren, Gorham & Lamont Inc.

course of action. The IS manager should always bear in mind, when considering motivation, that what is considered important by the computer professional is slightly different than what is valued by the general population. Ramon Mata Toledo and Elizabeth Unger have compared these values, as shown in Exhibit 12-7. The work of Mata Toledo and Unger suggest that some factors are important because

General Work Population	*Computer Professionals*
1. Achievement	1. Achievement
2. Recognition	2. Possibility for growth
3. Work itself	3. Work itself
4. Responsibility	4. Recognition
5. Advancement	5. Advancement
6. Salary	6. Supervision, technical
7. Possibility for growth	7. Responsibility
8. Interpersonal relations with subordinates	8. Interpersonal relations with peers
9. Status	9. Interpersonal relations with subordinates
10. Interpersonal relations with peers	10. Personal life
11. Supervision, technical	11. Interpersonal relations with superiors
12. Company policy and administration	12. Job security
13. Working conditions	13. Status
14. Personal life	14. Company policy and administration
15. Job security	15. Working conditions

EXHIBIT 12-7 Rank order of motivators for computer professionals and a more general work population.

Source: Ramon A. Mata Toledo and Elizabeth A. Unger, "Another Look at Motivating Data Processing Professionals," Department of Computer Science, Kansas State University, Manhattan, KA., p. 4.

their absence will discourage computer professionals, but these factors do not in themselves motivate. Exhibit 12-8 identifies some of these so-called "hygiene" factors. IS managers should ensure that hygiene factors are present so as to remove obstructions to productivity from the path of their employees.

Corrective Action   Sometimes employee performance falls outside acceptable bounds; it is then up to the IS manager to try to understand the cause of poor performance and to take corrective action. Often the problem is that the employee does not grasp the requirements of the job, or certain institutional obstacles are impeding his or her performance. The users may not be providing complete specifications in order for an analyst to finalize a project design step, for example. With the manager's help, the employee can be made to

Hygiene Factors	Motivators
1. Growth	1. Achievement
2. Technical supervision	
3. Interpersonal relations with peers	2. Work itself
4. Interpersonal relations with subordinates	
5. Salary	3. Recognition for work
6. Noninterference with personal life	
7. Interpersonal relations with superiors	4. Advancement
8. Job security	
9. Status	5. Responsibility
10. Company policy and procedure	
11. Working conditions	

EXHIBIT 12-8 Hertzberg's hygienes and motivators presented in rank order according to *Fitz-enz Study for Computer Professionals.*

Source: Ramon A. Mata Toledo and Elizabeth A. Unger, "Another Look at Motivating Data Processing Professionals," Department of Computer Science, Kansas State University, Manhattan, KA., p. 6.

appreciate acceptable levels of contribution. In *Analyzing Perform-ance Problems*, Robert Mager and Peter Pipe (1970) discuss a technique for assessing performance discrepancies. As indicated in Exhibit 12-9, training, practice, simplification, and personnel as-sessment are means of dealing with such discrepancies.

If the manager has diagnosed a problem that can be solved with the employee, he or she needs to help the employee admit the problem, ask the employee for a solution, and follow up on the employee's solution.

Employee Development

Because one of the key motivators of IS professionals is growth, it is crucial that IS managers devote sufficient attention to employee development. The benefits of doing so extend far beyond mere employee satisfaction or even retention. When the skills and abilities of employees improve, the quantity and quality of their work—that is, their productivity—will definitely rise. The returns on expendi-tures of time and money on employee development easily justify the decision to develop. For most IS departments the problem is to undertake development in the face of other urgent, immediate responsibilities.

Education   Because the field of IS is so volatile, education is widely accepted as a professional requirement. Yet too often companies do not treat it as important and, surprisingly, many IS professionals fail to push for ongoing education. Ignoring for a moment the individ-ual's responsibility to stay technically current, the IS manager should ensure that his or her organization fulfills its duty to keep its employees fluent in the tools of their trade. Undoubtedly, the IS manager and the department will benefit directly from the fresh ideas and motivation generated by educational programs.

Education can be formal or informal, outside the company or inside. It need not mean expensive, time-consuming training. For-mal off-site training has the advantage of being intensive, and a periodic change of venue is healthy. However, some formal training can be set up within the company for less money and with greater convenience. Moreover, it can be tailored and made specific to the environment.

Two varieties of training are common: outside instructor and self-taught training. Informal training can be even more tailored and integrated into the work process. This might include on-the-job training, professional reading programs, vendor briefing sessions, and many other techniques to make education more affordable and accessible.

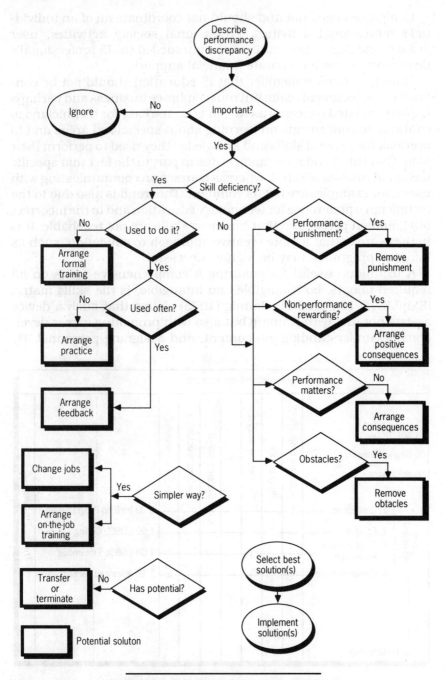

EXHIBIT 12-9 Assessing performance problems.

Source: Robert F. Mager and Pete Pipe, *Analyzing Performance Problems*, Belmont, CA: Fearon, 1970, p. 2.

Companies need not and should not coordinate all of an individual's educational activities. Professional society activities, user groups, and degree programs can be pursued at the IS professional's discretion but with corporate financial support.

Managers must remember that IS education should not be confined to the technical realm but must embrace business and perhaps industry-related concerns as well. It is far too easy for technicians to continue to concentrate on learning about specialized areas and to overlook the general skills and knowledge they need to perform their jobs. That this trend is common is due in part to the fact that specific technical courses abound, whereas courses on communicating with users, for example, are not as common. The trend is also due to the technician's preference for technology education and to the incorrect but common perception that business skills are not teachable. It is in these areas that a more creative approach to education, such as informal programs, may be highly successful.

A technique useful for ensuring a comprehensive focus on all required talents, both tangible and intangible, is the skills matrix (Exhibit 12-10). Fredrick Jahnig (1975) claims that such a device assists not just with training but also with promoting career development, understanding job content, and assigning personnel. By

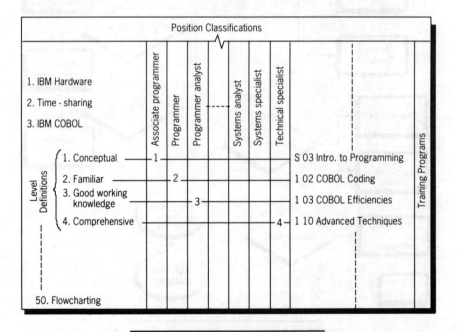

EXHIBIT 12-10 Skills matrix.

Source: Frederick F. Jahnig, "Skills Matrixing,"Excerpted from *Datamation*, September 1975, copyright © 1975 by Cahners Publishing Company.

relating education to a particular job use, this matrix can help the IS manager avoid a training trap—newly acquired knowledge with no immediate application. Without a chance to practice acquired skills, employees will quickly lose what they may have learned.

Career Development   A popular career-enhancement focus is on the managerial level. This has been unfortunate in many respects. As Dana Davis (1988) observes not every IS professional wants to or has the necessary skills to become a manager. For one thing, fast-track IS professionals often find the typical road to management slow and tedious. Moreover, there are very few management jobs in IS, relative to the number of professional jobs available and longevity is high. Consequently, the experience of most companies is that the odds that an IS employee will become a manager are disappointingly low.

The sad part of this saga is that most employees seek management positions only because of the supposed cachet they confer on the job. It is true that awarding managerial jobs was for a time the only way to keep employees' status, income, and other rewards on the rise—although most managers were happiest utilizing technical skills and few really looked forward to performing management tasks. Having realized this, many organizations have created a dual career-track environment, whereby advancement can continue without forcing a change in the nature of the work to which the IS professional is best

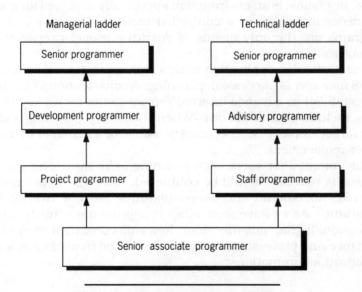

EXHIBIT 12-11 IBM dual ladder of advancement.

Source: Frederick P. Brooks, Jr., *The Mythical Man-Month*, copyright © 1975, Addison-Wesley Publishing Co., Inc., Reading Massachusetts. Figure 11.1 on page 119. Reprinted with permission.

suited. Frederick Brooks (1975) calls attention to this with an example from IBM, as shown in Exhibit 12-11.

For the individual looking for something more satisfying or more suited to his or her talents, lateral movement should be encouraged. Moving to a different though not more senior or lucrative position is one way for a seemingly marginal employee to remain useful within the organization. It can also inject excitement into that individual's work life.

Movement up the organizational ladder is certainly appropriate and even laudable. Many IS departments take pains to ensure that there is a succession plan. Exhibit 12-12 is a career ladder used by Michael Albrecht, Jr. (1987), which forms the basis for such a plan. It suggests that wherever possible senior vacancies should be filled internally through promotion. Of course, succession plans require that training and development of potential successors take place in advance so that skills will not be lacking when the time comes. Originally invented as a way to protect the organization against critical turnover, these plans are equally beneficial to employees, as they chart out likely career paths, set up promotional and career structures to support them, and aid in the development of skills necessary for eventual advancement.

Saul Gellerman (1973) argues that traditional, formal management training programs are often ineffective career-development tools. The only road to successful development of management skills, he claims, is an environment specifically designed for evolving the necessary skills in a controlled method. On-the-job training programs are the only means of ensuring proper preparation for managers.

One particular application of this technique especially useful to the IS manager is succession planning. A conscientious IS manager will establish in advance internal replacements for all key IS positions, including his or her own. When succession planning is shared with target employees, it becomes possible for a manager to train his or her replacement.

The potential for succession planning to be threatening (to both parties) is real but should be countered. After all, no promotion is assured, nor should succession planning assume overwhelming importance. As we have seen, other things are more important to IS professionals than advancement. Rewards consistent with job performance and professional abilities need to be treated as at least as important as promotions.

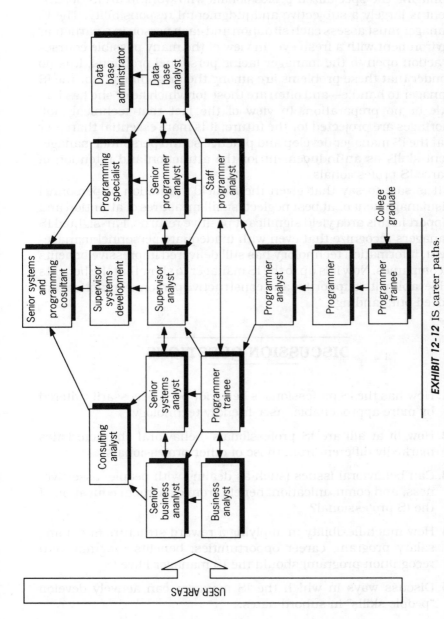

EXHIBIT 12-12 IS career paths.

Source: Michael J. Albrecht, Jr. "Managing Employee Careers," *Computerworld-In-Depth,* 1987, p. 26. "Copyright 1987 by the CW Publishing Inc. Framingham, MA. 01701. Reprinted from *Computerworld.*"

CONCLUSION

Managing the specialized professionals who work in an IS department is largely a subjective and judgmental responsibility. The IS manager must assess each situation and each person in a particular environment with a fresh eye. In view of the many possible courses of action open to the manager facing personnel problems, it is no wonder that these problems are among the most difficult for the IS manager to handle—and often are those for which he or she has had little or no preparation. In view of the fact that technical skill shortages are projected for the future, it is more essential than ever that the IS manager develop and practice sound personnel management skills as an inducement for the attraction and retention of scarce IS professionals.

It is safe to say that given the IS field's tradition of personnel mismanagement or at best neglect, small measures of attention and support in this area yield significant positive returns. Far-sighted IS managers recognize that even with inadequate personnel management, information technology has still delivered impressive benefits to companies. Now it is up to the IS manager to show that the benefits achievable with supportive and constructive personnel practices are indeed outstanding.

DISCUSSION QUESTIONS

1. How has the IS professional's behavior been necessarily altered by more approachable, user-friendly technology?

2. How (if at all) are IS professionals' behavioral characteristics markedly different from those of other professionals?

3. Can behavioral issues (such as dealing with people, assertiveness, and communication) benefit from classroom education of the IS professional?

4. How much flexibility in applying a reward structure (including salary program, career opportunities, benefits program, and recognition program) should the IS manager have?

5. Discuss ways in which the IS manager can actively develop "people skills" in subordinates.

6. If strategic responsibilities prevent the IS manager from personally interacting with the IS department staff, what actions can be taken to minimize personnel problems?

7. How do you explain the requirement for more attention to IS personnel issues on the one hand and Weinberg's claim that IS personnel tend to work independently and want management to leave them alone on the other?

8. "In the future, IS personnel will become a more diverse group and the IS personnel management problem will therefore become more complicated." Do you agree or disagree?

REFERENCES

Albrecht, Michael J. Jr. (1987). "Managing Employee Careers," *Computerworld-In-Depth*, pp. 21-32.

Baroudi, Jack J. (1985). "The Impact of Role Variables on IS Personnel Work Attitudes and Intentions," *MIS Quarterly* (December), pp. 341-357.

Brooks, Frederick P. Jr.(1975). *The Mythical Man-Month* (Reading, MA: Addison-Wesley), p. 119.

Cougar, J. D. ,and R. A. Zawacki (1978). "What Motivates DP Professionals?" *Datamation*, vol. 24, no. 9 (September), pp. 116-123.

Davis, Dana (1988). "But I Don't Want To Be a Manager," *Computerworld* (January 11), pp. 65-68.

Ferratt, Thomas W., and Larry E. Short (1988). "Are Information Systems People Different? An Investigation of How They Are and Should Be Managed," *MIS Quarterly* (September), pp. 427-443.

Gellerman, Saul W. (1973). "Developing Managers Without Management Development," *The Conference Board Record* (July), pp. 32-37.

Jahnig, Frederick F. (1975). "Skills Matrixing," *Datamation* (September), pp. 71-76.

Kaiser, Kate M., and Robert P. Bostrom (1982). "Personality Characteristics of MIS Project Teams: An Empirical Study and Action-Research Design," *MIS Quarterly* (December), pp. 43-60.

Licker, Paul S. (1985). "Breaking Down the Wall: MIS-User Job Rotation," *Journal of Information Systems Management* (Spring), pp. 10-16.

Lyons, Michael L. (1985). "The DP Psyche," *Datamation* (August 15), p. 103.

Mager, Robert F. and Pipe, Peter (1970). *Analyzing Performance Problems* (Belmont, CA: Fearon Publishers), p. 3.

Mata Toledo, Ramon A., and Elizabeth A. Unger ( ). "Another Look at Motivating Data Processing Professionals," Department of Computer Science, Kansas State University, Manhattan, pp. 1-7.

Middleton, Brett (1988). "Programmers: Not a Breed Apart," *Computerworld* (April 4), pp. 63-65.

Nolan, Richard L. (1981). "Managing the Human Resource," *Stage by Stage* vol. 2, no. 2, p. 2.

Weinberg, Gerald M. (1971). *The Psychology of Computer Programming* (New York: Van Nostrand Reinhold), pp. 45-200.

thirteen

☐

Information Systems Development Methodologies and Projects

295

The construction of information systems initially rested in the hands of a few clever specialists who, like other artisans, possessed high levels of inventiveness and craftsmanship. Their task was eased by the fact that these builders were responsible for determining the content as well as functionality of information systems.

But things have changed, and IS professionals no longer determine the functionality of users' systems. Indeed, the complexity of modern systems makes it difficult for individual professionals to construct systems on their own. Today's systems are neither self contained nor isolated. They must be integrated with surrounding systems and must also incorporate data and features from earlier predecessor systems.

The result has been the growth of development methodologies allowing an individual (or, more likely, a team) to construct a system properly by following guidelines tested over the years in many different system development projects. A popular analogy comes from the building trade. Whereas in the past a craftsperson could build a house by relying chiefly on intuition, modern housebuilders are teams of specialists who come together to do different tasks and who together can build many differing houses. For this to happen, the chief builder (project manager) follows similar procedures (such as blueprints and financing plans), for each house. Along the way there are reviews and approvals to refine the house and to limit risk. The chief builder, although probably familiar with the technology of the trade, is mainly responsible for ensuring that each house is built *on schedule, within budget*, and *according to specifications*. To do this, the chief builder must spell out clear rules and see that they are followed. The rules encourage early design decisions; subsequent decisions can then be made based on a sure foundation.

Although there are many ways to build a house, it is the similarities in contemporary house-building methods that are most pronounced. This is true of the development of traditional computer systems as well. All go through a similar life cycle, as shown in Exhibit 13-1. All system development methodologies, even those that look different, are ways of describing and controlling this same cycle. Some will parallel it step by step (or phase by phase to use popular system development terminology); others will combine several events into one phase or even one event into several measurable activities.

To illustrate the diversity of methodologies and to give you a flavor of the popular variety, in this chapter we will discuss an assortment of system development methodologies, all of which will refer to the process outlined in Exhibit 13-1.

System development methodologies have evolved to make contemporary system more productive, and continuing changes in both production and management methods will be forthcoming. It is up to the IS manager to anticipate the type and timing of these changes. As more sophisticated software is used, as more integration is required, as more turnkey products are installed, and as fewer technically skilled professionals are needed to perform systems and programming duties, carefully tailored management techniques must be in place to support this evolution.

Inception
    Preliminary

Feasibility study
    Existing procedures
    Alternative systems
    Cost estimates

Systems analysis
    Details of present procedures
    Collection of data on volumes, input/output files

Design
    Ideal system unconstrained
    Revisions to make ideal acceptable

Specification
    Processing logic
    File design
    Input/output
    Programming requirements
    Manual procedures

Programming

Testing
    Unit tests
    Combined module tests
    Acceptance tests

Training

Conversion and installation

Operations
    Maintenance
    Enhancements

EXHIBIT 13-1 The systems life cycle.

Source: Henry C. Lucas, Jr., The Analysis and Implementation of Information Systems, 2nd ed., New York: McGraw-Hill, copyright © 1981, p. 78. Reprinted with permission.

In this chapter we look first at system design methodological issues and then, more broadly, at system development projects themselves. We start with the goals of systems development methodologies (SDMs) and the relationship of the SDM and corporate priorities. Next, we consider means of incorporating standardized design methods into customized SDMs. The possible phases of an SDM are our next concern; from there, we launch into various development techniques and data conversion strategies.

Next, we turn to the actual systems development projects within which SDMs are practiced: large, traditional, maintenance projects, and other irregular or emergency projects. We discuss the functional objectives of most systems development projects and then examine issues of project initiation—an important step, as it happens—and scheduling concerns. We conclude with a look at important project management issues.

THE GOALS OF SYSTEMS DEVELOPMENT METHODOLOGIES

Most SDMs have many aims, some of which seem in conflict yet all of which must be kept in balance. The following sections discuss the goals (which are also, it is hoped, the benefits) of SDMs.

- Efficiency
- Communications
- Control
- Documentation
- Role Definition
- Consistency

Efficiency

As Exhibit 13-2 indicates, a certain degree of guidance and direction can definitely improve efficiency. However, it is also clear that rules and regulations can be overdone. Lengthy rule books or massive paperwork requirements may provide comprehensive constraints but will hardly allow systems development projects to be completed in a timely, efficient manner. If efficiency is a primary objective, some happy medium must be struck by the SDM. The task of finding this point is complicated by several factors. Fourth-generation languages, for example, do not require all the guidance and restrictions required by older languages such as COBOL. A data-dictionary coordination step is undertaken automatically by some new languages and is therefore redundant or detrimental if carried over intact from previous SDMs. At the same time, because the ease of use of new technology makes it (in theory) more productive, additional efficiencies to be gained through regimented procedures are more limited.

Communications

An SDM usually designates specific points during a project at which certain facts are to be communicated to others. This communication could involve both specific members of the project team and outside parties. Although there are a multitude of concerned participants and functions in any system development project, all can be grouped as management, users, or technicians. Obviously, each is concerned with different aspects of the project and each has different communications needs. Managers look for cost and schedule information, users for developments that affect their specifications, and technicians for design information. (Those persons who fall into more than one category typically have to balance several communications interests.) The SDM must facilitate a steady, reliable information flow among all parties.

Control

Controls can entail acquiring permission to proceed with a project (e.g., approvals for a spending plan) or being told how to proceed

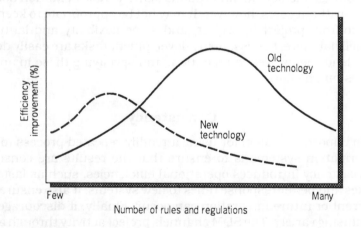

EXHIBIT 13-2 Systems development methodologies and efficiency.

(e.g., users specifying a preferred on-line dialogue). Although a liberal use of controls can instill a feeling of involvement and confidence and might prevent missteps, too-heavy controls can have negative effects on project schedule, cost, and content.

In most projects, the scarcest resource is the most heavily controlled. Thus, in cost-conscious environments, budget variance reports may be heavily used; in schedule-conscious settings reports on time expenditures will be frequently issued. The most difficult challenge for the project manager is to manage in such a way as to satisfy two or more control constraints. Achieving either budget or schedule performance goals is easier than satisfying them both.

Documentation

A byproduct of communications, documents are important enough to become separate SDM goals. Like blueprints, documents are useful to guide the construction of a product and ultimately become archival in nature. (Indeed, many documents are designed with a future use as standing documentation in mind.) Documentation can include users' manuals, systems overview information, operator instructions, maintenance programmer background information, restart and error recovery instructions, and more.

Role Definition

An SDM serves to define the roles of everyone in the system development project. By spelling out "who does what to whom," SDMs help reduce anxiety, minimize arguments over duties, and discourage inefficient, superfluous activity. Role definition does not come without costs, however. It may not be appropriate to keep roles static from project to project, and some flexibility and latitude is beneficial. Nevertheless, many development tasks are easily defined and lend themselves to repetition, and specifying these in an SDM saves much effort.

Consistency

One important reason for using a readily repeated process to build information systems is to ensure that the results are consistent. Consistency introduces operational efficiencies, such as faster run times and better response times to new systems. It also ensures that current or future integration can occur. Finally, it discourages any confusing variety. The SDM channels project activity through appropriate existing corporate processes such as data management, spending approvals, work assignments, and other typical organizational practices. A consistent SDM improves on the learning curve for future projects, allows comparisons of performance from one project to the other, and assists in future project planning.

SYSTEMS DEVELOPMENT METHODOLOGIES AND CORPORATE PRIORITIES

Each of the foregoing goals can be achieved, to a greater or lesser degree, by a thorough SDM. However, because some of these goals (efficiency and control, for instance) have contradictory components, the IS manager must answer some difficult questions in choosing the right SDM.

The first question to be answered concerns the priorities of the corporate environment. An SDM cannot accomplish everything, but it can be slanted toward specific organizational priorities and objectives. One way to begin is to identify the target beneficiaries of a planned system, along with attendant SDM features (see Exhibit 13-3). Emphases in one area can, however, be perceived as negligence in other areas. Exhibit 13-4 lists the trade-offs of an IS-dominated system development life cycle as compared with one that heavily favors users.

Another related way to begin is to identify corporate or other institutional factors necessitating trade-offs. Exhibit 13-5 schematizes two basic trade-off dilemmas. For instance, existing rules may give project team members the authority to adjust the development process and permission to make many decisions themselves. Approval of the network manager might be required only if, in the judgment of the project manager, significant changes to the network environment are planned. Making the rules more rigid would mean consistently requiring the network manager's approval, so that this person would in effect become the arbiter of "significant changes." An SDM can be written to be completely comprehensive, covering every project phase and every kind of project, or it can be restricted in its area of coverage to major (or simply typical) areas.

A final question concerns support of the corporate IS strategy. It is difficult to follow general, high-level guidance from above and simultaneously listen to and satisfy user needs from the bottom of the organization. An SDM must keep top-down planning and bottom-up design in balance and must also allow for constructive ways to resolve conflict. Exhibit 13-6 illustrates this dichotomy and indicates where cross-checks in the design process are necessary.

Regardless of the philosophy underlying it, every SDM has similar elements. Although some differences between phases may occur, radical inconsistencies or discontinuities should be avoided.

INCORPORATING STANDARDIZED DESIGN METHODS

In building SDMs, IS managers have two options at their disposal. The first is the option of purchasing flexible but predefined method-ologies. Several products, complete with integrated automated-productivity components, are on the market. In some instances the productivity tools, such as CASE products, can be purchased

Target Beneficiary	Area of Emphasis
Project manager	Project management tools
	Schedules
	Action plans
	Step-by-step procedures
Management	Escalation procedures
	Approval points
	Project reporting requirements
	Postevaluation reviews
Technical professional	Hardware determination
	Software determination
	Structured walk-throughs
	Detailed design reviews
	Performance testing
User	General design review and approval
	User testing/acceptance criteria
	User documentation
	Training

EXHIBIT 13-3 Target beneficiaries of a new system and areas of emphasis.

IS-dominated Development Life Cycle	User-dominated Development Life Cycle
Too much emphasis on data-base hygiene	Too much emphasis on problem focus
No recent new supplier or new distinct services (too busy with maintenance)	IS says out of control
New systems always must fit data structure of existing system	Explosive growth in number of new systems and supporting staff
All requests for service require system study with benefit identification	Multiple suppliers delivering services and frequent change in supplier of specific service
Standardization dominates, few exceptions	Lack of standardization and control over data hygiene and system
IS designs/constructs everything	Hard evidence of benefits nonexistent
Benefits of user control over development discussed but never implemented	Soft evidence of benefits nonexistent
Study always shows construction costs less than outside purchase	Few measurements/objectives for new system
Head count of distributed minis and development staff growing but surreptitiously	Technical advice of IS not sought or, if received, considered irrelevant
IS specializing in technical frontiers, not user-oriented markets	User buying design, construction, maintenance, and even operations services from outside
IS spending 80% on maintenance, 20% on development	User building networks to meet own needs (not corporate needs)
IS thinks it is in control of all	Some users growing rapidly in experience; other users feel nothing is relevant because they do not understand
Users express unhappiness	No coordinated effort for technology transfer or learning from experience
Portfolio of development opportunities firmly under IS control	Growth in duplication of technical skills
General management is not involved but concerned	Communications costs rising dramatically through redundancy

EXHIBIT 13-4 Two systems-development emphases and possible implications.

Source: Reprinted by permission of Richard D. Irwin, Inc. An exhibit from *Corporate Information Systems Management* by F. W. McFarlan and J. L. Kenny. copyright © 1983 by Richard D. Irwin, Inc.

separately and integrated into an existing, home-grown SDM. If such systems fit predefined needs, their purchase will save much time, provide a more comprehensive system, and save "reinventing the wheel" in several areas. These systems typically come with considerable help and advice on their use.

The other option is to incorporate standardized design methods and analytical techniques into the customized SDM. This might be one of the multitude of structured programming techniques, data diagramming methods, or top-down design techniques. Although many of these require considerable degrees of precision, each is purported to yield advantages in product integrity and work efficiencies. Many allow key areas, such as data flow, to be emphasized. In some cases, a popular method or technique will be familiar to new and existing employees as a result of academic training or previous experience.

THE PHASES OF A SYSTEMS DEVELOPMENT METHODOLOGY

Although there are many software development methodologies with from three or four phases up to twelve phases, the differences among them are largely fine points of emphasis and procedural variations. Even within this common framework, however, some important

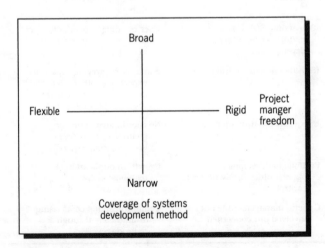

EXHIBIT 13-5 Basic systems development trade-off dilemmas.

choices remain. For example, one SDM might contain the following phases:

- Phase I   Problem definition
- Phase II   Feasibility study
- Phase III   Alternative selection
- Phase IV   Logical design
- Phase V   Physical design
- Phase VI   Implementation
- Phase VII   Postaudit

In contrast, another method might use a more limited but flexible approach consisting of these phases

- Phase I   Feasibility study
- Phase II   General and detail system design
- Phase III   Programming and procedures
- Phase VI   System acceptance
- Phase V   Implementation and support

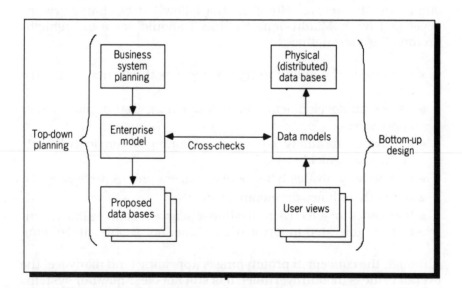

EXHIBIT 13-6 Top-down planning and bottom-up design.

Source: Fred R. McFadden and Jeffrey A. Hoffer, *Data Base Management*, Menlo Park, CA: Benjamin/Cummings, 1985, p.60.

The latter approach is likely to have simplified checkpoints and to entail less administrative overhead, at least in the beginning. Although it might be quite versatile in handling certain projects, it is less likely to be comprehensive in the types of projects it can easily handle. In contrast, the former method would involve a more disciplined approach to analyzing multiple options. Some IS managers that highly value activities such as training might see both approaches as flawed for imbedding this element within the larger phases and failing to give it explicit visibility.

SYSTEMS DEVELOPMENT TECHNIQUES

As systems development methodologies have evolved, many productive techniques have been used by creative IS managers. The following two alternatives have strong proponents. Of course, like other techniques they will continue to be refined.

Prototyping

Prototyping is a "trial balloon" approach. Because it is associated with other experimental approaches, it will be covered more thoroughly in Chapter 16. However, the follow list of characteristics developed by A. Milton Jenkins (1983) should serve to highlight prototyping's strengths:

- It provides the ability to try out ideas without incurring large costs.
- Its overall development cost is lower than that of many other approaches.
- It provides the ability to place a functioning system in the hands of the user quickly.
- It effectively divides labor between users and IS professionals.
- It greatly reduces development time.
- It provides for effective utilization of scarce resources (inefficiencies are tolerated in terms of machine, not people, utilization).

Although the concept of prototyping is appealing (and many feel the overall value is incontrovertible), it is still not clear how our systems development methods, project management methods, management controls, and so on must adjust to accommodate this new approach. Elimination of some procedures and overhead would seem to be in keeping with the economy of prototyping; however, a set of checks and balances is clearly in order.

Computer-Aided Software Engineering

Computer-aided software engineering (CASE) is a term applied to a group of tools used by IS professionals in the systems development process to more quickly and accurately design, display, integrate, and elaborate on technical products. Because the term and the technology are reasonably new, there are still variations in what different persons mean by CASE. Howard W. Miller (1988) describes CASE this way:

- It offers support for the common development life cycles, with built-in audit capabilities that ensure compliance.
- It is an information repository for storing the elements of the software engineering process including specifications, designs, graphics, and pseudo code.
- It offers a graphics interface for drawing structured diagrams, data-flow diagrams, and data structures.
- It comprises a highly integrated set of tools to automate every phase of the development life cycle.
- It automates code and dictionary generation from design specifications.
- It allows for prototyping of new designs and reverse engineering (i.e., converting existing software back into design specifications for modification and software regeneration).

These tools are more than just aids to productivity; they are redefining major portions of the software development process by collapsing activities (such as testing), introducing new flexibilities and integration, and facilitating communication. CASE is important as a strategic initiative because it affects both the efficiency and effectiveness of the SDM. Reducing the time between initiation and implementation of a system can result in significant strategic benefits.

As the technology continues to evolve, CASE tools are expected to correct deficiencies in current versions. Tony Percy (1988) of Applied Data Research notes the following limitations

- CASE works best on new projects. The tools that reverse-engineer existing systems for maintenance and enhancements are only now being developed.
- CASE tools do not impose the correct amount of discipline necessary for rigorous software development methodologies.
- Most CASE tools are limited to individual use and do not lend

themselves to shared activities and to common use of models and diagrams by a project team.

- CASE tools must integrate better with the mainframe environments where the complex products they help design will reside.
- CASE is not ready to support anticipated new technology (e.g., object-oriented data bases).
- CASE will need to make the transition from the innovative to the standardized.

Astute managers are watching CASE tools closely in order to assess when (and if) they will be able to deliver benefits to their organizations. For example, they are assessing whether CASE would have a role when applications are developed by desktop users. CASE will be adopted only when the potential benefits become attractive enough to deserve the organization's ongoing commitment to these tools.

Alternative Development Techniques

Michael Treacy (1988) has observed that traditional systems development techniques are appropriate in situations where there is a clear understanding of system-related needs and those needs are reasonably complex. Traditional methodologies stress accuracy and controls; and they permit a more top-down development of system features. Where the need is not well understood but potential complexity is reasonably limited, Treacy suggests that an evolutionary approach such as prototyping is useful in a trial-and-error mode. He goes on to point out, however, that this approach will not work where the need is poorly understood and the design will be highly complex, as indicated in Exhibit 13-7. For this situation, an approach called Innovative System Life Cycle is appropriate (see Exhibit 13-8). This more methodical method of constructing a system relies on the same process used by marketers to introduce new products. The idea is to develop the system in steps culminating in a IS product that has been adjusted to meet the requirements of the environment into which it is introduced. (A similar approach, described in Chapter 16, addresses the larger question of when EUC is appropriate.)

DATA CONVERSION STRATEGIES

The nature of information systems, needs for caution, needs of the user, urgency of implementation—all these contribute to the determination of how an organization is to move to a new system. Of course, where there is no prior system, a fresh start-up is possible. Occasionally, it is possible to initiate a replacement system from scratch, entering new data as needed. Generally, however, existing data must be moved electronically or manually into the files of replacement systems. Often this process is simultaneous with implementation so that data will be accurate as of the transition point.

When converting data is too monumental a task or when assimilation of new procedures is too intimidating, a phased implementation can be undertaken. However, this may complicate the conversion plan and introduce extra work and extra risk, especially for heavily integrated systems. Some IS managers use phased implementations when introducing risky technologies. By ensuring that a particular piece of the system works, the manager can more confidently decide to convert the remaining system.

For involved systems requiring substantial user training, a pilot system might be installed. This simulation actually tests the system in a fully employed, realistic mode. A more dramatic but perhaps more meaningful test is to run in parallel. This means that two systems, the old and the new, are used at the same time to process real information or transactions. The results are then compared to ensure that components that should not change do in fact remain the same. Both parallel runs and pilot systems require considerable user and IS department support as well as sturdy technical scaffolding.

Regardless of the conversion strategy adopted, the IS manager should be able to revert to the old one if users are surprised by some

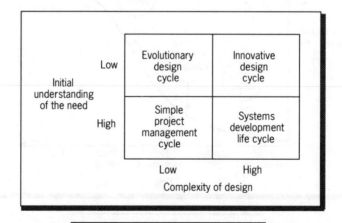

EXHIBIT 13-7 Appropriate systems design cycles.

Source: Michael Treacy, "Strategic Sales and Marketing Systems: A Development Approach," *The Consultant Forum* vol. 5, no. 1, Digital Equipment Corporation, Nashua, NH, 1988, p. 6. Reprinted with permission of the author.

unacceptable characteristic. Therefore, a well-designed "back-out" plan is needed, along with any necessary programs to effect it. Decision points should be analyzed ahead of time to identify those events that will mark progressively more costly milestones from which to retreat. For example, reverting to an old order-entry system after 1 week of entering orders in a new one might mean that those orders entered in the intervening week but remaining unprocessed would have to be re-entered into the old system for processing and then brought to the currency in which they existed in the new system. Clearly, the further one is from the start of conversion, the less practical it becomes to back out. However, backing out is essential during those first few cycles of the new system, should operation be seriously affected by a new piece of software.

No amount of testing and preparation seems to catch all problems. Minor problems can and should be corrected by systems and programming without unhooking the new system, but occasionally some problem is too big or too dangerous to correct on the fly.

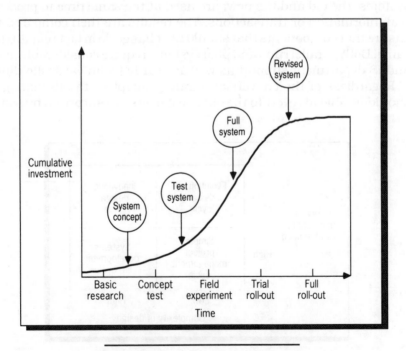

EXHIBIT 13-8 Innovative systems life cycle.

Source: Michael Treacy, "Strategic Sales and Marketing Systems: A Development Approach," *The Consultant Forum*, vol. 5, no. 1, Digital Equipment Corporation, Nashua, NH, 1988, p. 6. Reprinted with permission of the author

TYPES OF INFORMATION SYSTEMS DEVELOPMENT PROJECTS

Most SDMs are designed for and apply easily to major systems development projects with large scope, substantial resources, and complex activities. Such projects can easily bear the administrative overhead cost of the SDM process. However, not all SDMs are flexible enough to address other types of projects, such as those elaborated next.

Maintenance Projects

For the support or maintenance project, which is smaller and more limited than the major project, typically modified or even different procedures apply. The small size of such a project can exempt it from detailed management reporting. Similarly, its less important status usually means that a broad and thorough design review is either unnecessary or not worth the effort. And the maintenance project may have alternative approval cycles. For instance, the IS department traditionally exerts additional influence on the approval and solution process for maintenance projects, as the department is usually well versed in the hidden risks and long-term efficiencies of either postponements or superficial repairs.

Martin Buss (1981) warns of three risks encountered by firms that allow software to lapse into an outmoded condition.

1. Old software is risky. It creates unnecessary dependence on increasingly scarce personnel, hardware, and software support. Breakdowns become more likely. Moreover, obscure software is difficult to manage.
2. Outdated software helps the competition. If customers are lost, it may be impossible to attract new customers when software-based services are obsolete. If competitors have better support software, catching up becomes difficult.
3. Outmoded software is not cost effective. The costs for users to operate it, for programmers to support it, and for hardware to run it are all higher. Inadequate software can even foment personnel turnover, which is itself quite costly.

Despite the fact that it is sensible not to fall behind on software repair and correction, maintenance activity has a dangerous tendency to monopolize IS development time. The following are five approaches to avoiding maintenance where possible:

1. *First-time Accuracy*   If attention is paid to the accuracy and appropriateness of specifications before project implementation, many inconvenient changes can be avoided.

2. *User-Flexible Systems*   New technologies that allow users to take over elements such as report generation can help systems and programming get out of the business of performing necessary but trivial maintenance tasks.

3. *Ignoring Maintenance Requests*   This approach can be heartless but is often justified, as many requests are not of overwhelming business importance. Care must be exercised so that the occasional essential requirement is not overlooked.

4. *System Replacement*   Although no single change is crucial, collectively changes point to inadequate software. Careful monitoring of deterioration can lead to a decision not to continue patching the product but rather to replace it altogether. This can be planned through a technique known as "piggybacking" (Martin, 1987), where a replacement system is initiated while the old system is still healthy, so that the new one will be ready when deterioration accelerates (see Exhibit 13–9).

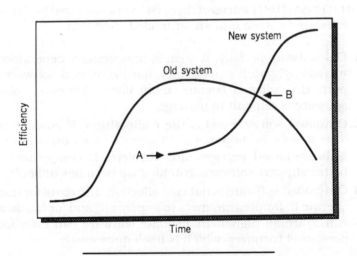

EXHIBIT 13-9 Piggybacking.

Source: Merle P. Martin, "The Human Connection in Systems Design - Part VI - Designing Systems for Change," *Journal of Systems Management*, July, 1987, p. 15. Copyright Journal of Systems Management 1987.

5. *Rationing Maintenance Resources* A compromise solution that does not entirely ignore the need for occasional change but does not permit wholesale commitment of systems and programming resources is to severely (and often arbitrarily) limit the amount of repair attention that a given system receives by restricting the personnel and hardware resources that are applied to it.

Other Projects

There are many "special cases" where projects are concerned. For instance, one different type of systems development project is the emergency project, which requires that approval be streamlined and documentation minimized. Usually, either separate design procedures are used or a standard SDM is revised to accommodate these special circumstances.

Other atypical projects may require revised design procedures. Such projects might include systems developed on personal computers, departmental computing solutions, and specialized applications of automation such as image processing or robotics. Once again, organizational priorities are an important factor in the choice of SDM. The IS manager will want to assess his or her environment to identify commonly occurring project types that may require immunity from SDM routines.

FUNCTIONAL OBJECTIVES OF INFORMATION SYSTEMS DEVELOPMENT PROJECTS

A precise statement of what the new system should contain is an obvious and critical element of any systems development project. One of the major responsibilities of the project manager is to see that such a statement is developed. How early on and in how much detail this statement is articulated will have significant implications for the approval, support, and management of the project—not to mention its final content. Specifying too much detail too early can discourage constructive improvements or can commit extensive resources to efforts that are later superceded. But postponing specification of system details can leave projects in an aimless or misdirected state.

Functional specifications can be generated by the key user in isolation or as a more participative venture. Specific responsibility for these specifications has the virtue of ensuring ownership, provided that guidelines are followed. However, system contents can usually benefit from ideas and suggestions from other quarters, and for practical reasons the final results should usually include input from the IS department, other users, and often senior management. Some feel it is best to gather and incorporate this input up front; others maintain that a clear statement of the features of the optimum system is needed before additional input is solicited and compromises are reached.

Senior management is very unlikely to support an IS development project without some statement of the benefits it will confer. With some projects these benefits can be expressed in terms of the strategic support a new system will offer. The preferred practice,however, is to quantify the expected results. This allows a basis for comparison so that management can determine if the investment is justified. The project manager must decide who should be responsible for quantifying the benefits. Because most benefits will accrue to users' areas and users typically request the new systems, it falls to the user to commit to and be responsible for achieving these benefits. The project manager may be called on to help justify project costs by validating these benefits, coordinating other benefits outside the arena of a particular user, and tracking costs.

Some project managers segment the benefits so each is paired with its costs, though this can be complicated by intermeshed costs and benefits. Itemizing project elements this way allows for alternative approaches or for a "cafeteria selection" of separate system features.

PROJECT INITIATION

Project initiation is an especially crucial time because decisions made early in the project have the most wide-ranging effects. Errors made at this stage cost the most to fix and conversely the most costly mistakes can be avoided at this time. The right decisions made at project initiation can do more to determine the destiny of the project than latter decisions. This is because initiation is the point at which the widest range of outcomes are still possible or at which any potential outcome can be achieved with the least adjustment, as Exhibit 13-10 suggests.

Regardless of type, there are many ways that projects can be activated. It is common for projects to be launched by a senior management steering committee. After reviewing proposals containing cost/benefit information, this management group is able to make informed decisions on which projects to do and which to dismiss or at least defer.

Another method, which introduces the advantage of perspective, uses the IS planning process to identify future potential projects and to create a departmentwide work plan that suggests the proper timing of each potential project. Yet another substantially different approach builds on the advantages of a charge-back environment. Because each IS departmental function has a budget, each can independently authorize IS development activity. This method usually involves planning within the IS department and may apply best to minor projects with reasonably limited resource requirements.

It is not unusual for a committee composed of middle managers to be responsible for the authorization of maintenance projects, with some other mechanism responsible for major projects. Similarly, an

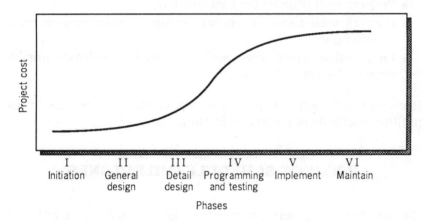

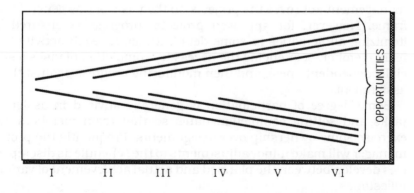

EXHIBIT 13-10 The effects of decision making early in an IS development project

information center might be expected to try handling user PC-based problems before users are permitted to proceed with their own solutions. Even emergency projects usually require some authorization before initiation and an even more elaborate approval process before a permanent solution is effected.

Approval methods usually are selected to match the types of potential projects, the IS department's level of sophistication, and the management style of the organization. However, a study by J. D. McKeen and Tor Guimaraes (1985) suggests that some approval methods might be biased. In particular, steering committees may have a tendency to favor the following

- Projects that are large (in terms of worker-hours to develop and total number of users).
- Projects with little vertical integration.
- Projects with formal proposals complete with written cost/benefit analysis.
- Projects that can demonstrate both tangible as well as intangible benefits for the organization.

Because other methods may have similar biases, it is wise to use multiple methods of project activation.

PROJECT SCHEDULE/MILESTONES

Usually, IS development projects have general schedules with specific milestones for benefits and budgetary outlays, and senior management approves the projects on the basis of this general time frame. However, for approved projects, progress is ensured by itemizing all activities in some detail, assigning each activity to a team member, sequencing the necessary completion of tasks (especially dependent ones), and then monitoring progress against these assignments.

Some degree of participation is generally advised in assigning tasks and setting completion dates so that team members can exercise some ownership over assignments. Frequently the project manager will make minor adjustments to the schedule as discrepancies develop between the planned and actual achievement of various milestones.

The project manager's level of involvement differs from project to project, but he or she needs to strike a balance between interfering with team productivity and falling out of touch with schedules and progress. Mark Teagan and Liz Young (1988) of Keane Associates recommend following an "80-hour rule," according to which the project manager divides tasks into segments of roughly 80 person-hours of effort each. Thus, the work is split into manageable pieces that the project manager can track more readily.

PROJECT MANAGEMENT ISSUES

Although the IS manager is responsible for planning the direction of and seizing opportunities to use technology, it is the project manager whose implementation efforts bring the expected benefits of the technology to the organization. If the IS manager is the field general, then the project manager is the commanding officer on the front lines. Because this position is critical, the right person must be placed appropriately in each project manager slot and must correctly employ the best tactics at his or her disposal.

The activities of the project manager seem to oscillate between full-time management and actual task performance. Naturally, at the extremes of project size, the choices are clear. Large projects clearly demand someone who can devote all of his or her time to administering the project—communicating, overseeing, making decisions, and so forth. For a small project this level of administration would be overkill. Between these two extremes, the appropriate activities of the project manager depend on the environment, the corporate management style, and the available project managers.

The required skill set will be determined in part by whether the project manager has direct supervisory responsibility for the project team or a weaker advisory or "dotted-line" responsibility. For substantial projects, many advocate the control implicit in a direct supervisory role. Again, however, this is often impractical for smaller projects.

Who Should Manage an Information Systems Development Project?

One of the ongoing controversies within the IS department is whether the user or an IS professional should manage an IS development project. Although having the user serve as project manager helps ensure involvement and ownership, the IS professional would arguably understand better those activities under his or her direction. Many organizations avoid this controversy by using some form of dual leadership. Although this does tend to emphasize the cooperative nature of a project, decisive direction and action can be hampered without a clear, logical delineation of responsibilities.

Moreover, the controversy over who should direct development projects does not stop at the choice between user and IS professional. Many believe that the ideal project manager is a department head with the authority to make important system-related decisions even though this individual's actual project management role might be part-time. Others believe that a full-time project manager is required and that this person can be delegated the necessary authority to make important decisions.

Another alternative is having an outside consultant manage the effort. This is consistent in situations where outsiders have been brought in to deal with the technical areas of a project. It can also allow some independence and objectivity in instances where decision making is political and controversial. However, many companies oppose such practices on the grounds that an outsider does not have enough organizational knowledge, organizational accountability, or project ownership.

Speed Versus Thoroughness

A project manager, facing numerous tactical considerations regarding project content, might decide to minimize the project's size and content in order to complete the project quickly. (Care must be taken to ensure that attempts to reduce the volume of work does not inadvertently jeopardize the quality of the remaining project.) He or she might also decide to expand the project, adding control activities and content to make the project more comprehensive in terms of both the final outcome and the process that produces it. Using a particular SDM, the organization will lean toward one extreme or the other at the time of project approval; however, within these extremes the project manager still has room for his or her own preferences.

The project cost structure will be affected by the choice of tactic. Exhibit 13-11 shows that projects of similar content can incur different costs, depending on the project's time frame. A project that is rushed will incur extra costs and waste, including additional one-time help, extra coordination, and overtime, not to mention the cost of errors and inefficiency caused by haste. At the opposite extreme, projects extended for too long a period will suffer rising costs resulting from the need to continually refresh earlier work, to repair the team structure, and to maintain extended communication and administration—plus any inefficiency caused by casualness. The optimum time frame will minimize costs by using the most efficient means of project completion regardless of time frame. Additional timing changes compelled by other reasons will only increase potential costs. Each project should be evaluated to determine where in the range of lapsed times its more economical schedule lies.

Project Budget Estimation

Assuming that the project manager has the experience and skills to approximate the size and duration of a proposed project, there is still the ticklish task of incorporating a risk factor into the budget estimate. Some project managers believe in leaving themselves a healthy margin for error for unforeseen difficulties. Although this does afford protection, it presents other problems. The first is the possibility that the project could be "priced out of the market": Senior management, on seeing the high costs, might turn down the request for approval. Even if approved, the project with an overly wide error-margin may set up a suspicious, adversarial attitude in senior managers.

Another risk of high estimates is that they tolerate and can encourage inefficiency. In themselves, high estimated budgets offer no real incentive for team members to work as quickly and accurately as they can. If the built-in overhead factor is not actually used, the project manager may appear unable to plan resource utilization accurately and may risk a certain loss of personal credibility.

Other problems stemming from the practice of excessive estimates (known as "padding") include inconsistent corporate risk policies and the compounded incorporation of safety factors. Of course, there is the argument that project goals should be as ambitious and

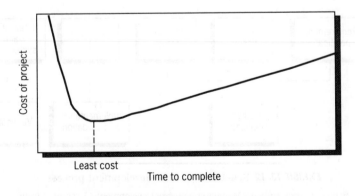

EXHIBIT 13-11 Relationship of project cost to lapsed completion time

demanding as possible in order to enforce productivity. Yet project managers often maintain that they must include some margin for error, else their organizations may suffer unexpected project delays. Some suggest that working under overly rigorous or unrealistic target milestones tends to decrease, not increase, productivity. In the end, it is up to the project manager to determine the right balance.

Staffing the Project

Needs for specialized (and occasionally unique) IS skills are as varied as the many projects proposed. The usual drawbacks to specialization are compounded by timing considerations; acquiring specialized skills at critical times is very difficult to do without introducing certain inefficient uses of those skills. Generalists, however, often lack certain uncommon but vital skills required by particular projects at particular points.

A solution is to contract outside for selected skills. One downside of this (and any other specialized solution, for that matter) is the additional difficulty of educating newcomers and integrating them, socially and functionally. Another problem is that acquired skill and knowledge will be lost when the project is completed and they leave.

An environment set on maximizing the use of its skilled employees will arrange to have critical people busy on other assignments until they are needed by the project and to ensure that as their project commitment ends, another scheduled use of their time has already been lined up. Of course, some flexibility is prudent, given the uncertain nature of most projects. It is also important that specialists not be reassigned to other activities just when they are needed for training and system modifications.

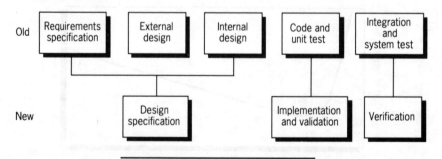

EXHIBIT 13-12 Redefinition of the development process.

Source: Patrick Brown, "Managing Software Development." Excerpted from *DATAMATION*, April 15, 1985 © 1985 by Cahners Publishing Company.

CONCLUSION

Until recently the process of developing new information systems through specific methodologies has been one of the most ritualized and, next to programming, the most identifiable undertakings of the IS professional. This task promises to become harder as managers must now allow for rapid-fire technological advances. The challenge to the IS and project manager is compounded by the fact that no successful SDMs have yet been established as universally successful responses to IS-related change. And yet changes to our traditional processes are essential if we are to increase our efficiency, flexibility, and our cost effectiveness. This is the intent of the newer technologies. Patrick Brown (1985) predicts the inevitable truncation of methods, as illustrated in Exhibit 13-12.

These changes cannot come at the expense of greater risk, less control, or reduced involvement of others within the organization. That would be conceding important contributions that IS has worked hard to deliver to our organizations.

The need for the IS manager to manufacture solutions to problems and continue the string of productivity improvements is not a new requirement. It has been the lot of the IS management function and will be so as long as change is expected in the area of technology. It is fortunate that the experiences and the roles of IS managers prepare them to be so resourceful.

DISCUSSION QUESTIONS

1. What are some of the ways that CASE or prototyping tools might alter traditional systems development methodologies?

2. Do you believe that specific project approval methods encourage the selection of certain types of IS development projects? How would you explain such a phenomenon?

3. Is it possible to justify a project when cost/benefit analysis is not appropriate? How would you go about doing so?

4. Compare the two sets of project phases listed in the early part of this chapter. What are some of the strengths and weaknesses of each?

5. Do you agree with the opinion that the project manager's role is of paramount importance? Explain why or why not.

6. Is it right for a project manager to "pad" a project estimate? Is the manager protecting the company or him/herself?

REFERENCES

Brown, Patrick (1985). "Managing Software Development," *Datamation* (April 15), p. 135

Buss, Martin D. J. (1981). "Penny-Wise Approach to Data Processing," *Harvard Business Review* (July-August), pp. 111-117.

Jenkins, A. Milton (1983). "Prototyping: A Methodology for the Design and Development of Application Systems," Indiana University, Division of Research, School of Business, (April).

Martin, Merle P. (1987). "The Human Connection in System Design, Part VI—Designing Systems for Change," *Journal of Systems Management* (July), pp. 14-18.

McKeen, J. D., and Tor Guimaraes (1985). "Selecting MIS Projects by Steering Committee," *Communications of the ACM* (December), pp. 1344-1352.

Miller, Howard W. (1988). "Understanding CASE Technology," *Mainframe Journal* (May/June), pp. 44-47.

Percy, Tony (1988). "What CASE Can't Do Yet," *Computerworld* (June 20), pp. 59-60.

Teagan, Mark, and Liz Young (1988). "The Dynamics of Prototyping," *Computerworld* (August 8), pp. 53-55.

Treacy, Michael (1988). *The Consultant Forum*, vol. 5, no. 1 (TTB1-3/F06), Digital Equipment Corporation.

fourteen

□

Information Systems as a Functional Entity: Issues and Opportunities

Nothing is more certain about IS management in the future than the fact that it will change. As the chapters in this part have indicated, the IS manager must be capable of making continual adjustments in skills, style, and techniques that can effectively accommodate change on all fronts. This challenge appears enormous; however, there are ways to predict the "fronts" of necessary change. First of all, past trends can be extrapolated to suggest future needs. Thus, the necessity for increased attention to the content of top IS-management positions, increased integration of the demands of a broadening constituency, and greater emphasis on the IS department's contributions to the core business can all be logically inferred from past experiences.

In addition, by observing the actions of peers and competitors, keeping abreast of current technical and professional literature, and paying attention to general trends in management, IS managers can anticipate the kinds of changes they will face and prepare for a climate that grows ever more complex, exciting, and challenging.

In this chapter we begin with the changing technical climate and examine ways in which IS managers can forecast IS technological developments. We then turn to the changing functional role of the IS department. The chapter ends with a discussion of managing the IS portfolio.

FORECASTING TECHNOLOGY

Timing Hardware and Software Acquisitions

All technology tends to improve in fits and starts. As much as vendors try to avoid it, at some time in the life of a product, dramatic improvement can be accomplished only through a radical metamorphosis or replacement. This alternately results in periodic quiescent phases for the product. These phases, however, usually have the advantage of a degree of product stability and reliability to recommend them. The difference in the two stages is an important consideration in selecting hardware or software.

Many believe that computer products must be acquired solely on the basis of their current attributes. If they do the job for which they have been selected, other qualities are unimportant. There are, however, economic imperatives that argue otherwise.

The decision to buy used or new is an economic as well as an aesthetic one. If you chose to buy used equipment, you must not only look for the lowest price but must also estimate the future value of the used technology. And new technology purchased at list price will, of course, depreciate over time as even newer technology is announced or anticipated.

Moreover, if soon-to-be-outmoded hardware or software is installed, the value of the software (in terms of compatibility) and the real market value of the hardware will decline. Although one might choose to avoid the costs of upgrading, there are other costs: those of not being able to continue expanding a system's features, of attracting a staff that knows and wants to work with older technology, and of keeping obsolete products in working order.

Many larger IS departments that can afford a hardware strategy based on equipment value choose one of two extreme strategies. One is to buy only the latest technology and sell it when newer products are announced, before its price drops too much. The other approach is to buy old, fully devalued equipment and use it as long as it is serviceable. The equipment is basically worthless when the department has finished with it, but little value will be lost in terms of price declines. The difference in the buying price and the selling price, divided by the period of use, may make this strategy worthwhile. Exhibit 14-1 illustrates patterns in the decline of the market value of computers.

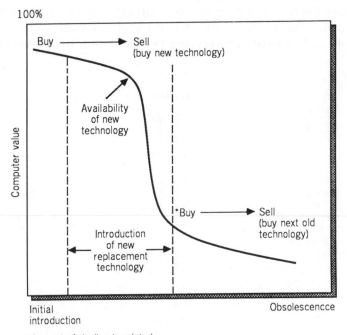

EXHIBIT 14-1 Decline in the market value of computers.

Yet another strategy is to lease the products instead of buying them. A product's position in its life cycle, in conjunction with the period of need, can guide a company's decision to lease or buy equipment, as Exhibit 14-2 illustrates.

Many factors go into determining which course to follow. These factors include the organization's financial goals, the perceived value of money, tax laws, need for flexibility, and risk-avoidance postures.

Positioning the Information Systems Department for Evolution

IS managers like to have systems that can keep up with improvements in technology. Achieving this requires wisdom and work on the part of the IS department, which must select a vendor who can meet current needs and stay in touch with new technology appropriate to the company. Obviously, this selection entails a personality match as well, as some companies may not want to keep pace with a leading-edge vendor and may prefer instead the relaxed approach of a more conservative supplier.

As has been stressed in earlier chapters, the IS manager should be knowledgeable about the general state of technology and the competitive health of various vendors. In essence, the manager must

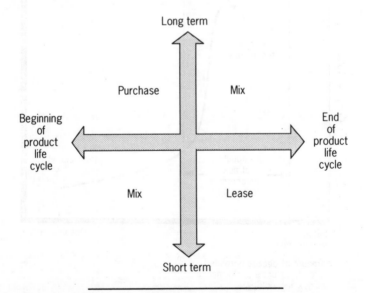

EXHIBIT 14-2 Factors affecting the decision to lease or buy computer equipment.

Source: Third Party Market Update, CIS: Syracuse, N. Y., April 1988. Reprinted with permission.

be an industry analyst, aware of vendor or product popularity and financial performance as well as technological trends.

We have seen how important it is to not become too financially committed to technology in transition. Similarly, too heavy a functional or emotional reliance on obsolete products increases the difficulty of shedding them. No amount of prescience can substitute for paying close attention to the work of technology management. This work entails applying all improvements and upgrades to the product, keeping all applications in good repair, and taking the time and trouble to use important new product features. New technology is rarely dropped in a department's lap; rather, the IS manager has to be prepared to take advantage of it when the opportunity arises.

Dealing with Integration

As we have seen, new technology increasingly integrates many elements. Exhibit 14-3 shows, as an example, the integration by fourth-generation languages of several previously separate functions. Although this integration is often helpful from the standpoint of use, it does complicate the process of keeping everything current. Many changes may need to be orchestrated more or less simultaneously, or a massive product replacement may need to occur periodically, with attendant difficulties for those individual users who do not need the improvements. For these and other reasons, many IS

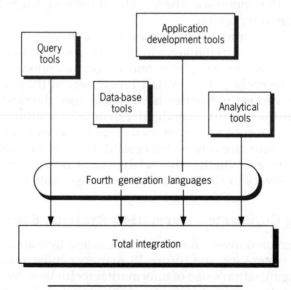

EXHIBIT 14-3 Software Evolution

managers are selecting and designing systems that are not integrated. This choice allows for separate evolutionary paths as well as greater isolation from security breaches, system failures, and performance problems.

THE CHANGING FUNCTIONAL ROLE OF THE INFORMATION SYSTEMS DEPARTMENT

In previous chapters we have seen the heightened role that the IS department can play in the modern organization. We have also noted the potential implications of that role for the behavior and performance of IS professionals. As the IS department's role at the corporate level continues to change, so too will its functional role. The following sections examine several key areas of change.

Evolving Infortmation Systems Managerial Skills

The IS manager has been and will continue to play a more senior, executive role within the organization. Essentially, the perspective of the IS manager must become executive in nature, so that the manager's methods of directing the IS department can stay in tune with overall business and organizational goals and needs. To this end, the IS leader must develop an acute ability to separate the critical from the important, the vital from the meaningful, and the essential from the popular.

Richard Nolan and Bruce Rogow (1983) have categorized the broad abilities of the IS manager in the 1970s and contrasted them with skills needed in the 1980s and beyond as shown in Exhibit 14–4. More recently (1988), Nolan has observed that competitive pressures in various industries have encouraged the push of the IS manager into the executive spotlight. As complex solutions—be they reductions in inventory or increased organizational or global communications—are found to be successful, they set the standard for all like businesses. Whether they wish to be or not, IS managers are now major players in the success of their organizations.

Setting Corporate Information Systems Standards

Although personal involvement and "managing by walking around" will still be necessary, the future IS manager must more directly influence organization's use of information technology by establishing specific policies and procedures. As the territory for which the IS

	EDP Manager 1973	New Breed Information Systems Manager (late 1970s)	Computing Functional Executive 1980
Views himself as	Technologist	An operating manager	A functional executive
Approach	"Hands on"	Closely involved	"Hands off"
Role model	"We"	"Us"	Others
Personality	Strong-willed	Direct	Flexible, diplomatic
Short term	Tomorrow	3-6 months	This year
Long term	One year	12-24 months	5-10 years
Develops expertise	Centrally	Concentrated	Distributed in units
Deliverable	Report	System	Organizational change
Rallying point	Expertise	Force of personality	Common vision
Demands	Personal loyalty	Departmental loyalty	Loyalty to common vision
How to do it	One way	Several ways	Many alternatives
Technology perspective	One legitimate, others dangerous	Limited	Many deserve consideration, consideration with control
Thinking	"Right"	Pragmatic	Abstract
Political base	Functional	Narrow, built by service	Broad, built through relationships
Facilitate change by	Installing technology	Policy is law	Guidelines
Constituent base	Professionals	Narrow	Widening
Decisions reached	Independently	Rapidly--without consensus	By negotiation, conflict resolution
Attention focused	Project	Targeted, some alienation	Broadly, open doors
Senior management	Limited interaction	Executes initial concerns	Leads, counsels
Assistance to units	Control	Audit, review	Common exposures, opportunities

EXHIBIT 14-4 The IS manager's leadership attributes in the 1970s and beyond.

Source: Richard L. Nolan and Bruce J. Rogow, Stage by Stage vol. 3, no. 3, Fall 1983 Copyright © 1983 Nolan, Norton & Co., Lexington, MA. All right reserved. Reprinted with permission.

department is responsible increases and as more actual development falls to user departments to undertake, the IS department will rely increasingly on setting rules and guidelines, however liberal, to exert its influence. Tailoring appropriate policies requires strategic vision, political sensitivity, and a keen awareness of behavioral issues.

Experimenting with New Technology

The pressure to make increasingly productive use of information technology is not the only motivation to try new technical ideas; human curiosity prompts many people to flirt with change. Information technology's increasing effectiveness, successful track record, and inherently attractive labor saving qualities have made it an appealing target for experimentation and change.

The IS manager must set an organizational strategy that is characterized by the right blend of aggressiveness and caution. On the one hand, experimentation, although encouraging new uses, also has the potential of wasting or misdirecting effort and defusing a rigorous pursuit of benefits. Too much control, on the other hand, can stifle the kind of creativity that uncovers obscure but revolutionary applications of technology. Moreover, overly heavy control may discourage even clear-cut and obviously beneficial applications.

As illustrated in Exhibit 14-5, if one accepts that too little technology will decrease technical benefits because fruitful opportunities for automation will be neglected, but too much technology will decrease benefits by encouraging wasteful and inappropriate usages, then it follows that some hypothetical middle ground—the "optimum" in the exhibit—will maximize the benefits of technology. The goal of the IS manager is to find that optimum point.

IS managers who opt for controls have a bias toward accepting less technology. They would rather avoid inappropriate usage even at the expense of overlooking beneficial but less obvious applications. In contrast, IS managers who encourage experimentation (through policies, standards, and practices) have an opposite bias toward more technology. Naturally, the best policy of control strikes a prudent balance. The selection of a policy depends heavily on the corporate culture, driving business forces, and other circumstances. Still, the choice reveals a lot about the IS managers as well as the organization.

The choice of approaches also reflects the IS managers' attitudes toward users. The experimental approach demonstrates a trust in the natural objectivity and unguided productivity of the users of technology. This attitude is very reminiscent of Theory Y. On the other hand, IS managers that favor control might simply believe, like Theory Z, that people need guidelines and structures so that efforts conform to the needs and directions of the organizations.

Another attitude exposed by the choice of policy is the manager's sensitivity to risk. Experimenters might be seen as risk-insensitive, whereas control-oriented managers might come across as risk-averse. Heavy control may suggest that the organization believes that only a few of the potential applications of technology will yield benefits that exceed investments; experimentation may indicate organizational confidence in the potential of most applications of technology paying off.

Increasing the Importance of Quality

As organizations become increasingly dependent on information technologies and attendant applications, systems that support key business activities must offer even greater reliability than is needed for "back-room" systems. And systems that support organizational strategies must be more precise and accurate than those that simply address administrative needs. Therefore, an increasing emphasis on quality assurance programs is necessary. Existing programs must shift their focus away from the correctness of the code and toward the appropriateness of the application.

The real challenge for the IS manager is to heighten the importance of quality programs without adding to the overhead (or

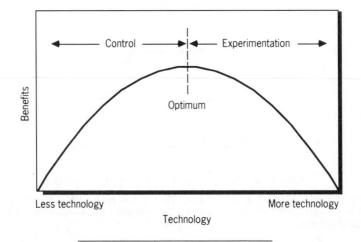

EXHIBIT 14-5 Control and experimentation in the introduction of new technology.

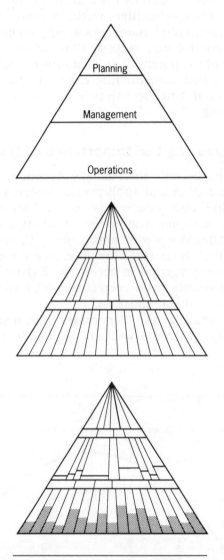

EXHIBIT 14-6 The evolution of an investment portfolio.

Source: Richard L. Nolan, "Principal DP Asset: The Applications Portfolio," *Stage by Stage*, vol. 1, no. 2, p. 4. Copyright © 1982, Nolan, Norton & Co., Lexington, MA. All rights reserved. Reprinted with permission.

subtracting from the efficiency) of the development process. Introducing new levels of quality—"doing things right"—should complement the process of getting systems targeted, developed, built, and running—"doing the right things."

The Need for New Relationships

As new kinds of systems evolve, new IS roles will evolve to support them. Whether these will be in addition to or instead of existing jobs is one question that has been explored elsewhere. The fact that some skills new to the IS function will be required, however, is becoming increasingly clear. With IS doing less and advising more, Sullivan-Trainor (1988) has identified consulting talents, both people skills and technical skills, that are being required within IS. These include

- Listening Skills
- Perspective
- Patience
- Technical Know-How
- Flexibility
- Enthusiasm

A newer approach toward dealing with users was cited by Sullivan-Trainor (1988) from a seminar offered by Arnoudse and Oullette—the HEAR model.

H   Accurately hear the clients words
E   Empathize with the client's situation
A   Analyze the user's problem
R   Respond to the situation

Such an empathetic approach is certainly consistent with but clearly more than the user-oriented service that IS has traditionally offered.

MANAGING THE PORTFOLIO OF INFORMATION SYSTEMS INVESTMENTS

An organization's investments in technology are necessarily complex and diverse. As we saw in Chapter 4, companies are being challenged to identify investments at progressively more strategic (and more highly leveraged) levels of corporate activity. However, this does not relieve the IS manager of the obligation to "invest," if only as a caretaker, in lower levels of the organization. The fact that a company might decide, as a point of strategy, to make aggressive investments in one functional area in no way means that investments will not be made in other less strategic areas. In fact, there may be alternative investment strategies in different areas and/or at different levels.

Richard Nolan (1981) has recognized that the IS manager actually presides over a portfolio of investments made across many levels and functions, all requiring different strategies. Exhibit 14-6 illustrates the evolution of an investment portfolio. The first drawing indicated that investment can be made in systems at three different levels. The assortment of functions available for investment (e.g., marketing, manufacturing), each potentially with system investment opportunities in all three levels, is shown in the second diagram. Each segment in the now divided pyramid represents the potential for investment consistent with the organization's strategic plan. The disproportionate size of the various wedges is indicative of the disproportionate opportunities that confront each organization. The last diagram shades a portion of each wedge to represent actual level of investment. This allows the IS manager to visualize where investment penetration is being made compared to the opportunities for investment. Like any portfolio, a balanced approach to investing will minimize risks and harvest the relatively easy benefits of building tools in previously unimproved areas. However, this analysis will quickly indicate at a glance if a company is investing their IS resources in an unbalanced and pedestrian way, as the sample company in the third diagram seems to be doing.

Although functional department investment is of initial importance to organizations, David P. Norton (1984) has pointed out that the nature of the investment may transcend functional alignments and may be a more important dimension along which to measure investment. Exhibit 14-7 shows that within any IS departmental functions or levels, IS products can be classified according to the following five application segments.

1. *Institutional Functions:* Transaction or procedural systems that reflect an organization's business processes.
2. *Professional Support:* Computing support for groups of professionals (e.g., secretaries, engineers, programmers).
3. *Physical Automation:* Automation of physical flows and processes.
4. *External Products:* Systems and information that serve as value-added products or services to customers.

   5. *Infrastructure:* Investments made in foundation technology
   such as data architecture and network architecture.

The junction of functional user areas and application segments
indicates to the IS manager the appropriate level of investment, as
shown in Exhibit 14-8.

   This analysis allows comparison to general industry levels or
specific competitors and permits historical comparison and management discussion. The process of categorizing spending by application segment encourages the IS manager to recognize important
differences in various investments, differences that might otherwise
remain hidden. This in turn helps the IS manager find the most
appropriate means of organizing, measuring, and controlling each
segment. Exhibit 14-9 shows some measurement alternatives in the
areas of spending, user segmentation, and output for various
application segments.

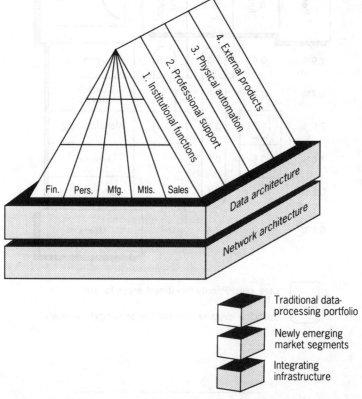

Traditional data-
processing portfolio

Newly emerging
market segments

Integrating
infrastructure

EXHIBIT 14-7 Product segmentation's impact on the applications portfolio.

Source: David P. Norton, "The Economics of Computing in Advanced Stages: Part II—A New
Framework for Management," *Stage by Stage*, vol. 4, no. 3, Fall 1984, p. 3. Copyright Nolan, Norton
& Co.., Lexington, MA. All rights reserved. Reprinted with permission.

For the IS manager increasingly called on to allocate scarce resources across a broad area so as to meet the demands of a multifaceted business strategy, to minimize risk, and to maximize returns, tools such as the Nolan and Norton application portfolio model are valuable techniques for staying in charge of the control and communication process.

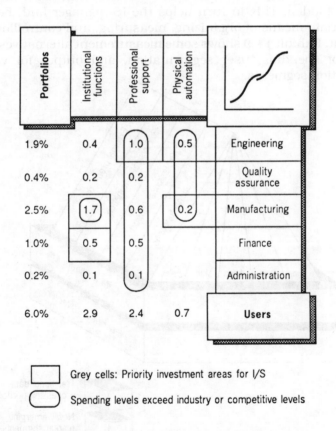

	Portfolios	Institutional functions	Professional support	Physical automation	
	1.9%	0.4	1.0	0.5	Engineering
	0.4%	0.2	0.2		Quality assurance
	2.5%	1.7	0.6	0.2	Manufacturing
	1.0%	0.5	0.5		Finance
	0.2%	0.1	0.1		Administration
	6.0%	2.9	2.4	0.7	**Users**

☐ Grey cells: Priority investment areas for I/S

⬭ Spending levels exceed industry or competitive levels

EXHIBIT 14-8 Alignment of spending and business strategy for one company.

Source: David P. Norton, "The Economics of Computing in Advanced Stages: Part IV—Focusing on the Investment," *Stage by Stage*, vol. 5, no. 1, Spring 1985, p. 6. Copyright Nolan, Norton & Co., Lexington, MA. All rights reserved. Reprinted with permission.

CONCLUSION

The techniques for successfully introducing change are varied. Users' acceptance of change may hinge on their respect for and trust in the IS manager or on their belief that new projects are their own idea. Alternatively, it may require constantly emphasizing the benefits of new tools. Offering proof through experimentation is a popular approach to gaining users' confidence, as is the use of "guinea pigs" to attract others to the technology. Even fairly heavy-handed management may play an effective role. Depending on the audience, of course, a variety of such techniques may be needed.

Selecting improved business solutions often requires maintaining some link to the familiar or traditional. Voice-prompted computer systems frequently retain keyboard entry as an optional feature so new users have recourse to something they know well. Old commands and features are sometimes retained in upgraded systems so that new users will not feel on completely unfamiliar ground. Tipping the hat to tradition serves useful psychological and political purposes. Yet too much caution and risk avoidance can slow the

Portfolios	Institutional functions	Professional support	Physical process	External product	Infrastructure
Input (spending) measure	I/S spending as percent of sales	I/S spending per person	I/S spending per unit of output	I/S spending as percent of product sales	Spending on infrastructure as percent of I/S spending
User segmentation scheme	Functional department (e.g., accounting)	Job family (e.g., brokers)	Physical process (e.g., letters mailed)	Product line (e.g., commercial paper)	X
Output (return) measure	Output per support staff (e.g., transactions per empoyee)	Output per professional (e.g., revenue per employee)	Output per direct employee (e.g., letters processed per employee)	X	X

EXHIBIT 14-9 Different metrics appropriate for each protfolio segment.

Source: David P. Norton, "The Economics of Computing in Advanced Stages," Stage by Stage, vol. 4, no. 4, Winter 1985, p. 6. Copyright Nolan, Norton & Co.., Lexington, MA. All rights reserved. Reprinted with permission.

realization of returns in costly new systems. The IS department is ever vigilant for opportunities for ensuring progress without increasing stress or inciting rejection of new technologies.

Contemporary IS managers sometimes run into difficulty because they continue to follow the advice or practice of a previous era. Elements of tradition, once sound, slowly and imperceptibly become obsolete. Successful IS managers have recognized the need for ongoing flexibility and alertness; change, as we have seen, comes swiftly.

DISCUSSION QUESTIONS

1. Given current trends in hardware introduction, is the task of managing IS hardware apt to become easier or more difficult?

2. What areas of the IS department are likely to change in response to current integration trends?

3. How might the background of the IS manager of the future differ from IS manager's of today? What about the background and career path of other professionals within the IS department?

4. Would functional area executives respond favorably to the categorization by application segment? Why or why not?

5. How difficult would the mechanics (quantifying spending by segment, measuring industry investment levels, and so forth) of the applications portfolio process be to implement? Why?

6. What impact will the increased emphasis on standards and quality have on the organization of the IS department? What functions within the department will be affected the most?

7. What are some of the differences in tracking software technology as opposed to hardware technology?

REFERENCES

Nolan, Richard L.,(1981). "Principal DP Asset: The Applications Portfolio," *Stage by Stage* vol. 1, no. 2 (Lexington, MA.: Nolan, Norton & Co.).

Nolan, Richard L., (1988). "MIS in the Next Decade," *Information Week* (January 4), pp. 26-28.

Nolan, Richard, and Bruce J. Rogow (1983). *Stage by Stage* vol. 3, no. 3 (Fall) (Lexington, MA: Nolan, Norton & Co.).

Norton, David P. (1984). "The Economics of Computing in the Advanced Stages," *Stage by Stage* vol. 4, nos. 3-5 (Fall through Spring) (Lexington, MA.: Nolan, Norton & Co.).

Sullivan-Trainor, Michael (1988). "Not Just Another End-User Liaison," *Computerworld* (March 21), pp. 95-97.

SUGGESTED STUDENT PROJECTS

1. Select a company. Investigate and comment on its IS personnel management process, highlighting the areas covered in Chapter 12.

2. Analyze the SDM of an specific organization, including the following:

   ■ Evolution of current methodology
   ■ Alignment of current methodology with business and IS department strategies
   ■ How new technologies have affected methodology
   ■ Recommendations for improvements

3. Pick one of the following industries and comment on the trends in that industry as they affect management. Look ahead toward the late 1990s and predict future impacts of that industry.

   ■ Desktop publishing
   ■ Minicomputers
   ■ Micro-based fourth-generation languages
   ■ Videodisk technologies
   ■ CASE tools and methodologies
   ■ Image processing
   ■ Artificial intelligence
   ■ Computer-integrated manufacturing

4. Pick two companies and one of the following islands of technology:

   ■ Desktop publishing
   ■ Word processing center
   ■ CAD/CAM
   ■ Graphics
   ■ Robotics

and compare and contrast each company's program, including the following:

   ■ Is it centralized or decentralized in the organization?
   ■ Where does it report in the organization?
   ■ How is it managed?
   ■ Advantages/disadvantages of each
   ■ Recommendations

5. Conduct an extensive literature search on one of the following topics and write an expository paper that summarizes the body of knowledge on that topic.

- IS organizational structures
- Systems development methodologies
- System design techniques
- Conversion strategies
- Decision models for prioritizing a portfolio of application development projects
- Strategic information systems planning

Supplementary Reading List

(1982). "John Diebold Talks About Information Management," *Computerworld* (December 6), pp. 2ff.

(1984). "Rejuvenating Your Old Systems," *EDP Analyzer*, vol. 22, no. 3, (March), pp. 1-14.

(1986). "Developing High Quality Systems Faster," *EDP Analyzer*, vol. 24, no. 6, (June), pp. 1-11.

(1987). "Guiding Distributed Systems," *EDP Analyzer*, vol. 25, no. 11 (November), pp. 1-16.

(1987). "The Role of Business Systems Groups," *EDP Analyzer* Vol. 25, no. 8 (August), pp. 1-16.

(1987). "Why Software Prototyping Works," *Datamation* (August 15), pp. 97ff.

(1988). "Trends in Artificial Intelligence," *I/S Analyzer*, vol. 26, no. 2 (February), pp. 1-16.

Adamski, Lee (1985). "Prototyping," *Computerworld* (May 6), pp. ID25ff.

Alloway, Robert M. (1980). "A Practical Approach to Strategic Planning for the DP Department," Center for Information Systems Research, Alfred P. Sloan School of Management, Massachusetts Institute of Technology,Cambridge, MA, CISR 52.

Alloway, Robert M. (1980). "User Managers' Systems Needs," , Center for Information Systems Research, Alfred P. Sloan School of Management, Massachusetts Institute of Technology, Cambridge, MA, CISR No. 56, Sloan WP No. 1125-80

Alloway, Robert M., and Jerome T. Nolte (1979). "Planning Skill Development for Systems Analysts,", Center for Information Systems Research, Alfred P. Sloan School of Management, Massachusetts Institute of Technology, Cambridge, MA, CISR No. 56, Sloan WP No. 1125-80.

Ansoff, H. Igor (1987). "Strategic Management of Technology," *Journal of Business Strategy*, vol. 7 (Winter), pp. 28-39.

Arvey, Richard D., and Joseph C. Hoyle (1973). "Evaluating Computer Personnel," *Datamation* (July), pp. 69-73.

Ball, Michael (1988). "MIS Hiring and Training: In Search of Business Savvy," *Computerworld* (April 4), pp. 57-61.

Bander, Diana (1986). "Building a Better Project Manager," *Computerworld*, May 26, pp. 69-78.

Bardwick, Judith (1987). "How Executives Can Help 'Plateaued' Employees," *Management Review* (January), pp. 40-46.

Benjamin, Robert I., et al. (1984). "Information Technology: A Strategic Opportunity," *Sloan Management Review* (Spring), pp. 3-10.

Bergeron, Francois (1986). "Factors Influencing the Use of DP Chargeback Information," *MIS Quarterly* (September), pp. 225-237.

Boar, Bernard H. (1985). "Application Prototyping: Trade Guesses for Experience," *Computerworld* (March 4), pp. 45ff.

Boar, Bernard (1986). "Application Prototyping: A Life Cycle Perspective," *Journal of Systems Management* (February), pp. 25-31.

Bowman, Brent, et al. (1981). "Modeling for MIS," *Datamation* (July), pp. 155ff.

Brady, Sharon E. (1987). "Getting a Hand On Maintenance Costs," *Datamation* (August 15), pp. 62-71.

Brand, Eric (1988). "What's In, What's Out," *Datamation* (January 15), pp. 94-100.

Bruns, William J., and Warren F. McFarlan (1987). "Information Technology Puts Power in Control Systems," *Harvard Business Review* (September-October), pp. 89-94.

Burch, John (1986). "Information Systems' Building Blocks," *Journal of Systems Management* (March), pp. 7-11.

Choudhury, Nandan, et al. (1986). "Chargeout of Information Systems Services," *Journal of Systems Management* (September), pp. 16-21.

Clement, Andrew, and C. C. Gotlieb (1987). "Evolution of an Organizational Interface: The New Business Department at a Large Insurance Firm," *ACM Transactions on Office Information Systems*, vol. 5, no. 4 (October), pp. 328-339.

Colter, Mel A. (1984). "A Comparative Examination of Systems Analysis Techniques," *MIS Quarterly* (March), pp. 51-66.

Connolly, James (1984). "Prototyping Seen Easing End-User Request Backlog," *Computerworld* (May 7), p. 12.

Coombes, T. S. (1986). "Ten Key Elements of Information Systems Productivity," *Journal of Systems Management* (April), pp. 34-37.

Cougar, J. Daniel (1986). "E Pluribus Computum," *Harvard Business Review* (September-October), pp. 87-91.

Daft Richard L., and Robert H. Lengel (1986). "Organizational Information Requirements, Media Richness and Structural Design," *Management Science*, vol. 32, no. 5, pp. 554-571.

Daly, Edmund B. (1979). "Organizing for Successful Software Development," *Datamation* (December), pp. 107ff.

Dansker, Benjamin, et al. (1987). "Issues Management in the Information Planning Process," *MIS Quarterly* (June), pp. 223-230.

Dearden, John (1987). "The Withering Away of the IS Organization," *Sloan Management Review* (Summer), pp. 87-91.

Deardon, John, and Nolan, Richard L. (1973). "How to Control the Computer Resource," *Harvard Business Review* (November-December), pp. 68-78.

De Geus, Arie P. (1988). "Planning as Learning," *Harvard Business Review* (March-April), pp. 70-74.

Demb, Ada Barbara (1975). "Centralized versus Decentralized Computer Systems: A New Approach to Organizational Impacts," Center for Information Systems Research, Massachusetts Institute of Technology, Cambridge, MA, CISR Report 12.

Denton, Keith (1988). "Decision-Making Technology," *Production and Inventory Management Review*, vol. 8, no. 1, pp. 35-37.

Dickson, Gary W., et al. (1984). "Key Information Systems Issues for the 1980's," *MIS Quarterly* (September), pp. 135-159.

Diebold, John (1984). "Six Issues That Will Affect the Future of Information Management," *Data Management* (July), pp. 10-14.

Dos Santos, Brian L. (1986). "A Management Approach to Systems Development Projects," *Journal of Systems Management* (August), pp. 35-41.

Er, M. C. (1987). "The Impact of Information Technology on Organizations," *Journal of Systems Management* (April), pp. 32-36.

Er, M. C. (1987). "Prototyping, Participative and Phenomenological Approaches to Information Systems Development," *Journal of Systems Management* (August), pp. 12-16.

Falce, T. (1985). "Changing Role of Management Information Systems and Office Automation," *Journal of Systems Management* (May), pp. 26-29.

Ferratt, Thomas W., and Larry E. Short (1986). "Are Information Systems People Different: An Investigation of Motivational Differences," *MIS Quarterly* (December), pp. 377-387.

Firdman, Henry Eric (1988). "Expert Systems: Are You Already Behind?" *Computerworld* (April 18), pp. 99-105.

Forcht, K. A., et al. (1987). "Emerging Roles of the MIS Professional: Technocrat or Change Agent," *Journal of Systems Management* (November), pp. 10-17.

Gallant, John (1986). "Prototyping Seen As Tool for Applications Refinement," *Computerworld* (March 4), p. 18.

Gilhooley, Ian A. (1987). "Productive Systems Development With Prototyping," *Journal of Information Systems Management* (Spring), pp. 15-22.

Gish, James (1984). "Improving MIS/DP Productivity," *Infosystems* (February), p 87.

Goldstein, David K., and John C. Rockart (1984). "An Examination of Work-Related Correlates of Job Satisfaction in Programmer/Analysts," *MIS Quarterly* (June).

Goodhue, Dale L., et. al. (1988). "Managing the Data Resource: A Contingency Perspective," *MIS Quarterly* (September), pp. 373-392.

Gordon, Carl L., et al (1987). "Toward a Standard Systems Development Life Cycle," *Journal of Systems Management* (August), pp. 24-27.

Grant, F. J. (1984). "Missing: Top Management," *Computerworld* (September 10), pp. 41-48.

Gremillion, Lee L., and Philip Pyburn (1983). "Breaking the Systems Development Bottleneck," *Harvard Business Review* (March-April), pp. 130-137.

Hamburger, Cindy (1986). "Project Planning on a Human Scale," *PC World* (April), pp. 154-162.

Hammer, Michael (1987). "Strategic Systems: Right From Wrong," *InformationWEEK* (September 28), pp. 28-33.

Harrison, Teresa S. (1985). "Techniques and Issues in Rapid Prototyping," *Journal of Systems Management* (June), pp. 8-13.

Hartog, Curt, and Martin Herbert (1986). "1985 Opinion Survey of MIS Managers: Key Issues," *MIS Quarterly* (December), pp. 351-361.

Hartog, Curt, and Robert A. Rouse (1987). "A Blueprint for the New IS Professional," *Datamation* (October 15), pp. 64-69.

Hurst, Rebecca (1987). "CASE Systems Near Fruition," *Computerworld-Focus* (July 8), pp. 27-38.

Isenberg, Daniel J. (1984). "How Senior Managers Think," *Harvard Business Review* (November-December), pp. 81-90.

Janson, Marius A., and L. Douglas Smith (1985). "Prototyping for Systems Development: A Critical Appraisal," *MIS Quarterly* (December), pp. 305-315.

Janulaitis, M. Victor (1984). "Are the Risks Worth Taking?" *Computerworld* (August 13), pp. 13ff.

Jenster, Per V. (1987). "Using Critical Success Factors in Planning," *Long Range Planning*, vol. 20, no. 4, pp. 102-109.

Kaiser, Kate M., and William R. King (1980). "The Manager-Analyst Interface in Systems Development," Graduate School of Business, University of Pittsburgh, Working Paper Series WP-435.

Kaplan, Robert S. (1986). "Must CIM Be Justified By Faith Alone?" *Harvard Business Review* (March-April), p. 95.

Kanter, J. (1986). "The Role of Senior Management in MIS," *Journal of Systems Management* (April), pp. 10-24.

Khosrowpour, M. (1985). "MIS Leadership in Transit," *Journal of Systems Management* (November), pp. 18-21.

Kimmerly, William (1987). "Toward Spontaneous Computing," *Computerworld* (October 12), pp. 111-115.

Kirkley, John (1988). "The Restructuring of MIS: Business Strategies Take Hold," *Computerworld* (March 21), pp. 79-93.

Kling, Rob, and Suzanne Iacono (1984). "The Control of Information Systems Development After Implementation," *Communications of the ACM*, vol. 27, no. 12 (December), pp. 1218-1226.

Kull, David (1986). "Anatomy of a 4GL Disaster," *Computer Decisions* (February 11), pp. 58-65.

Lantz, Kenneth (1986). "The Prototyping Methodology: Designing Right the First Time," *Computerworld* (April 7), pp. 69-72.

Lasden, Martin (1981). "Overcoming Obstacles to Project Success," *Computer Decisions* (December), pp. 114ff.

Lecht, Charles P. (1987). "Management Styles: Japan vs. the U.S.," *Computerworld* (October 26), pp. 21-22.

Lederer, Albert L., and Aubrey L. Mendelow (1987). "Information Resource Planning: Overcoming Difficulties in Identifying Top Management's Objectives," *MIS Quarterly* (September), pp. 389-399.

Loev, Gerald, and Glenn Mangurian (1984). "Alternatives to Replacing Obsolete Systems," *Journal of Information Systems Management* (Fall), pp. 89-93.

Lowry, Christina, and Robert Little (1985). "The Perils of Prototyping," *Cause/Effect* (July), pp. 4-8.

Lucas, Henry C., Jr. (1978). "The Evolution of an Information System: From Key-Man to Every Person," *Sloan Management Review*, vol. 17, no. 2, pp. 39-52.

Mannino, Paul V. (1987). "A Presentation and Comparison of Four Information Systems Development Methodologies," *ACM Sigsoft Software Engineering Notes*, vol. 12, no. 2 (April), p. 25.

Markus, Lynne, and Neils Bjorn-Anderson (1987). "Power Over Users: Its Exercise by System Professionals," *Communications of the ACM*, vol. 30, no. 1 (June), pp. 498-504.

Martin, Jason (1985). "From Analysis to Design," *Datamation* (September 15), pp. 129-135.

Martin, Josh (1981). "Choosing a Management Style," *Computer Decisions* (December), pp. 79ff.

Martin, Merle P. (1986). "The Human Connection in Systems Design: Part I— The Elusive User," *Journal of Systems Management* (October), pp. 6-29.

Martin, Merle P., and James E. Trumbly (1987). "A Project Accountability Chart (PAC)," *Journal of Systems Management* (March), pp. 6-9.

Mazzucchelli, Louis (1985). "Structured Analysis Can Streamline Software Design," *Computerworld* (December 12), pp. 80-86.

Merlyn, Vaughan (1987). "The Backlog Stops Here," *Computerworld* (June 22), pp. 61-66.

Murray, John P. (1987). "The Issue of Quality Assurance: Can We Afford Not to Do It Right the First Time?" *System Development*, vol. 7, no. 1 (January), pp. 1-7.

Necco, Charles R., et al. (1987). "Systems Analysis and Design: Current Practices," *MIS Quarterly*, vol. 11, no. 4 (December), pp. 461-476.

Nolan, Richard L. (1973). "Computer Data Bases: The Future Is Now," *Harvard Business Review* (September-October), pp. 98-114.

Nolan, Richard L. (1977). "Controlling the Costs of Data Services," *Harvard Business Review* (July-August), pp. 114-124.

Nolan, Richard L., et. al. (1988). "Ten Principles Transform I/S Operation Into Information Utility," *Data Management* (January), pp. 18-28.

O'Dell, Peter (1986). "Development Methods Meld," *Computer Decisions* (March 25), pp. 38ff.

Opliger, Edwin B. (1985). "Identifying Microcomputer Concerns," *EDP Journal*, vol. 1, pp. 43-66.

Otten, Klaus W. (1984). "Information Resources Management: Management Focus on the Value of Information and Information Work," *Journal of Information & Image Management* (August), pp. 9-14.

Owen, Darrell E. (1986). "Information Systems Organizations—Keeping Pace with the Pressures," *Sloan Management Review* (Spring), pp. 59-68.

Owen, Darrell E. (1987). "IRM: Obstacles Toward Success," *Journal of Systems Management* (April), pp. 16-18.

Owens, Elizabeth L. (1987). "DP Personalities Discourage Office Politics," *Data Management* (July), p. 21.

Packer, Michael, and Janice Brodman (1988). "A Competitive Strategy for the Rest of Us," *Computerworld* (April 11), pp. 69-73.

Page-Jones, Meilir (1985). "Staff Development Requires Education, Promotion and Motivation," *Data Management* (October), pp. 32-37ff.

Phan, Dien, et. al. (1988). "The Search for Perfect Project Management," *Computerworld/In Depth*, September 26, pp. 95-100.

Philips, Roger (1988). "Productivity Tools Sit Idle," *Computerworld*, February 1, pp. 53-55.

Pottruck, David S. (1980). "How to Keep 'Distributed' DP Pros Happy," *Computer Decisions* (September), pp. 90-92.

Quang, Pham Thu (1986). "MERISE: A French Methodology for Information Systems Analysis and Design," *Journal of Systems Management* (March), pp. 21-24.

Radding, Allan (1987). "All Action, No Talk?" *Computerworld* (May 18), pp. 81-87.

Reimel, J. Christopher (1985). "The Value of Information and Its Relationship to Microcomputers and Data Base," *The EDP Auditor Journal*, vol. 11, pp. 32-37.

Rockart, John F., and Michael S. Scott-Morton (1984). "Implications of Changes in Technology for Corporate Strategy," *Interfaces*, vol. 14, no. 1 (January-February), pp. 84-95.

Saunders, Carol Stoak (1986). "Impact of Information Technology on the Information Systems Department," *Journal of Systems Management* (April), pp. 18-24.

Schneyman, Arthur H. (1986). "Organizing Information Resources," *Information Management Review*, vol. 1, no. 1 (Summer), pp. 35-45.

Schuff, Fred (1987). "Coding Software—The Right Way," *Journal of Information Systems Management* (Winter), pp. 76-81.

Seilheimer, Steven D. (1987). "Importance of the Human Factor in the Information System Life Cycle," *Journal of Systems Management* (July), pp. 24-27.

Severson, Eric, and Kenneth A. Kozar (1988). "A Business Approach to Cracking the Application Backlog," *Journal of Information Systems Management* (Winter), pp. 17-21.

Shank, Michael E., and Andrew C. Boynton (1985). "Critical Success Factor Analysis as a Methodology for MIS Planning," *MIS Quarterly* (June), pp. 121-129.

Shevlin, Jeffrey L. (1984). "Evaluating Alternative Methods of Systems Analysis," *Data Management* (April), pp. 22-25.

Silhan, Peter A. (1987). "Learning to Avoid MIS Design Cop-Outs," *Journal of Systems Management* (July), pp. 35-39.

Smith, Peter M. (1985). "A Prototyping Case Study," *Journal of Information Systems Management* (Summer), pp. 20-25.

Snow, Martin A. (1986). "Taming the Micro Revolution: The Need for Policy," *The EDP Auditor Journal*, vol. 8, pp. 1-5.

Snyders, Jan (1981). "Grow Your Own Managers," *Computer Decisions* (November), pp. 178-198.

Spock, Robin E. (1985). "Break with Tradition," *Datamation* (May 1), pp. 111-114.

Sroka, John M., and Martha H. Rader (1986). "Prototyping Increases Chance of Systems Acceptance," *Data Management* (March), pp. 12-19.

Stewart, George (1982). "Program Generators," *Popular Computing* (September), pp. 112-120.

Sumner, Mary, and Jerry Sitek (1986). "Are Structured Methods for Systems Analysis and Design Being Used?" *Journal of Systems Management* (June), pp. 18-23.

Synders, Jan, and Martin Lasden (1980). "Managing Programmers to Work Harder and Happier," *Computer Decisions* (October), pp. 34-48.

Synnott, William R., William H. Gruber (1981). *Information Resource Management: Opportunities and Strategies for the 1980's*, (New York: Wiley).

Tait, Peter, and Iris Vessey (1988). "The Effect of User Involvement on System Success: A Contingency Approach," *MIS Quarterly* (March), pp. 91-108.

Tate, Paul (1988). "Risks! The Third Factor," *Datamation* (April 15), pp. 58–64.

Tricker, R. I. (1982). "How to Plan Information Strategy," *Management Today* (September), pp. 62ff.

Walsh, John J., and Jerome Kanter (1988). "Toward More Successful Project Management," *Journal of Systems Management* (January), pp. 16-21.

Whieldon, David (1981). "Organizing MIS/DP to Meet the New Challenges," *Computer Decisions* (October), pp. 156-176.

Winer, Charles R. (1984). "Improving Productivity and User Satisfaction Depends on Structured Systems," *Data Management* (November), pp. 36-39.

Withington, Frederic G. (1987). "Managing Your IS Pros," *Datamation* (October 15), pp. 73-81.

Zachman, J. A. (1987). "A Framework For Information Systems Architecture," *IBM Systems Journal*, vol. 26, no. 3, pp. 276-292.

Zachmann, William F. (1988). "Centralization vs. Decentralization: Finding the Appropriate Balance," *InfoWorld*, p. 68.

Zahniser, Richard A. (1985). "What Do You Mean...Structured??" *Small Systems World* (June), pp. 28-32.

Zmud, Robert W. (1984). "Design Alternatives for Organizing Systems Activities," *MIS Quarterly* (June), p. 93.

□ PART IV □

INFORMATION SYSTEMS AS A USER–SUPPORT ENTITY

$\mathbf{J}$ust as the IS department's relationship with corporate-level managers has changed so has its relationship with the end-user community changed—and rather dramatically in fact. In less than 10 years the end user has changed from being a nuisance for IS managers who espoused a philosophy of a strong centralized IS function, to being a partner of sorts with IS managers who accept the movement toward a user-driven computing environment. Every indication points to an even more expansive role for the end user as well as what might be called a "strategic bonding" among the elements of the corporate/IS/end-user triad.

The goal of an equal partnership between the IS professional and the end user is generally accepted by senior and IS managers, but the machinery to accomplish it is not yet in place. The major responsibility for putting this machinery in place rests with the IS manager, although strong support is needed from end-user managers. Part IV examines these evolving relationships, identifies certain key problem areas, and points to some plausible solutions.

CHAPTER 15
The Role of Information Systems As a User-Support Entity

CHAPTER 16
End-User Applications Development

CHAPTER 17
Organizing Information Systems to Support
End-User Computing

CHAPTER 18
Information Systems As a User Support Entity:
Issues and Opportunities

SUGGESTED STUDENT PROJECTS

SUPPLEMENTARY READING LIST

fifteen

□

The Role of Information Systems as a User-Support Entity

The Importance of End-User Computing to the Organization

Management Concerns Regarding End-User Computing

Who Is The End User?

Adopting Information Technology: Information Systems and End-User Perceptions

Information Systems Managerial Support of End-User Computing

End-User Computing Opportunities

End-User Computing Risks

Conclusion

Discussion Questions

References

James C. Wetherbe and R. L. Leitheiser (1985) defined end-user computing (EUC) as "the use and/or development of information systems by the principal users of the systems' outputs or by their staffs." Richard Ball (1987) offers the following broad working definition of EUC:

> **End-user computing refers to the use of computing technology in which the end user plays a dominant role in the definition, development and creation of automated processing and output. The end user assumes responsibility for tasks traditionally carried out by the MIS department. End-user computing may occur on any computing technology (that is, it is not limited to the personal computer) and may be done by anybody, including MIS staff.**

EUC arose as a result of three somewhat independent events. First, through the 1960s and well into the 1970s, the IS department gained a reputation for being consistently late and over budget with application systems that seldom met the needs of the user. Even in the face of such poor service, the backlog of requested systems grew, on average, to at least 3 and sometimes as many as 5 years of work. The combination of major backlog levels and slow response time was obviously intolerable and had to be addressed.

Second, in the 1970s hardware and software technologies began to change rapidly. The emergence of fourth-generation languages (4GLs) and the microcomputer seemed to provide a way out for the frustrated user. With these powerful tools, users saw a way to design and develop their own systems, thus avoiding the crippling applications development bottleneck.

Third, one of the user's early problems was a lack of computer-literate staff to develop new systems. Although some of the more energetic user staffs started to learn development techniques on their own, it was colleges, universities, and vendors that provided the missing ingredient. Colleges and universities were beginning to graduate computer-literate business students who could join functional departments and help managers launch systems development efforts. And vendors were beginning to develop training courses and low-cost, "user friendly" packages and interfaces to facilitate end users' initial interactions with computers.

It may have been an accident of history that these events all occurred simultaneously and resulted in the emergence of EUC. One might also speculate that if IS departments had been able to meet user needs effectively, end users may not have evolved as we know them today, and the industry might have followed a different course.

In any event, end users have emerged as a very powerful and important factor in the strategic and competitive use of information technology in the modern organization. In fact, EUC ranks second only to strategic IS planning as an important issue for the IS manager (Dickson et al., 1984).

This chapter begins by considering the importance of EUC to the organization and certain specific management concerns relating to EUC, broken into three managerial elements: user, IS, and senior management. From here we move to a thorough description of the various types of end users. Next, we contrast the perceptions held by the IS department and end users with regard to adopting new information technology. Then, after looking into ways in which the IS manager can support EUC, we end with an examination of opportunities and risks associated with this new form of computing.

THE IMPORTANCE OF END-USER COMPUTING TO THE ORGANIZATION

Managers generally agree that EUC is an important variable in the total computing equation of the organization. From the benefit/beneficiary matrix (see Chapter 2) we learned that the company's competitive position is strengthened when individual efficiency is improved through office automation and special purpose software designed to reduce the labor intensity of routine, repetitive tasks. Overall effectiveness and thus competitive position are enhanced through the use of sophisticated applications and software packages designed to improve management's decision-making ability.

The resulting productivity gains also favorably affect the value chain in areas that have strategic payoff. For example, the use of a data-base management package to track and analyze sales by lead source can lead to a revision of shipping schedules that in turn will result in both faster service to more active accounts and service differentiation from other competitors—a strategic gain for the company. Although this chain of events is not strictly causal, it is clear that EUC can and does have strategic value.

At the senior-management, IS, and end-user levels of a business, the planning process must integrate EUC as a strategic weapon in the corporate arsenal. This is easier said than done; EUC is generally an ad hoc activity and hence difficult to budget. For budget planning purposes it needs to be viewed in much the same light as a typical research and development function.

MANAGEMENT CONCERNS REGARDING END-USER COMPUTING

For both the organization and its managers, it is crucial that the strategic potential of EUC be realized. However, although senior, IS, and end-user managers all have a vested interest in accomplishing this goal, they do not share identical concerns about EUC. The following sets of questions are typical of those that managers in each area ask about EUC.

Senior Management

- Have we identified areas of strategic opportunity for EUC?
- Are we taking full advantage, across the organization, of our EUC efforts?
- Have we identified the targeted benefits?
- Does the planning process incorporate EUC as a strategic option?
- Is the organization configured to support EUC?
- Are enough resources being allocated to EUC?

IS Management

- Have the developers followed accepted analysis, design, and programming standards?
- Are EUC systems appropriately documented?
- Have user managers made provisions for the maintenance of their systems?
- Have any strategic opportunities been missed by not consulting with the IS department?
- Should any of the users' systems be part of the corporate systems portfolio?
- Have users taken advantage of existing corporate data or developed their own?

User Management

- Are appropriate design standards in place, and are control methods satisfactory?
- Are systems development methods being followed?
- Are the benefits of EUC being fully realized?

In addition, senior management is also concerned with fostering an organizational culture and managerial environment conducive to EUC. This suggests placing the justification for EUC with the end-user manager. In that way, various value-added criteria can be used as valid measures for the justification and prioritization of end-user developed applications. An entrepreneurial environment (structured along the lines of projects, task forces, and strategic business units) also encourages EUC.

For IS management, the challenge is to allow end-user units sufficient autonomy but not at the expense of the necessary controls, standards, and policies needed to ensure that EUC complements other corporate activity. And for user managers, the challenge is four fold:

- To maintain a corporate perspective in managing the EUC activity in their units.
- To ensure proper compliance with IS departmental practices.
- To ensure that hardware/software acquisitions are compatible with corporate standards and supportable by the IS department.
- To provide appropriate planning and support for EUC in their units.

The ultimate success of EUC depends heavily on user management. The relationships of the three elements are schematized in Exhibit 15-1, which emphasizes the critical role of the user manager in ensuring successful EUC activity.

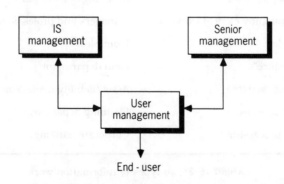

EXHIBIT 15-1 The relationships among managers in an EUC environment.

WHO IS THE END USER?

In the broadest sense, anyone (secretary, accounting clerk, supervisor, manager, president) who uses a computer can be called an end user. Panko and Sprague (1984) identify two types of end users:

1. Type I: An "information worker" who is told what to accomplish and the steps to accomplish it.
2. Type II: An "information worker" who must understand general goals and then figure out how to attain them.

The kinds of work that each type performs helps distinguish them, as Exhibit 15-2 shows. However, this typology tends to oversimplify the complex management issues relating to EUC. A better approach is to define end users from the standpoint of the computing skills they offer and to intersect these skills with the types of information these workers process. John Rockart and L.Flannery (1983)

Type I	*Type II*
High volume of transactions	Low volume of transactions
Low cost (value) per transaction	High value (cost) per transaction
Well-stuctured procedures	Ill-structured procedures
Output measures defined	Output measures less defined
Focus on process	Focus on problems and goals
Focus on efficiency	Focus on effectiveness
Handling of "data"	Handling of concepts
Predominantly clerical workers	Managers and professionals
Examples:	Examples:
"Back office"	Loan department
Mortgage services	Asset/liability management
Payroll processing	Planning department
Check processing	Corporate banking

EXHIBIT 15-2 Two types of information work.

Source: McNurlin, Barbara C. and Ralph H. Sprague, Jr., *Information Systems Management in Practice*, Englewood Cliffs, N.J.: Prentice-Hall, 1986, p. 10.

following such an approach, identify six types of end users: nonprogramming, command-level, programming-level end users, functional-support, EUC-support personnel and data-processing programmers.

Nonprogramming End Users

This type of end user uses applications systems developed by others. The developers may be personnel in their own department (i.e., programming-level end users) or from the IS department (i.e., data-processing programmers). The nonprogramming end user uses the computer by responding to a series of menus and/or prompts for very specific information. He or she has little understanding of the computer beyond routine interactions with the system. Airline reservation clerks and department store cashiers are typical representatives of this end-user category. This user is clearly a Type I information worker as defined by Panko and Sprague. Nonprogramming end users were the earliest and, for a long time, the only type of end user that the traditional IS department anticipated serving.

Command-Level End Users

This user differs from the nonprogramming user in that the system he or she uses is partially or totally command driven, hence more under his or her control. This type of system is clearly more powerful than a menu-driven system in the sense that the user has more flexibility. To use it, the user must form a query statement that the system then interprets and executes. The information retrieved may be a single record or a summary of data from a subset of records meeting conditions specified by the user. The user must have a working knowledge of the command-driven language (usually part of the data-base management system). Some applications may require porting retrieved data to a word processing or graphics package for later printing within some type of report or document. Thus, this user may need an elementary knowledge of operating systems.

As new software becomes available, the command-level end user will make more sophisticated use of computers. Financial analysts and marketing researchers are typical representatives of this category of end user.

Programming-Level End Users

A typical user in this category has the ability to design and write programs in compiler or interpreter languages and to produce custom-designed reports and analyses. Often the systems this user develops will be used by nonprogramming or command-level end users. Programming-level end users are usually attached to a single business department and are not part of the IS department. They tend to develop exceptional skills in one or perhaps two application packages and will frequently have more expertise with the package than do the personnel in the IS department who are assigned to support uses of the package.

The term "power user" is sometimes applied to these end users. As we will see later, these information technology gatekeepers will prove to be a valuable resource for the IS department in providing EUC support services. Much of those user's development efforts are for their own purposes, although they will often provide informal support to others in their department.

Functional-Support Personnel

This group of end users is almost always found in functional departments. These users are technically skilled but view themselves as functional rather than IS specialists. They can write programs in compiler-based languages but seldom use anything other than end-user languages. They often serve as a liaison with the IS department and represent their functional departments on systems development project teams. These users typically develop systems for use by others.

End-User Computing Support Personnel

These users are usually assigned to an information center and are specialists in one or more end-user programming packages. They offer general support to new users (nonprogramming and command-level end users). Training at the introductory and advanced levels with a specific package is their main responsibility; they are usually weak in function-specific applications. They also offer support to command-level and programming-level end users in data extraction and package choice, as well as occasional systems-development advice.

Data Processing Programmers

This is the most frequently overlooked of the end-user groups. These users are exactly like Cobol programmers except that they program in end-user languages at a high skill level. Their needs are very different from those of the other types. Productivity training and automated software design, code generators, and related technologies are their principle areas of need. They are the real experts in end–user languages but frequently lack a functional business orientation. Larger companies often set up information centers (sometimes called development centers) to meet the needs of this group.

It may not be apparent at first glance that the data-processing programmer would be considered an end user. To see that this user does belong in the taxonomy, note the parallel between programming end users and data-processing programmers as depicted in Exhibit 15-3. Tools are the most significant area of similarity. Although 4GLs and microcomputer packages are used by both end-user types, the depth of understanding and usage of each is quite different. The

	Programming-Level End-User	Data-Processing End-User
Problem	Solve a business problem or make as business decision	Design, code, test, debug, and document program(s)
Tools	Prototyping 4GLs Microcomputer packages	Prototyping 4GLS Microcomputer packages Programming languages Design aids Documentation tools
Support resources	User guides Training classes	Programmer manuals Training classes
Staff resources	Power users Functional-support personnel Programming-level end users	Programmers Systems analysts Systems programmers Operations staff
Organizational support	Information center	Development center

EXHIBIT 15-3 Similarities between programming-level and DP programming end users.

programming-level end user ordinarily learns only those commands needed to solve a particular problem. The data-processing user, on the other hand, generally has a working knowledge of the entire language and often makes creative and sometimes complex use of the commands. The support and training needs of each end user type differ in terms of sophistication; the programming-level user needs more structured help than does the data-processing end user.

It is important to distinguish between EUC and another category of computer use: personal computing. Personal computing can generally be thought of as computing that benefits only the individual and is not part of departmental or corporate systems portfolios. Most employees in the information sector are very individualistic and will often create personalized procedures for accomplishing a given task. If they use the computer as part of those procedures, that use is personal computing. When they leave their positions or companies, the loss of their procedures typically goes unnoticed by their organization.

Personal computing is very different from EUC in that it is not an integral part of an employee's responsibilities, departmental work flow, or reporting requirements. Often, such computer usage will be unknown even to an employee's immediate supervisor or manager. This type of computing activity is of little interest in our study of the management of EUC. However, it must be recognized as an important activity because it will often be the beginning of much broader usage of computing that will have value to the organization.

ADOPTING INFORMATION TECHNOLOGY: INFORMATION SYSTEMS AND END-USER PERCEPTIONS

An interesting comparison with obvious managerial consequences is that between the end user and IS department perceptions regarding appropriate usage of information technology. Exhibit 15-4 is a grid allowing us to compare the two groups on the basis of their needs for old versus new technology. The situation in each of the four categories of the grid is dynamic and can present senior, IS, and user managers with complex challenges. A mismatch (i.e., categories B or C) obviously indicates a problem, but even in cases where there is agreement (i.e., categories A or D), a problem may arise, as we will see. The following sections briefly describe the grid and offer prescriptive measures in cases of mismatch or incorrect positioning.

The Technology Adoption Grid

Category A Senior management is faced with a significant question if both the end user and the IS department are using old technology: Does this usage reflect the correct corporate strategy? If the answer is yes, there is no immediate problem, but time may cause this strategy to be incorrect. In that case, change will need to come from the IS manager, who is best positioned to understand and address the need for a technology upgrade. (Of course, if the use of the old technology is inherently ill-advised, senior management needs a new IS manager.)

Category B The IS manager's actions dictate the outcome of situations in this category. Although the IS department may be correctly promoting and adopting new technologies, the end-user may not be doing so because the IS department has failed to educate the user. This situation can, of course, be aggravated if the end-user community refuses to accept new technology. Alternatively, the IS department may have incorrectly positioned a new technology in the company and may thus be meeting (and rightly so) resistance on the part of the end user. In this case, some intervention on the part of senior management may be needed.

Category C The end user is probably frustrated with a situation in this category. Here the user may have found effective and efficient uses of a new technology only to discover that the IS department is clinging to old ways. Category C companies were common in the early days of EUC. Organizations that are incorrectly placed in this

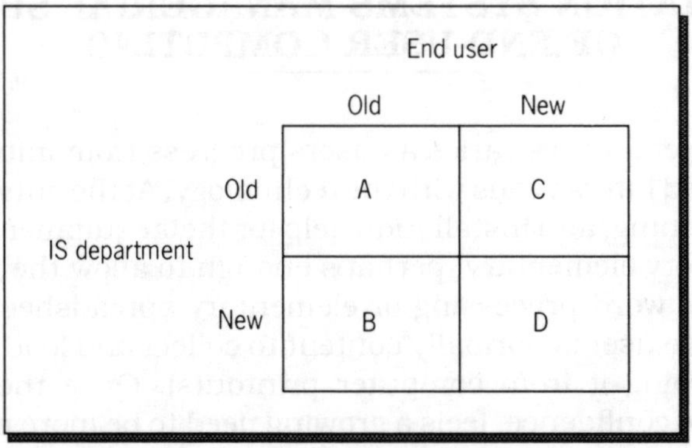

EXHIBIT 15-4 The information technology adoption grid.

category may require strong directives from senior management. The refusal of the IS department to accept end users as legitimate partners in the systems development effort is characteristic of Category C situations, as is a probable adversarial relationship between the department and end-user management.

Category D In Category D situations, senior management may have allowed both the IS department and the end user to sweep the company into acquiring the latest technologies when some other less ambitious strategy might have been more appropriate. In this case a return on the technology investment will not be realized. A strong, persuasive IS manager may be the root cause of the problem. On the positive side, the fact that both end users and the IS department are using a new technology can put the company in a position to exploit that technology for strategic advantage.

It would be very difficult to devise a single management approach, systems development methodology, or planning system to satisfy the needs of each end-user type. Clearly, the training support that management provides each type will vary considerably. Managers interacting with any of these end users must be sensitive not only to the type of computer work they do but also to the level of computer understanding that each has. Moreover, successful relationships among senior management, IS management, and end-user management depend primarily on whether each has an accurate perception of the role of information technology in the business of the company. If any one of the three does not, the company is automatically in a situation where some serious change will be required if it is to remain competitive.

INFORMATION SYSTEMS MANAGERIAL SUPPORT OF END-USER COMPUTING

Support for end users varies as users progress from initial to more sophisticated interactions with the technology. At the outset the user requires training, and installation help for their equipment. Training is usually very elementary, perhaps enough to allow the user to get started with word-processing or elementary spreadsheet skills. At this point the user is normally content to collect and load data (even by transcribing it from computer printouts). Once the user has gained some confidence, feels a growing need to be more productive, and has an insight into more sophisticated applications, he or she will soon ask for access to corporate-level data bases. A new set of training requirements emerge and, more importantly, IS management enters a new stage in its relationship with the now educated user (i.e., the command-level user). Issues of standards, data security, and data integrity, once of secondary importance, are now of primary importance. The data requirements for this user's applications are complex, as data management issues also begin to surface.

By this time the end user will be developing his or her own application systems, and issues of conformance to accepted design, testing, and documentation standards will surface. What was initially a simple managerial task becomes demanding and complex as the user is in a position to ask for (and exert influence to get) more access and more say in EUC policy formation. The end user now approaches computing as an investment and wants to be sure to get the maximum return. To further complicate the issue, not all such end users are at an identical level of computing; hence, determining the appropriate level of management support is not a trivial exercise.

John Henderson and Michael Treacy (1986) define the four fundamental issues facing the IS manager as they consider the management and support of EUC. The first is the necessary support infrastructure (i.e., educational mechanisms, implementation, and leadership). Decisions regarding this infrastructure depend on the type of users in the organization. The fact that end users also provide a support structure for one another further complicates the issue.

Users tend to prefer informal support mechanisms; thus, if someone in a neighboring office can answer a user's question, that person will be approached first, before a trip across the building is made or a telephone call is placed. The IS department, in contrast, prefers a more formal approach to support. Clearly, it is easier to allocate resources and plan for service levels if the degree and frequency of help requests are known. One thing is for certain: a centralized organizational structure cannot possibly meet the needs of such a diverse and interdependent end-user constituency.

The second issue facing the IS manager concerns the technological infrastructure. Here, decisions about hardware, software, and communications equipment must be made. As we already know, standards dominate this area. On the one hand, care must be exerted to not constrain the end user to the point where this user will have little incentive or opportunity to be creative. On the other hand, too few standards will make support, cross-functional sharing of systems and data, the integration of applications into the systems portfolio, and the establishment of competitive advantage unlikely.

The third issue is that of data infrastructure; here again, standards in data, data bases, integrity, and security are important. As the user becomes more sophisticated and makes more complex demands, the data infrastructure becomes more significant. Access to corporate data makes the end user far more productive, hence more likely to contribute to the strategic positioning of the organization.

The fourth and final issue deals with the economic evaluation and justification of EUC. This is a very difficult area because forecasts of costs or benefits associated with EUC are not usually available. Furthermore, the benefits of innovation are not immediately identifiable. Perceived value or value added are the best measures available, even though they are more subjective than quantitative. Cost/benefit frameworks also are not appropriate because they tend to inhibit creativity rather than encourage it.

To further complicate the issue, these four issues are dynamic; as organization and EUC evolve, their relative importance will shift. Exhibit 15-5 illustrates the change in importance of each issue over time. The important task for the IS manager is assessing how the management and support of EUC, in the face of these issues, must change, and anticipating the appropriate alignment of management support strategies.

It also helps to think about management strategies from the following four perspectives: implementation, marketing, operations, and economics. Exhibit 15-6 identifies these different perspectives, which are not unlike the stages in the Nolan model (see Chapter 2). They are sequential from the point of view of entry, but not all organizations will pass through all stages.

Effective implementation entails getting the new user excited about using computers as productivity-improvement tools. To accomplish this, the IS department must offer a wide range of learning opportunities for functional units as well as individuals. A centralized information center staffed by in-house consultants who eagerly seek out users and offer one-on-one help is a good start. This also gives consultants a chance to learn about users' specific functional needs and areas where computing may be used to advantage.

Knowledge of users' functional areas allows for a transition to a marketing-oriented perspective. Here, the emphasis is on growth and market penetration using systems with strategic value to the organization. The organization is developing an understanding of applications of the technology. To best accomplish this transition, a centralized, direct support service is needed.

Eventually, senior management will begin to ask for accountability. Departments will have to account for their investments in technology, and, as a result, the need for a centralized support service will diminish and be supplanted by the need for more standardization and formal planning. As the organization becomes more comfortable with its new approach to EUC, EUC will become part of the corporate strategic plan. Chapter 18 discusses this important corporate issue in greater detail.

END-USER COMPUTING OPPORTUNITIES

As end users increase their knowledge of computing through on-the-job use, they help improve overall organizational efficiency and effectiveness and ultimately contribute to competitive advantage.

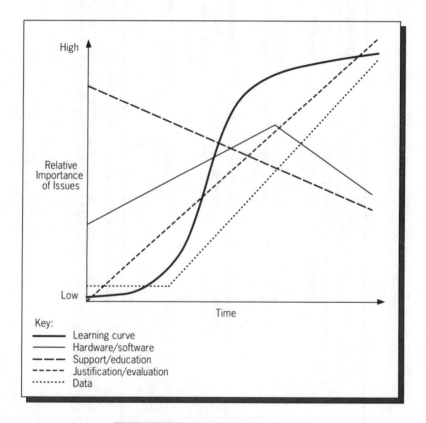

EXHIBIT 15-5 The significance of IS management issues relating to EUC as measured over time.

Source: John C. Henderson and Michael E. Treacy, "Managing End-User Computing for Competitive Advantage," *Sloan Management Review*, vol. 28, no. 2, Winter 1986, p. 6. Reprinted by permission of the publisher. Copyright 1986 by the Sloan Management Review Association. All rights reserved.

	Implementation	Marketing	Operations	Economic
Objective	Increase usage and user satisfaction	Market growth and market penetration	Integration and efficiency	Competitive advantage
Strategy	Opportunistic: supportive; Educational	Value-added products and services; Base building	Standards automation	Link IS plan strategy; Targeted investment
Structure	Centralized help centers; Roving consultants	Local direct support group	Centralized formal planning; Decentralized support	Distributed operations
Control mechanisms	Innovators	Departmental accountability	Centralized policies	Formal justification; Organizational incentives

EXHIBIT 15-6 Different perspectives on the management of EUC.

Source: John C. Henderson and Michael E. Treacy, "Managing End-User Computing for Competitive Advantage," *Sloan Management Review,* vol. 28, no. 2, Winter 1986. p. 8. Reprinted by permission of the publisher. Copyright 1986 by the Sloan Management Review Association. All rights reserved.

Thus, as seen from the corporate vantage point, there certainly is a relationship between EUC and a leading competitive edge. But advantages accrue at other levels, too, as indicated in the following sections.

Opportunities at the Information Systems Department Level

IS departments have traditionally been plagued by a shortage of qualified analysts and programmers. By having end users do their own development work, IS departments "off-load" to the user some of the pressure for ad hoc query and report generation. This in turn relieves some of the pressure on the IS staff, which can then devote its time more productively to larger projects. In many cases end users know their system requirements and can turn directly to system implementation, thus avoiding the requirement-specification phase and reducing development time.

One of the major problems associated with implementation is getting users to buy into the system—to assume the responsibility for its successful implementation. Users who develop their own systems have a vested interest in them and will do whatever they can to see that the systems development effort comes to a successful conclusion.

Opportunities at the End-User Level

End-users would list the following as EUC benefits (Wetherbe and Leitheiser, 1985):

1. The lead times for development requests from the user department are much shorter than those set by the IS department.

2. By doing their own systems development, end users have more control over systems and their use.

3. EUC can provide services not available from the IS department.

4. IS departmental procedures are not appropriate for small applications.

5. End-users gain more flexibility as a result of EUC.

6. The systems developed will better meet users' needs.

END-USER COMPUTING RISKS

Although there are many opportunities to be exploited with EUC, a number of risks exist, too. Gordon Davis (1984) discusses in detail some of the risk areas briefly reported next.

Elimination of Analyst Functions

When users design and develop their own systems, they do not take advantage of the diverse skills of the IS department's technical support staff. Design walk-throughs and data architecture reviews by a group of peers are standard in many settings, but these will not happen for user-designed and -implemented systems.

Another area of concern is end-user enforcement of standards and policies. Such enforcement is mandatory in the IS department but is unlikely to happen with any consistency and regularity in the end-user department.

Incomplete Specifications of System Requirements

The techniques and experiences of the analyst are invaluable when it comes to specifying system requirements completely and accurately. Although users may do a fair job with the specifications they do identify, it is likely that these specifications will not be complete. Experience is the best teacher in this area, and the typical end user has little of it.

Reduced Quality Assurance and System Stability

Because it has to live with its mistakes, the systems development staff is very aware of quality-related issues. They are concerned about data integrity, conformance to data definition and design standards, complete system and subsystem testing, clear documentation, and so forth. Initial investments of time to ensure a quality system results in less maintenance effort for "bug fixing" and easier system modification. In general, end users do not have the same level of commitment to system quality. The most obvious result is a higher-than-average maintenance effort.

In addition, end users have difficulty defining systems requirements. Pieces and parts of the system may be inadvertently left out so that the system will need to be retrofitted. The system will continually be in a state of flux so that its users are constantly having to relearn and change work patterns. Any productivity benefits that the system may have to offer will be cancelled out by the impact of the instability. By working with the IS department much of this system overhead could be avoided.

Proliferation of Unrelated Systems

Users have their own interests at heart and are usually not aware of the overall corporate systems portfolio and data resources when they are designing their own systems. As a result, they often unknowingly replicate data and/or systems that are in the corporate portfolio. Their applications may be new to the organization and, if combined with an already existing system, might have significant strategic value. User systems seldom communicate with other applications in the corporate portfolio. The result is the creation of disjointed "islands of applications" that may seem to serve the needs of single departments but are not integrated and thereby leveraged to meet other users' needs.

A related problem is the proliferation of data that are redundant, undocumented, obsolete, incorrect, and generally of little value. Such data reside in individual systems but are not otherwise used by other departments.

CONCLUSION

Developing a program to support and control EUC requires a partnership of senior management, IS management, and user management. EUC presents numerous opportunities as well as inherent risks, as we have seen. The opportunities include contributions to the organization's strategic goals, relief for an ongoing programmer shortage, and a variety of benefits that accrue to the user groups with their own computing expertise. The risks are related to the users' lack of understanding of formal systems development methods.

Education could certainly solve the problem except that the systems development process for EUC will not be the same as the traditional development process.

DISCUSSION QUESTIONS

1. Compare and contrast the training and support needs for each type of end user. What would you identify as the major challenge to IS management in providing the needed types of training and support?

2. Develop a strategy for making end users an extension of the support function of the IS department. How might you, as IS manager, implement that strategy? Be specific.

3. Expand the technology adoption grid to include senior managers as a third dimension. Discuss the organizational implications of either correct or incorrect assessments by these managers of old versus new information technologies.

REFERENCES

Ball, Richard, (1987). "Harnessing End-User Computing Without Hindering It," Computerworld (October 26), pp. 91–100.

Davis, Gordon B. (1984). "Caution: User Developed Systems Can Be Dangerous to Your Organization," MISRC-WP-82-04, MIS Research Center, University of Minnesota, Minneapolis, Minnesota.

Dickson, G. W., R. L. Leitheiser, J. C. Wetherbe, and M. Nechis (1984). "Key Information Systems Issues for the 1980's," MIS Quarterly (September), pp. 135–154.

Henderson, John C., and Michael E. Treacy (1986). "Managing End-User Computing for Competitive Advantage," Sloan Management Review, vol. 28, no. 2 (Winter), pp. 3–14.

Panko, R. R., and R. H. Sprague (1984). "Implementing Office Systems Requires a New DP Outlook," Data Management (November), pp. 40–42.

Rockart, John F., and L. Flannery (1983). "The Management of End User Computing," Communications of the ACM, vol. 26, no. 10 (October), pp. 776–784.

Wetherbe, J. C., and R. L. Leitheiser (1985). "Information Centers: A Survey of Services, Decisions, Problems, and Successes," Journal of Information Systems Management, vol. 2, no. 3 (Summer), pp. 3–10.

sixteen

□

End-User Applications Development

The forward-thinking IS manager welcomes end users who want to develop their own systems. Having users do so helps alleviate the programmer shortage problem, and programmers are able to spend their time on larger projects. There is, however, a high price to pay: The IS department must establish standards and controls on user systems-development activities and then monitor compliance with

371

those standards. Although the IS manager is supposed to ensure that end-user systems have been developed in accordance with principles, many users do develop systems regardless of the procedures and controls established by the IS department and it would be naive to assume that the end-user community will blindly follow these procedures and controls. Most users find them cumbersome, complex, sometimes unnecessary, and generally a hindrance to getting a system up and running quickly.

It is legitimate to ask whether a user-developed system should even meet the same standards as IS-developed systems. The answer is probably not—but what standards should be met, and how can compliance be verified?

This issue is critical to the growth and success of end-user computing (EUC), which must be folded into the strategic plan of the organization if it is to have any long-term impact. How should this happen? What will the IS department do when end-users develop the systems that do not work and for which no documentation exists? These and related questions raise a number of difficulties for the IS manager.

This chapter starts off with a look at implementing systems development procedures for EUC. We discuss the responsibilities first of the IS department and then of end-user management with regard to systems development, and then we turn to implementation of policy and procedure. Next, we explore the life cycle of the user-developed system and go on to discuss prototyping in some detail.

Our focus then shifts to controls, both hard and soft. We end with a discussion of certification of user-developed systems—coming full circle, in a sense, to the issue of the IS department's responsibilities regarding this rapidly emerging area of EUC.

IMPLEMENTING END-USER SYSTEMS DEVELOPMENT PROCEDURES

The development and implementation of policies and procedures for end-user systems development presents two different areas of concern for both IS management and end-user management. First, to develop acceptable policies and procedures, both parties in the end-user systems-development life cycle must understand their responsibilities. Second, simply stating policy and procedure and then expecting automatic compliance is naive; however, expecting the IS department to be end-user policy enforcers is unrealistic.

The IS department must become a facilitator and true partner with the end user. As facilitator, the IS department must help users take full advantage of new information technology. This can be done through user groups coordinated by IS staff; it can also be done by keeping users aware of the strategic direction of new technology as it applies to the organization. As a true partner, the IS department must realize that end users are going to develop their own systems with or without the support of the department; therefore, the IS department cannot and should not try to do everything. In forming this partnership, both the IS department and end-user departments must agree on separate responsibilities.

Senior management's philosophy and the corporate culture must also be taken into account. Many CEOs want all computing expertise to reside with the IS manager so that this manager is free to implement necessary controls and standards with the full support of senior management. Other senior managers may insist on tight controls and approvals via the chain of command. In such environments the end user is often very passive, and little happens until senior management makes a move. In these cases the IS manager would be foolish to attempt to implement standards that give the end user discretionary power regarding technology usage and applications development. In the final analysis, the IS manager must implement standards and controls that are compatible with the culture and philosophy of the organization.

THE DEVELOPMENT RESPONSIBILITIES OF THE INFORMATION SYSTEMS DEPARTMENT

The responsibilities of the IS department with respect to end-user systems development range primarily over areas that have corporate impact rather than specific business-function impact. These responsibilities include the establishment of policy and standards, data administration, communications, technology research, and training and education.

Setting Corporate Policy and Standards

At the corporate level, policies that govern all aspects of computing—including privacy, security, access privileges, and the ethical use of computing resources—must be established. In addition, standards must be established in such areas as hardware, software, data definition, data communications, systems analysis and design, and documentation. This is not easily accomplished. Standards are as much guidelines as anything else, and their purpose is not to constrain the end user but rather to create an environment in which users can be more productive and effective in their systems development efforts. If the end user is truly convinced of this, the problem of standards enforcement will be significantly reduced. Therefore, end-user management should be involved in the development of standards and must agree to them. Consensus will arise as a compromise between control and autonomy. Because end-user management will ultimately be responsible for enforcement, if it is not convinced of the value of the standards it is unlikely to support their enforcement.

Standards should not be applied unilaterally across the organization or without regard to specific situations. The IS department must be sensitive to whether the system to be developed has short-term or long-term business or strategic implications. If short-term, some variance from standards might be allowed; if long-term, a more rigid enforcement may be in order. In many cases a system may have strategic value only if it can be quickly implemented. In these cases some variances might be allowed so that opportunities are not missed simply because of delays in imposing a development methodology. Exhibit 16-1 is an example of standards as they might be developed for the end-user systems-development life cycle.

Steps in the Systems Development Life Cycle	End-User Control
Problem definition	Problem statement is reviewed by IS for possible integrations with existing systems portfolio
Feasibility study	IS reviews the design for a better alternative using existing technology
Systems design	Design walk-through with appropriate IS staff
	Data definition and data-base design review
Implementation	Consulting available to assist user
Testing	IS creates test data and signs off on valid test completion
Documentation	IS accepts documentation for systems portfolio

EXHIBIT 16-1 Standards for the end-user systems-development life cycle.

Data Administration

The IS department is clearly responsible for defining the corporate data structure as well as providing the environment in which those data can be maintained and made accessible to the organization. The data architecture must be appropriate for the needs of the organization, and decisions regarding its structure should involve the user. Users must be able to look to the IS department for help, advice, and consulting with regard to data design for their systems.

Communications

By defining the hardware and software alternatives within which users must operate, the IS department makes it possible for data communications to take place across the organization. Anything short of that creates a barrier to the truly strategic use of information and systems by others in the organization. One of the major problem areas for IS is the creation of a "seamless" data environment for the user. As data are more distributed across the network, it is important to remove as many barriers to data communication as possible.

Technology Research

The ideal strategic planning process is business driven, but without functional managers who are also computer fluent, this process will not happen. A technology-driven process, as we saw in Chapter 5, is not the answer, either. It is the responsibility of the IS department to keep the organization informed of the latest technologies as they presently or might in the future apply to the organization. A series of "white papers," focused on specific end-user system requirements, is one means of fulfilling that responsibility. At the same time, the IS department should establish an R&D effort, in conjunction with the appropriate functional departments and strategic business units, to investigate and try out new information technologies. A proactive partnership with the end user can significantly diminish the likelihood of missing strategic opportunities.

Training and Education

Managers and users always have a need for training and education that can be best provided by the IS department. Present end-user needs are typically for education in all aspects of the systems development life cycle, including documentation, testing, and maintenance. These are areas that the end user has traditionally ignored, largely as a result of ignorance of their value for the entire development effort. Much of the process and procedure of IS-developed systems is inappropriate for user-developed systems and for systems developed with 4GL tools.

THE DEVELOPMENT RESPONSIBILITIES OF END–USER MANAGEMENT

By assuming responsibility for their own applications development and report generation, user departments also become responsible for a number of other computing activities that traditionally have been undertaken by the IS department. Often, this is recognized too late. With authority to control systems also comes a responsibility to support them, which the following sections delineate.

Applications Management

Decisions regarding which applications to develop, and what the priorities of the application development portfolio should be, are the responsibility of the end-user manager. As with decentralized applications development, having the user assume this responsibility confers certain benefits. Better allocation of personnel and other resources is possible, and cost/benefit analysis is easier. The actual policies and procedures used by the functional department can be tailored to meet the needs of that department. However, applications development cannot be totally divorced from corporate policy and procedure. Where the application involves other departments, systems development needs to take place in accordance with policy and procedure established at the corporate level. The issue of who is in charge of cross-departmental development projects is not easily resolved. Systems designed and projects managed by committee are not the solution.

Implementation

The implementation phase of systems development is also the responsibility of the end-user department. If the system is to be used by several people in the department or functional area, the developer's department is responsible for systems design and testing, documentation, and training. Again, this process will not take place independent of established IS policy and procedure. For example, design reviews and/or walk-throughs may be jointly conducted by the IS and user departments. The IS department may also assume some responsibility for signing off on the system test phase. Once the system is put into production, the user developer also assumes responsibility for ongoing support. This support takes the form of software maintenance, additional training for new hires, perhaps a user group, system changes in response to new report requests, and so on. The IS department can play an important role in the initial training of user-developers in the complete systems development life cycle.

Operational Responsibility

Perhaps the most difficult responsibility for the end user to assume involves areas not visible to the typical user, including back-up procedures, error detection and correction, file maintenance, and quality assurance. Left to their own devices, end users usually realize the importance of these operational responsibilities only after suffering the consequences of not fulfilling them. Losing a large data file or application program for which there was no backup, is a common problem—-and hard way to learn the lesson. The IS department should be responsible for educating the end user in all aspects of applications management, including operational activities.

THE IMPLEMENTATION OF POLICY AND PROCEDURE

Allan Sewell (1987) discusses the shift in responsibility for policy and procedure from the IS department to the functional units. Although the IS department is clearly responsible for the development of policy and procedure, Sewell maintains that it is not responsible for its implementation. Because policy and procedure are developed in concert with user management, it should be straightforward for user managers to assume responsibility for implementation. They will have been educated as to the value and benefit of meaningful policy and procedure and should be willing participants in their implementation, particularly in light of the fact that policy and procedure can be tailored to the specific needs of the user department.

When applications systems cross departmental or business-unit lines, implementing policy and procedure can become more complex. However, user management can nonetheless ensure conformance with corporate policy and procedure so as to preserve the integrity of the system. The IS department's responsibilities thus end with integrating data and systems among departments and establishing uniform corporate policies, procedures, and communication.

Sewell provides some guidelines that will facilitate this transfer of responsibility:

1. An open communications link must be established between the IS department and systems personnel in the user department. This link will help resolve questions of procedure.
2. Procedures must exist to update corporate data so that user-derived data will also be kept up to date.
3. One person in each user area must be given responsibility for operations, for maintenance of critical data, and for communicating procedural matters.
4. The IS department should establish a small liaison staff to be responsible for communicating with user departments. Ideally, the notion of "one-stop-shopping" for the user department should be established. (The idea of a "help desk," introduced in Chapter 10, is one possibility.)

John Rockart (1987) advocates that line management must take the lead in systems development, with the IS department moving into a support role. He bases his argument on the fact that the IS manager cannot possibly know enough about each functional area and the strategies of its manager to design appropriate systems. The functional manager must learn enough about the technology to recognize and seize strategic opportunities. For this to happen, a partnership between functional and IS managers is needed in order to integrate strategic systems across organizational boundaries. Rockart calls the result a "Wired Society" and concludes that achieving it requires transforming not only the way we do business but also the organizational structure itself. (This is discussed in detail in Chapter 17.)

THE LIFE CYCLE OF END-USER SYSTEMS DEVELOPMENT

Applications development has largely moved away from transactions-oriented systems and into control or strategic systems at the middle and senior management levels. Many system needs at this level are not well-defined. The user manager often has only a vague description of the system and what it needs to do, is often unsure of exactly how the decision process works, and is therefore not able to write a statement of the problem, as the traditional systems development life cycle would require. On the other side, the systems analyst does not have enough understanding of the user's functional area to assist with problem definition, either. Linear systems development methods are not adequate for such ill-defined kinds of development projects in which the problem cannot be defined in sufficient detail, a feasibility study makes no sense, cost/benefit analysis is out of the question, and analysis and programming phases have been incorporated with the use of 4GL tools.

What is needed is a methodology that allows defining the system to be part of the development stage. This is precisely what so-called adaptive techniques are designed to do. Such methodologies allow the definition of the system to change as part of the development process itself; that is, in the act of developing the system the developer arrives at a more detailed definition of the system. Based on the new definition, the system design is altered, and the process continues until another more definitive statement can be made that leads to yet another version of the system. The process stays underway until such time as the user manager is satisfied that either the objective has been met or the process seems to be leading nowhere, in which case the project is abandoned.

Sometimes projects are pursued on the basis of rather vague notions on the part of the user manager regarding added or perceived value. It is easy to see why the IS manager might be uncomfortable with this approach: there is no time-line for completion and no specification of deliverables or estimate of resources to be committed to the project. However, the process does encourage learning on the part of both the user manager and the developer; fewer fixed-cost commitments to projects that are ultimately scrapped; faster response time to the need for a working version of the system; and much shorter development time, which is extremely valuable for systems with solid strategic value.

Prototyping

Two basic types of prototypes can be used in the systems development process: throwaway prototypes and operational prototypes. A third type, iconic prototypes, are physical or simulation models of some system (clay models of cars operating in a wind tunnel, for example) and are not appropriate for information systems development.

Throwaway Prototypes With these, a model of the system is built using a nonprocedural language. Once the prototype system meets user-defined needs, it is discarded and replaced with an operational version that is usually written in a third-generation procedural language to take advantage of certain machine efficiencies. There are cases, however, where the production version may be written in the same 4GL in which the prototype is written. For the user this use of prototyping may be difficult to grasp, as the throwaway prototype is a working version of the system. From the IS perspective, the prototype is built quickly for the sole purpose of defining an effective system. In contrast, the production version (using the same 4GL) is written for efficiency, and to add robustness and the necessary operational components (error recovery, backup procedures, etc.).

Throwaway prototypes are useful in research and development situations and where the final system will be heavily used and response time or machine efficiency is important. Once the system features and capabilities have been sufficiently defined and accepted by the end user, the prototype has served its purpose and may be discarded. The actual production software is developed in accordance with traditional development methodologies. Prototyping is therefore used in place of the system-development phases of problem definition, feasibility assessment, alternative selection, and logical design.

Operational Prototypes These prototypes are written in a 4GL that will also be the production language for the completed system. The system evolves through several versions from very simplified to very sophisticated. During each evolutionary cycle a working version of the system is in operation. As the system evolves it takes on more and more of the characteristics of the final system. The process ends when the user is satisfied that the system meets defined needs or decides that the system is not converging to an acceptable solution. In the later case the system is aborted, usually at less cost than that of its traditionally developed counterpart.

Operational prototypes are working versions of part of the final system that will eventually evolve into the full system. These prototypes are appropriate to develop when it is important to get something to the end user quickly. Two operational-prototyping scenarios are typical: (1) when the user is the CEO, a senior manager, or someone whose continued interest in the project is critical to the development effort, and (2) when the problem is ill-defined or involves new users, or there is little familiarity with the problem area. In this second case the prototype serves as the learning environment for both the user and the system builder.

The Advantages of Prototyping Prototyping has many advantages over more conventional, linear systems development methodologies. It allows a system to be up and running quickly, usually within days. Because many of the needed systems have strategic value, it is important to get something up fast; the "strategic window" may be very narrow. Prototyping is usually less costly than linear alternatives. If, early in the revision cycle, it is discovered that the system will not be able to meet end-user needs, it can be abandoned with little cost. Linear methods require problem definition and feasibility study followed by cost/benefit analysis and, finally, a decision as to whether or not to develop the system. The time and cost involved in these activities may be extensive, and there may still be nothing to show for the effort in the way of system output.

For needs that cannot be accurately defined or involve areas unfamiliar to both the end user and the system builder, prototyping is an excellent learning device for both parties. It helps them better understand one other, the problem, and its solution. Unlike the traditional systems development life cycle, prototyping must have meaningful end-user involvement; this is a design feature. Traditional methods have always been a problem for the IS department in that meaningful user involvement is difficult to achieve even if consciously planned for.

It is clear that prototyping fits the need for strategic systems development very nicely. Many strategic systems cannot be accurately defined by the end user and are approached more as R&D than as development projects. They involve considerable speculation, risk, and "fuzziness." By not incurring large expenses and by getting a system up and running quickly, prototyping helps reduce the risk factor.

The Disadvantages of Prototyping For the systems and programming manager, the major disadvantage of prototyping is the lack of defined deliverables and a completion deadline. Senior management is likely to have similar concerns, as most of the control mechanisms that managers are used to are missing. The general feeling among senior managers is that the process is still ill-defined and subjective. With so many projects vying for top priority, many managers feel that it is difficult to justify open-ended allocations of system-builder time.

When is Prototyping Appropriate? Making a choice between the traditional systems development life cycle and prototyping is relatively straightforward. Many of the systems currently needing development are intended to aid middle- and senior-level managerial decision-making. For the most part this involves semistructured or unstructured situations. Often the end user cannot provide a detailed definition of system requirements, and the usual systems development methodologies may fail. Prototyping is used successfully in these cases.

A. Milton Jenkins (1983) identifies the following as appropriate situations in which prototyping should be used:

- When traditional life-cycle methods are not responsive enough to time constraints
- When the project can be decomposed into manageable subprojects
- When the user cannot clearly define the system requirements
- When user satisfaction (and timely results) are important
- When the user or builder wants to try out a new idea
- When the application is a decision support system (DSS)
- When the application will be low usage

Jenkins (1983) also identifies situations in which the use of prototyping is inappropriate:

- When the IS staff is not fully familiar with prototyping tools
- When data resources are not readily available
- When software resources are not readily available
- When IS management is not willing to provide the needed staff resources and support
- When the user and/or builder will not commit the necessary development time

The Prototyping Methodology

The early work of Peter Keen (1980) gives a conceptual model for a prototyping development methodology that Keen defines as "middle out" (see Exhibit 16-2). The end user describes only a small part or single feature of what the final system will have to generate. From this information, the system builder (usually a programmer/analyst) quickly creates an initial version of the system. The end user works with this first version long enough to be able to describe enhancements and/or revisions. These are passed on to the system builder, who generates version two, three, four, and so on. While the end user is passing through these stages, the system builder is learning more about the user's problem and is thus better able to work with the user to finalize the product. The revision process may continue indefinitely, or the project may be terminated at any stage on the basis of the user's conclusion that the prototype is not converging to the required system.

At some point the user may be satisfied that the system is acceptable for production status. One of two things can happen at this point: either the prototype becomes the operational version of the system or the prototype is discarded and a system is rewritten using a third-generation language. Exhibit 16-3, adapted from Jenkins (1983), is a schematic of this prototyping development method.

In many cases the end user is also the systems builder. In other cases the system builder may be an end-user programmer or one of the functional support personnel. In both cases the IS department is not directly involved in the development effort; standards and controls will therefore be needed.

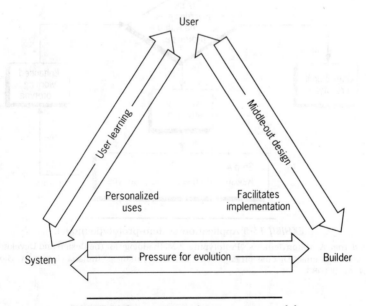

EXHIBIT 16-2 A conceptual prototyping model.

Source: Peter Keen, "Decision Support Systems: A Research Perspective," Center for Information Systems Research, Massachusetts Institute of Technology, Cambridge, MA, March, 1980, CISR 54, p. 12.

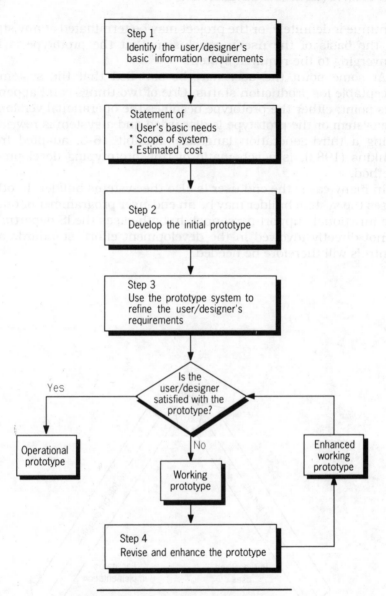

EXHIBIT 16-3 Application system prototype model.

Adapted from: A. Milton Jenkins, "Prototyping: A Methodology for the Design and Development of Application Systems," Discussion Paper 227, School of Business, Indiana University, Bloomington, IN, April 1983.

HARD AND SOFT CONTROLS

Whatever development process the end user might use, a well-defined set of controls and standards is necessary. These are developed under the direction of the IS department with the full cooperation of user management. As we have seen with respect to policy and procedure, by having user management participate in the definition process, the IS department can be sure that the controls and standards developed will be acceptable, workable, and enforceable.

Controls and standards are obviously needed to protect the interests of the organization as a whole. At the same time, it is important not to stifle the interest, enthusiasm, and creative processes of the end user. Furthermore, because there are several classes of users to consider, it is very likely that one set of standards and controls will not be appropriate for all. Add to this the possibility that the application type may determine the type of controls and standards needed, and the problem becomes quite complex.

Hard Controls

Richard Ball (1987) describes a model for developing a set of controls and standards. His model is based on the premise that appropriate controls and standards are a function of system complexity and risk. Ball classifies application traits as data attributes, application attributes, and project attributes. Data attributes include volume considerations, scope (individual, departmental, or corporate), retention requirements, and use (normal business functions or critical decisions). Application attributes include the technology used by the application, be it a single-user or multi-user system, and whether its use is scheduled or as needed. Project attributes are basically sizing characteristics, such as time to develop.

The second dimension Ball considers is risk. He defines three risk categories: A (low-risk, small applications for personal use), B (medium-risk, departmental or corporate level computing), and C (high-risk, large-end-user development efforts that have strategic impact). Attributes and risk categories can be arrayed in a matrix, as shown in Exhibit 16-4.

An application is placed in the risk category corresponding to its highest ranking on any of the attributes. The standards vary dramatically from class A to class C applications; this takes into account the fact that users developing class A applications are likely to be relatively unsophisticated as compared to users developing

	Class A	Class B	Class C
Data attributes	"Personal" Nonstrategic Low volume Independent	Departmental High volume Used by other programs	Strategic or sensitive Used to update Used to update corporate data base
Application attributes	"Personal" Stand-alone Low complexity	"Corporate" Used by more than one person	Complex "Yellow" or "red" technology Updates corporate data base
Project attributes	One to five workdays No formal project management warranted	Six to 20 workdays Some project approval, project management warranted	Twenty-one to 40 workdays Formal project approval, project management More than 40 workdays-- use system development standards

	General standards	Class A standards plus	Class B standards plus
Associated standards	Use passwords Back-up data Use common sense Label	Controls analysis recommended Must document Must register with end-user computing applications library Label	Controls analysis required Feasibility and cost-benefit analysis Data base administrator's approval to update corporate data base Label
Examples	Electronic mail Word processing Data-base query Simple spreadsheet	Spreadsheet used on a scheduled basis Data-base reporting program used by more than one person	Micro DBMS application Complex spreadsheet Simple spreadsheet, used for critical decision support

EXHIBIT 16-4 The application matrix.

Source: Copyright by CW Publishing Inc., Framingham, MA 01701—Reprinted from *Computerworld.*

class C applications. The needs of each user type will be very different. For example, a user developing a class C application may not be acquainted with the various control, cost, and feasibility analyses that are required. Obviously, the IS department has a responsibility to see that this end user has the tools needed to implement such a set of standards. It is also responsible for seeing that these standards are widely accepted and enforced. For this to happen, end users and their managers will have to cooperate in the development of the standards.

Compliance with these standards will come about only because they have broad support. Ball (1987) gives some suggestions for ensuring that compliance. He urges that user supervisors, user coordinators, or the information center be made responsible for ensuring compliance. He also suggests that EDP internal auditors be made aware of these standards and assist in checking for compliance.

Soft Controls

Hard controls are necessary in the areas of hardware, software, and communications. Soft controls, in contrast, create the necessary bonding between the IS department and the end-user department. J. Daniel Cougar (1987) lists a number of these soft controls, which are discussed in the following sections.

Maintenance The IS department can encourage users to pick from among a specified number of hardware and software alternatives by offering to maintain only those devices on an approved list. In extreme cases perhaps only one family of devices or one vendor's equipment is listed. Of course, the department needs to take into account varying user needs in determining this list. Being too conservative will constrain users and encourage noncompliance; being too liberal will place an undue burden on the IS department with regard to hardware and software maintenance.

Centralized Purchasing By centralizing the purchasing function, the IS department can negotiate quantity discounts that can be passed on to the user. There may also be some leverages that accrue to the purchaser simply because of the larger orders placed. Being a volume customer can only help in dealing with current or potential vendors. Lower prices will certainly be an inducement to user managers on a tight budget or with large quantities to purchase.

Training By providing training on a selected collection of software products, the IS department can encourage users to work within that set. This will also create user groups for each of the major software products. Users will still have a need for specialized software not widely used in the organization, but with good planning a major part of the organization's software needs can be met by a relatively small collection of products. Users, especially those not overly sophisticated, will find comfort in knowing that specialized help is available if they need it.

Shared Data To develop strategic systems, the user will eventually need to access and share data from different functional areas of the organization. The IS department can anticipate this need and step forward with appropriate file-sharing software. If the IS department is successful in creating a "seamless environment," users will be encouraged to develop systems that will be compatible across user departments.

Centralized Software Control The IS department should maintain the current release of all supported software and keep users up to date with the latest versions. This preserves software compatibility and consistency across user areas and also makes it easier to maintain the software.

Systems Development Training Most users have no background in application development methods. Feasibility studies, logical design, data-base design, data dictionaries, and so forth are new concepts to most users. They are going to develop their own applications regardless of what the IS department does to help or hinder them. The IS department can help the user acquire good systems development habits by providing extensive training in application development. This gives the department an opportunity to instill corporate policies and procedures regarding applications development, which in turn will leave users better equipped to manage their own future development projects. The IS department also benefits in those cases where maintenance of the system may come under departmental jurisdiction at some later point.

Communications The IS department should do whatever it can to create a reliable communications system among users. Electronic mail services should be provided to PC users just as they are provided to mainframe users. Product-specific user groups can also be effective in encouraging compliance with supported software packages. The user's peer group is very influential for user decision-making; the new user may well decide to follow peer group advice and go with a supported package if it offers an apparent value or benefit.

Soft controls are clearly initiatives taken by the IS department to convince users that conformance to policy and procedures is in their best interest. If these controls are properly used, the user will feel drawn, not forced, to conform.

CERTIFYING USER-DEVELOPED SYSTEMS

The IS department will want to certify that a user-developed system meets standard for several reasons:

- To ensure compatibility with existing and planned applications portfolios
- To see that the system conforms to corporate data architecture
- To see that the system can be integrated with existing systems for strategic benefit
- To ensure that appropriate system and user documentation exists
- To see that the system can be maintained by the IS department, if necessary.

Although the systems development process is well defined for third-generation-based systems, the same cannot be said for fourth-generation-based systems. End-user software has reached a level of sophistication such that the user has little more to do than define a collection of data tables, load data, invoke a report generator, and produce a variety of summary reports. All of this may be done through a menu-driven system so that the user never considers alternative solutions, data definition, data modeling, choice of software, system flows, and so on. Because the user's main objective is to get a system up and running quickly, many traditional systems development practices appear to run counter to this objective and are bypassed by users who either do not know about them or chose to ignore them. This situation may be dealt with in part by educating users about the systems development life cycle. User management will help ensure compliance to standards. As a final check, the IS department must verify that the system does meet established standards and can be put in the corporate portfolio.

There are three levels of certification to consider. The first involves areas that have been defined as personal computing; they are mentioned here for the sake of completeness, but in fact there is no need for standards at this level. Even if standards were contemplated, there would be no way to enforce them or to certify compliance. The second level concerns user-developed systems that are for the benefit of a single department; these may be required to meet only those standards specified by the manager of that department, who is responsible for the proper use of resources and the accomplishment of departmental goals and objectives. The third level of certification concerns those systems which have use outside the department developing them. Information reported from the data and system developed in one department and used by another must be correct. Departments benefitting from other users' systems may not have the luxury of verifying the integrity and correctness of data that produced the information on which they will make decisions and take action. It is therefore essential that such systems be certified by the IS department.

As Robert Peterson (1987) notes, the certification of a system involves both the product of the system and the process that was used to create the system. Product certification involves verifying that the data are correctly defined and retrieved, calculations are correct and consistent with corporate practices, and information is correctly reported from these calculations. Process certification compares development procedures used against established development procedures and notes any variances. Once a system has been certified, it is cataloged into corporate libraries and follows the same life cycle as would any other IS-developed system. The accepted maintenance procedures that apply to IS-developed systems also apply to certified end-user-developed systems. EDP auditors will apply the same scrutiny as well.

Peterson notes a few exceptions. If the certified system is seldom used, certification is no longer necessary. Responsibility for making and communicating changes lies with the user department, which should approve and manage all changes. In these cases the role of the IS department is basically custodial.

Peterson also lists four requirements for a successful certification program. There must be a well-defined set of policies, procedures, and standards that users have agreed to follow. A portfolio of certified systems must be published, and it should contain information to help the user decide whether an existing system can be used in place of the one contemplated. The incentive for users to seek certification must be clearly known. Finally, user managers must actively support the program, not only by promoting it but also by acting as "gatekeepers" in their departments. The user manager is the link between the IS department and the end user with respect to ensuring compliance with standards.

CONCLUSION

The emergence of EUC, and more importantly, the rapid growth in user-developed systems, has brought a number of tough issues to the desk of the IS manager. Although it is generally agreed that end users should be encouraged and supported in their efforts at application development, ways of doing so are not immediately apparent. Clearly, a set of standards must be established that are rigid enough to afford reasonable safeguards yet not so rigid as to encourage noncompliance.

Various methods have been proposed for the development and enforcement of standards. For them to be successful, the user manager must be a full partner in their development and senior management must commit the necessary resources and managerial support. On a broader scale, the user must be accepted as a partner with the IS department so that the full strategic benefit of information technology can be realized. The user–IS partnership is therefore an essential part of any corporate IS strategy.

DISCUSSION QUESTIONS

1. How would you implement controls and standards for an end-user applications development procedure?

2. How might you integrate EUC into the IS strategic planning process?

3. Discuss the new role of user management in EUC. What are the major issues? As IS manager, how might you help a user manager prepare for his or her new role?

4. Modify the linear systems development process so it is appropriate for user-developed systems. Consider only cases in which 4GLs are used. Include appropriate controls and check points. Discuss your proposal, identifying its strengths and weaknesses.

REFERENCES

———(1987). "Rockart Exhorts Line to Lead," Computerworld (July 27), pp. 59ff.

Ball, Richard (1987). "Harnessing End-User Computing Without Hindering It," Computerworld (October 26), pp. 91-100.

Cougar, J. Daniel (1987). "End-user Computing: Investing for High Returns," Computerworld (May 25), pp. 67-72.

Jenkins, A. Milton (1983). "Prototyping: A Methodology for the Design and Development of Application Systems," Discussion Paper 227, School of Business, Indiana University, Bloomington.

Keen, Peter (1980). "Decision Support Systems: A Research Perspective," Center for Information Systems Research, Massachusetts Institute of Technology, Cambridge. CISR 54, Sloan WP 1117-80.

Peterson, Robert (1987). "Giving End-Users the MIS Seal of Good System Building," Computerworld (June 1), pp. 83-87.

Sewell, Allan (1987). "Departmental Computing: Distributing the Power," Datamation (October 15), pp. 83ff.

seventeen

☐

Organizing Information Systems to Support End–User Computing

393

In deciding how to organize support services to be provided to systems users, the IS manager must strike a balance between control of end-user activity and respect for end-users' freedom to pursue independent computing interests. The trend in end-user computing is toward decentralization into departmental computing units and work-group computing units, along with the emergence of what have come to be called "power users"—those who have become corporate experts on a particular package as a result of their interest in and experience with it. Such users become known to other users who then seek them out for answers to questions on package utilization. The IS department often depends on power users to serve as an extension of the information center and as advisors on various computing questions related to their areas of expertise. In some cases, power users may actually become "technology gatekeepers" for the organization, advising the IS department on specific technological issues.

We begin this chapter by looking closely at the control/autonomy issue. Three distinctive approaches can be identified: one that is laissez-faire, one that is monopolistic, and a third based on the information center.

We then turn to a discussion of organizational structures to support EUC. This leads to a more focused look at the information center—its goals and the scope of its services and some key management issues relating to the information center.

Our attention shifts again, to the issues of departmental and work-group computing. We end by looking at ways to organize for work-group computing.

END-USER COMPUTING: CONTROL VERSUS AUTONOMY

To be effective in supporting EUC, the organizational structure must take into account two opposing objectives. The control objective is to develop appropriate policies and procedures to ensure that users' systems development activities are consistent and compatible with the corporate IS function. Procedures have been defined previously for the number and types of microcomputers, training requirements, the type of support services offered, communications standards, software standards, hardware/software acquisition policy, data security, and related issues.

Meeting the control objective also entails developing a staff to help the end user consider feasible options and alternatives. The role is not new. Henry Lucas (1986) has suggested that the end user assume the role of project manager even for those development projects where the systems and programming staff does the analysis, design, and programming. When first proposed, Lucas's idea was met with skepticism and mistrust: it was a process that could easily be abused, so that the end user would be merely a figurehead and not really a principal player on the development team. However, Lucas's notion has turned out to be a very good strategy. (See Chapter 13 for more discussion on project management options.)

The second objective relates to end-user autonomy. The organizational structure must allow the end user to have control over the entire systems development process, including the creative part of the process—for it is here that the user first has an opportunity to buy into the system. Empirical studies of factors that lead to implementation success identify user ownership as an essential ingredient. Getting users involved early and keeping them in control is the best way to generate that sense of ownership. Along with that sense of ownership comes a vested interest in the success of the project.

Thomas Gerrity and John Rockart (1986) propose a management structure called the "managed free economy" that strikes a balance between these two objectives. Their controls are designed not to create barriers to end-user development activities but rather to provide a structure for those activities. By adhering to guidelines, users will receive maximum support when they need it, will be able to tie into the corporate data and systems portfolio, and will be able to take advantage of any expertise that may have been developed in other user departments or within the IS staff itself.

As EUC first emerged on the corporate scene, IS managers tended to ignore these new users, reasoning that their interest was faddish and would be short lived. It was relatively easy for the IS department to isolate these users and not worry about them. Even if they did not go away, they would not be able to make a serious contribution to the computing activities of the organization. Many IS managers also thought that the new users would soon become frustrated with trying to use the new tools and would go back to their old ways. Remember, the end user had almost no experience in systems development and few had any expertise in programming. However, vendors came to the rescue with training, "user-friendly" software, and enhanced capability and functionality in microcomputer hardware. Yet even when users seemed to be enjoying some success, many IS managers still resisted and ignored them. That, as it turns out, was a big mistake. This hands-off attitude was definitely the wrong one to assume.

Other IS managers adopted a totally different defensive strategy. Their objective was tight control. They instituted policies and procedures that all but made it impossible for the end user to do anything. Exhibit 17-1 is an example of an actual request form that one microcomputer support group required all users to complete before any development support would be allocated. It must have been developed with the thought that if this form did not stop users from requesting help, nothing would!

These control-focused IS managers may have eliminated the risk associated with EUC, but they threw the proverbial baby out with the bathwater in the process. A more middle-of-the-road approach was taken by those IS managers who tried to encourage end users to conform to hardware and software standards and policy. The message was this: If you (users) buy this hardware/software, we (IS staff) will support you. The support offered by the IS department was strictly reactive, however. Its basis was risk avoidance, not user support.

What is needed is a management approach that combines enough control features to reduce risk to the organization and enough autonomy to keep users excited about "doing their own thing." Too much control will stifle users' creative energies and initiative; too much autonomy will risk the possibility that users will head off in directions not consistent with the rest of the organization.

For senior managers the challenge is a bit different. They must avoid the pitfalls of technology-focused approaches and develop a business-driven strategy for managing EUC. Despite the importance of EUC, such a strategy has not yet been developed in most companies (Gerrity and Rockart, 1986). Three approaches commonly used to support EUC are described in the following sections.

The Laissez-Faire Approach

The earliest reaction of IS management to overtures from fledgling computer users was, as we have seen, to ignore them. The strategy was simple: Leave these users alone, do not offer much help, pay them lip service, and eventually they will give up out of frustration and failure. The microcomputer will be a passing fad that will soon disappear from corporate America, and things will return to their pre-micro days.

That, as we all know, did not happen. In fact, to let end users do whatever they choose was and is to court disaster. First of all, there are so many alternatives for both hardware and software that specialists are needed to determine what is best in a given situation.

DATE: _____

DEPT: _____   DIVISION: _____

USER CONTACT

(For proposed system) _____   EXTENSION: _____

Weekly time commitment (in hours) to the development of the proposed system: _____ hrs./week.

R:Base System V training dates:

_____   _____   _____   _____

Session I   Session II   Session I   Session II

_____   _____   _____

Introduction to R:Base   Advanced R:Base

Required completion date for proposed system: _____

Description of current system: _____

_____

Current System Deficiencies: _____

_____

Objectives of Proposed System: _____

_____

Benefits Expected from the Proposed System: _____

_____

Consequences if Proposed System is not Developed: _____

_____

(Please attach additional sheet if necessary)

SIGNATURES:

User Contact: _____

Departmental Manager   _____

Departmental Director   _____

Please include a statement as to the relative importance of this application to the division: _____

_____

_____

Project Accepted: _____ Denied: _____

Consultant assigned to project: _____

EXHIBIT 17-1 A sample user request form for microcomputer support.

Furthermore, if users go off in diverse directions, the chances of achieving compatibility in hardware and/or software are nil. Without coordination at the top, the organization is bound to miss opportunities to integrate user applications into effective information systems for the benefit of everyone. In the final analysis, strategic opportunities will surely be forgone.

The Monopolistic Approach

This approach advocates strong control over the user. The strategy here is also simple: If the IS department keeps a very tight reign on what the user can and cannot do, then there will be no surprises, and the user will be confined to a relatively limited set of computing activities. Life for the IS department will remain relatively unaffected by users because their computing activity will be too low-level to affect the rest of the organization's computing activity.

This strategy has tended to fail for several reasons. Strong control requires that a staff be available to enforce it; and most organizations adopting this approach have not had such staffs. As the cost of computing has dropped, the need to maximize hardware efficiency has become irrelevant—hence strong controls on hardware acquisition have become unnecessary. The use of 4GLs and other application packages have reduced dramatically the need for detailed documentation and for controls on that aspect of the system. Moreover, users have become so much more sophisticated that they now feel quite competent; they are much less likely to bow to strong controls initiated by the IS department and are even less likely to submit their system needs to an overly long backlog for systems and programming development. On its own, the IS department has little real leverage using the monopolistic approach; this strategy must ultimately fail. If senior management endorses it, the user will withdraw and do nothing—and so the organization loses. If senior management does not endorse it, the IS department would be foolish to press the issue, as it would have little leverage in a confrontation where the user could invoke the support of senior management. The IS department needs to develop a set of controls and policies that are compatible with the organizational philosophy, that everyone can live with, and that everyone agrees to live with.

The Information Center Approach

The information center approach is perhaps the most popular, in that it offers both support and control. But it, too, has shortcomings that are not immediately obvious. By its very nature it is a centralized structure, yet we have seen that decentralized structures are the trend of the future because they can better serve end-users needs. The staff in most information centers has very sound product knowledge and training skills but lacks either functional experience or sufficient function-specific knowledge. Even though the mission of information centers is not to do applications development, they suffer from not being able to utilize meaningful examples from users' functional areas as enticements for their training sessions. Finally, the information center is organized as a reactive entity and as such does not offer strategic initiatives to the user.

THE "MANAGED FREE ECONOMY" APPROACH

The objective of the organization that supports EUC is to strike a balance between the extremes of monopolistic and laissez-faire approaches. Gerrity and Rockart (1986) provide perhaps one of the best suggestions to date of how this may be accomplished. They suggest a model that they call the managed free economy. It has five components designed to strengthen the end-user community.

Articulating an End-User Strategy

It is important that users understand the computing environment in which they have to work. Part of that environment consists of the hardware and software support that they receive from the IS department. By having the IS department specify the computing strategy, the user is better able to design systems consistent with that strategy. Another important part of the environment is the organization's strategic technological direction; again, helping users understand this direction better equips them to plan for the future.

Defining the User/Information Systems Working Relationship

A working partnership arises when both the IS department and the end user try to develop a set of policies and procedures that define the computing environment. This represents a radical departure from the days when the IS department told users what the rules of the game were going to be—an approach destined for failure. It has become clear, from experiences in involving users in the systems development process, that a sense of ownership is critical to implementation success. The same is true, as we have seen, with regard to giving the user an equal role and responsibility in policy and procedure specification.

Developing Critical End-User Systems and Applications

The responsibility for bringing new technologies to end-user applications and systems belongs to the IS department. In this new partnership, IS technical experts disseminate information on new and emerging technologies that have relevance to the critical needs of the end user. (These critical needs are defined as part of the exercise of identifying corporate and departmental critical success factors.) Dissemination of information takes place as part of the environmental analysis step in the strategic planning process; the "white papers" that are part of the initial corporate and departmental planning process can provide that information.

Armed with technology updates, user management must seek out opportunities for individual or departmental efficiency, effectiveness, or innovation that may lead to competitive advantage. Although this multifaceted process identifies only certain application projects, at least it provides some input for the strategic plan.

Integrating the Support Organization

It is essential that a separate organizational entity, devoted exclusively to end-user support, be established. The users must be absolutely convinced that they are not second-class citizens in the eyes of the IS department, and anything short of a separate support function would risk causing that perception. The traditional information center is not sufficient; the solution must go beyond that, focusing rather on the type of support given.

Emphasizing Education

The support personnel must, of course, be technically competent. More importantly, however, they must understand that they are dealing with novices who may be somewhat awed by computing and may bring certain anxieties to the workstation. To be most effective in the long run, the IS department has to educate the end user. Some of this education can be provided through in-house training workshops, but the most effective (and, unfortunately, most costly) learning takes place as a specific application need (brought by the end user to the IS department's doorstep) is addressed.

An impatient user-support professional may become frustrated with the user's slow progress up the learning curve but must not give in to the urge to simply hand the solution to the user. Keeping users in the tutoring mode is important. The benefits of education reveal themselves as users gradually undertake the struggle to solve problems on their own.

Education involves reaching out beyond immediate needs for systems development. The IS department should continually offer executive training and briefing sessions as well as regularly offering both training and briefing sessions to middle-level and line managers. As they learn more about technological trends and capabilities, these managers will be in a better position to formulate the strategy set and take advantage of strategic opportunities.

AN ORGANIZATIONAL STRUCTURE FOR SUPPORTING END-USER COMPUTING

Hugh Watson and Houston Carr (1987) suggest a three-tiered organizational structure for supporting EUC (see Exhibit 17-2). It seems to work well with the ideas put forth by Gerrity and Rockart. Watson and Carr's structure has three units or groups: the corporate model unit, the decision support systems (DSS) unit, and the information center.

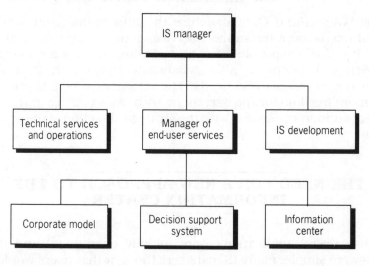

EXHIBIT 17-2 An organizational structure for supporting EUC.

Source: Reprinted by permission. Adapted from Hugh J. Watson and Houston H. Carr, "Organizing for Decision Support Systems: The End-User Services Alternative," *Journal of Management Information Systems*, vol. 4, no. 1, Summer 1987, p. 91.

The Corporate Model Unit

The corporate model unit enhances the corporate plan through a planning exercise specifically designed to support EUC. This exercise includes a definition of needs by the end user and an examination of existing data and systems by the manager of the corporate model unit. Solutions to specific user problems are then identified, and additional opportunities that the new application may create for others are also noted. The process also includes planning for the integration of the end-user's application into the corporate systems portfolio.

The Decision Support Systems Unit

The decision support systems (DSS) group works closely with the user in the development of systems that utilize appropriate corporate computing and information resources. Just as the corporate model unit is the planning function for EUC, so the DSS group is its implementation function. With this unit Watson and Carr recommend development support rather than training in the use of development tools; the unit thus represents an extension of traditional end-user support services.

The Information Center

In the Watson and Carr structure the information center offers typical microcomputer support services (but not development advice). Its chief responsibilities are training in package use and answering questions. It also assists end users with their data acquisition problems and needs. The information center provides maximum freedom for the user along with expert advice and development support consistent with the strategic direction of the organization.

THE NEED FOR A NEW APPROACH TO THE INFORMATION CENTER

Because users' applications were initially operational and their needs were simple, many IS managers thought that users would be satisfied with a reactive type of support in training and with simple applications development advice. Therefore, the information center was viewed as relatively unimportant by many IS managers who for years had more serious problems to deal with, such as the growing applications backlog and general user dissatisfaction with the output from systems and programming. But the situation has shifted dramatically in the last few years, as we have seen. In looking for ways to use computers for strategic purposes, users have posed new problems centering on corporate sharing and integration of data, access to external data bases, and the building of significant DSS and expert systems for competitive advantage. The transition has been from one of personal computing for individual productivity to one of systems to serve the complex needs of departmental and work-group computing units. The centralized support services that marked the early history of the information center seem inadequate for present-day user-support needs.

Information center managers need to consider their mission not as one of helping users acquire a degree of computer literacy but rather of developing a support structure for EUC that will serve the strategic needs of the organization. Thus, the mission of an information center is to promote, support, control, and manage end-user computing (White and Christy, 1987). By so doing, the information center improves the effectiveness and efficiency of the end user and thereby contributes to the competitive position of the organization.

White and Christy suggest that the information center formally state its goals and objectives, define control policy and security procedures, and develop means of improving effectiveness and efficiency. Each of these areas is discussed next.

A Formal Statement of Goals and Objectives

Thomas Gerrity and John Rockart (1986) and John Rockart and L. Flannery (1983) argue that in its statement of goals and objectives, the information center should actively promote the growth of EUC and make known its benefits. The information center's commitment to these goals and objectives is measured by the provision of resources and services to the end user.

Formal Control Policy and Security Procedures

For the end user to be productive while conforming to reasonable standards and practices, the information center needs to specify the rules of the game. E. B. Opliger (1985), J. C. Reimel (1985), and M. A. Snow (1985) stress the importance of review and approval processes for users requesting computing resources and proposing applications that involve the use of sensitive data. For new system requests, standards and procedures for data access and handling as well as documentation should also be established. Many users have little understanding of the concepts and procedures associated with systems design, development, control, and audit procedures. A program to educate them about proper applications development would be highly beneficial.

Methods to Improve Effectiveness and Efficiency

Tor Guimaraes and Vasudevan Ramanujam (1986) and Merle Martin (1986) enumerate activities that the information center can sponsor to help users of computing resources become more effective and efficient. Basic training as well as advanced seminars and workshops in the end-user tools supported by the information center are obvious suggestions. In addition to applications development tools, users must learn about systems design and development methodologies. Traditional systems development concepts as well as prototyping and other adaptive methods are helpful. Rather than formal seminars and workshops, the information center might teach development methodologies by working with users on actual projects and using these projects as vehicles for teaching development methods. The trap to avoid here, of course, is creating the system for the end user rather than using it as a teaching vehicle.

Apart from its teaching responsibilities, the information center can provide data access procedures that minimize the need for the users to understand the intricacies of the operating system and data architecture. Finally, establishing good communications with the end-user community so as to keep abreast of its needs and problems is an important way to help users solve their problems.

THE SCOPE OF THE INFORMATION CENTER'S SERVICES

In general, in defining the scope of services to be provided, the information center manager should keep in mind the fact that the information center's mission does not include developing applications for the end user. Doing so simply moves the applications backlog from the systems and programming group to the information center. The sooner users can do their own development work, the easier it will be for the information center in the long run. What users learn from one application can be transferred to the next.

The following is a list of typical services offered by an information center:

- Training
- Consulting
- Technical and operations support
- Hotline
- Management of data
- Microcomputer software evaluation
- Debugging assistance
- Newsletter
- Information clearinghouse
- Documentation support for user applications

Training Services

The most obvious training needs of end users will be in the use of application packages. The information center typically offers training several times a year in a variety of supported packages. As the user community becomes more computer literate, its training needs shift toward problem analysis, data usage, application validation, and operations.

With *problem analysis* the information center consultant, with the help of the user, identifies the problem as well as the appropriate software to be used; without guidance from the information center in this type of analysis, users tend to try adapting the one package they know to every problem. *Data usage training* includes identifying and describing existing data and instructing users in how to access the data. Because many users are content to accept the systems as correct once it has generated a report in the desired format, *validation training* introduces the idea of systems testing before the user-developed system is placed in production status. Finally, *operations training* includes systems integration, backup/recovery, and error detection. These four types of training help the user do a better job and better meet the information needs of their functional area and the entire organization.

Consulting, Technical, and Operations Support Services

In the *consulting* category are a variety of services. At various stages of a user-developed project, the user needs short-term advice and help. This may range from a simple question regarding the choice of alternative designs to an entire design review, a critique of the approach taken, or a host of other issues.

In addition, users continually have a need for *technical and operations support*. They show the information center staff new products that they read about in trade publications and ask about these products' suitability for particular applications. In many cases users are already convinced that a new product is the right technology for them, and they need to be educated about its actual features or compatibility with existing technology. Some users need help with operations-related problem—perhaps a data access problem.

The *hotline* service is a common feature of many information centers. It has proven to be a very effective means of answering end-user "quickies"—questions about use of a command or interpretation of an error message, or "How do you ..." questions. Usually such queries are specific to a particular product and can be answered over the telephone. Electronic mail may also be used to both transmit questions and receive answers. In this way the power users may be pressed into service without committing to a fixed schedule.

Good *data management techniques* are strangers to most users. Although it is the responsibility of the information center to bring the user up to speed in his or her understanding of backups, security, and data modeling, often the end user will need some straightforward guidance in these areas. The basic concepts of data management can be taught to users. It is up to user management, however, to ensure that these practices are in fact in place. For this, periodic audits will often suffice.

A growing responsibility of the information center is *microcomputer software evaluation*. Knowing the needs of the end user, the information center evaluates application packages and advises the end user accordingly. Normally, the information center picks more than one package for a given category of application and supports the user through seminars and workshops in each one.

Until such time as users are experienced in applications development, they will have a need for *debugging assistance*. Finding and fixing logic problems is a service that every information center should offer. As users become more sophisticated, their questions tend to become fewer but more difficult. It is not unusual for several end users to actually become more knowledgeable about a particular package than the information center staff simply because they have used it far more often. Their expertise should be made available to other users through the information center and perhaps through locally run user groups for each of the major application packages in the organization. These groups tend to be very successful, as all the users are from the same organization, or even department, and have a shared understanding of the business as well as of problem-resolution techniques.

It is not uncommon to have a corporate *newsletter* for information center users. The newsletter carries articles on special uses and tricks that others have found. Articles on specific uses of application packages can give other users new ideas as to how they might meet their system needs.

As new and enhanced software continues to appear on the market, the need arises for some evaluation regarding its fit with the organization and its needs. This *information clearinghouse* function of the information center will continue to grow in importance, as the information center is an ideal conduit for information on new products and services.

Finally, the user manager needs help in generating and verifying completion of appropriate *documentation*. All too often the end user who develops and runs a new system then departs from the organization, leaving no documentation trail showing how the system runs and how it was designed and programmed. IS professionals understand the value of good documentation and should instill that same understanding in all users. A good training program on the various levels, use, and importance of documentation is a wise investment in time and energy.

INFORMATION CENTER MANAGEMENT ISSUES

The trend toward decentralization of end-user support services is firmly established, but what remains unclear is its effect on the organizational structure of the information center. To what extent should decentralization take place? Is training to remain centralized? What about the alternative of using external sources for training and package support? Will the information center evolve into a form quite different from what it is now? These and other questions are much on the minds of IS managers.

The following sections touch on some important management concerns relating to the information center.

Justifying the Information Center

Joanne Kelleher (1986) believes that mature information centers are challenged "to avoid being left in the shallows of micro installation and training while the corporation moves ahead toward the deeper waters of strategic information management." Older information centers, she contends, face three challenges of their own. The first is what she calls "the organizational challenge: avoiding dissolution." Having dispelled computer illiteracy, information centers must find new objectives—ones with strategic implications.

The second challenge is economic: "proving effectiveness," in Kelleher's words. She maintains that mature information centers often must "carry their own weight." Managers who find charge-back systems risky may try to prove their Centers' worth "more subtly, by winning friends in high places," Kelleher writes.

The final political challenge is to fulfill promises. Having failed "to meet some of the goals they once set for themselves," such as eliminating applications backlogs, Kelleher argues that "managers are rethinking their strategies and turning increasingly toward tasks such as executive training in which they feel more comfortable of success."

Charge-Back Systems

Prompted by growing pressures from senior management, information centers are turning to charge-back systems—that is, charging their users for services rendered. This transfers the burden of justifying the Center's existence to the user manager, who often applies value-added criteria.

The chief benefit of a charge-back policy is that it forces users to be judicious in their requests for help. It is hoped that this in turn will bring about an improvement in the use of computing resources as well as in the productivity of both end-user and information center staff. However, the danger is that new users may not understand the relationship between cost and benefit and may pass up an opportunity to use the information center, thereby forgoing major productivity gains. New users are often reluctant to incur charges when the risk of failure is looming; moreover, when they have to pay for services, users want to control the nature of those services. Some users also want the opportunity to use their information center budgets to purchase services outside the information center.

DEPARTMENTAL AND WORK-GROUP COMPUTING

Work-group computing is the final stage in the evolution of the applications development process from its roots in the traditional development activities of the IS department, as shown in Exhibit 17–3. Historically, as we have seen, applications development has been the responsibility of the IS department. Although users should have played an important role in applications development, it was not until the emergence of the microcomputer in 1976 and Visicalc in 1978 that such participation actually became a possibility.

From End-User to Departmental Computing

In many functional business departments, the person who became the "computer guru" or power user eventually involved other departmental members in computing—largely by virtue of that individual's early successes and willingness to help others. However, with the increase of corporate appetites for more sophisticated systems, it became necessary for departments to plan the development of integrated systems in their functional area. Data-base-oriented systems became essential to the success of the department.

Departmental computing involves creating a physical (or even a logical) computing resource in the functional department. This facility can take a variety of forms. It may be a small processor with several terminals attached, a PC local-area network, a host-connected systems with data locally resident on the host, or a file-server on the PC network. In addition to hardware, it may consist of departmentally based data and operations staff as well as systems development staff.

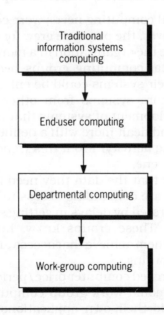

EXHIBIT 17-3 The evolution of work-group computing.

Many of the advantages of departmental computing are the same as those of decentralized computing; in fact, departmental computing is a form of decentralized computing, with the difference that the hardware is physically networked and the data are shared. In other words, the facility is functionally segregated but different from the distributed environment because there is a logical and/or physical relationship between users with a common functional responsibility. Functional department managers win by having both their information and information-processing capabilities accessible to their departments. They can determine their own priorities without regard for the needs of other user groups. They can do a better job of cost/benefit analysis and can be flexible in system changes.

For the IS manager, the prime advantage of this set up is that it allows the IS department to learn from users exactly what they need. Yet for the IS manager the situation can be a bit uncomfortable, because he or she is used to thinking of the IS department as a very structured entity. Departmental computing is more unstructured so that it can meet varying needs of the function that it supports. However, the progressive IS manager promotes such computing because he or she recognizes the potentially large benefits that can accrue to the organization.

From Departmental to Work-Group Computing

Initially, departmental computing needs were confined to one business unit; soon, however, the pressure grew for even more sophisticated systems to place the organization in a more favorable strategic position. Departmental computing groups began to see that the strategic benefit of their systems could be enhanced by integrating them with one or more systems from other departments. This necessitated the development of systems that transcended departmental boundaries and dealt more with a defined business activity, not a function-specific activity. From this trend, work-group computing came on the scene.

Work groups know that the data they need are in the corporate data bases, and they are demanding access to these data. Today's work groups are frustrated by delays in getting set up to "talk" to the corporate data base. These groups know, however, that the IS department can help them achieve that access and improve their use of departmental computing.

Trends toward improved computer price/performance and ease of use have clearly promoted work-group computing, and users are now encouraged to do their own applications development. This benefits the IS department, as we have seen; the situation is "win–win" with the groups needing each other. Yet although there are definite advantages to work-group computing, the IS manager must also be aware of certain disadvantages. The following appear to be among the more important ones:

- Resistance from the IS department can stifle the effort of the group and establish an adversarial relationship. (This is also true with departmental computing.)
- Work group members may have less expertise in systems design and implementation than IS department members and may therefore be less likely to develop systems that are easily maintained and modified.
- The work group may not adequately test the system; thus, there is a real potential for costly error and mistakes.
- The work group system is much more complex than a departmentally based system.
- Long-term system support and maintenance may be difficult to sustain.
- An agreement on standards is more difficult to establish, as functional and IS departments will have to give up some of their autonomy.
- There is typically no clear-cut leadership in development projects that span several departments.
- The system may not have an easily identified "home department;" this makes maintenance and application management more difficult to carry out effectively and in a timely manner.
- The process of changing a system tends to be more cumbersome and less responsive to the individual department's needs.

With work-group computing, the IS department must work hard to enforce standards, documentation, security, and controls. Because system development and processing activities occur beyond the normal purview of the IS department, it is more difficult for the department to know how things are being done and whether they are being done according to standards. The IS manager is therefore concerned with having a good set of clearly written, thoroughly explained standards, available to the user, and with ensuring that some attempt has been made to see that the user knows and enforces the standards. The IS manager might consider placing constraints on users who do not conform, although this approach would seem to be more punitive than constructive; another approach is to offer incentives in the form of support and training for user departments that do conform.

In addition, the IS manager is responsible more for the use of the information technology than for the technology itself. In a work group environment, it is difficult to hold the IS manager responsible for computing activity that he or she does not even know about and, indeed, has little opportunity to find out about unless the user reports it. With work-group computing there has been little transfer of IS managerial responsibility to user management, which creates problems for the IS department.

ORGANIZING FOR WORK-GROUP COMPUTING

Theresa Conlon (1987) reports that Prudential has tried to solve the technology transfer problem by creating the position of information systems executives and assigning about 30 of these executives to the business units. They are business (not systems) experts, and their job is to find ways of using the technology for applications consistent with Prudential's business direction and supportive of their own business efforts. The role of the IS department in such an environment is to maintain corporate data and systems while selling its support services to those units desiring aid, although these units remain free to do their own applications development. Most systems development is purchased from the IS department; business unit executives tend to focus on PC-based applications.

Such an environment fosters individual creativity and is a structure under which work-group computing can be successful. By definition, the work group is nearly self-sufficient and not unlike Peter Drucker's (1988) task-focused teams, briefly discussed in Chapter 7.

CONCLUSION

The ultimate objective of end-user computing is to take advantage of the strategic opportunities that such computing provides. To do this requires a form of comanagement, with both IS management and user management assuming responsibility and with IS functional units and the end-user support units acting as equal partners. Whatever organizational structure is chosen, it will have to take into account the emergence of decentralized support units in the form of departmental and work-group computing.

Even in the best of situations, numerous management questions remain. What support should remain centralized and what should be decentralized? Is a charge-back system the correct strategy in those cases where senior management wants some justification for support services? How can end-user computing be integrated into corporate-level strategic IS planning processes? The answers to these issues questions continue to be elusive.

DISCUSSION QUESTIONS

1. If the corporate philosophy regarding EUC is monopolistic, how would you as IS manager organize for effective end-user support? What if the corporate philosophy is laissez-faire?

2. What do you see as the mission and purpose of the information center in a computing environment dominated by departmental and work group computing and in which the strategic benefits of information technology are fully exploited?

3. Identify the transition problems that the IS professional staff might face as the IS department accepts the end user as an equal partner in corporate computing activity.

4. Describe the working and organizational relationship between the IS executive assigned to the business units and the CIO. Identify both the potential strengths and weaknesses of the relationship. To what extent should the CIO exert control over the IS executive?

REFERENCES

Conlon, Theresa (1987). "One User Swears by Centralized System; Another Opts For Change," *Management Information Systems Week* (June 1), pp. 23ff.

Drucker, Peter. (1988). "The Coming of the New Organization," *Harvard Business Review*, vol. 66, no. 1 (January-February), pp. 45–53.

Gerrity, T. P., and J. F. Rockart (1986). "End-User Computing: Are You a Leader or a Laggard?" *Sloan Management Review*, vol. 27, no. 4 (Summer), pp. 25–34.

Guimaraes, Tor, and Vasudevan Ramanujam (1986). "Personal Computing Trends and Problems: An Empirical Study," *MIS Quarterly* (June), pp. 179–185.

Kelleher, Joanne (1986). "Information Centers—Their Choice: Justify Existence or Go Out of Business," *Computerworld* (August 11), pp. 51ff.

Lucas, Henry C. (1986). *The Analysis, Design, and Implementation of Information Systems* 2nd ed., (New York: McGraw-Hill).

Martin, Merle P. (1986). "The Human Connection in Systems Design: Part I—The Elusive User," *Journal of Systems Management* (October), pp. 6–29.

Opliger, E. B. (1985). "Identifying Microcomputer Concerns," *The EDP Auditor Journal*, vol. 1, pp. 43–66.

Reimel, J. C. (1985). "The Value of Information and its Relationship to Microcomputers and Data Base," *The EDP Auditor Journal*, vol. 2, pp. 32–37.

Rockart, J. F., and L. S. Flannery (1983). "The Management of End-User Computing," *Communications of the ACM*, vol. 26, no. 10 (October), pp. 776–784.

Snow, M. A. (1985). "Taming the Microcomputer Revolution: The Need for Policy," *The EDP Auditor Journal*, vol. 2, pp. 1–4.

Watson, Hugh J., and Houston H. Carr (1987). "Organizing for Decision Support System Support: The End-User Services Alternative," *Journal of Management Information Systems*, vol. 4, no. 1, pp. 83–95.

White, Clinton E. Jr., and David P. Christy (1987). "The Information Center Concept: A Normative Model and A Study of Six Installations," *MIS Quarterly*, December, pp. 451–458.

eighteen

□

Information Systems as a User-Support Entity: Issues and Opportunities

The revolution that is taking place in information systems, especially as it relates to end-user computing, is threatening the very foundation of the IS department. Or is it? The old-guard IS manager is definitely threatened, but the contemporary IS manager is being

415

challenged. What is clear to both is that the end user is becoming a highly sophisticated "computerphile." Many end users are quite capable of linking information technology with the strategic direction of the organization and using it to create competitive advantages. It is clear that this technology is being used far more effectively now than in its early days. To operate efficiently and effectively in this new environment, the user needs a different type of support from the IS department. IS managers who cannot perceive this shifting need are destined to go the way of the dinosaurs; those who do perceive the shift are searching for appropriate responses and are destined to play a leading role in an exciting future.

We begin by looking at end-user computing in the short term: the role of the IS department in supporting user-developed systems and various means of restructuring the department for EUC. We then investigate some of the long-term implications of EUC, including the phenomenon of "spontaneous computing" and the emergence of the new executive user.

END-USER COMPUTING IN THE SHORT TERM

Supporting User-Developed Systems

There are several opportunities for the proactive IS manager in the story of end-user computing. The first relates to the development of a strategy to convert the IS department from a developer of application systems to a supporter of end-user applications development. Successful conversion requires a new partnership between the end user and the IS department. The challenge for the IS manager lies in becoming proactive in this partnership. A major challenge will be the specification of an end-user systems development life cycle—a life cycle not yet fully or consistently specified in many organizations. When such a methodology is in place, the challenge will be to provide serious training for the end user in the proper use of this new methodology.

Another opportunity facing the IS manager is really a challenge. Having established that both IS-developed and user-developed systems have important strategic value, the manager must answer two questions. The first is this: When should a system be developed by the IS department, as opposed to the end user? In cases where economies of scale exist, where the system will cross departmental or strategic business unit lines, where it will be subjected to stringent auditing requirements, or where corporate-level IS activity is involved, it is best to have the IS department develop the new system.

The second (and basically unanswered) question is this: How should computing resources be allocated between the IS department and users? Most strategic planning systems do not accommodate an applications development portfolio that includes both IS- and user-developed systems. The difficulty stems largely from the fact that many end-user applications resulted from a creative process not unlike that of many of the high-risk projects in a typical R&D portfolio. In fact, assigning projects to an R&D portfolio was one way of bypassing organizational constraints and might have been an early attempt at solving the support dilemma. Now, however, advocates of end-user applications urge that the organizational structure itself must be changed.

This position suggests the need for establishing a budget line to support new end-user ventures. The appropriate size of this budget relative to the total IS development budget has not been determined in most settings. An important management task, therefore, is that of assigning responsibility for this budget line.

Business Support Groups

Yet another opportunity for the IS manager concerns the business support group, a task force composed of functionally oriented business professionals who circulate throughout the organization looking for strategic opportunities. Such groups are created to unearth opportunities that functional business managers might not see. The business support group is funded much as an R&D group might be funded. Once its members identify areas of potential strategic benefit, they secure the necessary funding and support from the organization to experiment with their ideas and carry them to fruition.

Such groups are risky in the sense that not all their ideas will result in success. They do, however, help reduce the risk of missing valuable strategic opportunities. Funding such groups is tantamount to funding end-user ventures.

RESTRUCTURING THE INFORMATION SYSTEMS DEPARTMENT FOR END-USER COMPUTING

Some observers view the process of restructuring as a radical change occurring on several fronts. On the basis of client experience, Richard Nolan and his associates (1987) recommend a five-step cycle for restructuring the traditional hierarchical organization into one that supports new directions. They have defined downsizing, discovering growth, restructuring, rewarding performance, and validating the strategy as the five-step cycle. Each step is detailed in the sections that follow.

Downsizing

End-user computing has contributed to the narrowing of the base of the organizational triangle (see Exhibit 18-1). In effect, what has happened is that the need for support personnel has diminished with the spread of end-user computing throughout the organization. The increase in efficiency brought on by the microcomputer has reduced the need for clerical support positions. At the same time there has been a thinning of middle- management positions, largely as a result of more effective upward movement of information through the organization. According to Peter Drucker (1988), several layers of management exist only to clarify informational needs both up and down the organizational chain of command. Senior managers can have direct access to operational and control information; hence, the need for armies of middle-level managers is diminishing. This trend will continue as end-user computing becomes even more pervasive.

Discovering Growth

The establishment of a viable, innovative growth strategy is a major challenge for senior management. It will be facilitated through the assimilation of end-user computing into the systems portfolio. In this way information technology can provide further opportunities to affect efficiency, effectiveness, and product/service differentiation.

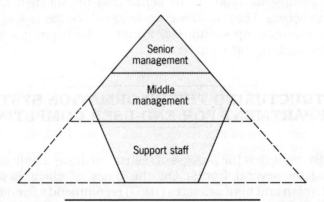

EXHIBIT 18-1 The organizational impact of end-user computing.

The business support group is one strategy for creating an organizational climate to exploit the new technology.

Restructuring

A hierarchical structure may have served the industrial-based economy, but it is not suitable for the information-based economy. A network structure, characterized by loosely coupled task forces, is more suitable. As Drucker explains it, task forces constitute a coalition of knowledge workers who collectively have all the expertise that they need to carry out their assigned responsibilities. By encouraging task forces, departmental computing, and work group computing, the IS department helps pave the way for the metamorphosis into the so-called information organization. The challenge given to IS is to anticipate task-force needs and design the appropriate hardware, software, data, and communications infrastructures. No small task!

Rewarding Performance

A hierarchical organization rewards performance through promotion, whereas the network structure must establish an alternative reward system. This transition will be difficult, as there is a long-standing tradition in most organizations of using promotion as the only visible sign of recognition. In the network structure, rewards will be salary increases and/or job rotation as a sign of successful task completion and as an opportunity to learn new skills and take on new challenges. [These ideas have been discussed on numerous occasions; Saul Gellerman (1973), for example, comments aptly on the reward structure in the context of developing future managers.]

For end users, the reward structure may include peer recognition and status as a power user. These users are increasingly invited to sit at the IS planning table as advisors, consultants, and even full partners in planning.

Validating the Strategy

Strategic planning must become a continuous exercise, must be business driven, and must be dynamic. What is accomplished should be measured against what has been planned, and against what the best companies in the same or different industries have done. Comparing the level of investment in computing across companies in the same industry and across different industries is a measure of corporate commitment to computing. Knowing what others are doing with new technology is important even if they are not mainstream competitors.

END-USER COMPUTING IN THE LONG TERM
Spontaneous Computing

The computer is on the way to becoming second nature to the knowledge worker, just as the telephone, calculator, and word processor are to the clerical worker. An environment of "spontaneous computing" is sure to become a reality for the present generation of knowledge workers. William Kimmerly (1987) defines spontaneous computing as an "environment so natural in its access and use that most end users will require little, if any, familiarity with the technical characteristics of computers in order to use the machines effectively." Spontaneous computing will require a change in emphasis for the IS department—away from traditional systems development and toward data management, integration of data management and the software development function, consulting support, and development of interfaces to integrate systems into the end-user environment. The IS department will continue to provide and support the information systems infrastructure (computer, data, and communications).

There are several opportunities for the IS department seeking to provide for spontaneous computing. The data-base environment will obviously be distributed, and standards for the design and development of these data bases will have long since been established. The challenge for the IS department will be to integrate these data bases into a network and thus provide for easy access and exchange among and between user groups. With the end user doing most of the applications development work, computer-aided software engineering (CASE) techniques will be needed. These tools are currently emerging within the IS department but have not yet reached the level of sophistication required for the end-user community. As these tools are developed, adaptive interfaces and expert systems will be used as help for the end user.

It is clear that the software development life cycle will have to be significantly upgraded in terms of efficiency and effectiveness if the end user is to be encouraged to develop systems. Needs also exist in the communications environment between the end user and distributed data and software. Seamless interfaces between systems, data bases, and software environments are necessary, and users must be shielded from the technical complexities of these environments.

Type III End Users

The executive is emerging as another type of end user, one whose needs are very different from those of the Type I and Type II end users defined by Ralph Sprague and Barbara McNurlin (1986). Exhibit 18-2 represents a revision of their original two categories into a new three-category scheme. The new Type II and Type III users are an outgrowth of the original Type II end user.

The Type III user is rather different from the other two, and his or her needs will be met in ways that are also very different. This user

Type I	Type II ,	Type III
Clerical workers	Professionals and middle managers	Senior managers
High volume of transactions	Moderate volume of transactions	Low volume of transactions
Frequent use	Little use	Very little use
Low value per transaction	Moderate value per transaction	High value per transaction
Routine and repetitive	Somewhat structured and repetitive	Unstructured and used once
Specific output	Control/analysis/report output	General directives, judgments, and initiative outputs
Efficiency focus	Effectiveness focus	Innovation and differentiation focus
Individual records	Summary of internal historical data	Highly aggregated and integrated internal and external data
Use of a single tool	Multiple tools with some integration	Large variety of highly integrated tools
Rote training	Somewhat structured and self-paced	Unstructured training with direct payoff

EXHIBIT 18-2 Future trends in end-user types.

typically spends very little time with the technology, uses a variety of simple but highly integrated tools, and views graphical displays of highly aggregated forecasted and historical data. This user's objective is to form general judgments and to develop strategic initiatives; therefore tools and data must be readily available and easy to use in very unstructured and nonrepetitive sessions. Clearly, this type of end user requires services, support, and systems that are totally different from any of those that the IS manager had to provide in the past. The tools that the IS department will need in order to accomplish this task are natural-language interfaces, expert systems, and artificial intelligence.

The strategy for designing systems for Type III users will involve examining corporate critical success factors to identify areas of interest chiefly to the executive. Using these CSFs, the IS department will be able to store highly aggregated extracts of the corporate data base and a variety of reporting options in a front-end processor to bring very sophisticated data modeling down to a few simple keystrokes. This major challenge has not yet been met.

CONCLUSION

The future of corporate computing is destined to lie in the hands of a strong, decentralized cadre of self-sufficient end users. The role of the IS department will continue to change to one of providing high-level support for policy, control, standards, and the maintenance of a sophisticated data-base and communications network. The end user's role, in contrast, will continue to change to one of developing strategic applications through departmental and work group entities that are self-sufficient and understand the critical link between technology and business strategy.

DISCUSSION QUESTIONS

1. At some point everyone will be an end user, hence no one will be an end user. Comment on this, addressing the implications for senior, IS, and end-user management in designing an appropriate organizational response to the disappearance of the end user. What would you expect the IS department to be like in this scenario?

2. What organizational changes might be needed (if any) to support Type III end users? Be specific.

3. Discuss the challenges to IS management as EUC migrates from departmental computing to work group computing. As an IS manager, how would you deal with these challenges?

4. What EUC management issues will arise in a spontaneous computing environment? How should IS management prepare for them?

REFERENCES

Drucker, Peter F. (1988). "The Coming of the New Organization," *Harvard Business Review*, vol. 66, no. 1 (January-February), pp. 45-53.

Gellerman, Saul (1973). "Developing Managers Without Management Development," *The Conference Board Record* (July), pp. 32-37.

Kimmerly, William (1987). "Toward Spontaneous Computing," *Computerworld* (October 12), pp. 111-115.

Nolan, Richard L. (1987). "What Transformation Is," Stage by Stage vol. 7, no. 5 (September-October), pp. 1-5.

Sprague, Ralph H., and Barbara C. McNurlin (eds.) (1986). Information Systems Management in Practice (Englewood Cliffs, NJ: Prentice-Hall).

SUGGESTED STUDENT PROJECTS

1. Pick a company having a well-established information center. Trace the development of the information center.

2. Identify a company that allows user developed systems in the corporate systems portfolio. Discuss the evolution of end-user developed systems in that company. Comment on their systems development process as well as the controls and procedures for end-user systems.

3. Identify a company in which departmental and/or work group computing exists. Trace its development paying particular attention to the relationships with the IS department in the areas of IS planning, user training, hardware/software acquisition policy, and systems development.

Supplementary Reading List

——(1984). "Coping With End User Computing," *EDP Analyzer* vol. 22, no. 2 (February), pp. 1-12.

——(1985). "Expanding End User Support," *EDP Analyzer* vol. 23, no. 6 (June), pp. 1-12.

——(1986). "End-User Computing," *Computerworld* (August 18), pp. 41–58.

——(1987). "Creating an Information Center Strategy," *EDP Analyzer*, vol. 25, no. 2 (February), pp. 1–12.

——(1987). "Why Software Prototyping Works," *Datamation* (August 15), pp. 97ff.

——(1987). "The Role of Business Systems Groups," *EDP Analyzer* vol. 25, no. 8 (August), pp. 1–16.

——(1988). "Work Group Computing Supports People, Not Applications," *Computerworld* (March 14), pp. 69–70.

Adamski, Lee (1985). "Prototyping," <u>Computerworld</u> (May 6), pp. ID/25ff.

Alavi, Maryam, and Ira R. Weiss (1985). "Managing the Risks Associated with End-User Computing," *Journal of Management Information Systems*, vol. 11, no. 1 (Winter), pp. 5-20.

Alavi, Maryam, et al. (1987). "Strategies for End-User Computing: An Integrative Framework," *Journal of Management Information Systems* vol. 4, no. 3 (Winter), pp. 28-49.

Alavi, Maryam, et al. (1988). "Managing End-User Computing as a Value-Added Resource," *Journal of Information Systems Management*, vol. 5, no. 3 (Summer), pp. 26-35.

Allen, Leilani (1984). "Who Are End Users?" *Computerworld* (November 19), pp. ID/19-ID/24.

Alloway, Robert M., and Judith A. Quillard (1983). "User Managers' Systems Needs," *MIS Quarterly* (June), pp. 27-41.

Arkush, Evelyn (1986). "Beyond End-User Computing: Managing in the Third Era," *Journal of Information Systems Management* vol. 3, no.2 (Spring), pp. 58-60.

Athappilly, Kuriakose, and Ron S. Galbreath (1986). "Practical Methodology Simplifies DSS Software Evaluation Process," *Data Management*, (February), pp. 10-17.

Ball, Richard (1987). "Harnessing End-User Computing Without Hindering It," *Computerworld* (October 26), pp. 91-100.

Benson, David H. (1983). "A Field Study of End User Computing: Findings and Issues," *MIS Quarterly* (December), pp. 35-45.

Boar, Bernard H. (1985). "Application Prototyping: Trade Guesses for Experience," *Computerworld* (March 4), pp. 45ff.

Boar, Bernard (1986). "Application Prototyping: A Life Cycle Perspective," *Journal of Systems Management* (February), pp. 25-31.

Brancheau, James C. et al. (1985). "An Investigation of the Information Center From the User's Perspective," *Association for Computing Machinery* vol. 16, no. 1, pp. 4-17.

Brinberg, Herbert R. (1984). "Effective Management of Information: How to Meet the Needs of All Users," *Management Review* (February), pp. 8-13.

Brzezinski, Ronald (1987). "When It's Time to Tear Down the Info Center," *Datamation* (November 1), pp. 73-82.

Carr, Houston H. (1987). "Information Centers: The IBM Model vs. Practice," *MIS Quarterly* (September), pp. 325-338.

Christy, David P., and Clinton E. White Jr. (1987). "Structure and Function of Information Centers: Case Studies of Six Organizations," *Information & Management* vol. 13, pp. 71-76.

Conlon, Theresa (1987). "One User Swears By Centralized System; Another Opts for Change," *Management Information Systems Week* (June 1), pp. 26ff.

Connolly, James (1984). "Prototyping Seen Easing End-User Request Backlog," *Computerworld* (May 7), p. 12.

Cougar, J. Daniel (1986). "E Pluribus Computum," *Harvard Business Review*, vol. 64, no. 5 (September-October), pp. 87-91.

Cougar, Daniel (1987). "End-User Computing: Investing for High Returns," *Computerworld* (May 25), pp. 67-72.

Crouse, Roger L. (1987). "Establishing Effective Information Center User Groups," *Journal of Information Systems Management,* vol. 4, no. 2 (Spring), pp. 41-47.

Efroymson, Sharon (1986). "Managing End-User Training," *Computerworld* (May 5), pp. 49-62.

Fleig, Clare P. (1985). "Managing Workgroup Computers: Dream or Nightmare?" *Information Week* (June 24), pp. 21-26.

Gallant, John (1986). "Prototyping Seen As Tool for Applications Refinement," *Computerworld* (March 4), p. 18.

Gerrity, Thomas P., and John F. Rockart (1986). "End-User Computing: Are You A Leader or A Laggard?" *Sloan Management Review* vol. 27, no. 4 (Summer), pp. 25-34.

Gerrity, Thomas, and John Rockart (1986). "Wanted: Effective Leaders to Manage End-User Computing," *Computerworld* (September 8), pp. 83-92.

Gibson, Michael L., and Lawrence S. Corman (1987). "User Programmer and Costs of The Misinformed User," *Journal of Systems Management* (May), pp. 23-29.

Gilges, Robert D. (1986). "End Users Take On New PC Tasks," *Computerworld/Focus* (April 16), p. 8.

Gilhooley, Ian A. (1987). "Productive Systems Development With Prototyping," *Journal of Information Systems Management,* vol. 4, no. 2 (Spring), pp. 15–22.

Guimaraes, Tor (1984). "The Evolution of the Information Center," *Datamation* (July 15), pp. 127-130.

Guimaraes, Tor (1987). "Prototyping: Orchestrating for Success," *Datamation* (December 1), pp. 101ff.

Guimaraes, Tor and Vasudevan Ramanujam (1986). "Personal Computing Trends and Problems: An Empirical Study," *MIS Quarterly* (June), pp. 179–185.

Hamilton, Rosemary (1987). "Information Centers Growing Up," *Computerworld* (July 20), p. 8.

Hamilton, Rosemary (1987). "Information Center Role Changes," *Computerworld* (August 10), pp. 25ff.

Hammond, L. W. (1982). "Management Considerations for an Information Center," *IBM Systems Journal*, vol. 21, no. 2, pp. 131-161.

Hardaker, Maurice, and Brian K. Ward (1987). "How to Make a Team Work," *Harvard Business Review*, vol. 65, no. 6 (November-December), pp. 112–119.

Harrison, Teresa S. (1985). "Techniques and Issues in Rapid Prototyping," *Journal of Systems Management* (June), pp. 8-13.

Head, Robert (1985). "Information Centers–Information Systems Divided They Stand," *Computerworld* (April 15), pp. ID/11-ID/15.

Henderson, John C., and Michael E. Treacy (1986). "Managing End-User Computing for Competitive Advantage," *Sloan Management Review* vol. 28, no. 2 (Winter), pp. 1-14.

Howard, Geoffry S., and G. Jay Weinroth (1987). "Users' Complaints: Information System Problems From The User's Perspective," *Journal of Systems Management* (May), pp. 30-34.

Huff, Sid L. et al. (1988). "Growth Stages of End User Computing," *Communications of the ACM*, vol. 31, no. 5 (May), pp. 542-549.

Janson, Marius A., and L. Douglas Smith (1985). "Prototyping for Systems Development: A Critical Appraisal," *MIS Quarterly* (December), pp. 305–315.

Janulaitis, M. Victor (1984). "Are the Risks Worth Taking?" *Computerworld* (August 13), pp. 13ff.

Jenkins, A. Milton, and Jack Fellers (1986). "An Annotated Bibliography on Prototyping," IRMIS Working Paper W613, School of Business, Indiana University, Bloomington.

Keen, Peter G. W., and Lynda A. Woodman (1984). "What to Do with All Those Micros," *Harvard Business Review*, vol. 62, no. 5 (September-October), pp. 142-150.

Kelleher, Joanne (1986). "Information Centers–Their Choice: Justify Existence or Go Out of Business," *Computerworld* (August 11), pp. 51-57.

Kimmerly, William (1987). "Toward Spontaneous Computing," *Computerworld* (October 12), pp. 111-115.

Kirkley, John (1988). "Are Top Execs Drowning in Data? SIC it to 'em," *Computerworld*, May 2, p. 19.

Kolodziej, Stan (1987). "Departmental Computing's Political Paradox," *Computerworld/Focus*, pp. 19-20.

Kraushaar, James M., and Larry E. Shirland (1985). "A Prototyping Method for Applications Development by End Users and Information Systems Specialists," *MIS Quarterly* (September), pp. 189-197.

Kull, David (1986). "Anatomy of a 4GL Disaster," *Computer Decisions* (February 11), pp. 58-65.

Lantz, Kenneth (1986). "The Prototyping Methodology: Designing Right the First Time," *Computerworld* (April 7), pp. 69-72.

Lasden, Martin (1980). "Games Played Between Users and Providers," *Computer Decisions* (October), pp. 72-86.

Lasden, Martin (1987). "Decision Support Systems–Mission Accomplished?" *Computer Decisions* (April 6), pp. 41-42.

Lauer, Joachim, and David M. Stettler (1987). "New Directions for Information Centers," *Journal of Systems Management* (October), pp. 6-11.

Lederer, Albert L., and Victoria L. Spencer (1988). "The Effective Information Center: Targeting the Individual User for Success," *Journal of Systems Management* (January), pp. 22-26.

Leitheiser, Robert L., and James C. Wetherbe (1986). "Service Levels: An Organized Approach to End-User Computing," *MIS Quarterly* (December), pp. 337-349.

Lowry, Christina, and Robert Little (1985). "The Perils of Prototyping," *Cause/Effect* (July), pp. 4-8.

Markus, Lynne, and Niels Bjorn-Andersen (1987). "Power Over Users: Its Exercise by System Professionals," *Communications of the ACM*, vol. 30, no. 1 (June), pp. 498-504.

Martin, Merle P. (1986). "The Human Connection in Systems Design: Part I–The Elusive User," *Journal of Systems Management* (October), pp. 6-29.

Merlyn, Vaughan (1987). "The Backlog Stops Here," *Computerworld*, June 22, pp. 61-66.

Metz, Galen (1988). "User Friendly Controls in the Information Center," *Journal of Information Systems Management*, vol. 5, no. 2 (Spring), pp. 25-31.

Miller, Howard (1987). "End Users Drive Benefit Analysis," *Computerworld* (August 10), pp. 59-62.

Millman, Zeeva, and Jon Hartwick (1987). "The Impact of Automated Office Systems on Middle Managers and Their Work," *MIS Quarterly* (December), pp. 479-489.

Munro, Malcolm C. et al. (1987). "Expansion and Control of End-User Computing," *Journal of Management Information Systems*, vol. 4, no. 3 (Winter), pp. 5-27.

Nelson, R. Ryan, and Paul H. Cheney (1987). "Training Today's User," *Datamation* (May 15), pp. 121-122.

Nelson, R. Ryan, and Paul H. Cheney (1987). "Training End Users: An Exploratory Study," *MIS Quarterly* vol. 11, no. 4 (December), pp. 547-559.

Oglesby, John N. (1987). "How to Shop for Your Information Center," *Datamation* (June 1), pp. 70ff.

Opliger, Edwin B. (1985). "Identifying Microcomputer Concerns," *EDP Journal*, vol. 1, pp. 43-66.

Peterson, Robert (1987). "Giving End Users the MIS Seal of Good System Building," *Computerworld* (June), pp. 83-86.

Podorowsky, Gary (1988). "A Practical Guide to the First Time User/Systems Developer," *Journal of Systems Management* (September), pp. 24-27.

Porter, Leslie R., and Janis L. Gogan (1988). "Coming to Terms with End-User Systems Integration," *Journal of Information Systems Management*, vol. 5, no. 5 (Winter), pp. 8-16.

Pottruck, David S. (1980). "How to Keep 'Distributed' DP Pros Happy," *Computer Decisions* (September), pp. 90-92.

Rinaldi, Damian, and Ted Jastrzembski (1986). "Executive Information Systems–Put Strategic Data at Your CEO's Fingertips," *Computerworld* (October 27), pp. 37-51.

Rivard, Suzanna, and Sid L. Huff (1988). "Factors of Success for End-User Computing," *Communications of the ACM*, vol. 31, no. 5 (May), pp. 552-560.

Rockart, John F., and Lauren S. Flannery (1983). "The Management of End-User Computing," *Communications of the ACM*, vol. 26, no. 10 (October), pp. 776-784.

Saarinen, Timo, et. al. (1988). "Strategies for Managing End User Computing," *Journal of Systems Management*, vol. 39, no. 8 (August), pp. 34-39.

Schussel, George (1987). "Application Development in the 5th Generation," *Datamation* (November 15), pp. 94-99.

Sewell, Alan (1987). "Departmental Computing: Distributing The Power," *Datamation* (October 15), pp. 82ff.

Seybold, Patricia B., and Judith S. Hurwitz (1987). "End Users Reap Technology's Benefits," *Computerworld/Focus* (May 6), pp. 43-46.

Smith, Peter M. (1985). "A Prototyping Case Study," *Journal of Information Systems Management*, vol. 2, no. 3 (Summer), pp. 20-25.

Snow, Martin A. (1986). "Taming the Micro Revolution: The Need for Policy," *The EDP Auditor Journal* vol. 8, pp. 1-5.

Spence, J. Wayne (1988). "End User Computing–The Human Interface," *Journal of Systems Management* (February), pp. 15-21.

Sroka, John M., and Martha H. Rader (1986). "Prototyping Increases Chance of Systems Acceptance," *Data Management* (March), pp. 12-19.

Stanton, Steven A. (1988). "End-User Computing: Power to the People," *Journal of Information Systems Management*, vol. 5, no. 3 (Summer), pp. 79-81.

Steerle, Jean, and Dick Bottomley (1988). "Channeling the End-User Computing Initiative: A Case Study," *Journal of Information Systems Management* vol. 5, no. 2 (Spring), pp. 49-55.

Sullivan-Trainor, Michael (1988). "Not Just Another End-User Liaison," *Computerworld* (March 21), pp. 95-97.

Sumner, Mary (1985). "Organization and Management of the Information Center," *Journal of Systems Management* (November), pp. 10-15.

Sumner, Mary (1986). "Cooperative Management Avoids Risk Imposed by User-Developed Applications," *Data Management* (June), pp. 12-16.

Sumner, Mary (1986). "User-Developed Applications: What Are They Doing?" *Journal of Information Systems Management*, vol.3, no. 4 (Fall), pp. 37-46.

Sumner, Mary R., and Robert Klepper (1987). "The Impact of Information Systems Strategy on End-User Computing," *Journal of Systems Management* (October), pp. 12-17.

Swider, Gaile A. (1988). "Ten Pitfalls of Information Center Implementation," *Journal of Information Systems Management*, vol. 5, no. 5 (Winter), pp. 22–28.

Tait, Peter, and Iris Vessey (1988). "The Effect of User Involvement on System Success: A Contingency Approach," *MIS Quarterly* (March), pp. 91-108.

Teagan, Mark, and Liz Young (1988). "The Dynamics of Prototyping," *Computerworld*, August 8, pp. 53-55.

Tucker, Michael (1987). "The Strategist and the PC," *Computerworld/Focus* (March 4), pp. 36-39.

Warner, Edward (1987). "Corporate ICs Increasingly Charging for Support," *InfoWorld* (September 28), p. 47.

Watson, Hugh J., and Houston H. Carr (1987). "Organizing for Decision Support System Support: The End-User Services Alternative," *Journal of Management Information Systems*, vol. 4, no. 1 (Summer), pp. 83-95.

Weber, E. Sue, and Benn R. Konsynski (1987). "Problem Management: Neglected Elements in Decision Support Systems," *Journal of Management Information Systems*, vol. 4, no. 3 (Winter), pp. 64-81.

Weisman, Randy (1987). "Six Steps to AI-Based Functional Prototyping," *Datamation* (August 1), pp. 71-72.

Wetherbe, James C., and Robert L. Leitheiser (1985). "Information Centers: A Survey of Services, Decisions, Problems, and Successes," *Journal of Information Systems Management*, vol. 2, no. 3 (Summer), pp. 3-10.

White, Clinton E. Jr., and David P. Christy (1987). "The Information Center Concept: A Normative Model and a Study of Six Installations," *MIS Quarterly* (December), pp. 451-458.

Withington, Frederic G. (1987). "4 Rules of DDP You Can't Break," *Datamation* (May 15), pp. 105-108.

Wright, Peter (1987). "Where the Competition Can't Hurt You: Beyond Functional Departments," *Information Management* (November-December), pp. 19-21.

Yaverbaum, Gayle J. (1988). "Critical Factors in the User Environment: An Experimental Study of Users, Organizations and Tasks," *MIS Quarterly*, vol. 12, no. 1 (March), pp. 75-88.

Zachmann, William F. (1988). "Information Systems Shouldn't Play 'Computer Cop' to Corporate End-Users," *InfoWorld* (March 28), p. 80.

Zink, Ronald A. (1984). "The Tilt To End-User Programming," *Computerworld* (July 23), pp. ID/5-ID/14.

PART V

THE FUTURE AND INFORMATION SYSTEMS MANAGEMENT

We have explored the various effects of information systems on the modern organization from corporate, internal, and end-user perspectives. Yet IS-related issues do not stop there. The influence of IS extends to the general work environment and even to the larger society in which businesses operate. As professionals we must explore these more expansive frontiers, mindful of our responsibility to react to input from, as well as influence these larger realms

Unlike corporate, departmental, or end-user allegiances, which can be said to yield identifiable results, devoting attention to the potential impacts of information technology on the workplace and on society at large is a task motivated primarily by professionalism and conscience. Our personal limitations notwithstanding, we represent a field of human activity and possibility with very significant and broad ramifications. The final chapters of this book examine issues relating to the most basic areas of impact: quality of work and quality of life.

CHAPTER 19

Quality of Work

431

CHAPTER 20
Quality of Life

SUGGESTED STUDENT PROJECTS

SUPPLEMENTARY READING LIST

nineteen

□

Quality of Work

■■■■

The Coming Work Environment

Changing the Nature of Work

The Demands of the New Work Environment

Conclusion

Discussion Questions

References

In light of the impressive and largely unexpected changes that computerization has wrought on our world, we might be tempted to say, "You ain't seen nothin' yet!" But although the general public is free to speculate idly on the world of the future, the IS manager is obligated to anticipate and react to real-life emerging trends in computerization. A futurist approach entails not just imagining what will happen but deciding how it should work and making it work that way.

This chapter begins with a look at the work environment of the future and the notions of electronic, "logical," and "paperless" offices. We then turn to the issue of how information technology has changed the nature of work; in particular, we focus on flexibility and on shifts in organizational structure.

The new work environment poses certain demands on IS managers with regard to creativity, productivity, and bottom-line impacts. We end by examining all these areas and the IS managers' possible responses.

433

THE COMING WORK ENVIRONMENT

The workplace is the frontier of technical change and the first place to register the effects of automation. Because the workplace is frequently the target of computerization, we tend to think of it as the only recipient—though it is not; in all corners of society, automated processes are influencing people and activity.

There are many theories as to how the work environment will be altered by new automated processes ranging from the physical to the conceptual. One school of thought, making much of the integration of the computer terminal, the telephone, the printer, and other as yet unimagined equipment, speculates on how we might use such functionality and how the work of tomorrow will be performed. To the extent that the workplace environment is defined by the tasks we perform, this type of thinking is useful; however, because it focuses on devices and their uses, it may not emphasize strongly enough the communications-dependent and group nature of future work.

An alternate school of thought examines where we will perform our work. The phrase "logical office" suggests that with the use of workstations that can communicate with general functions (such as document management, data management, and image management), a worker's office can be located anywhere that communications (e.g., telephones and radio transmission) exist. Thus, if work is structured correctly, employees might undertake all their activities in their homes (or anywhere else). Detractors of logical offices point out that the disadvantage is a lessening of the social dimension of the workplace.

Yet another viewpoint focuses on the concept of the "paperless office." Underlying this vision is the theory that all physical forms of information (text, image, and data) can be more cheaply, efficiently, and flexibly contained and manipulated in electronic form. Proponents of this view argue that paper itself gets in the way of our productivity and that with only a little imagination, the electronic capture of information can be extended to voice as well.

The point of this speculation is that old methods unconsciously restrict our efficiency and flexibility; the speed of electronic "lookup" and the ability to integrate information overcomes many of the management problems of paper. However, paper is straightforward, familiar, and easy to use. In the view of some, because paper may be the best way to keep things simple, paper will always have a place in the office of the future. Amy Wohl, one commentator on this viewpoint, humorously observed that, "the paperless office is about as practical as the paperless bathroom."

CHANGING THE NATURE OF WORK

As we saw in Chapter 2, management practice itself is evolving in the face of rapid technological advances. In many ways (ignoring for a moment the difficult challenges that accompany any change), the human dimension of the management task is being enhanced by automation. Clearly other factors are also at work. Thomas L. Brown, Ph.D. (1986) illustrates this new focus by comparing modern managerial values to traditional ones across a variety of issues, (see Exhibit 19–1 for part of his analysis).

Changes such as these to management methods will be necessary to accommodate the changing values of workers. In the future, workers are expected to be less loyal to a single company, to cultivate more interests outside of work, to expect employers to accommodate his or her special working needs, to expect their jobs to be satisfying and enriching, and more. As these or other trends develop, management is beginning to realize that not only structural and procedural changes to our management methods are called for, but fundamental shifts in employer/employee relations will be required.

Consequentially, several healthy trends can be detected. There is more tolerance for bottom-up ideas, more insistence on participation, and greater emphasis on human values. Work is increasingly cited for the contributions it makes to the worker's sense of worth and fulfillment. In actuality the picture is not so utopian, because worker trends are by no means obvious or consistent and effective solutions are not yet proven. Still, IS managers must nonetheless adjust their style and methods to promote such values and attitudes.

Work and Flexibility

Not all visions of future management are so benign. Tom Peters (1988), envisioning what the successful companies of the 1990s will look like, suggests the need for substantial and possibly painful adjustments. Peters indicates that successful firms will be:

- Flatter (having fewer layers of organization structure).
- Populated by more autonomous units (having fewer central staffs and more local authority).
- Oriented toward differentiation, producing high value-added goods and services and creating niche markets.
- Quality conscious.
- Service conscious.

Quality of Work			
Value	Management Issues	The Traditional Manager Answers	The Modern Manager Answers
1. Control	Who should be empowered to make decisions in the customer's interests?	Managers make the decisions.	The person closest to the work should make, or participate in, the decision.
2. Teamwork	Should people be interdependent? How strongly should people share tasks?	Workers should essentially work alone.	Workers should be part of a team; no worker is truly an island.
3. Communication	What's the best way to disseminate information about performance in meeting customer needs?	Managers, preferably at the top, make statements as required.	Everyone should be talking about customer requirements and satisfaction all the time.
4. Measurement	How should the organization measure progress in meeting customer requirements?	Managers track and keep records.	Everyone should measure how he or she is contributing to customer satisfaction.
5. Professionalism	Who is expected to reflect professionalism on the job?	Only managers, and selected specialists, should be considered professional.	Everyone has a "customer." Therefore, everyone ought to be considered as professional.
6. Organizational Economy	Who is responsible for understanding the budget and the impact of work in meeting budget targets?	Managers exclusively watch the bottom line and take appropriate actions	Everyone impacts the bottom line; everyone should be able to track that impact as far as possible.
7. Environment	What tools are needed? What is the right climate for work?	It's a workplace-only basic tools should be provided. The climate should be work-oriented, fairly sterile.	It's a workscape: It's up to employees to "paint" the right climate for getting work done; they must have the very best tools to do it.
Quality of Work Life			
8. Individual respect	How is appreciation for each employee as a unique human being best demonstrated?	Only senior people should be accorded this treatment; only senior people are "indispensable."	Each person is highly valued for the unique skills he or she brings to the enterprise.
9. Personal challenge	How does a manager provide a sense of challenge for employees to keep boredom from affecting work life?	Only people at higher levels need to be kept operationally sharp.	Anyone bored with his or her work affects the sharpness of the organization; challenge is necessary for everyone.
10. Growth	What is the best way to provide personal and professional growth—and for whom?	Growth is a benefit . People should come to work prepared to do the job; it's what you know that counts.	Learning is a constant requirement for growing. As people become charged up with new thinking, the organization also benefits.

11. Enthusiasm	Is enthusiasm a factor in productivity?	Enthusiasm is nice to have but not required; that's why people call it "work."	People who are not turned on will not be happy at their work or effective in doing it; enthusiasm should be emphasized.
12. Ethics	Are honesty and fairness important at all organizational levels?	One should run a company as fairly and honestly as can be effectively done.	People must feel that they are working for an ethical enterprise; ethics is a bedrock management issue.
13. Work/life balance	What is the right balance between time for work and time for personal interests?	One's personal life comes after the job is done—whenever that is.	An employee feels best when his life and his work mesh in a harmonious balance.
14. Rewards	What is the right system for rewards?	Pay and promotion are the two biggest factors in people's eexpectations of rewards from working.	There are as many possibilities for rewarding people as an organization can discover.

Quality of Management

15. Business and organizational understanding	Who should know the business and how it's organized?	Only top management needs a sense of the "big picture."	Everyone should understand that he or she is a piece of the main; no work can be done in a vacuum.
16. Relating job to society	Can employees relate their jobs to society?	This is essentially an executive concern as the senior manager relates the work of the full enterprise throughout society.	Every employee should see that the work of all accumulates to a final product or service, for which he or she should share in the credit.
17. Trust	How is trust established?	Trust is earned by each person over a long period of time.	It should be assumed that each person is credible unless proven otherwise.
18. Recognition	What is the best way to handle recognition?	Only when people separate from the organization can their contributions be recognized. Recognition should not be overdone.	People should be recognized as often as possible.
19. Relating past, present, and future	Who should know about the past, present, and future?	A sense of history can come only with tenure, an association with the organization over a period of time.	The history of the organization is an excellent way to stress traditions or the need for changes in the future, which ought to be fully shared.
20. Leadership	How does a leader set a vision for the organization?	A manager commands an army and must provide marching orders for the direction in which he wants the troops to march.	Vision relies on inspiration to become reality; thus, a leader should work on iterating the dreams of the people.
21. Spirit	Does the organization need a sense of "spirit"?	It's nice if something "magical" develops in the organization, but one can reach goals without it.	No enterprise is exactly like another; that's what provides the competitive edge. Spirit must be found or created.

EXHIBIT 19-1 The Brown values template: modern managerial values.

Source: Thomas L. Brown Ph.D., "When Values Collide," *Industry Week*, July 21, 1986, p. 31.

- More Responsive.
- Much faster at innovation.
- User of highly trained, flexible workers as a means of adding value.

Peters goes on to point out that technology will help bring about this change as it becomes instrumental in how goods and services are designed, manufactured, and distributed. The role that technology could play in non-product related components of this scenario—increasing flexibility or permitting fewer organizational layers for instance—is perhaps less obvious but equally important.

Work and the Organizational Structure

The flatter organization, as shown in Exhibit 19-2, is just one of many predictions currently being made about organizational structure. Another, which requires some exploration, is the movement toward the replacement of employees by automation. Many observers have speculated (some with delight and some with concern) that future organizations can be run with fewer people. To date, this has not

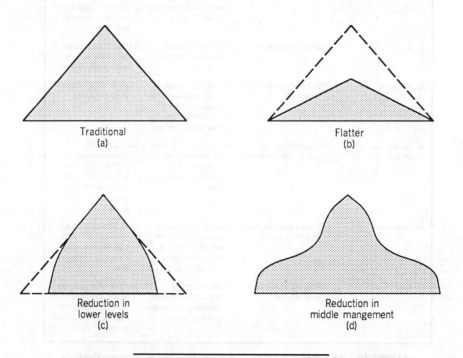

EXHIBIT 19-2 Various effects of IS on organizational structures.

been the case; jobs have changed and there has been transitional displacement, but in general, employment has remained stable. Yet some observers continue to affirm that organizational structure and composition will be altered drastically by improved technical solutions. Exhibit 19-2 illustrates an organization with reduced dependence on large numbers of lower-level employees. In this scenario middle managers would remain not so much directors of people as problem solvers, decision makers, and program managers.

According to another (diametrically opposed) theory, many management activities will be subject to automation. R. O. Mason (1987) defines five sequential groups of activities that occur in the managerial decision-making process and assigns each a name:

1. Source identifying entities of interest
2. Data recording attributes about each entity
3. Prediction drawing inferences from recorded data
4. Value evaluating inferences and choosing a course of action
5. Action taking a course of action

Using this taxonomy, it is possible to choose various points at which automation can interact with management activity, as shown in Exhibit 19-3. As automation becomes more potent, management tasks can be increasingly supplemented or assumed by computers. The impact on organizational structure is a reduction in the quantity of managers (see Exhibit 19-2d).

	Source	Data	Prediction	Value	Action
Alternative					
A	Information system			Management	
B	Information system				Management
C	Information system				Management
D	Information system				

EXHIBIT 19-3 Alternative interfaces between information systems and management.

Source: R. O. Mason, "Basic Concepts for Designing Management Information Systems In R. O. Mason and E. B. Swanson (eds.), *Measurements for Management Decisions, Journal of Systems Management*, November 1987, p. 14. Reprinted by permission.

Both scenarios—fewer lower-level workers and fewer managers—are possible. It is also possible that automation will have more than one organizational impact, which further complicates the future. One such possibility put forward by Peter Drucker (1988) is the increased use of task groups as a way to increase responsiveness. As such fluid organizational structures as task groups become more common approaches to career patterns, communication, authority, and so forth will have to be redefined.

THE DEMANDS OF THE NEW WORK ENVIRONMENT

Creativity

IS departments have successfully enhanced productivity in the past by instituting routine, repetitive processes. Although this has increased task proficiency, it has also cultivated mental habits that do not lead to "breakthrough" thinking. Innovative ideas cannot be mechanically produced; however, the emergence of novel, effective uses of computing show that revolutionary inventions are indeed possible. The IS manager must tap the creative potential of his or her subordinates by cultivating more flexible and imaginative thinking, at least in terms of the definition of a strategic direction for IS.

Left Brain/Right Brain Thinking Chapter 12 introduced left brain/right brain modes of thinking as one way to divide types of thought processes. This division of types of thought also provides a point of departure for defining the types of thinking that result in creativity. To review, the left hemisphere of the brain (in right-handed people) deals with information in a logical and analytical manner. The right hemisphere of the brain deals with information in an emotional and intuitive manner. The difference between art and science characterizes these extremes. Ian Oliver and Hilary Langford (1984) have delineated various specific differences, as shown in Exhibit 19-4.

IS professionals are generally assumed to be left-brain thinkers, in light of the historic duties of the IS department. (The difference in the two modes of thought can help explain why users and the IS department communicate so ineffectively and why new ideas sometimes are so poorly received within the IS department.) Because creative processes are not credited with being deductive or scientific, it is the right brain instinctive, impulsive traits that are consistent with the majority of inventions. Managers should be aware of and encourage the creative benefits of right-brain thinking, even when they might seem to be at odds with traits more typically associated with IS success.

Paradigms and Innovation   Often innovation is triggered simply by removing restrictions to the way we look at problems. Joel Arthur Barker (1985) recognizes this as he draws on the seminal work of Thomas Kuhn in developing the concept of the paradigm. A paradigm is a set of rules or boundaries that defines how we view the world around us. We need the structure of paradigms to tell us how to be successful but they can also block our view of ideas and solutions that do not fit our mental filters. Early data processing professionals learned to solve problems with mainframe solutions. They were successful in doing this so that is the mind set with which they approached problems. When mini- and micro-processors became practical (a paradigm shift in Barker's parlance), some of these professionals could not expand their rule base to accommodate these new ideas. The adage "If all you have is a hammer, every problem looks like a nail" is apropos.

Left Hemisphere	*Right Hemisphere*
Logical	Emotional
Verbal	Spatial
Objective	Subjective
Intellectual	Intuitive
Linguistic	Nonverbal
Analytical	Gestalt
Explicit	Implicit
Reductionistic	Holistic
Sequential	Simultaneous
Linear	Relational
Analytical	Synthetic

EXHIBIT 19-4 Two modes of thinking.

Source: I. Oliver and H. Langford, "Myths of Demons and Users," *Proceedings of the Australian Computer Conference*, November 1984, Australian Computer Society.

Barker makes several key points about paradigm change.

- New paradigms are created or discovered while the old paradigms they are replacing are still successful.
- The paradigm shifter is almost always an outsider whose new idea is almost always rejected initially.
- The paradigm pioneers who choose to follow a new paradigm early, make their decision to switch intuitively and without benefit of objective evidence.
- When people change their paradigms, their perceptions of the world change substantially. This paradigm effect explains why two people can see the same thing in very different ways.

It is because of paradigms that innovation frequently generates strong emotions. Innovation that enhances the prevailing paradigm is readily accepted and forcefully supported whereas innovation that changes the paradigm is fought with great vigor because it destroys the present investment. It is hard for some to throw out their old rules and learn to function under new guidelines. However, with the old rules now invalid, it is easy for the newcomer to compete more effectively.

IS managers need to understand more about paradigms and to become sensitive to the paradigms that define our way of thinking. In this way they might gain some control of them. Moreover, listening to new ideas helps to focus on and question our current rule base and consequentially builds mental flexibility. Management must also develop parallel structures to promote new paradigms while using the remaining vitality of mature paradigms as they plateau. This simultaneous process points out the need for "crossover" discussions between different groups and different fields—especially the technical and nontechnical. Otherwise, revolutionary change will not just be overlooked but likely will be energetically opposed.

Building a Creative Climate David Freedman (1987) points out that many IS departments—even some with impressive records of strategic breakthroughs—have not built the necessary "idea-nurturing environment." Creativity is a continual process and one that is most likely to happen if encouraged through teamwork, as James Wetherbe (1988) explains in detail. Outside assistance (e.g., training) can play a role in helping to cultivate ideas, as can internal processes such as innovation-enhancing techniques and brainstorming sessions.

Creativity-Enhancing Techniques   As we have observed, there is
no formula for producing an original idea. The following guidelines
have been identified by William Synnott (1987) as ones used by
various companies in their pursuit of a competitive edge:

- Foster corporate education.
- Find a champion.
- Establish new alliances; the marriage of different pieces of
  company knowledge can spark invention.
- Conduct market research.
- Collect competitive intelligence.
- Fund corporate research and development.
- Establish an IW (information weapons) group.
- Promote integrated planning.
- Create a SWAT team (special group for ad hoc assignments)
- Conduct brainstorming sessions.
- Set productivity targets.
- Do informal planning.
- Practice incrementalism: allow competitive systems to evolve.
- Create "trojan horses": transfer IS professionals into user or-
  ganizations to open the gates to IS planning.

Productivity

Setting Productivity Levels   We have emphasized the role of the
IS manager in contributing to productivity enhancement. Equally
important is the IS manager's role in communicating productivity
improvements to senior management. This is easier said than done.
For example, if the IS department increases its own productivity
potential by adopting a new technology, it has two basic options. It
can produce the same output with less input (by reducing staff,
perhaps) or it can produce more output with the same input. (Exhibit
19-5 illustrates these options.) The difficulty arises in communicating with senior managers about the choice. They understand reduction in input, as this can usually be communicated in terms of
measurable budget dollars. However, the output of an investment in
IS is usually less tangible; the benefits are often indirect and thus
harder to communicate. It is little wonder that given the choice of
options, senior management often opts for reduced input.

IS managers who are driven to maximize the effects of information
technology may prefer to produce more output, without appreciating

the need to recover an investment in new technology by reducing spending. The most objective approach is to think about the new productive capabilities of the IS department in terms of the level of productivity that satisfies corporate requirements for return on investment.

Determining Corporate Productivity Because IS investment decisions are made one at a time, proof of productivity is typically determined by specific and detailed measurements—of documents processed per worker, for instance. Traditionally, it has been assumed that high marks in each such measurement category somehow translate to overall high corporate productivity. Many companies, however, increase their level of IS spending without achieving noticeable commensurate improvements in overall productivity.

This leads to the conclusion that analyzing productivity at the highest level requires new tools. Peter Drucker (1988) recommends comparative techniques such as units of output per worker. This allows comparisons over time as well as across an industry. Paul Strassmann (1985) uses a computation method called value-added productivity analysis. Exhibit 19-6 shows how revenue can be reduced first by all "purchases" and then by the cost of capital and operational expenses, so that an amount of value added by management can be determined. The ratio of this figure to the cost of management becomes the measure of management's productivity.

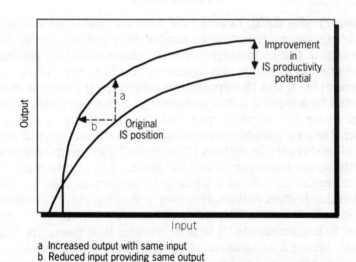

a Increased output with same input
b Reduced input providing same output

EXHIBIT 19-5   Option for reacting to enhanced productivity.

If one believes that IS investments improve corporate productivity, then one would expect management productivity to improve with higher levels of IS investment. Surprisingly, as Exhibit 19-7 shows, there is apparently no correlation between the two. This is a sobering finding for the enthusiastic IS manager, but it should be added that further analysis by Strassmann has shown that increased IS investment does result in increased management productivity for companies in superior strategic positions. Management of companies in inferior strategic positions, however, actually becomes less productive with increases in IS investment. This might be due to the general unimaginativeness of strategically inferior companies and a possible inability to think of breakthrough uses of technology. The latter companies are faced with a difficult dilemma: information technology might be the way to reverse a competitive disadvantage, but statistically speaking, such a commitment will probably only make things worse.

Revenue Contributions

Because merely assisting other strategic business units with strategic systems is not a sufficient raison d'etre for an IS department, many departments are being use as revenue-producing units. Companies such as Boeing, MacDonell Douglas, Southern Pacific, Pennzoil, Weyerhaeuser, Lockheed, and Security Pacific are assessing their IS resources and pursuing the commercial value of these resources. The IS entity is typically spun off as a separate corporate entity with its own revenue goals and sometimes with a highly

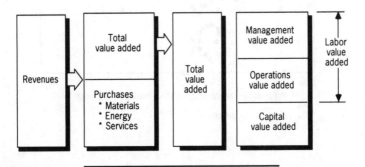

EXHIBIT 19-6 Value-added productivity analysis.

Source: Reprinted with permission of The Free Press, a Division of Macmillan, Inc., from *Information Payoff: The Transformation of Work in the Electronic Age* by Paul Strassman. Copyright © 1985 by The Free Press.

market-oriented charter. Possible marketing opportunities are broad and include the following:

- IS consulting and project assignments
- Software sales
- Time sharing and sale of computer time
- Computer equipment brokering
- Communications and transmission services
- Disaster recovery services
- Facilities management
- Training and education

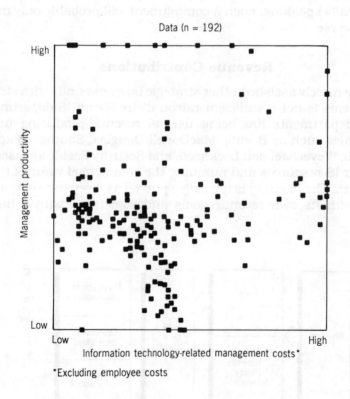

EXHIBIT 19-7 Relationship between IS expenditures and management productivity.

It is not clear if pursuing isolated strengths as market niche opportunities is a more successful tactic than selecting market opportunities that are consistent with overall corporate strategies and drawing on synergies. Moreover, there are several issues for the IS manager to consider before committing to turning the department into a revenue generator.

New Skill Requirements The skills needed to market services to the general public can differ from those used to market services within an organization. There may be more latitude in selecting alternative products and services, there may be a requirement for a purer sales orientation, and there may be less importance attached to nonmonetary performance, among other things. Consequently, the professional talents required may change. The IS manager will have to be more entrepreneurial and take more risks. Also IS project managers might, as a by product of selling to prospective customers, become more aggressive and thus forsake traditional prudence. Some would claim that these characteristics needed to be adopted in any case: the IS department should function as a business whether or not it has external markets. Others see such new skills as markedly different from those which an organization depends on for internal IS-related services.

Conflicting Responsibilities If revenue generation is to become an IS departmental responsibility, provisions should be made to prevent conflicts between external revenue opportunities and internal organizational needs. To avoid divided loyalties, some companies set up two organizations. This may be expensive, but it is effective; otherwise, the IS manager, in an effort to satisfy revenue targets, may ignore internal demands that have to do with the larger corporate good. Conversely, if external customers believe that resources or services may be preempted at any time by internal demands, they may not be willing to patronize so unreliable a vendor.

Narrowing of Scope The IS department provides a broad set of products and services to the organization it serves. If these are marketed to the general business community, the department must specialize in a limited number of products and services in order to compete effectively. Doing so will, however, cause a realignment of departmental skills. Unless care is taken, some of the products and services that the corporate users rely upon will be allowed to atrophy or, worse, be dropped altogether. Offering selected products to the market is appropriate; offering selected products to user constituents is not.

Professional Motivations   Some organizations believe that IS professionals would look favorably on working in a business unit that is an important revenue generator, where individual talents can be recognized and rewarded and where work can be more diversified and possibly more challenging. Others, however, believe that IS professionals do not typically enjoy the higher risks attached to marketing their products and services; do not identify with less scientific tasks such as marketing, customer service, and pricing; and do not like to "go where the revenue is." The IS manager must know his or her staff's views on these issues before embarking on a money-making course.

CONCLUSION

While the IS manager is busy trying to make a difference in his or her organization, information technology is rapidly transforming the overall work environment. Maintaining awareness of these trends is the least that is required of the responsible IS manager. At the most ambitious extreme, the IS manager can become instrumental in directing technological changes in the workplace. It is very important to remember, however, that hardware and software alone will not magically transform tomorrow's businesses. What counts are the specific ways in which these tools are used.

DISCUSSION QUESTIONS

1. Of the "electronic", "logical" and "paperless" office scenarios of the coming work environment, which do you feel best describes the future? Why?

2. Which organizational trend do you feel is most likely to evolve?

3. What types of organizational structure would best support a revenue-generating IS function?

4. Might fostering a creative environment damage the emphasis on caution and controls that is a part of most systems development environments? How can both needs be accommodated?

5. "There is no way to prove to senior managers that the IS department is productive; they just have to believe it." Why do you agree or disagree with this statement?

REFERENCES

Barker, Joel Arthur (1985). *Discovering the Future: The Business of Paradigms* (St Paul, MN: ILI Press).

Brown, Thomas L. (1986). "When Values Collide" *Industry Week* (July 21), pp. 29-32.

Drucker, Peter F. (1988). "The Coming of the New Organization," *Harvard Business Review* (January-February), pp. 45-53.

Freedman, David H. (1987). "Cultivating IS Creativity," *Infosystems* (July), pp. 24-27.

Mason, R. O. "Basic Concepts for Designing Management Information Systems," in R. O. Mason and E. B. Swanson (eds)., *Measurements for Management Decisions*.

Oliver, Ian, and Hilary Langford (1984). "Myths of Demons and Users," *Proceedings of the Australian Computer Conference* (November), Australian Computer Society.

Peters, Tom (1988). *Thriving On Chaos* (New York: Alfred A. Knopf), pp. 23-29.

Strassmann, Paul (1985). *Information Payoff: The Transformation of Work in the Electronic Age* (New York: Free Press).

Synnott, William R. (1987). *The Information Weapon* (New York: Wiley) pp. 87-91.

Wetherbe, James (1988). *Systems Analysis and Design* Third Edition, (St. Paul: West).

twenty

□

Quality of Life

Information technology affects just about everyone who works for or deals with businesses—and a good many other people, too. In short, this technology has in a short time significantly modified our environment. And whether or not they realize it, IS managers are playing an important part in changing the larger social landscape. For this reason it is part of their professional responsibility to pay attention to both the opportunities and the dangers that this technology poses.

This chapter begins with an examination of several areas to which IS managers must be particularly sensitive: computers and the law, computers and security, and computer literacy. These areas all have implications for society at large and for quality of life in general, as we will see.

We then turn to the broad question of responding to change. Here we look at how IS managers adapt their skills even in the face of predictions that their role will ultimately cease to be important (predictions, it should be noted, that we disagree with!). We end the chapter—and this book—with a discussion of professionalism, followed by a few parting words on the effects of the IS management profession.

COMPUTERS AND THE LAW

According to the I/S Analyzer (1988), "As companies make more use of information systems to run their business, sell services, offer advice, design products, and add value to their goods, there is greater likelihood that poor information practices could lead to harm—to themselves and their customers." The Analyzer identifies four areas of potential legal problems for business with poor control over their IS functions:

- Negligence
- Liability
- Protecting personal data
- Unfair business practices

Legislation dealing with the role of computers in business and in society has increased the obligation that companies have to use computers responsibly and has reinforced the importance of the IS manager's role. Some of the important trends in computer legislation are highlighted in the following sections.

The Freedom of Information Act

According to the Freedom of Information Act (FOIA), certain governmental and private organizations (e.g., credit bureaus) are required to make information on individuals available on request. The principle behind the FOIA is that personal information that can affect the lives of citizens should be available to them. Moreover, the fact that this information is computerized cannot prevent individuals from having access to it. In fact, where information is automated, there is growing pressure to require organizations to make this information available to citizens in electronic form (a new challenge for the IS manager).

The Privacy Act

The Privacy Act requires organizations to guard and protect the confidentiality of personal information so that it cannot be distributed in such a way as to cause individuals any harm. In some instances, businesses are prohibited from disseminating data such as personal phone numbers, mailing addresses, or salary information without receiving permission from the individuals to whom these data pertain. Computer security takes on a whole new meaning when legal requirements for both secrecy and authorized access are considered.

Roger A. Clarke (1988) observes that privacy legislation has not recognized the potential dangers that misuse of sophisticated IT presents. Current techniques of "dataveillance," the systematic use of personal data systems in the investigation or monitoring of the actions or communications of one or more persons, consists of two different techniques. Personal dataveillance, or monitoring identified individuals who have attracted attention, is normally what comes to mind when privacy protection is mentioned. It is where information on someone already identified is requested, screened for, or matched against. Although this is important to control, Clarke points out that it is really the less potentially damaging of the two.

Far more threatening is mass dataveillance, where groups of people are screened with the intent of singling out individuals who may be worth further surveillance. When coupled with the facilitative mechanism of coupling with other data bases, especially on an inferential basis, the results can be especially dangerous. The whole approach of mass dataveillance, Clarke believes, is arbitrary. Although he points out some benefits to such techniques, there are many more dangers that should cause us to think very carefully as a society about the extent to which we allow the use of such techniques.

The Foreign Corrupt Practices Act

As a response to corporate bribery incidents abroad, Congress passed legislation placing personal liability for improper business conduct on boards of directors and corporate officers. Thus, any failure to take prudent management action to protect corporate informational assets presents the stockholders with a mode of legal recourse. Because information and strategic systems represent important areas of exposure to businesses, strategies to minimize risks (such as disaster recovery programs) become essential.

International Issues

The legislation referred to above are U.S. laws. Organizations operating in other countries must be cognizant of differing legislation. A particularly complicated issue has become transborder data flows, the movement of digital information across international borders. Other countries see information as a real asset and national resource. This can include not just scientific data or meaningful demographic information but even the financial and operating results of companies with multicompany locations. Some countries want to monitor; others want to tax, control and otherwise restrict its leaving their country. However, the use of voice-grade phone lines to move data makes this control of practical difficulty. There are signs of many countries making reasonable compromises in their requirements for control. However, this might change. After all, many of these countries have already shown an astute appreciation for the power of information as reflected in their own highly advanced local privacy legislation.

It is too early to see how laws and other pending legislation will evolve. However, businesses clearly have legal obligations with respect to information and its storage, retrieval, and processing. IS managers must be highly sensitive to issues of legal exposure and would be wise to prepare for more governmental controls in the area of IS.

COMPUTERS AND SECURITY

The growing number of people familiar with computers and the rapid spread of computer technology (especially telecommunications) increases the chances that someone will intentionally or inadvertently violate the integrity of a corporate computer system. The IS manager is clearly charged with preventing such an occurrence.

Computer crime is of major concern to businesses—yet the term itself is vague. It has traditionally included theft of programs and information, unauthorized use of computer resources, and damage to software and information. As technology is used more broadly, opportunities for illegal use of computers to aid in the theft of money or goods are increasing. Breaching computer systems to gain access to unauthorized areas even puts trespassing on the growing list of computer crimes.

Computer crime contains "gray areas." It is unclear, for example, whether casual after-hours use of corporate computing resources actually deprives the company of anything tangible and constitutes a crime. Some professionals argue that these ambiguous areas are more properly ethical considerations.

Corporate awareness of security risks is increasing; however, as we have seen, security controls must be reasonable and must permit authorized activities to take place conveniently. Moreover, businesses should see security as a investment and spend only as much on protection as the risk warrants.

Beyond managing the mechanics of such a security program, the IS department should set the standard for scrupulous respect for the sanctity of information resources. Professional standards contribute to this attitude. Another means available to the IS manager would be to make ethical values an important hiring requirement. Apart from the very practical problem of not easily assessing ethics, a more diabolic contradiction stymies this well intentioned approach. Many of the other traits we normally seek out in job searches and reward in employees have shown up as being consistent traits of most computer criminals and "hackers." They have tended to be young, technically astute, inquisitive, energetic (even "workaholics"), independent workers, self-motivated, stimulated by a challenge, persistent; in short, highly talented IS professionals. Clearly what separates the valued performer with these strengths from the miscreant is a set of values that guides them to use their skills constructively. The challenge to the IS profession is not simply to be able to identify the presence of such rectitude but to instill it in our fellow professionals.

COMPUTER LITERACY AND EDUCATION

As we have seen, IS managers can help promote the effective use of technology by making sure that other less technically experienced people find technology approachable. The most obvious way to do so is to build user-friendly systems. An equally important but usually overlooked means is to educate others in the organization, including end users, managers, and of course senior executives. Education implies more than training on specific systems or orientation on an IS plan; it entails building real familiarity with a technology and its uses. Many people must be taught not to view technologically motivated changes with trepidation; not everyone embraces such changes without careful, empathetic teaching to help them overcome their anxieties or skepticism. Education thus has value beyond simply establishing computer literacy in a given employee.

Certainly, knowing the buzzwords and understanding the mechanics of technology can help some users feel part of the technical revolution. For others with more personal concerns, however, education has to be aimed at the job-performance level. These persons need to experiment with and really see technology at work—making their lives easier. Being shown that people control technology, not the other way around, is essential for such persons; it lies at the heart of any good computer literacy program.

RESPONDING TO CHANGE

The list of external factors that influence IS is already long and complicated, and IS managers need to accept the fact that this list will only become longer. Apart from government intervention (in the form of legislation), industry cooperation, new vendors, and foreign competition are all factors that will exert a powerful influence on the information technology, marketplace and, indirectly, on the individual IS department. The list of issues is likely to expand. From the basic concerns of computer science, technology, and the attendant skills, we have moved to some far-reaching areas: health and safety concerns, ergonomics, environmental issues, historical preservation, quality of the work life, societal impacts, and other subjects that remind us how ambitious and topical the IS field has become. For these reasons, IS managers who successfully complete the transition to corporate executive will still find themselves engaged in a process of ongoing intellectual broadening. They must become conversant in social, legal, and medical issues, to name only a few.

It is easy to find evidence for the prediction that information technology will find its way into even more facets of our society than it already has. Persons with IS management skills will have to adapt tried-and-true solutions to new settings, including previously unautomated industries, professional sports, nonprofit organizations— even, some might argue, the home of the future. This adaptation cannot be done haphazardly; the penalties for failure are high.

One prediction that IS managers have trouble handling is that they will become unnecessary. The reasoning is that if technology becomes simplified enough, it can be purchased and managed by anyone; there will be no need for the special attentions of IS management. In other words, just about everyone will become an IS manager of sorts. The IS department will disappear, and even the IS manager's staff duties would be absorbed eventually by an enlightened, capable general-management population (trained, naturally, by the to-be-retired IS manager!).

Of course, it is hard to guarantee that this will not happen. We know that some metamorphosis, as yet unknown, is quite probable. However, the likelihood that IS management will completely disappear is remote. Even if information technology becomes so sophisticated that it "manages itself" and all general managers suddenly develop sound IS-related skills, some corporate-level entity separate from functional groups will be needed to establish autonomous controls, to stabilize cross-functional processes, and to provide long-range leadership. The IS manager will then assume a new and different role. For organizations that accept that information is a resource, a distinct function to manage it has always and will always make sense. Exhibit 20-1 shows the IS department and other resource-management departments.

Regardless of the fate of the IS department, the IS manager must approach the future with a constructive attitude. Organizations expect maximum benefits from their use of technology and for the IS manager this expectation should be more important than concerns about the direction of his or her job. In the first place, any lessening of the IS manager's importance is quite remote; in the second, professionalism compels the manager to do whatever is good for the organization.

PROFESSIONALISM

IS managers have a responsibility to their organizations to develop and maintain skills appropriate for the successful completion of their work. However, they also have a responsibility themselves: to develop a well-rounded set of skills so as to meet the challenges they face now and will face in the future. These twin responsibilities have

Resource	Responsible Department
Money	Finance
Labor	Human resources
Material	Material management
Machines	Manufacturing/facilities
Information	Information systems

EXHIBIT 20-1 Resource management departments of an organization.

three components: knowledge and behavior, human values, and ethics.

Knowledge and Behavior

We have seen (in Chapter 8) that IS managers need a sound understanding of technology, industry, and management. Because each manager has somewhat different interests and professional-development needs, programs for professional development at advanced levels tend to be customized. They consist frequently of formal and informal constructs and activities, including professional reading, groups and circles of professional friends and acquaintances who meet to discuss important questions. The key ingredient in the ongoing development of professional knowledge is an aggressively acquisitive and analytical mind.

The IS manager whose skills are constantly improving makes use not only of greater knowledge but also of a set of behaviors that allow him or her to apply this knowledge properly. The very act of proactively pursuing knowledge in itself builds an attitude of assertiveness and initiative that is more and more requisite in today's IS manager. The act of dealing with other professionals serves to hone the interpersonal skills so important to the IS manager in a business context. As we have seen, the choice of proactive or reactive behaviors is a tricky one. Various behaviors must be practiced frequently in professional settings (on the job and off) before they are learned.

Human Values

One of the most damaging themes with which IS managers have had to contend is that of the computer as dehumanizing. Starting with the idea that computers will inevitably take away jobs, many people have felt that there is something demeaning about a computerized environment.

This attitude is not necessarily incorrect. Automation in some industries has indeed been intended to eliminate jobs and has been implemented by insensitive technicians who, by focusing on the technology, have ignored the human factor. The history of systems implementation has not always been pretty; it reveals that computers can be and have been used in brutally impersonal ways.

The ultimate challenge to IS managers is to show that technology can and must be used in supportive, humanizing ways. Work that is made more interesting, easier, safer, cleaner, and more valuable supports and emphasizes human values. Because too often technical values have been stressed, IS professionals sometimes have to be trained in the importance of people in making systems work. This importance is reinforced as stronger, more sympathetic bonds are built with users and as more ergonomic, "human-engineered" systems are developed. The day is fast approaching when proper preparation for IS management will entail not the study of technology but the study of people.

Ethics

One of the distinctions between a profession and a trade is the fact that the professional must do more than just apply his or her specialized skills; he or she is obliged to exercise ethical judgment in deciding how those skills are to be wielded. Part of this obligation is the universal imperative to which everyone is bound, to perform work according to an unstated but important set of rules of personal behavior. The dignity of another human being must not be violated, for example, whether the professional is installing computer systems, running a billion-dollar corporation, or selling hamburgers. Dishonesty, taking advantage of others, and exploiting a position for unfair advantage are always wrong; no one's professional standing divorces him or her from accountability to certain codes of conduct.

In addition, many professionals (doctors and lawyers, for instance) play special roles and encounter special circumstances where unique ethical guidelines must be developed. James Young (1988) has observed that IS managers are among this group of professionals. Although the overlap is great, ethics should not be confused, as many commentators do, with computer crime. The act of breaking the law might be unethical to some, but the act, jaywalking as an extreme example, might not violate our generally accepted dictates of conscience. Conversely, some behaviors, lying for instance, might not be illegal but might be considered as unethical by many.

Unlike laws, ethical guidelines evolve from the beliefs and codes of each individual professional as well as through the conventions of common practice, which solidify over time. An example is the concept of software protection. Before there were laws to guide IS professionals, they understood that software is the product of someone's imagination and efforts and must be viewed with respect. In the minds of the earliest IS professionals, software was a tangible thing. But there were (and still are) fine points in the treatment of software that leave the definition of "respect" unclear. When is copying software warranted, and when is it inappropriate? When is software distinctly someone's property, and when is it merely an expression of commonly available concepts? Specific code for sorting records is a patentable product whereas the concept of sorting is general knowledge. In between lie many ambiguous areas. Is a specific sorting technique protectable, for instance? What about the concept of screen icons as user prompts? If they are ownable, who should own them, the first person who thought of the idea or the person who put it into practice? (It is interesting to note that only when commonly agreed upon ethical values could not be derived was the IS profession forced to resort to software pirating laws in order to determine once and for all proper behavioral values.)

Similar but broader dilemmas confront the IS manager. What are our responsibilities to users and businesses to conceal or reveal data? How do we balance our duty to introduce change with our responsibility to protect our organizations from risk? How do we rationalize any conflicts between our obligations to users of technology and our fealty to businesses? What are our obligations to enlighten others about the benefits of IS, and when does this become self-serving proselytizing? R. Mason has grouped issues such as these into key areas that he calls four ethical issues of the information age. They are

1. *Privacy* What information about one's self or one's associations must a person reveal to others, under what conditions and with what safeguards? What things can people keep to themselves and not be forced to reveal to others?

2. *Accuracy* Who is responsible for the authenticity, fidelity and accuracy of information? Similarly, who is to be held accountable for errors in information and how is the injured party to be made whole?

3. *Property* Who owns information? What are the just and fair prices for its exchange? Who owns the channels, especially the airways, through which information is transmitted? How should access to this scarce resource be allocated?

4. *Accessibility* What information does a person or an organization have a right or a privilege to obtain, under what conditions and with what safeguards?

As long as IS managers retain both the knowledge of and responsibility for the increasingly pivotal managerial areas surrounding technology, the obligation for well-considered ethical standards of management practice and behavior will fall squarely on these managers' shoulders.

CONCLUSION

The yardsticks for evaluating the effects of the IS management profession should be nothing less than the changes in our lives brought about by intelligent, benign uses of technology. Choices need to be made about the degree and direction of technological usage, and our profession should help society as a whole make these choices. Enlarging on the role we have constructed at the corporate level, we must strike balance between leadership and service. We must avoid playing the role of "high priests of technology," and we must certainly also avoid handing decisions to others with less understanding of the important issues.

The IS management profession should not strive for homogeneous principles; this would clearly be unhealthy. However, unless we test our diversity against reality and unless we take seriously the differing ideas of all our colleagues, we will sacrifice the naturally healthy process of evolution on which we have been embarked as a group. Professional societies are, of course, a major way to encourage the continuation of this process. However, IS professionals must go beyond merely structural methods. IS practitioners must view themselves as professionals and respond to one another in ways that build on their common backgrounds.

In addition to the sense of community that IS professionals should feel, there should also be a private feeling of satisfaction for each professional. More than ever, IS professionals can see the difference they are making for their organizations and, beyond those four walls, for the larger culture in which we all participate. There is no reason for today's IS professional to suffer from a sense of obscurity and lack of appreciation; where such attitudes still exist, they are the result of a failure of the IS manager to communicate the enormous potential of IS. As such obstacles are overcome and growing numbers of people perceive IS's positive effects, the professional will become one to be truly proud of, to get highly excited about, and to enjoy on large and small levels alike.

DISCUSSION QUESTIONS

1. Does IS management as a profession have a duty to establish ethical standards that should guide the behavior of individual IS managers, or should ethical standards be a personal matter to be determined individually?

2. Because the professional development of IS managers improves individuals and enhances their careers, should companies support it? Or is it much more the individuals' responsibility than that of their companies?

3. Do you believe that latent computer criminals appear as highly desirable employees? Are their possibly other traits which might serve as warning signs to the IS manager?

4. Does the resistance of some users to new systems reflect a fear of new technology specifically or of change in general? Should the IS manager deal with these two types of fear differently?

5. As society grows more familiar with information technology, does this familiarity make the IS manager's job of directing the effects of technology harder or easier? Why?

REFERENCES

———(1988). "Information and the Law" *I/S Analyzer*, Vol 26, no. 1, (January), pp. 1-12.

Clarke, Roger A. (1988). "Information Technology and Dataveillance" *Communications of the ACM*, Vol 31, no. 5,(May), pp. 498-512.

Mason,R. (1986). "Four Ethical Issues of the Information Age," *MIS Quarterly*, (March), pp. 5-12.

Young, James (1988). "In Defense of MIS's Honor," *Computerworld Focus*, Vol 22, no. 01a (January), p. 6.

SUGGESTED STUDENT PROJECTS

1. Obtain a copy of the statement of ethics of a professional society and analyze it in light of your own assessment of the needs of the profession.

2. Prepare an analysis of recent or proposed computer legislation including recommendations for further action. Base your analysis on real or potential computer crimes.

3. Pick a company that uses the IS arm for revenue generation. Assess the degree to which they have been successful. Identify factors that might contribute to these results.

4. Select a company that has an active process to encourage creativity within the IS department. Assess the degree to which the process has been successful and recommend improvements if any.

Supplementary Reading List

Applegate, Lynda M., et. al. (1988). "Information Technology and Tomorrow's Manager" *Harvard Business Review*, vol. 66, no. 6 (November-December), pp. 128-136.

Atkins, William (1985). "Jesse James at the Terminal," *Harvard Business Review* (July-August), pp. 82-87.

Brand, Eric (1988). "What's In, What's Out," *Datamation* (January 15), pp. 94-100.

Diebold, John (1984). "Six Issues That Will Affect the Future of Information Management," *Data Management* (July), pp. 10-14.

Hartog, Curt, and Martin Herbert (1986). "1985 Opinion Survey of MIS Managers: Key Issues," *MIS Quarterly* (December), pp. 351-361.

Kidder, Tracy (1981). *The Soul of a New Machine* (Boston: Little, Brown).

Marchand, Donald A., and Forest W. Horton Jr. (1986). *Infotrends.* (New York: Wiley).

Naisbitt, John. (1982). *Megatrends* (New York: Warner).

Summers, R. C. (1984). "An Overview of Computer Security," *IBM Systems Journal,* vol 23, no. 4, pp. 309-323.

Toffler, Alvin (1980). *The Third Wave* (New York: William Morrow).

name index

□

A

Albrecht, Michael Jr., 290
American Airlines, 69
American Hospital Supply, 69, 72
Anthony, R. N., 32
Austin, Nancy, 83

B

Bakos, Yannis, 51, 66, 67
Ball, Richard, 352, 385, 387
Barker, Joel Arthur, 441, 442
Baroudi, Jack J., 279
Benjamin, Robert, 66, 126
Boeing, 445
Bostrom, Robert P., 274
Brancheau, James, 59
Brooks, Frederick, 290
Brown, Patrick, 321
Brown, Thomas L., 435
Buchanan, Jack, 261–263
Bullen, Christine, 23, 24
Buss, Martin J. D., 311

C

Carr, Houston H., 401, 402
Cash, James, 62, 129
Cecchi, W. J., 146
Chandler, Alfred, 251
Christy, David P., 403
Citicorp, 70, 71

Clarke, Roger A., 452
Colgate-Palmolive, 72
Conlon, Theresa, 412
Cougar, J. Daniel, 387
Crescenzi, Adam, 48, 53, 54

D

Davis, Dana, 289
Davis, Gordon, 32, 99, 289, 368
Dickson, Gary, 28–30, 35, 152, 353
Drucker, Peter, 130, 131, 412, 418, 419, 440, 444

E

ECONOMOST, 71
EDP Analyzer, 128

F

Ferratt, Thomas W., 272
First Boston Corporation, 71
Flannery, L. S., 356, 403
Freedman, David H., 442

G

Gantz, John, 155
Gellerman, Saul W., 290, 419
Gerrity, Thomas P., 395, 396, 399, 401, 403
Gibson, Cyrus, 17, 22, 27, 30, 31, 35, 103

subject index

Printed by
Fong & Sons Printers Pte Ltd